NINTH EDITION

The Prentice Hall Essential Guide for College Writers

STEPHEN REID
Colorado State University

Prentice Hall

Boston Columbus Indianapolis New York San Francisco Upper Saddle River
Amsterdam Cape Town Dubai London Madrid Milan Munich Paris Montreal Toronto
Delhi Mexico City Sao Paulo Sydney Hong Kong Seoul Singapore Taipei Tokyo

Senior Acquisitions Editor: *Brad Potthoff*
Senior Development Editor: *Marion B. Castellucci*
Senior Marketing Manager: *Sandra McGuire*
Senior Media Producer: *Stefanie Liebman*
Project Coordination, Text Design, and Electronic Page Makeup: *Nesbitt Graphics, Inc.*
Senior Art Director: *Anne Nieglos*
Cover Designer: *Laura Gardner*
Image Permission Coordinator: *Angelique Sharps*
Photo Researcher: *Pearson Image Resource Center/ Teri Stratford*
Senior Operations Specialist: *Mary Ann Gloriande*
Printer and Binder: *Courier Corporation*
Cover Printer: *Coral Graphic Services, Inc.*

For permission to use copyrighted material, grateful acknowledgment is made to the copyright holders on pages C-1–C-2, which are hereby made part of this copyright page.

Library of Congress Cataloging-in-Publication Data
Reid, Stephen
    The Prentice Hall essential guide for college writers / Stephen Reid. — 9th ed.
        p. cm.
    Rev. ed. of: Prentice Hall guide for college writers, Stephen Reid, 8th ed. c2008.
    Includes index.
    ISBN 978-0-205-80210-4
    1. English language—Rhetoric—Handbooks, manuals, etc. 2. Report writing—Handbooks, manuals, etc. 3. College readers. I. Reid, Stephen, 1940- Prentice Hall guide for college writers. II. Title. III. Title: Essential guide for college writers.
    PE1408.R424 2010
    808'.042—dc22
                                        2009052056

1 2 3 4 5 6 7 8 9 10—CRK—13 12 11 10

Student Edition ISBN-13: 978-0-205-80210-4
Student Edition ISBN-10:   0-205-80210-9

Prentice Hall
is an imprint of

www.pearsonhighered.com

Brief Contents

Contents

6 ANALYZING AND DESIGNING VISUALS   145

7 EXPLAINING   183

Thematic Contents

The Prentice Hall Essential Guide for College Writers contains selections from almost 100 writers, artists, and photographers. Thematic clusters of essays, articles, editorials, Web sites, cartoons, poems, short fiction, and images are indicated below. An asterisk (*) indicates a complete essay.

ENVIRONMENTAL ISSUES

Preface

Ready or not, teachers of writing find themselves ushered or perhaps even beamed into a New Media world. In some cases, we have a technological head start on our students; in other cases, we are scrambling to catch up with their knowledge of and facility with hybrid texts. The Internet, with its Web sites, databases, blogs, tweets, YouTube videos, and Facebook pages, is quickly becoming the dominant medium, and it features an amazing array of genres, images, photographs, video clips, sound bites, and other forms of digitized communication. The public and academic writing for which we prepare our students is also a rapidly evolving target.

Thus a major goal of teaching writing in the twenty-first century is, in fact, to teach students traditional critical reading and writing skills while adapting to rapidly evolving digital media. One of the most crucial challenges is helping students find and evaluate a variety of media sources in a Web 2.0 world dominated by Google and Wikipedia. Students need to be familiar not just with databases, visuals, videos, Powerpoint presentations, and Web sites, but they also need to know how to analyze these media so they can employ them in an effective rhetorical manner for a variety of audiences, purposes, and genres. Our students may be digital natives, but they are often rhetorical novices.

Providing students with a firm grounding in rhetorical matters is still the best way to teach students to write in twenty-first century electronic environments. The WPA Outcomes Statement for First-Year Composition (available at the WPA Council Web site) outlines five key goals: building students' *rhetorical knowledge* of purpose, audience, genre, cultural context, voice, and tone; improving students' *critical thinking, reading, and writing* skills; developing students' strategies for *writing processes*; helping students develop their *knowledge of conventions*; and helping students learn how to *compose in electronic environments*. Clearly, the first of these goals—building rhetorical knowledge of purpose, audience, genre, and cultural context—is crucial to the last goal—helping students learn how to analyze electronic texts so that they can compose effectively in electronic environments. Therefore a major goal of *The Prentice Hall Essential Guide for College Writers* is to teach students how to integrate traditional rhetorical skills into a digital world—in particular into the Web 2.0 world where students currently live, work, and play. This concise, portable edition focuses on these important rhetorical skills.

KEY FEATURES OF THE TEXT

Logical Sequence of Purpose-Based Chapters

Within the rhetorical situation, aims and purposes help guide the reader to select appropriate genres, organizational strategies, appeals to audience, and appropriate styles. Early chapters in *The Prentice Hall Essential Guide for College Writers* focus on observing, remembering, critical reading, and analyzing visuals while later chapters emphasize exposition and argumentation (explaining, evaluating, problem solving, arguing, and researching).

Focus on Writing Processes

Every major chapter contains guidelines for writing, journal exercises, reading and writing activities, collaborative activities, peer response guidelines, revision suggestions, and professional and student samples to assist students with their work-in-progress within their rhetorical situation.

Journal Writing

Throughout the text, write-to-learn activities help writers improve their critical reading skills, warm up for each assignment, and practice a variety of invention and shaping strategies appropriate for understanding their purpose, audience, genre, and social context.

Emphasis on Student Writing

The text showcases student writing, featuring the work of student writers from several colleges and universities. The text contains *ten full-length student essays,* several of which are accompanied by sample prewriting materials, rough drafts, peer response sheets, and postscripts. Many of these essays are source-based and include Works Cited lists.

Professional Writing

Twenty-six professional essays on topics often related to new media literacy, ranging from plagiarism detection programs to *Slumdog Millionaire,* are included in the text. Featured professional writers include Margaret Atwood, Deborah Tannen, Gary Stix, Daniel Kammen, Manohla Dargis, and Rebecca Moore Howard.

- **A *Casebook on Web 2.0* in Chapter 10, Arguing, features three essays about the risks and benefits of Wikipedia.** These pieces engage students in critical reading about accuracy and reliability issues on Wikipedia and help them become more informed users of Web content.
- **A *Casebook on Climate Change* in Chapter 5, Reading,** includes essays on reversing climate change and using renewable energy sources and a Web site on changing personal lifestyles to reduce our carbon footprint.

Alternate Thematic Table of Contents

The professional and student essays, articles, and images in each chapter combine to create thematic clusters of topics that recur throughout the text: Web 2.0 Literacies, Race and Cultural Diversity, Gender Roles, Technology and the Internet, Environmental Issues, Education, Literacy and Language, Advertising and the Media, Social Issues, and Cultural Explorations.

Chapter Opening Images

Google street views, Wikipedia graphics, Web pages, climate change graphics, and modern and pop art introduce ideas and images that are picked up in the essays, visuals, and journal ideas in every chapter. These images give visible focus to contemporary literacies.

At-a-glance Graphics

Information graphics highlight key content for students throughout the text.

- **Techniques Charts** summarize techniques and procedures for different types of writing.
- **Writing Assignment Charts** show the genres appropriate for writing to personal, academic, and public audiences.
- **Source Evaluation Charts for print, online database, and open Web sources** (such as blogs) help students with their research as they write for a variety of personal, public, and academic audiences.

Marginal Quotations

Nearly a hundred short quotations by composition teachers, researchers, essayists, novelists, and poets personalize for the inexperienced writer a larger community of writers still struggling with the same problems that each student faces.

STRUCTURE OF *THE PRENTICE HALL ESSENTIAL GUIDE FOR COLLEGE WRITERS*

The text contains eleven sequenced chapters that gradually build students' rhetorical knowledge and skills. Initial chapters focus on writing process and rhetorical situations; middle chapters give students practice and facility with invention, descriptive and narrative writing, critical reading skills, and basic skills for analyzing images and visuals. The next group of chapters focuses on argument skills for personal, academic, and public audiences. The final chapter helps students conduct research for a variety of purposes and audiences.

Chapter 1: An Introduction to Myths and Rituals for Writing

Chapter 1, "Writing Myths and Rituals," discounts some common myths about college writing courses, introduces the notion of writing rituals, and outlines the variety of journal writing used throughout the text. Writing process rituals are crucial for all writers but especially so for novice writers. Illustrating a variety of possible writing rituals are testimonies from a dozen professional writers on the nature of writing. These quotations continue throughout the book, reminding students that writing is not some magical process, but rather a madness that has a method to it, a process born of reading, thinking, observing, remembering, discussing, and writing.

Chapter 2: An Orientation to Rhetorical Situation and to Writing Processes

Chapter 2, "Situations, Purposes, and Processes for Writing," grounds the writing process in the rhetorical situation. It shows how audience, genre, subject, and context work together with the writer's purpose to achieve a rhetorical end. It demonstrates how meaning evolves from a variety of recursive, multidimensional, and hierarchical activities that we call the *writing process*. Finally, it reassures students that, because individual writing and learning styles differ, they will be encouraged to discover and articulate their own processes from a range of appropriate possibilities.

Chapters 3 to 10: Aims and Purposes for Writing

The text then turns to specific purposes and assignments for writing. Chapters 3 through 6 ("Observing," "Remembering," "Reading," and "Analyzing and Designing Visuals") focus on invention and critical reading strategies. These chapters introduce genres and situations for writing that build students' rhetorical repertoires: observing people, places, objects, and images; remembering people, places, and events; developing critical reading and responding strategies; and developing critical reading strategies for visuals and rhetorical principles for designing visuals.

Chapters 7 through 10 ("Explaining," "Evaluating," "Problem Solving," and "Arguing") emphasize subject- and audience-based purposes and occasions for writing. The sequence in these chapters moves the student smoothly from exposition to argumentation (acknowledging the obvious overlapping), building on the strategies and repertoires of the previous chapters. The teacher may, in fact, use Chapters 7 through 10 as a minicourse in argument, teaching students how to develop and argue claims of fact and definition, claims of cause and effect, claims about values, and claims about solutions or policies. To support the text's emphasis on digital literacy, Chapter 9, "Problem Solving," presents a debate between John Barrie and Rebecca Moore Howard on whether teachers should use plagiarism detection devices such as Turnitin.com to combat plagiarism.

Chapter 11: Researching

Chapter 11, "Researching," supports the reading, writing, and researching strategies presented in the first ten chapters. This chapter helps students plan their research projects, find and critically evaluate print, online database, and open Web documents, record key content and bibliographic information, and document their sources using MLA or APA style. In keeping with the text's emphasis on information literacy and critical reading and evaluation of texts, this chapter demonstrates important contemporary strategies students need while selecting and focusing their research projects, collecting and evaluating sources, integrating sources into their projects, and avoiding plagiarism. A "behind-the-scenes" examination of Wikipedia shows students how entries are edited and why there are risks involved in using Wikipedia as a source. Up-to-date documentation instruction and examples based on the 2009 *MLA Handbook for Writers of Research Papers* and the 2009 *Publication Manual of the American Psychological Association* provide students with the latest models of correct MLA and APA style.

SUPPLEMENTS FOR INSTRUCTORS AND STUDENTS

Instructor's Manual: Teaching Composition with *The Prentice Hall Essential Guide for College Writers*

This instructor's manual, written by Stephen Reid, is designed to complement the text with additional classroom activities and ideas, as well as detailed discussion of effective strategies for the teaching of written expression skills. The manual also includes chapter commentaries, answers to discussion questions, and sections on composition theory, policy statements, lesson plans, collaborative writing, writing in a computer classroom, teaching ESL writers, small group learning, write-to-learn exercises, reading/writing exercises, journal assignments, suggestions for student conferences, and ideas for responding to and evaluating writing.

mycomplab MyCompLab

MyCompLab empowers student writers and facilitates writing instruction by uniquely integrating a composing space and assessment tools with market-leading instruction, multimedia tutorials, and exercises for writing, grammar, and research.

Students can use MyCompLab on their own, benefiting from self-paced diagnostics and a personal study plan that recommends the instruction and practice each student needs to improve her writing skills. The composing space and its integrated resources, tools, and services (such as online tutoring) are also available to each student as he writes.

MyCompLab is an eminently flexible application that instructors can use in ways that best complement their courses and teaching styles. They can recommend it to students for self-study, set up courses to track student progress, or leverage the power of administrative features to be more effective and save time.

The assignment builder and commenting tools, developed specifically for writing instruction, bring instructors closer to their student writers, make managing assignments and evaluating papers more efficient, and put powerful assessment within reach. Students receive feedback within the context of their own writing, which encourages critical thinking and revision and helps them to develop skills based on their individual needs.

Learn more at www.mycomplab.com.

CourseSmart eTextbook

The Prentice Hall Essential Guide for College Writers is also available as a CourseSmart etextbook. This is an exciting new choice for students, who can subscribe to the same content online and search the text, make notes online, print out reading assignments that incorporate lecture notes, and bookmark important passages for later review. For more information, or to subscribe to the CourseSmart etextbook, visit www.coursesmart.com.

Other Supplements

Pearson English has a wide array of other supplementary items—some at no additional cost, some deeply discounted—that are available for packaging with this text. Please contact your local Pearson representative to find out more.

ACKNOWLEDGMENTS

Because teaching writing is always a situated enterprise, I would like to thank the members of the composition faculty and staff at Colorado State University whose teaching expertise and enthusiasm have improved every page of the text: Kate Kiefer, Sarah Sloane, Lisa Langstraat, Tobi Jacobi, Carrie Lamanna, and Sue Doe. Many of the innovative teaching strategies, resources, and syllabi developed by Colorado State University composition faculty members are available at http://writing.colostate.edu.

In addition, I wish gratefully to acknowledge Dominic DelliCarpini, Writing Program Administrator at York College of Pennsylvania, who expertly developed the research strategies in Chapter 11, "Researching," and materially contributed to the focus on Web 2.0 materials throughout the book.

Many other key suggestions came from the following teachers who offered excellent advice: Jeanette Adkins, Tarrant County College; Young Eui Choi, Richland College; Joseph Rocky Colavito, Butler University; Jennifer Pooler Courtney, University of North Carolina Charlotte; Kevin R. Martin, Cochise College; LeRoy H. Miller, Northern Kentucky University; Missy Nieveen Phegley, Southeast Missouri State University; Coretta Pittman, Baylor University; and Chrishawn Speller, Seminole Community College. I wish to thank them for their thorough, honest, constructive, and professional guidance.

For the expert crew at Pearson Education, I am especially grateful. Phil Miller, a fine editor and friend, has enthusiastically supported this text from the start. Brad Potthoff provided an excellent vision as well as continuing support, while Marion Castellucci did a wonderfully thorough and professional job as development editor.

Finally, I wish to thank my family for their continued personal and professional support.

—STEPHEN REID
Colorado State University

The Prentice Hall Essential Guide for College Writers

Mark Shasha
Beach Reader

Beach Reader was painted by award-winning artist, actor, and author Mark Shasha. In this chapter, Journal Exercise 7 on page 11 invites you to analyze this painting and relate it to places where you like to read or write.

Writing Myths and Rituals

For me, the most effective writing ritual is to gather up all of my stuff—legal pad and pencil, notes, and dictionary—and get on my bike, ride to campus, and set myself up in the art lounge in the student center. During the week, I'll do this in the evening after dinner. On a weekend, I go any time from 10 A.M. to midnight. I don't write effectively at home because there are always distractions. Some people will be moving around and I'll go see who they are and what they're doing, or I'll go get a cup of coffee or a piece of toast, or I'll snap on the TV, ignoring that tiny voice inside saying, "Get busy—you have to get this done!" So what makes the art lounge better? Simple—no distractions. I can lay out all of my stuff, get a cup of coffee, and go to work. All around me people are doing the same thing, and somehow all of those hardworking people are an encouragement. The art lounge is always quiet, too—quieter than the library—and it doesn't smell like the library.

One myth about writing I have believed my whole life is that "good writers are born, not made." My attitude when beginning this writing course was one of apprehension and dread. I wondered if I *could* improve my writing, or if I was destined to receive B's and C's on every essay for the rest of my life. This writing class has given me concrete examples and suggestions for improvement—not just grammar or essay maps. The freewriting is such a great help that whenever I'm stuck, I immediately turn to my ten-minute freewriting to open up blocked passages. Once I get past my writer's block, I see that I can be a good writer.

> " A writer is someone who writes, that's all. "
> —GORE VIDAL, NOVELIST AND SOCIAL COMMENTATOR

> " I've always disliked words like *inspiration*. Writing is probably like a scientist thinking about some scientific problem or an engineer about an engineering problem. "
> —DORIS LESSING, AUTHOR OF ESSAYS AND FICTION, INCLUDING *THE GOLDEN NOTEBOOK*

> " I always worked until I had something done and I always stopped when I knew what was going to happen next. That way I could be sure of going on the next day. "
> —ERNEST HEMINGWAY, JOURNALIST AND NOVELIST, AUTHOR OF *THE OLD MAN AND THE SEA*

A S YOU BEGIN A COLLEGE WRITING COURSE, YOU NEED TO GET RID OF SOME MYTHS ABOUT WRITING THAT YOU MAY HAVE BEEN PACKING AROUND FOR SOME TIME. DON'T ALLOW MISCONCEPTIONS TO RUIN A GOOD EXPERIENCE. HERE ARE A FEW COMMON MYTHS ABOUT WRITING, followed by some facts compiled from the experiences of working writers.

MYTH: "Good writers are born, not made. A writing course really won't help my writing."

FACT: *Writers acquire their skills the same way athletes do—through practice and hard work.* There are very few "born" writers. Most writers—even professional writers and journalists—are not continually inspired to write. In fact, they often experience "writer's block," the stressful experience of staring helplessly at a piece of paper, unable to think or to put words down on paper. A writing course will teach you how to cope with your procrastination, anxiety, lack of "inspiration," and false starts by focusing directly on solving the problems that occur during the writing process.

MYTH: "Writing courses are just a review of boring grammar and punctuation. When teachers read your writing, the only thing they mark is that stuff, anyway."

FACT: *Learning and communicating—not grammar and punctuation—come first in college writing courses.* Knowledge of grammar, spelling, punctuation, and usage is essential to editing, but it is secondary to discovering ideas, thinking, learning, and communicating. In a writing course, students learn to revise and improve the content and organization of each other's writing. *Then* they help each other edit for grammar, punctuation, or spelling errors.

MYTH: "College writing courses are really 'creative writing,' which is not what my major requires. If I wanted to be another Shakespeare and write poetry, I'd change my major."

FACT: *Writing courses emphasize rhetoric, not poetry.* Rhetoric involves practicing the most effective means or strategies for informing or persuading an audience. All writing—even technical or business writing—is "creative." Deciding what to write, how to write it, how best to get your reader's attention, and how to inform or persuade your reader requires creativity and imagination. Every major requires the skills that writing courses teach: exploring new ideas, learning concepts and processes, communicating with others, and finding fresh or creative solutions to problems.

MYTH: "Writing courses are not important in college or the real world. I'll never have to write, anyway."

FACT: *Writing courses do have a significant effect on your success in college, on the job, and in life.* Even if you don't have frequent, formal writing assignments in other courses, writing improves your note-taking, reading comprehension, and thinking skills. When you do have other written tasks or assignments, a writing course teaches you to adapt your writing to a variety of different purposes and audiences—whether you are writing a lab report in biology, a letter to an editor, a complaint to the Better Business Bureau, or a memorandum to your boss. Taking a writing course helps you express yourself more clearly, confidently, and persuasively—a skill that comes in handy whether you're writing a philosophy essay, a job application, or a love letter.

The most important fact about writing is that you are already a writer. You have been writing for years. A writer is someone who writes, not someone who writes a nationally syndicated newspaper column, publishes a bestseller, or wins a Pulitzer Prize. To be an effective writer, you don't have to earn a million dollars; you just have to practice writing often enough to get acquainted with its personal benefits for you and its value for others.

WARMING UP   Freewriting

Put this book aside—right now—and take out pencil or pen and a piece of paper. Use this free exercise (private, unjudged, ungraded) to remind yourself that you are already a writer. Time yourself for five minutes. Write on the first thing that comes to mind—*anything whatsoever*. Write nonstop. Keep writing even if you have to write, "I can't think of anything to say. This feels stupid!" When you get an idea, pursue it.

When five minutes are up, stop writing and read what you have written. Whether you write about a genuinely interesting topic or about the weather, freewriting is an excellent way to warm up, to get into the habit of writing, and to establish a writing ritual.

Writing Fitness: Rituals and Practice

Writing is no more magic or inspiration than any other human activity that you admire: figure skating at the Olympics, rebuilding a car engine, cooking a gourmet meal, or acting in a play. Behind every human achievement are many unglamorous hours of practice—working and sweating, falling flat on your face, and picking yourself up again. You can't learn to write just by reading some chapters in a textbook or by memorizing other people's advice. You need help and advice, but you also need practice. Consider the following parable about a Chinese painter.

> A rich patron once gave money to the painter Chu Ta, asking him to paint a picture of a fish. Three years later, when he still had not received the painting, the patron went to Chu Ta's house to ask why the picture was not done. Chu Ta did not answer but dipped a brush in ink and with a few strokes drew a splendid fish. "If it is so easy," asked the patron, "why didn't you give me the picture three years ago?" Again, Chu Ta did not answer. Instead, he opened the door of a large cabinet. Thousands of pictures of fish tumbled out.

Most writers develop little rituals that help them practice their writing. A ritual is a *repeated pattern of behavior* that provides structure, security, and a sense of

> 66 My idea of a prewriting ritual is getting the kids on the bus and sitting down. 99
> —BARBARA KINGSOLVER
> AUTHOR OF *PRODIGAL SUMMER*

66 Writing is [like] making a table. With both you are working with reality, a material just as hard as wood. Both are full of tricks and techniques. Basically very little magic and a lot of hard work are involved. . . . What is a privilege, however, is to do a job to your own satisfaction. 99
—GABRIEL GARCÍA MÁRQUEZ,
NOBEL PRIZE–WINNING AUTHOR OF *ONE HUNDRED YEARS OF SOLITUDE*

progress to the one who practices it. Creating your own writing rituals and making them part of your regular routine will help reduce that dreaded initial panic and enable you to call upon your writing process with confidence when you need it.

PLACE, TIME, AND TOOLS

Some writers work best in pen and ink, sprawled on their beds in the afternoon while pets snooze on nearby blankets. Others are most comfortable with their keyboards and word processors at their desks or in the computer lab. Legal-sized pads help some writers produce, while others feel motivated by spiral notebooks with pictures of mountain streams on the covers. Only you can determine which place, time, and tools give you the best support as a writer.

The place where you write is also extremely important. If you are writing in a computer lab, you have to adapt to that place, but if you write a draft in long-hand or on your own laptop, you can choose the place yourself. In selecting a place, keep the following tips in mind.

- **Keep distractions minimal.** Some people simply can't write in the kitchen, where the refrigerator is distractingly close, or in a room that has a TV in it. On the other hand, a public place—a library, an empty classroom, a cafeteria—can be fine as long as the surrounding activity does not disturb them.
- **Control interruptions.** If you can close the door to your room and work without interruptions, fine. But even then, other people often assume that you want to take a break when they do. Choose a place where you can decide when it's time to take a break.
- **Have access to notes, journal, textbooks, sources, and other materials.** If the place is totally quiet but you don't have room to work or access to important notes or sources, you still may not make much progress. Whatever you need—a desk to spread your work out on, access to notes and sources, extra pens, or computer supplies—make sure your place has it.

The time of day you write and the tools you write with can also affect your attitude and efficiency. Some people like to write early in the morning, before their busy days start; others like to write in the evening, after classes or work. Whatever time you choose, try to write regularly—at least three days a week—at about the same time. If you're trying to get in shape by jogging, swimming, or doing aerobics, you wouldn't exercise for five straight hours on Monday and then take four days off. Like exercise, writing requires regular practice and conditioning.

Your writing tools—pen, pencil, paper, legal pads, four-by-six-inch notecards, notebooks, computer—should also be comfortable for you. Some writers like to make notes with pencil and paper and write drafts on computers; some like to do all composing on computers. As you try different combinations of tools, be aware of how you feel and whether your tools make you more effective. If you feel comfortable, it will be easier to establish rituals that lead to regular practice.

66 Writers are notorious for using any reason to keep from working: overresearching, retyping, going to meetings, waxing the floors—anything. 99
—GLORIA STEINEM,
FORMER EDITOR OF *MS. MAGAZINE*

Rituals are important because they help you with the most difficult part of writing: getting started. So use your familiar place, time, and tools to trick yourself into getting some words down on paper. Your mind will devise clever schemes to avoid writing those first ten words—watching TV, texting a friend, drinking some more coffee, or calling a classmate and whining together about all the writing you have to do. But if your body has been through the ritual before, it will walk calmly to your favorite place, where all your tools are ready (perhaps bringing the mind kicking and screaming all the way). Then, after you get the first ten words down, the mind will say, "Hey, this isn't so bad— I've got something to say about that!" And off you'll go.

FRANK AND ERNEST ©by Bob Thaves

Copyright © 1987 by Bob Thaves. Reprinted with the permission of Bob Thaves.

Each time you perform your writing ritual, the *next* time you write will be that much easier. Soon, your ritual will let you know: "*This is where you write. This is when you write. This is what you write with.*" No fooling around. Just writing.

ENERGY AND ATTITUDE

Once you've tricked yourself into the first ten words, you need to keep your attitude positive and your energy high. When you see an intimidating wall starting to form in front of you, don't ram your head into it; figure out a way to sneak around it. Try these few tricks and techniques.

- **Start anywhere, quickly.** No law says that when you sit down to write a draft, you have to "begin at the beginning." If the first sentence is hard to write, begin with the first thoughts that come to mind. Or begin with a good example from your experience. Use that to get you going; then come back and rewrite your beginning after you've figured out what you want to say.

- **Write the easiest parts first.** Forcing yourself to start a piece of writing by working on the hardest part first is a sure way to make yourself hate writing. Take the path of least resistance. If you can't get your thesis to come out right, jot down more examples. If you can't think of examples, go back to brainstorming.

- **Keep moving.** Once you've plunged in, write as fast as you can—whether you are scribbling ideas out with a pencil or hitting the keys of a computer. Maintain your momentum. Reread if you need to, but then plunge ahead.

- **Quit when you know what comes next.** When you do have to quit for the day, stop at a place where you know what comes next. Don't drain

> ❝I am by nature lazy, sluggish and of low energy. It constantly amazes me that I do anything at all. ❞
> —MARGARET ATWOOD, WHO HAS MANAGED TO PRODUCE NUMEROUS BOOKS OF FICTION AND POETRY

66Since I began writing I have always played games. . . . I have a playful nature; I have never been able to do things because it is my duty to do them. If I can find a way to do my duty by playing a game, then I can manage. 99

—MARIA IRENE FORNES, OBIE AWARD–WINNING PLAYWRIGHT

66I carry a journal with me almost all the time. . . . 99

—NTOZAKE SHANGE, AUTHOR OF THE PLAY *FOR COLORED GIRLS WHO HAVE CONSIDERED SUICIDE WHEN THE RAINBOW IS ENUF*

the well dry; stop in the middle of something you know how to finish. Make a few notes about what you need to do next and circle them. Leave yourself an easy place to get started next time.

One of the most important strategies for every writer is to *give yourself a break from the past and begin with a fresh image.* In many fields—mathematics, athletics, art, engineering—some people are late bloomers. Don't let that C or D you got in English back in tenth grade hold you back now like a ball and chain. Imagine yourself cutting the chain and watching the ball roll away for good. Now you are free to start fresh with a clean slate. Your writing rituals should include only positive images about the writer you are right now and realistic expectations about what you can accomplish.

- **Visualize yourself writing.** Successful athletes know how to visualize a successful tennis swing, a basketball free throw, or a baseball swing. When you are planning your activities for the day, visualize yourself writing at your favorite place. Seeing yourself doing your writing will enable you to start writing more quickly and maintain a positive attitude.
- **Discover and emphasize the aspects of writing that are fun for you.** Emphasize whatever is enjoyable for you—discovering an idea, getting the organization of a paragraph to come out right, clearing the unnecessary words and junk out of your writing. Concentrating on the parts you enjoy will help you make it through the tougher parts.
- **Set modest goals for yourself.** Don't aim for the stars; just work on a sentence. Don't measure yourself against some great writer; be your own yardstick. Compare what you write to what *you* have written before.
- **Congratulate yourself for the writing you do.** Writing is hard work; you're using words to create ideas and meanings literally out of nothing. So pat yourself on the back occasionally. Keep in mind the immortal words of comedian and playwright Steve Martin: "I think I did pretty well, considering I started out with nothing but a bunch of blank paper."

KEEPING A JOURNAL

Many writers keep some kind of notebook in which they write down their thoughts, ideas, plans, and important events. Some writers use a journal, a private place for their day-to-day thoughts. Other writers create weblogs, or "blogs," a more public place for their ideas. Both journals and blogs can be a "place for daily writing." If you choose a private, written journal, you can later select what you want others to read; if you use your blog, your thoughts and ideas are there for others to read and respond to. Whatever medium you choose, use it as part of your daily writing ritual. In it can go notes and ideas, bits and pieces of experience, or responses to essays or books you're reading. Sometimes journals or blogs are assigned as part of your class work. In that case, you may do in-class, write-to-learn entries, plans for your essays, postscripts for an essay, or reflections on a portfolio.

Your journal or blog can be a place for formal assignments or just a place to practice, a room where all your "fish paintings" go.

As the following list indicates, there are many kinds of journal entries. They fall into three categories: *reading entries, write-to-learn entries,* and *writing entries.*

1. Reading entries help you understand and actively respond to student or professional writing.
2. Write-to-learn entries help you summarize, react to, or question ideas or essays discussed in class.
3. Writing entries help you warm up, test ideas, make writing plans, practice rhetorical strategies, or solve specific writing problems.

All three kinds of journal writing, however, take advantage of the unique relationship between thinking, writing, and learning. Simply put, writing helps you learn what you know (and don't know) by shaping your thoughts into language.

READING ENTRIES

- **Prereading journal entries.** Before you read an essay, read the headnote and write for five minutes on the topic of the essay—what you know about the subject, what related experiences you have had, and what opinions you hold. After you write your entry, the class can discuss the topic before you read the essay. The result? Your reading will be more active, engaged, and responsive.
- **Double-entry logs.** Draw a line vertically down a sheet of paper. On the left-hand side, summarize key ideas as you reread an essay. On the right-hand side, write down your reactions, responses, and questions. Writing while you read helps you understand and respond more thoroughly.
- **Essay annotations.** Writing your comments in the margin as you read is sometimes more efficient than writing separate journal entries. Check out the author on Google and look up any unfamiliar terms or references. Also, in a small group in class, you can share your annotations and collaboratively annotate a copy of the essay.
- **Vocabulary entries.** Looking up unfamiliar words in a dictionary and writing out definitions in your journal will make you a much more accurate reader. Often an essay's thesis, meaning, or tone hinges on the meanings of a few key words.
- **Summary/response entries.** Double-entry logs help you understand while you reread, but a short one-paragraph summary and one-paragraph response after you finish your rereading helps you focus on both the main ideas of a passage and your own key responses.

WRITE-TO-LEARN ENTRIES

- **Lecture/discussion entries.** At key points in a class lecture or discussion, your teacher may ask you to write for five minutes by responding to a few questions: What is the main idea of the discussion? What one question would you like to ask? How does the topic of discussion relate to the essay that you are currently writing?

> **"**The most valuable writing tool I have is my daybook. . . . I write in my lap, in the living room or on the porch, in the car or an airplane, in meetings at the university, in bed, or sitting down on a rock wall during a walk. . . . It is always a form of talking to myself, a way of thinking on paper. **"**
>
> —DONALD MURRAY, JOURNALIST, AUTHOR OF BOOKS AND ESSAYS ABOUT WRITING

- **Responses to essays.** Before discussing an essay, write for a few minutes to respond to the following questions: What is the main idea of this essay? What do you like best about the essay? What is confusing, misleading, or wrong in this essay? What strategies illustrated in this essay will help you with your own writing?
- **Time-out responses.** During a controversial discussion or argument about an essay, your teacher may stop the class, take time out, and ask you to write for five minutes to respond to several questions: What key issue is the class debating? What are the main points of disagreement? What is your opinion? What evidence, either in the essay or in your experience, supports your opinion?

Writing Entries

- **Warming up.** Writing, like any other kind of activity, improves when you loosen up, stretch, get the kinks out, practice a few lines. Any daybook or journal entry gives you a chance to warm up.
- **Collecting and shaping exercises.** Some journal entries will help you collect information by observing, remembering, or investigating people, places, events, or objects. You can also record quotations or startling statistics for future writing topics. Other journal entries suggested in each chapter of this book will help you practice organizing your information. Strategies of development, such as comparison/contrast, definition, classification, or process analysis will help you discover and shape ideas.
- **Writing for a specific audience.** In some journal entries, you need to play a role, imagining that you are in a specific situation and writing for a defined audience. For example, you might write a letter of application for a job or a letter to a friend explaining why you've chosen a certain major.
- **Revision plans and postscripts.** Your journal is also the place to keep a log—a running account of your writing plans, revision plans, problems, and solutions. Include your research notes, peer responses, and postscripts on your writing process in this log.
- **Imitating styles of writers.** Use your journal to copy passages from writers you like. Practice imitating their styles on different topics. Also, try simply transcribing a few paragraphs. Even copying effective writers' words will reveal some of their secrets for successful writing.
- **Writing free journal entries.** Use your journal to record ideas, reactions to people on campus, events in the news, reactions to controversial articles in the campus newspaper, conversations after class or work, or just your private thoughts.

WARMING UP   Journal Exercises

Choose three of the exercises below and write for ten minutes on each. Date and number each entry.

1 Make an "authority" list of activities, subjects, ideas, places, people, or events that you already know something about. List as many topics as you can. If your reaction is "I'm not really an *authority* on anything," then imagine you've met someone from another school, state, country, or historical period. With that person as your audience, what are you an "authority" on?

2 Choose one activity, sport, or hobby that you do well and that others might admire you for. In the form of a letter to a friend, describe the steps or stages of the process through which you acquired that skill or ability.

3 In two or three sentences, complete the following thought: "I have trouble writing because . . ."

4 In a few sentences, complete the following thought: "In my previous classes and from my own writing experience, I've learned that the three most important rules about writing are . . ."

5 Describe your own writing rituals. *When, where,* and *how* do you write best?

6 Write an open journal entry. Describe events from your day, images, impressions, bits of conversation—anything that catches your interest.

7 Look again at the chapter opening work of art, *Beach Reader,* by Mark Shasha. Mark Shasha is an award-winning artist, author, and actor who travels much of the year to talk to children about the world of reading, writing, and drawing. Describe how Shasha uses color, light, balance, and focus in his painting to create an inviting place for reading, writing, or just relaxing.

Mona Lisa Barn
Dennis Weimer.
Layne Kennedy,
Photographer

The picture above, taken by photographer Layne Kennedy, shows a famous Mona Lisa barn painting on a farm near Cornell, Wisconsin. Mona Lisa's shirt has been repainted to celebrate Wisconsin's victory in the 1994 Rose Bowl. A freewriting assignment on page 23 invites you to describe the purpose, audience, and genre of this image.

Situations, Purposes, and Processes for Writing

A veteran smoker, you have become increasingly irritated at the nonsmoking regulations that have appeared in restaurants, businesses, and other public places. And it's not just the laws that are irritating, but the holier-than-thou attitude of people who presume that what's good for them should be good for you. Non-smoking laws seem to give people license to censure your behavior while totally ignoring their own offensive behavior: polluting the atmosphere with hydrocarbons, fouling the aquifers with fertilizers, and generally corrupting the social air with odors of false superiority. So after one particularly memorable experience, you write a letter to the editor of the local paper, intending not only to express your own frustration but also to satirize all those smug do-gooders.

As a Chinese-American woman growing up in America, you decide to write about the difficulty of living in two cultures. You recall how, during your childhood, you rebelled against your mother when she insisted that you learn about your Chinese heritage. You remember how much you hated your Chinese school and how embarrassed you were that your mother could not speak English properly. As you grew older, however, you realized the price you paid for your assimilation into American culture. After discussing this conflict with your friends, you decide to describe your experiences to others who share them or who may want to know what you learned. At that point, you write an autobiographical account of your experiences and post it on the Web.

> " First and foremost I write for myself. Writing has been for a long time my major tool for self-instruction and self-development. "
> —TONI CADE BAMBARA, AUTHOR OF *THE SALT EATERS*

> " How do I know what I think until I see what I say? "
> —E. M. FORSTER, AUTHOR OF *A PASSAGE TO INDIA*

THE WRITING FOR THIS COURSE (AND THE STRUCTURE OF THIS TEXTBOOK) ASSUMES THAT WRITING IS VALUABLE FOR TWO RELATED REASONS. FIRST, WRITING ENABLES YOU TO LEARN ABOUT SOMETHING, TO HELP YOU OBSERVE YOUR SURROUNDINGS, TO REMEMBER IMPORTANT IDEAS AND events, and to record and analyze what you see and read. Second, writing is an important means to communicate with your readers, to explain or evaluate an idea, to offer a solution, or to argue your point of view. These two reasons for writing are usually related. If you want to persuade others to agree with your point of view, you'll be more effective if you reflect on how your personal observations, memories, experiences, and things you've read and heard might help you convince your readers. Whatever you write, however, you are always writing in a particular situation or context. Understanding how your goals as a writer relate to the writing situation and to your own processes for writing is the focus of this chapter.

The Rhetorical Situation

As you begin this writing course, consider how you and your writing fit into a larger context. Anytime you write an e-mail response, a letter to your friends, a posting on your Facebook page, an essay for your English or history class, an application for a job, a letter to the editor, or an entry in your journal, you are in the middle of a rhetorical situation. If rhetoric is the "art of using language effectively or persuasively," then the rhetorical situation is the overall context in which your writing occurs.

ELEMENTS OF THE RHETORICAL SITUATION

The key parts of the rhetorical situation are you, the writer; the immediate occasion that prompts you to write; your intended purpose and audience; your genre or type of writing; and the larger social context in which you are writing. Because these key terms are used repeatedly in this course, you need to know exactly what each term means and how it will help guide your writing.

● **THE WRITER**   You are the writer. Sometimes you write in response to an assignment, but at other times, you choose to write because of something that happened or something that made you think or react. In college or on the job, you often have writing assignments, but in your life, you are often the one who decides to write when you need to remember something, plan, remind others, express your feelings, or solve a problem.

● **THE OCCASION**   The occasion is whatever motivates you to write. Often you are motivated by an assignment that a teacher or a boss gives you. Sometimes, however, a particular event or incident makes you want to write. The cause may be a conversation you had with a friend, an article you read, or something that happened to you recently. The occasion is simply the immediate cause or the pressing need to write, whether assigned to you by someone else or just determined by you to be the reason for your desire to write.

● **PURPOSE**   Your purpose in writing is the effect you wish to have on your intended audience. Major purposes for writing include **expressing** your feelings; investigating a subject and **reporting** your findings; **explaining** an idea or concept; **evaluating** some object, performance, or image; **proposing a solution** to a problem; and **arguing** for your position and responding to alternative or opposing positions.

● **AUDIENCE**   Your knowledge about your intended audience should always guide and shape your writing. If you are writing for yourself, you can just list ideas, express your thoughts, or make informal notes. If you are writing to explain an idea or concept, you should think about who needs or wants to know about your idea. To whom do you want to explain this idea? Are they likely to be novices or experts on the topic? Similarly, if you are arguing your position, you need to consider the thoughts and feelings of readers who may have several different points of view. What do they believe about your topic? Do they agree or disagree with your position, or are they undecided?

● **GENRE**   The genre you choose is simply the kind, type, or form of writing you select. Everyone is familiar with genres in literature, such as poems, novels, and plays. In nonfiction, typical genres are essays, memoirs, magazine articles, and editorials. In college, you may write in a variety of genres, including e-mail, personal essays, lab reports, summaries, reviews of research, analytical essays, argumentative essays, and even scientific or business reports. Sometimes, you may need to write multigenre or multimedia reports with graphic images or pictures. For community service learning or on the job, you may write reports, analyses, brochures, or flyers. As a citizen of the community, you may write letters to the editor, responses to an online discussion forum, or letters to your representative.

The genre you choose helps create the intellectual, social, or cultural relationship between you and your reader. It helps you communicate your purpose to your reader or makes possible the social action you wish to achieve. If your purpose is to analyze or critique material you are reading in a class, an essay is a genre suitable to your purpose and your intended audience (your teacher and your peers in class). A lab report is a different genre, requiring your notes, observations, and hypothesis about your experiment, presented for members of a scientific community. Finally, the purpose of a one-page brochure for your

> ❝ Every genre positions those who participate in a text of that kind: as interviewer or interviewee, as listener or storyteller, as a reader or a writer, as a person interested in political matters, as someone to be instructed or as someone who instructs; each of these positionings implies different possibilities for response and for action. ❞
>
> —GUNTHER KRESS,
> AUTHOR OF *LITERACY IN THE NEW MEDIA AGE*

> 66 A rhetorically sound definition of genre must be centered not on the substance or form of discourse but on the action it is used to accomplish. 99
>
> —CAROLYN MILLER,
> TEACHER AND AUTHOR OF
> *GENRE AS SOCIAL ACTION*

community crisis center, for example, may be to advertise its services to a wide audience that includes college students and members of the community. The point is to learn what readers expect of each genre and then choose—or modify—a genre that is appropriate for your purpose and audience. Learning which genres are appropriate for each writing situation and learning about the formal features of each genre (such as introduction, presentation of information, paragraphing, and vocabulary) is a key part of each writing task. Remember, however, that genres have rules but are not rulebound. Every text should have recognizable features of a genre but also individual variation appropriate for that particular occasion.

● **CONTEXT**   As both a reader and a writer, you must consider the rhetorical and social context. When you read an essay or other text, think about the **author**, the **place of publication**, the **ongoing conversation** about this topic, and the larger **social or cultural context**. First, consider who wrote an essay and where it appeared. Was the essay a citizen's editorial in the *New York Times,* a journalist's feature article in *Vogue,* a scientist's research report in the *New England Journal of Medicine,* or a personal essay on an individual's Web site? Often, who wrote the article, what his or her potential bias or point of view was, and the place of publication can be just as important as what the article says. Next, consider the ongoing conversation to which this essay contributes. What different viewpoints exist on this topic? Which perspectives does this essay address? Finally, the larger sense of culture, politics, and history in which the article appears may be crucial to your understanding.

Similarly, when you write an essay, think about where it might be read or published and what conversation already exists on the topic. What cultural or political points of view are represented in the conversation? How does that ongoing conversation affect what you think? How does your own cultural, political, ethnic, or personal background affect what you believe? Understanding and analyzing the larger rhetorical and social context helps you become a better reader and writer.

WHY THE RHETORICAL SITUATION IS IMPORTANT

So, you understand each of the elements of the rhetorical situation, and you see how they are interconnected. But how does that knowledge help you as a writer? The answer is both easy and difficult. The easy part is that every decision you make as a writer—how to begin, how much evidence you include, how you organize, whether you can use "I" in your writing, what style or tone you should use—depends on the rhetorical situation. The style and organization of a lab report is different from an essay, which is different from a brochure. If you've ever asked your teacher, "Won't you just tell me what you want?" the answer to that question always is, "Well, it depends." It depends on what is appropriate for the purpose, audience, genre, and context. And that is where the difficult part of writing begins: learning which genres, styles, and methods of organization are appropriate for each writing situation. To learn the various approaches to writing and how they are most effectively used is the reason that you continually read and practice writing the major genres taught in your composition class.

FREEWRITING: INVENTORY OF YOUR WRITING

Before you read further in this chapter, take out a pen or open a computer file and make a list of what you have written in the last year or two. Brainstorm a list of all the genres you can think of: shopping lists for a trip, letters to family or friends, applications for jobs, school essays, personal or professional Web sites, science projects, or memos for your boss. Then, for one of your longer writing projects, jot down several sentences describing the situation that called for that piece of writing—what was the occasion, purpose, and audience? What form or genre did your writing take? How did that genre help define a relationship between you and your reader? Where did you write it, and what was your writing process?

Purposes for Writing

Getting a good grade, sharing experiences with a friend, or contributing to society may be among your motives for writing. However, as a writer, you also have more specific rhetorical purposes for writing. These purposes help you make key decisions related to your audience and genre. When your main purpose is to express your feelings, you may write a private entry in your journal. When your main purpose is to explain how your sales promotion increased the number of your company's customers, you may write a formal sales report to your boss. When your main purpose is to persuade others to see a movie that you like, you may write a review for the local newspaper. In each case, the intended rhetorical purpose—your desire to create a certain effect on your audience—helps determine what you write and how you say it.

> 66 The writer may write to inform, to explain, to entertain, to persuade, but whatever the purpose there should be first of all, the satisfaction of the writer's own learning. 99
> —DONALD MURRAY, TEACHER AND PULITZER PRIZE–WINNING JOURNALIST

WRITER-BASED PURPOSES

Because writing is, or should be, for yourself first of all, everything you write involves at least some purpose that benefits you. Of course, expressing yourself is a fundamental purpose of all writing. Without the satisfaction of expressing your thoughts, feelings, reactions, knowledge, or questions, you might not make the effort to write in the first place.

A closely related purpose is learning: Writing helps you discover what you think or feel, simply by using language to identify and compose your thoughts. Writing not only helps you form ideas but actually promotes observing and remembering. If you write down what you observe about people, places, or things, you can actually "see" them more clearly. Similarly, if you write down facts, ideas, experiences, or reactions to your readings, you will remember them longer. Writing and rewriting facts, dates, definitions, impressions, or personal experiences will improve your powers of recall on such important occasions as examinations and job interviews.

SUBJECT- AND AUDIENCE-BASED PURPOSES

> **I think writing is really a process of communication. . . . It's the sense of being in contact with people who are part of a particular audience that really makes a difference to me in writing.**
> —SHERLEY ANNE WILLIAMS, POET, CRITIC, AND NOVELIST

Although some writing is intended only for yourself—such as entries in a diary, lists, class notes, reminders—much of your writing will be read by others, by those readers who constitute your "audience."

- You may write to *inform* others about a particular subject—to tell them about the key facts, data, feelings, people, places, or events.
- You may write to *explain* to your readers what something means, how it works, or why it happens.
- You may write to *persuade* others to believe or do something—to convince others to agree with your judgment about a book, record, or restaurant, or to persuade them to take a certain class, vote for a certain candidate, or buy some product you are advertising.
- You may write to *explore* ideas and "truths," to examine how your ideas have changed, to ask questions that have no easy answers, and then to share your thoughts and reflections with others.
- You may write to *entertain*—as a primary purpose in itself or as a purpose combined with informing, explaining, persuading, or exploring. Whatever your purposes may be, good writing both teaches and pleases. Remember, too, that your readers will learn more, remember more, or be more convinced when your writing contains humor, wit, or imaginative language.

> **Writing, as a rhetorical act, is carried out within a web of purpose.**
> —LINDA FLOWER, TEACHER AND RESEARCHER IN COMPOSITION

COMBINATIONS OF PURPOSES

In many cases, you write with more than one purpose in mind. Purposes may appear in combinations, connected in a sequence, or actually overlapping. Initially, you may take notes about a subject to learn and remember, but later you may want to inform others about what you have discovered. Similarly, you may begin by writing to express your feelings about a movie that you loved or that upset you; later, you may wish to persuade others to see it—or not to see it.

Purposes can also contain each other, like Chinese boxes, or overlap, blurring the distinctions. An explanation of how an automobile works will contain information about that vehicle. An attempt to persuade someone to buy an automobile may contain an explanation of how it handles and information about its body style or engine. Usually, writing to persuade others will contain explanations and basic information, but the reverse is not necessarily true; you can write simply to give information, without trying to persuade anyone to do anything.

SUBJECT, PURPOSE, AND THESIS

The *thesis, claim,* or *main idea* in a piece of writing is related to your purpose. As a writer, you usually have a purpose in mind that serves as a guide while you gather information about your subject and think about your audience. However, as you collect and record information, impressions, and ideas you gradually narrow your subject to a specific topic and thus clarify your purpose. You bring your purpose into sharper and sharper focus—as if progressing on a target from the outer circles to the bull's-eye—until you have narrowed your purpose down to a central thesis. The thesis is the dominant idea, explanation, evaluation, or recommendation that you want to impress upon your readers.

The following examples illustrate how a writer moves from a general subject, guided by purpose, to a specific thesis or claim.

Subject	Purpose	Thesis, Claim, or Main Idea
Childhood experiences	To express your feelings and explain how one childhood experience was important	The relentless competition between my sisters and me changed my easygoing personality.
Social networking sites	To inform readers about how to set privacy settings on MySpace and Facebook	The default settings on MySpace and Facebook will not always protect your online privacy.
Carbon footprint	To persuade readers to reduce their carbon footprint	Americans should take ten important steps to reduce their carbon footprint when they are at home, when they shop, and when they travel.

Purpose and Audience

Writing for yourself is relatively easy; after all, you already know your audience and can make spontaneous judgments about what is essential and what is not. However, when your purpose is to communicate to other readers, you need to analyze your audience. Your writing will be more effective if you can anticipate what your readers know and need to know, what they are interested in, and what their beliefs or attitudes are. As you write for different readers, you will select different kinds of information, organize it in different ways, or write in a more formal or less formal style.

FREEWRITING: WRITING FOR DIFFERENT AUDIENCES

Before you read further, get a pen or pencil and several sheets of paper and do the following exercise.

1. For your eyes only, write about what you did at a recent party. Write for four minutes.

2. On a second sheet of paper, describe for the members of your writing class what you did at this party; you will read this aloud to the class. Stop after four minutes.

3. On a third sheet of paper, write a letter to one of your parents or a relative describing what you did at the party. Stop after four minutes.

AUDIENCE ANALYSIS

If you are writing to communicate to other readers, analyzing your probable audience will help you answer some basic questions.

- What genre should I choose? What genre—or combination of genres—would best enable me to communicate with my audience?
- How much information or evidence is enough? What should I assume my audience already knows? What should I not tell them? What do they believe? Will they readily agree with me, or will they be antagonistic?
- How should I organize my writing? How can I get my readers' attention? Can I just describe my subject and tell a story, or should I analyze everything in a logical order? Should I put my best examples or arguments first or last?

- Should I write informally, with simple sentences and easy vocabulary, or should I write in a more elaborate or specialized style, with technical vocabulary?

Analyze your audience by considering the following questions. As you learn more about your audience, the possibilities for your own role as a writer will become clearer.

1. **Audience profile.** How narrow or broad is your audience? Is it a narrow and defined audience—a single person, such as your Aunt Mary, or a group with clear common interests, such as the zoning board in your city or the readers of *Organic Gardening?* Is it a broad and diverse audience: educated readers who wish to be informed on current events, American voters as a whole, or residents of your state? Do your readers have identifiable roles? Can you determine their age, sex, economic status, ethnic background, or occupational category?

2. **Audience–subject relationship.** Consider what your readers know about your subject. If they know very little about it, you'll need to explain the basics; if they already know quite a bit, you can go straight to more difficult or complex issues. Also estimate their probable attitude toward this subject. Are they likely to be sympathetic or hostile?

3. **Audience–writer relationship.** What is your relationship with your readers? Do you know each other personally? Do you have anything in common? Will your audience be likely to trust what you say, or will they be skeptical about your judgments? Are you the expert on this particular subject and the readers the novices? Or are you the novice and your readers the experts?

4. **Writer's role.** To communicate effectively with your audience, you should also consider your own role or perspective. Of the many roles that you could play (friend, big sister or brother, student of psychology, music fan, employee of a fast-food restaurant, and so on), choose one that will be effective for your purpose and audience. If, for example, you are writing to sixth-graders about nutrition, you could choose the perspective of a concerned older brother or sister. Your writing might be more effective, however, if you assume the role of a person who has worked in fast-food restaurants for three years and knows what goes into hamburgers, french fries, and milkshakes.

Writers may write to real audiences, or they may create audiences. Sometimes the relationship between writer and reader is real (sister writing to brother), so the writer starts with a known audience and writes accordingly. Sometimes, however, writers begin and gradually discover or create an audience in the process of writing. Knowing the audience guides the writing, but the writing may construct an audience as well.

Purpose, Audience, and Genre

In addition to considering your purpose and audience, think also about the possible forms or genres your writing might take. If you are writing to observe or remember something, you may want to write an informal essay, a letter, a memoir, or even an e-mail to reach your audience. If you are writing to inform your readers or explain some idea, you may write an article, essay, letter, report, or pamphlet to best achieve your purpose and address your audience. Argumentative writing—writing to evaluate, persuade, or recommend some position or course of action—takes place in many different genres, from e-mails, blogs, and letters, to reviews and editorials, to proposals and researched documents. As you select a topic, consider which genre would most effectively accomplish your purpose for your intended audience.

Below are some of the common genres that you will read or write while in college, on the job, or as a member of your community. Each genre has certain organization and style features that readers of this genre expect. Knowing the genre that you are writing or reading helps answer questions about how to write or how to respond to a piece of writing.

Genre	Conventions of Organization and Style
Personal essay	Some narrative and descriptive passages Informal; uses first-person "I" Applies personal experience to larger social question
Research review	Uses concise, accurate summary May be an annotated bibliography or part of a larger thesis Adheres to MLA, APA, Chicago styles
Argumentative essay	Makes a claim about a controversial topic Responds to alternative or opposing positions Carefully considers audience Supports claims with evidence and examples Uses reasonable tone Has formal paragraphing
Laboratory report	May be informal description of materials, procedures, and results May be formal organization with title, abstract, introduction, method, results, and discussion

Brochure	Mixes graphics, text, visuals
	Visually arresting and appealing layout
	Concise information and language
Letter to the editor	Refers to issue or topic
	States opinion, point of view, or recommendation
	Usually concise to fit into editorial page
Posting to an electronic forum	Connects to specific thread in discussion
	May be informal style
	Flaming and trolling occur, but are often censured
E-mail, text message or tweet	Usually short
	Informal and personal style
	Often without salutation, caps, or punctuation
	May use emoticons such as :-), :-(, :-.) (Cindy Crawford), or 8(:-) (Mickey Mouse), or acronyms such as BTW, LOL, FYI, or THX

FREEWRITING: PURPOSE, AUDIENCE, GENRE, AND CONTEXT IN AN IMAGE

Before you read further in this chapter, analyze the rhetorical elements in the photograph by Layne Kennedy that appears at the beginning of this chapter. What is the purpose of this barn painting? Who was the intended audience? How would you describe this genre of art? What was the social and cultural context in which this painting appeared? (Use Yahoo!, Google, or your favorite search engine to discover background information.) Overall, how effective is this painting at achieving its rhetorical purpose for its audience and context? Explain.

Analyzing the Rhetorical Situation

To review, the rhetorical situation consists of the writer, the occasion, the purpose and audience, the genre and the context. Sometimes several of these are assigned to the writer, but at other times, the writer chooses a purpose, audience, and genre. The key point to remember is that these terms are all interrelated and interconnected. Your overall purpose often depends on your selected audience. Deciding on a particular audience may mean choosing a particular genre. Thinking about the context and conversation surrounding a particular topic may help you be more persuasive for your selected audience. Writing and revising require reconsidering and revising each of these elements to make them work harmoniously to achieve your rhetorical goal.

The following scenarios illustrate how the writer's purpose, the occasion, the audience, genre, and context work together to define the rhetorical situation. In the following descriptions, identify each of the key parts of the rhetorical situation.

> A student who transferred from a community college to a 4-year school had to give up her well-paying job and move 75 miles to attend a state institution. The cost of getting her degree ballooned to nearly $10,000 per year. She decides to write a letter to send to her state senator arguing that some 2-year schools in her state should be able to grant bachelor's degrees for high-achieving students. She cites precedents in several states, including California and Florida. Although she acknowledges that such a policy would change the mission of community colleges, she tries to persuade her senator that in these difficult economic times, students need options for getting a degree that do not leave them with thousands of dollars of debt to repay.

> In response to a request by an editor of a college recruiting pamphlet, a student decides to write an essay explaining the advantages of the social and academic life at his university. According to the editor, the account needs to be realistic but should also promote the university. It shouldn't be too academic and stuffy—the college catalog itself contains all the basic information—but it should give high school seniors a flavor of college life. The student decides to write a narrative account of his most interesting experiences during his first week at college.

PURPOSE, AUDIENCE, AND CONTEXT IN TWO ESSAYS

The two short essays that follow appeared as columns in newspapers. Both relate the writers' own experiences. They are similar in genre but have different purposes, they appeal to different readers, and they have different social and cultural contexts. First, read each essay just to understand each writer's point of view. Then reread each essay, thinking particularly about each writer's main purpose, his or her intended audience, and the social and cultural context surrounding each topic.

PROFESSIONAL WRITING

The Struggle to Be an All-American Girl

Elizabeth Wong

It's still there, the Chinese school on Yale Street where my brother and I used to go. Despite the new coat of paint and the high wire fence, the school I knew 10 years ago remains remarkably, stoically the same. *1*

Every day at 5 p.m., instead of playing with our fourth- and fifth-grade friends or sneaking out to the empty lot to hunt ghosts and animal bones, my brother and I had to go to Chinese school. No amount of kicking, screaming, or pleading could dissuade my mother, who was solidly determined to have us learn the language of our heritage. *2*

Forcibly, she walked us the seven long, hilly blocks from our home to school, depositing our defiant tearful faces before the stern principal. My only memory of him is that he swayed on his heels like a palm tree, and he always clasped his impatient twitching hands behind his back. I recognized him as a repressed maniacal child killer, and knew that if we ever saw his hands we'd be in big trouble. *3*

We all sat in little chairs in an empty auditorium. The room smelled like Chinese medicine, and imported faraway mustiness. Like ancient mothballs or dirty closets. I hated that smell. I favored crisp new scents. Like the soft French perfume that my American teacher wore in public school. *4*

Although the emphasis at the school was mainly language—speaking, reading, writing—the lessons always began with an exercise in politeness. With the entrance of the teacher, the best student would tap a bell and everyone would get up, kowtow, and chant, "sing san ho," the phonetic for "How are you, teacher?" *5*

Being ten years old, I had better things to learn than ideographs copied painstakingly in lines that ran right to left from the tip of a *moc but,* a real ink pen that had to be held in an awkward way if blotches were to be avoided. After all, I could do the multiplication tables, name the satellites of Mars, and write reports on "Little Women" and "Black Beauty." Nancy Drew, my favorite book heroine, never spoke Chinese. *6*

The language was a source of embarrassment. More times than not, I had tried to disassociate myself from the nagging loud voice that followed me wherever I wandered in the nearby American supermarket outside Chinatown. The voice belonged to my grandmother, a fragile *7*

...continued The Struggle to Be an All-American Girl, **Elizabeth Wong**

woman in her seventies who could outshout the best of the street vendors. Her humor was raunchy, her Chinese rhythmless, patternless. It was quick, it was loud, it was unbeautiful. It was not like the quiet, lilting romance of French or the gentle refinement of the American South. Chinese sounded pedestrian. Public.

In Chinatown, the comings and goings of hundreds of Chinese on their daily tasks sounded chaotic and frenzied. I did not want to be thought of as mad, as talking gibberish. When I spoke English, people nodded at me, smiled sweetly, said encouraging words. Even the people in my culture would cluck and say that I'd do well in life. "My, doesn't she move her lips fast," they would say, meaning that I'd be able to keep up with the world outside Chinatown. 8

My brother was even more fanatical than I about speaking English. He was especially hard on my mother, criticizing her, often cruelly, for her pidgin speech—smatterings of Chinese scattered like chop suey in her conversation. "It's not 'What it is,' Mom," he'd say in exasperation. "It's 'What is it, what is it, what is it!'" Sometimes Mom might leave out an occasional "the" or "a," or perhaps a verb of being. He would stop her in mid-sentence: "Say it again, Mom. Say it right." When he tripped over his own tongue, he'd blame it on her: "See, Mom, it's all your fault. You set a bad example." 9

After two years of writing with a *moc but* and reciting words with multiples of meanings, I finally was granted a cultural divorce. I was permitted to stop Chinese school. 10

I thought of myself as multicultural. I preferred tacos to egg rolls; I enjoyed Cinco de Mayo more than Chinese New Year. 11

At last, I was one of you; I wasn't one of them. 12

Sadly, I still am. 13

PROFESSIONAL WRITING

I'm O.K., but You're Not

Robert Zoellner

The American novelist John Barth, in his early novel, *The Floating Opera,* remarks that ordinary, day-to-day life often presents us with embarrassingly obvious, totally unsubtle patterns of symbolism and meaning—life in the midst of death, innocence vindicated, youth versus age, etc. 1

The truth of Barth's insight was brought home to me recently while having breakfast in a lawn-bordered restaurant on College Avenue near the Colorado State University campus. I had asked to be seated in the 2 smoking section of the restaurant—I have happily gone through three or four packs a day for the past 40 years.

As it happened, the hostess seated me—I was by myself—at a little *3* two-person table on the dividing line between the smoking and non-smoking sections. Presently, a well-dressed couple of advanced years, his hair a magisterial white and hers an electric blue, were seated in the non-smoking section five feet away from me.

It was apparent within a minute that my cigarette smoke was bugging *4* them badly, and soon the husband leaned over and asked me if I would please stop smoking. As a chronic smokestack, I normally comply, out of simple courtesy, with such requests. Even an addict such as myself can quit for as long as 20 minutes.

But his manner was so self-righteous and peremptory—he re- *5* minded me of Lee Iacocca boasting about Chrysler—that the prompt-ings of original sin, always a problem with me, took over. I quietly pointed out that I was in the smoking section—if only by five feet—and that that fact meant that I had met my social obligation to non-smokers. Besides, the idea of morning coffee without a cigarette was simply incon-ceivable to me—might as well ask me to vote Republican.

The two of them ate their eggs-over-easy in hurried and sullen si- *6* lence, while I chain-smoked over my coffee. As well as be hung for a sheep as a lamb, I reasoned. Presently they got up, paid their bill, and stalked out in an ambiance of affronted righteousness and affluent propriety.

And this is where John Barth comes in. They had parked their car— *7* a diesel Mercedes—where it could be seen from my table. And in the car, waiting impatiently, was a splendidly matched pair of pedigreed poodles, male and female.

Both dogs were clearly in extremis, and when the back door of the *8* car was opened, they made for the restaurant lawn in considerable haste. Without ado (no pun intended), the male did a doo-doo that would have done credit to an animal twice his size, and finished off with a leisurely, ruminative wee-wee. The bitch of the pair, as might be ex-pected of any well-brought-up female of Republican proclivities, con-fined herself to a modest wee-wee, fastidious, diffident, and quickly executed.

Having thus polluted the restaurant lawn, the four of them mar- *9* shalled their collective dignity and drove off in a dense cloud of blue smoke—that lovely white Mercedes was urgently in need of a valve-and-ring job, its emission sticker an obvious exercise in creative writing.

As I regretfully watched them go—after all, the four of them had *10* made my day—it seemed to me that they were in something of a hurry, and I uncharitably wondered if the husband was not anxious to get home in order to light the first Fall fire in his moss-rock fireplace, or apply the

...continued I'm O.K., but You're Not, **Robert Zoellner**

Fall ration of chemical fertilizer to his doubtlessly impeccable lawn, thus adding another half-pound of particulates to the local atmosphere and another 10 pounds of nitrates and other poisons to the regional aquifers. But that, of course, is pure and unkindly speculation.

In any case, the point of this real-life vignette, as John Barth would 11 insist, is obvious. The current controversy over public smoking in Fort Collins is a clear instance of selective virtue at work, coming under the rubric of, what I do is perfectly OK, but what you do is perfectly awful.

QUESTIONS FOR WRITING AND DISCUSSION

1 Choosing only one adjective to describe your main reaction to each essay, answer the following question: "When I finished the _____ [Wong, Zoellner] essay, I was _____ [intrigued, bored, amused, irritated, curious, confused, or _____] because _____. Explain your choice of adjectives in one or two sentences.

2 Referring to specific passages, explain the purpose and state the thesis or main point of each essay.

3 What personality or role does each writer project? Drawing from evidence in the essay, describe what you think both writers would be like if you met them.

4 Both of these essays appeared in newspapers. What kind of reader would find each essay interesting? What kind of reader would not enjoy each essay? For each essay, find examples of specific sentences, word choices, vocabulary, experiences, or references to culture or politics that would appeal to one reader but perhaps irritate another.

5 These two essays are similar in genre—they are both informal essays narrating personal experiences and explaining what each writer discovered or learned. There are differences, however, in structure and style. What differences do you notice in the way each essay begins and concludes, in the order of the paragraphs, and in vocabulary or style of the sentences?

6 Each essay has a particular social, cultural, and political context. Describe this context for both essays. Then identify at least three other viewpoints that exist in the cultural, social, or political conversations that surround each of these topics. (For example, what are different points of view about multicultural or bilingual education? What arguments exist both for and against smoking in privately owned business establishments?) How

effective is each writer in responding to the ongoing cultural, social, or political context or conversation?

Dimensions of the Writing Process

Processes for writing vary from one writer to the next and from one writing situation to the next. Most writers, however, can identify four basic stages, or dimensions, of their writing process: collecting, shaping, drafting, and revising. The writing situation may precede these stages—particularly if you are assigned a subject, purpose, audience, and form. Usually, however, you continue to narrow your subject, clarify your purpose, meet the needs of your audience, and modify your form as you work through the dimensions of your writing process.

> **❝**I don't see writing as communication of something already discovered, as "truths" already known. Rather, I see writing as a job of experiment. It's like any discovery job; you don't know what's going to happen until you try it. **❞**
>
> —WILLIAM STAFFORD, TEACHER, POET, AND ESSAYIST

COLLECTING

Mark Twain, author of *The Adventures of Huckleberry Finn*, once observed that if you attempt to carry a cat around the block by its tail, you'll gain a whole lot of information about cats that you'll never forget. You may collect such firsthand information, or you may rely on the data, experience, or expertise of others. In any case, writers constantly collect facts, impressions, opinions, and ideas that are relevant to their subjects, purposes, and audiences. Collecting involves observing, remembering, imagining, thinking, reading, listening, writing, investigating, talking, taking notes, and experimenting. Collecting also involves thinking about the relationships among the bits of information that you have collected.

> **❝**The writing process is not linear, moving smoothly in one direction from start to finish. It is messy, recursive, convoluted, and uneven. Writers write, plan, revise, anticipate, and review throughout the writing process. **❞**
>
> —MAXINE HAIRSTON, TEACHER AND AUTHOR OF ARTICLES AND TEXTBOOKS ON WRITING

SHAPING

Writers focus and organize the facts, examples, and ideas that they have collected into the recorded, linear form that is written language. When a hurricane hits the Gulf Coast, for example, residents of Texas, Louisiana, Mississippi, Alabama, and Florida are likely to collect an enormous amount of data in just a few hours. Rain, floods, tree limbs snapping in the wind, unboarded windows shattering, sirens blaring—all of these events occur nearly simultaneously. If you try to write about such devastation, you need to narrow your focus (you can't describe everything that happened) and organize your information (you can't describe all of your experiences at the same time).

The genre of the personal essay, weaving description in a chronological order, is just one of the shapes that a writer may choose to develop and organize experience. Such shaping strategies also help writers collect additional information and ideas. Reconstructing a chronological order, for example, may suggest some additional details—perhaps a wet, miserable-looking dog running through the heavy downpour—that you might not otherwise have remembered.

DRAFTING

> 66 We must and do write each our own way. 99
> —EUDORA WELTY, NOVELIST AND ESSAYIST

At some point, writers actually write down a rough version of what will evolve into the finished piece of writing. Drafting processes vary widely from one writer to the next. Some writers prefer to reread their collecting and shaping notes, find a starting point, and launch themselves—figuring out what they want to say as they write it. Other writers start with a plan—a mental strategy, a short list, or an outline—of how they wish to proceed. Whatever approach you use in your draft, write down as much as possible: You want to see whether the information is clear, whether your overall shape expresses and clarifies your purpose, and whether your content and organization meet the needs and expectations of your audience.

REVISING

When writers revise rough drafts, they literally "resee" their subjects—and then modify drafts to fit new visions. Revision is more than just tinkering with a word here and there; revision leads to larger changes—new examples or details, a different organization, or a new perspective. You accomplish these changes by adding, deleting, substituting, or reordering words, sentences, and paragraphs. Although revision begins the moment you get your first idea, most revisions are based on the reactions—or anticipated reactions—of the audience to your draft. You often play the role of audience yourself by putting the draft aside and rereading it later when you have some distance from your writing. Wherever you feel readers might not get your point, you revise to make it clearer. You may also get feedback from readers in a class workshop, suggesting that you collect more or different information, alter the shape of your draft to improve the flow of ideas, or clarify your terminology. As a result of your rereading and your readers' suggestions, you may change your thesis or write for an entirely different audience.

Editing—in contrast to revising—focuses on the minor changes that you make to improve the accuracy and readability of your language. You usually edit your essay to improve word choice, grammar, usage, or punctuation. You also use a computer spell-check program and proofread to catch typos and other surface errors.

THE WHOLE PROCESS

In practice, a writer's process rarely follows the simple, consecutive order that these four stages or dimensions suggest. The writing process is actually recursive: It begins at one point, goes on to another, comes back to the first, jumps to the third, and so forth. A stage may last hours or only a second or two. While writing a letter to a friend, you may collect, shape, revise, and edit in one quick draft; a research paper may require repeated shaping over a two-week period. As writers draft, they may correct a few mistakes or typos, but they may not proofread until many days later. In the middle of reorganizing an essay, writers often reread drafts, go back and ask more questions, and collect more data. Even while editing, writers may throw out several paragraphs, collect some additional information, and draft new sections.

In addition to the recursive nature of the writing process, keep in mind that writing often occurs during every stage, not just during drafting and revising. During collecting, you will be recording information and jotting down ideas. During shaping, you will be writing out trial versions that you may use later when you draft or revise. Throughout the writing process, you use your writing to modify your subject, purpose, audience, and form.

The most important point to keep in mind is that the writing process is unique to each writer and to each writing situation. What works for one writer may be absolutely wrong for you. Some writers compose nearly everything in their heads. Others write only after discussing the subject with friends or drawing diagrams and pictures.

During the writing process, you need to experiment with several collecting, shaping, and drafting strategies to see what works best for you and for a particular piece of writing. As long as your process works, however, it's legitimate—no matter how many times you backtrack and repeat stages. When you are struggling with a piece of writing, remember that numerous revisions are a normal part of the writing process—even for most professionals.

Circling back over what you have already written—to sharpen your thesis, improve the organization, tighten up a paragraph, or add specific details to your examples—is likely to be the most time-consuming, yet worthwhile, part of your writing process. Most professional writers testify to the necessity and value of writing numerous drafts. When you are reworking a piece of writing, scrawling revisions over what you had hoped would be your finished product, remember what Nobel laureate Isaac Bashevis Singer once pointed out: "The wastepaper basket is the writer's best friend."

WARMING UP   Journal Exercises

The following exercises will help you review and practice the topics covered in this chapter. In addition, you may discover a subject for your own writing. Choose three of the following entries, and write for ten minutes on each.

1 Reread your "authority" list from Chapter 1. Choose one of those topics and then explain your purpose, identify a possible audience, and select a genre you would use.

2 From the resources available to you at home or on your computer, find examples of four different genres, such as advertisements, pamphlets, letters, articles, letters to the editor, and so forth. For each sample genre, identify the purpose, audience, and context. Bring these samples to class and be prepared to explain the rhetorical situation for each genre and why each sample is or is not effective.

3 **Writing Across the Curriculum.** If you have already been given a writing assignment in another course, explain the purpose, the intended audience, and the genre for that assignment. Be prepared to explain in class (or in a discussion forum) how you plan to complete that assignment.

4 During the first week of the term, one of your friends, Mark Lindstrom, is in an accident and is hospitalized. While still under the effects of anesthesia, he scribbles the following note for you to mail to his parents.

> Dear Mom and Dad,
>
> I arrived here last week. The trip was terrible. Dr. Stevens says that my leg will be better soon. My roommate is very strange. The police say my money is gone forever.
>
> Please send $1,500 to my new address right away.
>
> Thanks!
>
> Your loving son
>
> Mark

Because you were at the accident and can fill in the details, Mark asks you to explain everything to his parents. Write a short letter to them. Next, write a paragraph to your best friend that describes what happened to Mark.

A Writing Process at Work: Drafting and Revising

While drafting and revising, writers frequently make crucial changes in their ideas and language. The first scribbled sentences, written primarily for ourselves, are often totally different from what we later present to other people in final, polished versions. Take, for example, the final version of Abraham Lincoln's Gettysburg Address. It begins with the famous lines "Four score and seven years ago our fathers brought forth on this continent a new nation. . . ." But his first draft might well have begun, "Eighty-seven years ago, several politicians and other powerful men in the American Colonies got together and decided to start a new country. . . ." It is difficult to imagine that language ingrained in our consciousness was once drafted, revised, drafted again, and edited, as the author or authors added, deleted, reordered, and otherwise altered words, sentences, and ideas. In fact, it usually was.

Carl Becker's study of the American Declaration of Independence assembles the early drafts of that famous document and compares them with the final version. Shown below is Thomas Jefferson's first draft, with revisions made by Benjamin Franklin, John Adams, and other members of the Committee of Five that was charged with developing the new document.

Rough Draft of the Opening Sentences
of the Declaration of Independence
Thomas Jefferson

When in the course of human events it becomes necessary for ~~a~~ ^one^ people to dissolve the political bands which have connected them with another, and to ~~advance from that subordination in which they have hitherto remained, & to~~ assume among the powers of the earth the ~~equal & independent~~ ^separate and equal^ station to which

the laws of nature & of nature's god entitle them, a decent respect to the opinions

of mankind requires that they should declare the causes which impel them to ~~the change~~ ^the separation.^

We hold these truths *to be* ~~sacred & undeniable; that~~ ^self-evident^ all men are created equal ~~& independent;~~ that ~~from that equal creation they derive in rights~~ ^they are endowed by their creator with^ inherent

rights; that   these
& inalienable among ~~which~~ are ~~the preservation of~~ life, ~~&~~ liberty, & the pursuit

of happiness. . . .

The Final Draft of the Opening Sentences of the Declaration of Independence, as Approved on July 4, 1776

When in the Course of human events, it becomes necessary for one people

to dissolve the political bands which have connected them with another, and to

assume among the powers of the earth, the separate and equal station to which

the Laws of Nature and of Nature's God entitle them, a decent respect to the

opinions of mankind requires that they should declare the causes which impel

them to the separation.

We hold these truths to be self-evident, that all men are created equal, that

they are endowed by their Creator with certain inalienable Rights, that among

these are Life, Liberty and the pursuit of Happiness.

? QUESTIONS FOR WRITING AND DISCUSSION

1. Select one change in a sentence that most improved the final version of the Declaration of Independence. Explain how the revised wording is more effective.

2. Find one change in a word or phrase that constitutes an alteration in meaning rather than just a choice of "smoother" or more appropriate language. How does this change affect the meaning?

3. Upon rereading this passage from the Declaration of Independence, one reader wrote, "I was really irritated by that 'all men are created equal' remark. The writers were white, free, well-to-do, Anglo-Saxon, mostly Protestant males discussing their own 'inalienable rights.' They sure weren't discussing the 'inalienable rights' of female Americans or of a million slaves or of

nonwhite free Americans!" Revise the passage from the Declaration of Independence using this person as your audience.

4 On the Internet, visit the National Archives at http://www.nara.gov to see a photograph of the original Declaration of Independence and learn how the Dunlap Broadside of the Declaration was read aloud to troops. What does this historical context add to what you know about the Declaration of Independence? Do the revisions help make the document more revolutionary or propagandistic? In addition, this site has other treasures from the National Archives including the police blotter listing Abraham Lincoln's assassination, the first report of the *Titanic*'s collision with an iceberg, and Rosa Parks's arrest records. Do you think these documents are as important to our history and culture as the Declaration itself? Explain.

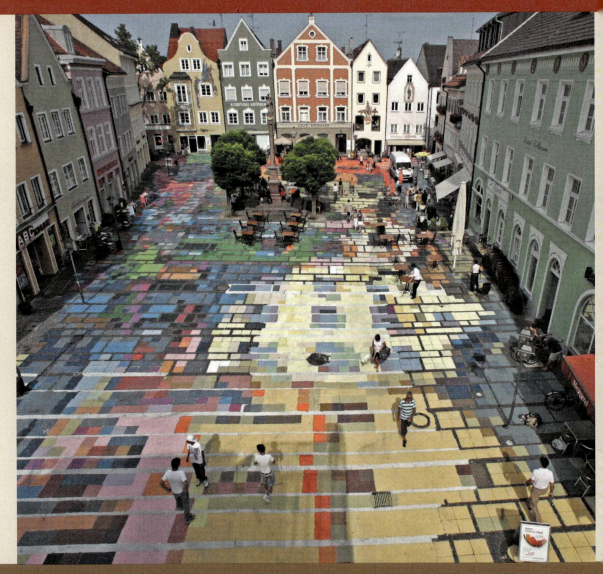

Street painting
Weilheim, Germany
Diether Endlicher/AP
Wide World Photos

This street painting was completed in 2008 by art students in Weilheim, Germany, to replicate a painting of the same square done 99 years earlier by artist Vassily Kandinsky. After observing the details of the painting in this photograph, respond to journal entry 5 on page 45.

Observing

3

In the far corner of a friend's living room is a lighted aquarium. Instead of water, the aquarium has a few inches of white sand, a dish of water, and a small piece of pottery. When you ask about the aquarium, your friend excitedly says, "You mean you haven't met Nino?" In a matter of seconds, you have a small, tannish-brown snake practically in your lap, and your friend is saying, "This is Nino. She—or he—is an African sand boa." You imagined that all boa constrictors were huge snakes that suffocated and then swallowed babies. "Actually," replies your friend, "Nino is very shy. She prefers to burrow in the sand." The snake is fascinating. It is only fifteen inches long, with a strong, compact body and a stub tail. Before it burrows into your coat pocket, you observe it closely so you can describe it to your younger brother, who loves all kinds of snakes.

In the physics laboratory, you're doing an experiment on light refraction. You need to observe how light rays bend as they go through water, so you take notes describing the procedure and the results. During each phase of the experiment, you observe and record the angles of refraction. The data and your notes will help you write up the lab report that is due next Monday.

> My task . . . is, by the power of the written word, to make you hear, to make you feel—it is, before all, to make you see.
>
> —JOSEPH CONRAD, AUTHOR OF *HEART OF DARKNESS* AND OTHER NOVELS

> Seeing is of course very much a matter of verbalization. Unless I call my attention to what passes before my eyes, I simply won't see it.
>
> —ANNIE DILLARD, NATURALIST AND AUTHOR OF *PILGRIM AT TINKER CREEK*

Observing is essential to good writing. Whether you are writing in a journal, doing a laboratory report for a science class, or writing a letter to the editor of a newspaper, keen observation is essential. Writing or verbalizing what you see helps you discover and learn more about your environment. Sometimes your purpose is limited to yourself: you observe and record to help you understand your world or yourself better. At other times, your purpose extends to a wider audience: you want to share what you have learned with others to help them learn as well. No matter who your audience is or what your subject may be, however, your task is to see and to help your readers see.

Of course, observing involves more than just "seeing." Good writers draw on all their senses: sight, smell, touch, taste, hearing. In addition, however, experienced writers also notice what is *not* there. The smell of food that should be coming from the kitchen but isn't. A friend who usually is present but now is absent. The absolute quiet in the air that precedes an impending storm. Writers should also look for *changes* in their subjects—from light to dark, from rough to smooth, from bitter to sweet, from noise to sudden silence. Good writers learn to use their previous *experiences* and their *imaginations* to draw comparisons and create images. Does a sea urchin look and feel like a pincushion with the pins stuck in the wrong way? Does the room feel as cramped and airless as the inside of a microwave oven? Finally, good writers write from a specific point of view or role: a student describing basic laws of physics or an experienced worker in a mental health clinic describing the clientele.

The key to effective observing is to *show* your reader the person, place, object, or image through *specific detail*. Good description follows the advice of experienced writers: *Show, don't tell.* Showing through vivid detail allows the reader to reach the conclusions that you may be tempted to just tell them. If your reader is going to learn from your observations, you must give the *exact details that you learned from,* not just your conclusions or generalizations. Even in writing, experience is the best teacher, so use specific details to communicate the look, the feel, the weight, the sights and sounds and smells.

Although effective description depends on detailed observation, what we already know about the subject—and what we can learn during our observations—can be crucial. The people, places, objects, or images that we observe are often difficult, complex, or contested. They do not give up their meaning in our first glance. If we look at an Impressionist painting, are we seeing pretty colors in shimmering light or just careless, undisciplined brushwork? If we see workers in a field planting or harvesting crops, is it a natural agricultural scene or the exploitation of Japanese internment workers? A key part, then, of effective observation is learning and reading about what we see. An observant eye requires a critical, inquiring mind.

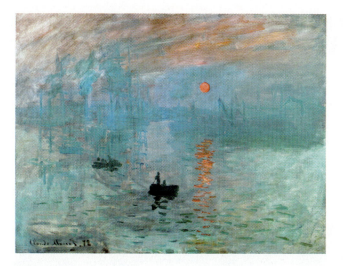

Claude Monet, *Impression: Sunrise*, 1872. This painting gave the Impressionists their name.

Ansel Adams, farm, farm workers, Mount Williamson in background, 1943. Photograph of Japanese-American Internment, Manzanar Relocation Center, California.

Whether you are a tourist describing the cliff dwellings at Mesa Verde, a student in a chemistry class writing up your laboratory experiment, a social worker observing working and housing conditions of agricultural workers, or a volunteer observing at a community crisis center, your task is to critically observe and then describe your subject—to show your readers, to make them *see*.

> ❝The real voyage of discovery consists not in seeking new landscapes but in having new eyes.❞
>
> —MARCEL PROUST, AUTHOR OF *REMEMBRANCE OF THINGS PAST*

Techniques for Writing About Observations

The short passages on the following pages use specific techniques for observing people, places, objects, or images that are described here. In all of the passages, the writer *narrows* or *limits* the scope of the observation and selects specific details that support the *dominant idea* of the passage. The dominant idea reflects the writer's purpose for that particular audience. As you read each passage, notice how the authors use the techniques listed below for making their writing more vivid and effective.

Techniques for Writing About Observations

Technique	Tips on How to Do It
Giving sensory details (sight, sound, smell, touch, taste)	Use *sensory descriptions, comparisons,* and *images.* "Zoom in" on crucial details. Also include *actual dialogue* and *names of things* where appropriate.
Describing what is *not* there	Sometimes keen observation requires stepping back and noticing what is *absent,* what is *not* happening, or who is *not* present.
Noting changes in the subject's form or condition	Even when the subject appears static—a landscape, a flower, a building—look for evidence of changes: a tree being enveloped by tent worms, a six-inch purple-and-white iris that eight hours earlier was just a green bud, a sandstone exterior of a church being eroded by acid rain.
Learning about your subject	An observant eye requires a critical, inquiring mind. Read about your subject. Google key ideas or terms. Ask other people or experts on the subject. Probe to find what is *unusual, surprising,* or *controversial* about your subject.
Writing from a distinct point of view	Good writers assume a distinct role. A lover and a botanist, for example, see entirely different things in the same red rose. *What* is seen depends on *who* is doing the seeing.

Focusing on a dominant idea	Focus on those details and images that clarify the main ideas or discoveries. Discovery often depends on the *contrast* between the writer's expectations and the reality.

These techniques for observing are illustrated in the following two paragraphs by Karen Blixen, who wrote *Out of Africa* under the pen name Isak Dinesen. A Danish woman who moved to Kenya to start a coffee plantation, Blixen knew little about the animals in Kenya Reserve. In this excerpt from her journals, she describes a startling change that occurred when she shot a large iguana. (The annotations in the margin identify all six observing techniques.)

In the Reserve I have sometimes come upon the Iguana, the big lizards, as they were sunning themselves upon a flat stone in a riverbed. They are not pretty in shape, but nothing can be imagined more beautiful than their coloring. They shine like a heap of precious stones or like a pane cut out of an old church window. When, as you approach, they swish away, there is a flash of azure, green and purple over the stones, the color seems to be standing behind them in the air, like a comet's luminous tail.

Role: A newcomer to the Reserve

Comparisons, images, and sensory details

Once I shot an Iguana. I thought that I should be able to make some pretty things from his skin. A strange thing happened then, that I have never afterwards forgotten. As I went up to him, where he was lying dead upon his stone, and actually while I was walking the few steps, he faded and grew pale, all color died out of him as in one long sigh, and by the time that I touched him he was grey and dull like a lump of concrete. It was the live impetuous blood pulsating within the animal, which had radiated out all that glow and splendor. Now that the flame was put out, and the soul had flown, the Iguana was as dead as a sandbag.

Changes in condition

Learning about the subject

What is not there

Dominant idea: Now colorless and dead

OBSERVING PEOPLE

Observing people—their dress, body language, facial features, behavior, eating habits, and conversation—is a pastime that we all share. In a *Rolling Stone* article, for example, Brian Hiatt describes U2 lead singer Bono in his native Dublin. Notice how the descriptive details and images work together to create the dominant impression of Bono as a famous, high-energy rock star, conversationalist, and global philanthropist.

Bono rounds a corner onto a narrow Dublin street, boots crunching on old cobblestone, sleek, black double-breasted overcoat flapping in the January breeze. . . . He's running late for his next appointment, which is not unusual in what must be one of the most overstuffed lives on the planet: "part-time" rock stardom; global advocacy for Africa's poor that's won him nominations for the Nobel Peace Prize; various multinational business and charitable ventures; an op-ed column for The New York Times; and four kids with Ali Hewson, his wife of 26 years. "I find it very hard to leave home," he says, "because my house is full of laughter and songs and kids."

Interviewing Bono is like taking an Alaskan husky for a walk—you can only suggest a general direction, and then hold on for dear life. Over an 80-minute lunch at a favorite Dublin restaurant, Eden, he repeatedly goes off on wild, entertaining tangents, which tend to include names such as Bill Clinton, Microsoft co-founder Paul Allen, genomic researcher Craig Venter and Archbishop Desmond Tutu (Bono calls him "the Arch"). He tosses out one killer sound bite after another, blue eyes moving like tropical fish behind today's pinkish-purple shades.

He eats his chicken breast in big bites, avoiding the potatoes, talking with his mouth full—and when the chicken is gone, he dips a finger into the sauce and licks it off, more than once. "We began this decade well—I think we'll end it better," he says, sitting on a white chair at a white table in a restaurant that's otherwise empty— apparently because management has cleared it out for him. "Wouldn't it be great if, after all these years, U2 has their heyday? That could be true of a painter or a filmmaker at this stage."

OBSERVING PLACES

In the following passage, John Muir describes California and the Yosemite Valley as it looked over 130 years ago. John Muir, of course, was the founder of the Sierra Club, whose first mission was to preserve the vision of Yosemite that Muir paints in the following paragraphs. Notice how Muir uses all of the key techniques for observing as he vividly describes the California Sierra.

Arriving by the Panama steamer, I stopped one day in San Francisco and then inquired for the nearest way out of town. "But where do you want to go?" asked the man to whom I had applied for this important information. "To any place that is wild," I said. This reply startled him. He seemed to fear I might be crazy and therefore the sooner I was out of town the better, so he directed me to the Oakland ferry.

So on the first of April, 1868, I set out afoot for Yosemite. It was the bloom-time of the year over the lowlands and coast ranges; the landscapes of the Santa Clara Valley were fairly drenched with sunshine, all the air was quivering with the songs of the meadow-larks, and the hills were so covered with flowers that they seemed to be painted. Slow indeed was my progress through these glorious gardens, the first of the California flora I had seen. Cattle and cultivation were making few scars as yet, and I wandered enchanted in long wavering curves, knowing by my pocket map that Yosemite Valley lay to the east and that I should surely find it.

Looking eastward from the summit of the Pacheco Pass one shining morning, a landscape was displayed that after all my wanderings still appears as the most beautiful I have ever beheld. At my feet lay the Great Central Valley of California, level and flowery, like a lake of pure sunshine, forty or fifty miles wide, five hundred miles long, one rich furred garden of yellow *Compositae*. And from the eastern boundary of this vast golden flower-bed rose the mighty Sierra, miles in height, and so gloriously colored and so radiant, it seemed not clothed with light, but wholly composed of it, like the wall of some celestial city. Along the top and extending a good way down, was a rich pearl-gray belt of snow; below it a belt of blue and dark purple, marking the extension of the forests; and stretching along the base of the range a broad belt of rose-purple; all these colors, from the blue sky to the yellow valley smoothly blending as they do in a rainbow, making a wall of light ineffably fine. Then it seemed to me that the Sierra should be called, not the Nevada or Snowy Range, but the Range of Light.

In general views no mark of man is visible upon it, nor anything to suggest the wonderful depth and grandeur of its sculpture. None of its magnificent forest-crowned ridges seems to rise much above the general level to publish its wealth. No great valley or river is seen, or group of well-marked features of any kind standing out as distinct pictures. Even the summit peaks, marshaled in glorious array so high in the sky, seem comparatively regular in form. Nevertheless the whole range five hundred miles long is furrowed with canyons 2,000 to 5,000 feet deep, in which once flowed majestic glaciers, and in which now flow and sing the bright rejoicing rivers.

OBSERVING OBJECTS

In observing an inanimate object such as a cookie, Paul Goldberger—architecture critic for *The New York Times*—brings his special point of view to his description. He totally ignores the cookie's taste, ingredients, and calories, focusing instead on the architectural relationships of function and form. Goldberger's architectural perspective helps focus his observations, creating a dominant idea for each passage.

Sugar Wafer (Nabisco)

There is no attempt to imitate the ancient forms of traditional, individually baked cookies here—this is a modern cookie through and through. Its simple rectangular form, clean and pure, just reeks of mass production and modern technological methods. The two wafers, held together by the sugar-cream filling, appear to float . . . this is a machine-age object.

Fig Newton (Nabisco)

This, too, is a sandwich but different in every way from the Sugar Wafer. Here the imagery is more traditional, more sensual even; a rounded form of cookie dough arcs over the fig concoction inside, and the whole is soft and pliable. Like all good pieces of design, it has an appropriate form for its use, since the insides of Fig Newtons can ooze and would not be held in place by a more rigid form. The thing could have had a somewhat different shape, but the rounded tip is a comfortable, familiar image, and it's easy to hold. Not a revolutionary object but an intelligent one.

> **"**For Godsake, keep your eyes open. Notice what's going on around you. **"**
> —WILLIAM BURROUGHS, NOVELIST

WARMING UP   Journal Exercises

The following topics will help you practice close, detailed observation and may possibly suggest a subject for your assignment on observing. Read the exercises and then write on the two or three that interest you the most.

1. Go to a public place (library, bar, restaurant, hospital emergency room, gas station, laundromat, park, shopping mall, hotel lobby, police station, beach, skating rink, beauty salon, city dump, tennis court, church, etc.). Sit and observe everything around you. Use your pencil to help you see, both by drawing sketches and by recording sensory details in words. What do you see that you haven't noticed before? Then *narrow* your attention to a single person, *focus* on a restricted place, or *zoom* in on a single object. What do you see that you haven't noticed before?

2. In one of your classes, use your repeated observations of the total learning environment (the room, the seating arrangements, the blackboards, the audiovisual or computer equipment, the teacher, the daily teaching or learning rituals, and the students) to speculate on who has authority, how knowledge is created or communicated, and what the learning goals are for this course.

3 **Community Service Learning Project.** If you are working on a community-service learning project, for your first assignment, go and observe the place, people, and setting for the agency. Start by taking double-entry notes in your journal. On the left-hand side, record visual and sensory details; on the right-hand side, record your reactions and impressions. Use these notes for a description of your agency that will go in your final portfolio for your learning project.

4 Go to a gallery, studio, or museum where you can observe sculpture, paintings, or other works of art. Choose one work of art and draw it. Then describe it as fully as possible. Return to the gallery the next day, reread your first description, observe the work again, and add details that you didn't notice the first time.

5 Study the chapter-opening photograph of the Weilheim, Germany, street painting on page 36. Then go to Google images and enter "Vassily Kandinsky Weilheim" and examine the original painting of the buildings in that square. How accurately has the street painting on page 36 captured the original Kandinsky image? Because the street painting is not an exact replication, what are the differences between the image on the street and the original Kandinsky painting you found on Google? Consider the details, the color saturation, the use of rectangular blocks, and the overall style. Explain these differences, citing specific details from both the original Kandinsky painting and the photograph of the street art.

PROFESSIONAL WRITING

Take This Fish and Look at It

Samuel H. Scudder

In this essay, Samuel H. Scudder (1837–1911), an American entomologist, narrates his early attempts at scientific observation. Scudder recalls how a famous Swiss naturalist, Louis Agassiz, taught him the skills of observation by having him examine a fish—a haemulon or snapper—closely, carefully, and repeatedly. Agassiz, a professor of natural history at Harvard, taught his students that both factual details and general laws are important. "Facts are stupid things," he said, "until brought into connection with some general law." Scudder, writing about his studies under Agassiz, suggests that re-peated observation can help us connect facts or specific details with general laws. The essay shows us an important lesson that Scudder learned: To help us see, describe, and connect, "A pencil is one of the best of eyes."

It was more than fifteen years ago that I entered the laboratory of *1* Professor Agassiz, and told him I had enrolled my name in the Scientific School as a student of natural history. He asked me a few questions about

...continued Take This Fish and Look at It, **Samuel H. Scudder**

my object in coming, my antecedents generally, the mode in which I afterwards proposed to use the knowledge I might acquire, and, finally, whether I wished to study any special branch. To the latter I replied that, while I wished to be well grounded in all departments of zoology, I purposed to devote myself specially to insects.

"When do you wish to begin?" he asked.   2

"Now," I replied.   3

This seemed to please him, and with an energetic "Very well!" he   4
reached from a shelf a huge jar of specimens in yellow alcohol. "Take this fish," he said, "and look at it; we call it a haemulon; by and by I will ask what you have seen."

With that he left me, but in a moment returned with explicit instruc-   5
tions as to the care of the object entrusted to me.

"No man is fit to be a naturalist," said he, "who does not know how   6
to take care of specimens."

I was to keep the fish before me in a tin tray, and occasionally mois-   7
ten the surface with alcohol from the jar, always taking care to replace the stopper tightly. Those were not the days of ground-glass stoppers and elegantly shaped exhibition jars; all the old students will recall the huge neckless glass bottles with their leaky, wax-besmeared corks, half eaten by insects, and begrimed with cellar dust. Entomology was a cleaner science than ichthyology, but the example of the Professor, who had unhesitatingly plunged to the bottom of the jar to produce the fish, was infectious; and though this alcohol had a "very ancient and fishlike smell," I really dared not show any aversion within these sacred precincts, and treated the alcohol as though it were pure water. Still I was conscious of a passing feeling of disappointment, for gazing at a fish did not commend itself to an ardent entomologist. My friends at home, too, were annoyed when they discovered that no amount of eau-de-Cologne would drown the perfume which haunted me like a shadow.

In ten minutes I had seen all that could be seen in that fish, and   8
started in search of the Professor—who had, however, left the Museum; and when I returned, after lingering over some of the odd animals stored in the upper apartment, my specimen was dry all over. I dashed the fluid over the fish as if to resuscitate the beast from a fainting fit, and looked with anxiety for a return of the normal sloppy appearance. This little excitement over, nothing was to be done but to return to a steadfast gaze at my mute companion. Half an hour passed—an hour—another hour; the fish began to look loathsome. I turned it over and around; looked it in the face—ghastly; from behind, beneath, above, sideways, at three-quarter's view—just as ghastly, I was in despair; at an early hour I concluded that lunch was necessary; so, with infinite relief, the fish was carefully replaced in the jar, and for an hour I was free.

On my return, I learned that Professor Agassiz had been at the 9
Museum, but had gone, and would not return for several hours. My fellow-
students were too busy to be disturbed by continued conversation.
Slowly I drew forth that hideous fish, and with a feeling of desperation
again looked at it. I might not use a magnifying-glass; instruments of all
kinds were interdicted. My two hands, my two eyes, and the fish: it
seemed a most limited field. I pushed my finger down its throat to feel
how sharp the teeth were. I began to count the scales in the different
rows, until I was convinced that was nonsense. At last a happy thought
struck me—I would draw the fish; and now with surprise I began to discover new features in the creature. Just then the Professor returned.

"That is right," said he; "a pencil is one of the best of eyes. I am glad 10
to notice, too, that you keep your specimen wet, and your bottle corked."

With these encouraging words, he added: "Well, what is it like?" 11

He listened attentively to my brief rehearsal of the structure of parts 12
whose names were still unknown to me: the fringed gill-arches and movable operculum; the pores of the head, fleshy lips and lidless eyes; the lat-
eral line, the spinous fins and forked tail; the compressed and arched
body. When I finished, he waited as if expecting more, and then, with an
air of disappointment:

"You have not looked very carefully; why," he continued more 13
earnestly, "you haven't even seen one of the most conspicuous features of
the animal, which is plainly before your eyes as the fish itself; look again,
look again!" and he left me to my misery.

I was piqued; I was mortified. Still more of that wretched fish! But 14
now I set myself to my task with a will, and discovered one new thing
after another, until I saw how just the Professor's criticism had been. The
afternoon passed quickly; and when, towards its close, the Professor inquired:

"Do you see it yet?" 15

"No," I replied, "I am certain I do not, but I see how little I saw 16
before."

"That is next best," said he, earnestly, "but I won't hear you now; put 17
away your fish and go home; perhaps you will be ready with a better answer in the morning. I will examine you before you look at the fish."

This was disconcerting. Not only must I think of my fish all night, 18
studying, without the object before me, what this unknown but most visible feature might be; but also, without reviewing my discoveries, I must give
an exact account of them the next day. I had a bad memory; so I walked
home by Charles River in a distracted state, with my two perplexities.

The cordial greeting from the Professor the next morning was reas- 19
suring; here was a man who seemed to be quite as anxious as I that I
should see for myself what he saw.

"Do you perhaps mean," I asked, "that the fish has symmetrical sides 20
with paired organs?"

...continued Take This Fish and Look at It, **Samuel H. Scudder**

His thoroughly pleased "Of course! Of course!" repaid the wakeful 21 hours of the previous night. After he had discoursed most happily and enthusiastically—as he always did—upon the importance of this point, I ventured to ask what I should do next.

"Oh, look at your fish!" he said, and left me again to my own devices. 22 In a little more than an hour he returned, and heard my new catalogue.

"That is good, that is good!" he repeated; "but that is not all; go on"; 23 and so for three long days he placed that fish before my eyes, forbidding me to look at anything else, or to use any artificial aid. "Look, look, look," was his repeated injunction.

This was the best entomological lesson I ever had—a lesson whose 24 influence has extended to the details of every subsequent study; a legacy the Professor had left to me, as he has left it to so many others, of inestimable value, which we could not buy, with which we cannot part.

A year afterward, some of us were amusing ourselves with chalk- 25 ing outlandish beasts on the Museum blackboard. We drew prancing star fishes; frogs in mortal combat; hydra-headed worms, stately craw- fishes with gaping mouths and staring eyes. The Professor came in shortly after, and was as amused as any at our experiments. He looked at the fishes.

"Haemulons, every one of them," he said; "Mr. _____ drew them." 26

True; and to this day, if I attempt a fish, I can draw nothing but 27 haemulons.

The fourth day, a second fish of the same group was placed beside 28 the first, and I was bidden to point out the resemblances and differences between the two; another and another followed, until the entire family lay before me, and a whole legion of jars covered the table and surround- ing shelves; the odor had become a pleasant perfume; and even now, the sight of an old, six-inch worm-eaten cork brings fragrant memories.

The whole group of haemulons was thus brought in review; and 29 whether engaged upon the dissection of the internal organs, the prepa- ration and examination of the bony framework, or the description of the various parts, Agassiz's training in the method of observing facts and their orderly arrangement was ever accompanied by the urgent exhorta- tion not to be content with them.

"Facts are stupid things," he would say, "until brought into connec- 30 tion with some general law."

At the end of eight months, it was almost with reluctance that I left 31 these friends and turned to insects; but what I had gained by this outside experience has been of greater value than years of later investigation in my favorite groups.

vo·cab·u·lar·y

In your journal, write down the meanings of the italicized words in the following phrases.

- my *antecedents* generally (**1**)
- *Entomology* was a cleaner science than *ichthyology* (**7**)
- dared not show any *aversion* (**7**)
- to *resuscitate* the beast (**8**)
- instruments of all kinds were *interdicted* (**9**)

- movable *operculum* (**12**)
- I was *piqued* (**14**)
- with my two *perplexities* (**18**)
- his repeated *injunction* (**23**)
- *hydra-headed* worms (**25**)
- the urgent *exhortation* (**29**)

QUESTIONS FOR WRITING AND DISCUSSION

1 If you have taken any science classes with laboratory sections, describe any observing techniques you used while completing the lab assignments. What were you asked to observe? What were you asked to record? How were these sessions similar to or different from Scudder's experience? Explain.

2 Follow Professor Agassiz's advice about observing: Without looking again at the essay, record in writing what you found to be the most memorable parts of the essay. What parts seemed most vivid? Explain.

3 Apply Scudder's technique of *repeated observation* to his own essay. Read the essay a second time, carefully, looking for techniques for recording observations. Use a pencil to help you read, by underlining or making brief notes. What do you notice on the second reading that you did not see in the first?

4 What is the purpose of this essay? To inform us about fish? To explain how to learn about fish? To persuade us to follow Professor Agassiz's method? To entertain us with college stories? In your estimation, what is the primary purpose?

5 Describe the genre and intended audience for this essay. Review the list of genres on pages 22–23. What features of the essay (such as content, dialogue, paragraphing, narrative voice) help indicate the genre of this piece? Who is the intended audience? Which sentences most clearly address the intended audience?

6 "Facts are stupid things," Agassiz says, "until brought into connection with some general law." Reread paragraph 8. What is the "general law" about scientific observation—or, in this case, the *dominant idea*—created by the specific details describing Scudder's first session with his fish? Explain.

Observing: The Writing Process

ASSIGNMENT FOR OBSERVING

Do a piece of writing in which you observe a specific person, place, object, and/or image. Your goal is to show how specific, observed details create a dominant impression about the person, place, object, image, or overall scene. For this assignment, remember that *repeated observation* is essential. Choose a specific place, scene, environment, group of people, or recurring event that *you can observe several times* during your writing process.

Though your initial purpose is to observe, you also need to think about a possible audience and genre. The chart below will help you choose a genre that will be appropriate and effective for your purpose and audience:

- A personal audience includes yourself, family, and close friends.
- An academic audience includes teachers, students, and anyone connected to an academic setting.
- A public audience includes people who are typically addressed through newspapers, magazines, newsletters, online articles or blogs, advertisements, and business publications.

Audience	Possible Genres for Descriptive Writing
Personal Audience	Journal, letter, blog, social networking site, email, scrapbook, multigenre documents
Academic Audience	Academic essay, science lab report, essay exam, business observation, technical report, online essay, class forum posting, multigenre documents.
Public Audience	Newspaper, magazine, or Internet article, editorial, newsletter, pamphlet, flyer, public blog, wiki posting, multigenre documents

CHOOSING A SUBJECT

If one of your journal entries suggested an interesting subject, try the collecting and shaping strategies. If none of those exercises caught your interest, consider the following ideas.

- **Think about your current classes.** Do you have a class with a laboratory—chemistry, physics, biology, engineering, animal science, horticulture, industrial sciences, physical education, social work, drawing, pottery—in which you have to make detailed observations? Use this assignment to help you in one of those classes: Write about what you observe and learn during one of your lab sessions.

- **Seek out a new place on campus that is off your usual track.** Check the college catalog for ideas about places you haven't yet seen—a theater where actors are rehearsing, a greenhouse, a physical education class in the martial arts, a studio where artists are working, a computer laboratory, or an animal research center. Or visit a class you wouldn't take for credit. Observe, write, and learn about what's there.

- **From a magazine that you read, choose an advertisement or an image to describe.** Start by observing the composition or arrangement of the

"Write about dogs!"

figures and the use of color, lines, balance, and contrast in the advertisement or work of art. *Your goals are to describe this image in detail and to analyze the effectiveness of this image in its rhetorical context.* As part of the rhetorical context, consider the artist or sponsor, the occasion, the purpose and intended audience, the genre, and the cultural context of this image. (See Chapter 6 for additional help.)

As you write on your subject, consider a tentative audience and purpose. Who might want to know what you learn from your observations? What do you need to explain? What will readers already know? Jot down tentative ideas about your subject, audience, and purpose. Remember, however, that these are not cast in concrete: You may discover some new idea, focus, or angle as you write.

COLLECTING

Once you have chosen a subject from your journal or elsewhere, begin collecting information. Depending on your purpose, your topic, or even your personal learning preferences, some activities will work better than others. However, you should *practice* all of these activities to determine which is most successful for you and most appropriate to your topic. During these collecting activities, go back and *reobserve your subject.* The second or third time you go back, you may see additional details or more actively understand what you're seeing.

> 66 We don't take in the world like a camera or a set of recording devices. The mind is an agent, not a passive receiver. . . . The active mind is a composer and everything we respond to, we compose. 99
> —ANN BERTHOFF,
> AUTHOR AND TEACHER

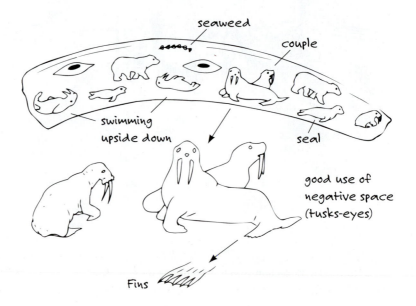

● **SKETCHING**   Begin by *drawing* what you see. The essayist Samuel Scudder says that pen or pencil can be "the best of eyes." Your drawing doesn't have to be great art to suggest other details, questions, or relationships that may be important. Instead of trying to cover a wide range of objects, try to focus on one limited subject and draw it in detail.

Here's an example. Writing student Brad Parks decided to visit an Eskimo art display at a local gallery. As part of his observing notes, he drew these sketches of Eskimo paintings. As he drew, he made notes in the margins of his sketches and zoomed in for more detail on one pair of walruses.

● **TAKING DOUBLE-ENTRY NOTES**   Taking notes in a double-entry format is a simple but effective system for recording observed details. At the top of the page, write the place and time of your observation and your perspective, role, or point of view. Place a vertical line down the middle of a page in your journal. On the left-hand side, write down description and sensory details. On the right-hand side, record your reactions, thoughts, ideas, and questions.

● **ANSWERING QUESTIONS**   To help you describe the person, place, object, or image, write a short response in your journal to each of the following questions.

- What exactly is it? Can you *define* this person, place, object, or image? If it's an object, are its parts related? Who needs it, uses it, or produces it?
- How much could it change and still be recognizable?
- Compare and contrast it. How is it similar to or different from other comparable people, places, things, or images?
- From what points of view is it usually seen? From what point of view is it rarely seen?

● **FREEWRITING**   *Freewriting* means exactly what it says. Write about your subject, nonstop, for five to ten minutes. Sometimes you may have to write, "I can't think of anything" or "This is really stupid," but keep on writing. Let your words and ideas suggest other thoughts and ideas. For observing, the purpose of freewriting is to let your imagination work on the subject, usually *after* you have observed and recorded specific details. Freewriting on your subject will also develop more *associations* or *comparisons* for the right-hand side of your double-entry log. It should also help you to identify a dominant idea for your details.

SHAPING

To focus once again on the shaping process, consider your subject, purpose, and audience. Has your purpose changed? Can you narrow your subject to a specific topic? You may know the answers to some questions immediately; others you may not know until after you complete your first draft. Jot down your current responses to the following questions.

- **Subject:** What is your general subject?
- **Specific topic:** What aspect of your subject interests you? Try to narrow your field or limit your focus.
- **Purpose:** Why is this topic interesting or important to you or to others? From what point of view will you be writing? What is the *dominant idea* you are trying to convey?
- **Audience:** Who are your readers? Are you aiming for a personal, an academic, or a public audience? What are these readers like, and why might they be interested in your topic?
- **Genre:** What specific genre might best serve your purpose and reach your intended audience? Experiment with a couple of genres to see which one might be most effective.
- **Context:** What is the cultural, political, social, or personal context in which this person, object, or image appears? How does that context affect your subject? How does the context affect you?

With answers to these questions in mind, you should experiment with several of the following genre possibilities and organization strategies. These genres and strategies not only will organize your specific examples but also may suggest related ideas to improve your description.

As you practice these strategies, try to *focus* on your subject. In a profile of a person, for example, focus on key facial features or revealing habits or mannerisms. If you're writing about a place or an event, narrow the subject. Describe, for instance, the street at night, a spider spinning a web in a windowsill, a man in a laundromat banging on a change machine, a bird hovering in midair, a photograph, a fish. Write in depth and detail about a *limited* subject.

With a limited subject, a shaping strategy such as spatial order, chronological order, or comparison/contrast will organize all the specific details for your audience. Shaping strategies give you ways of seeing relationships among the many bits of your description and of presenting them in an organized manner for your reader. Seeing these relationships will also help you discover and communicate the dominant idea to your reader.

● **SPATIAL ORDER**   Spatial order is a simple way to organize your descriptive details. Choose some sequence—left to right, right to left, bottom to top—and describe your observed details in that sequence. In the following description of his "trashed" dorm room, Dale Furnish, a student who was the victim of a prank, uses spatial order. The italicized words illustrate the spatial order.

As I walked in the door, I could hardly believe that this scene of destruction used to be my room. *Along the left-hand wall,* nearly hiding my desk and mirror, was a pile of beer cans and bottles, paper cups, and old crumpled newspapers. The small window *on the far wall* was now covered with the mattress of the bed, and the frame of the bunk bed stood on end. The clothes closet, *to the right of the window,* looked as though it were a giant washing machine which had just gone through spin cycle—clothes were plastered all over, and only four hangers remained, dangling uselessly on the pole. *On the right wall,* where the bed had been, was the real surprise. Tied to the heating pipe was a mangy looking sheep. I swear. It was a real sheep. As I looked at it, it turned to face me and loudly and plaintively said, "Baaaa." *Behind me,* in the hall, everyone began laughing. I didn't know whether to laugh or cry.

● **CHRONOLOGICAL ORDER**   Chronological order is simply the time sequence of your observation. In the following passage, Gregory Allen, writing from his point of view as a five-foot-six-inch guard on a basketball team, describes sights, sounds, and his feelings during a pickup game. The italicized words emphasize the chronological order.

The game *begins.* The guy checking me is about 6'1", red hair, freckles, and has no business on the court. He looks slow, so I decide to run him to tire him. I dribble twice, pump fake, and the guy goes for it, thinking that he's going to block this much smaller guy's shot. *Then* I leap, flick my wrist, and the ball glides through the air and flows through the net with a swish as the net turns upside down. I come down and realize that I have been scratched. *Suddenly,* I feel a sharp pain as sweat runs into the small red cut. I wipe the blood on my shorts and *continue playing* the game. *After* that first play, I begin to hear the common song of the game. There's the squeak of the high-top Nike sneakers, the bouncing ball, the shuffle of feet. *Occasionally,* I hear "I'm open!" "Pass the ball!" "Augghh!" And *then,* "Nice play, man!"

● **COMPARISON/CONTRAST**   If what you've observed and written about your subject so far involves seeing similarities or differences, you may be able to use comparison/contrast as a shaping strategy—either for a single paragraph or for a series of paragraphs. The following two paragraphs, for example, are taken from Albert Goldman's biography of Elvis Presley, titled *Elvis.* In these paragraphs, Goldman's dominant idea depends on the striking contrast between what he finds on the front lawn of Graceland, the rock star's mansion in Memphis, and what he notices when he steps through the front door.

Prominently displayed on the front lawn is an elaborate creche. The stable is a full-scale adobe house strewn with straw. Life-sized are the figures of Joseph and Mary, the kneeling shepherds and Magi, the lambs and ewes, as well as the winged annunciatory angel hovering over the roof beam. Real, too, is the cradle in which the infant Jesus sleeps.

When you step through the ten-foot oak door and enter the house, you stop and stare in amazement. Having just come from the contemplation of the tenderest scene in the Holy Bible, imagine the shock of finding yourself in a *whorehouse!* Yet there is no other way to describe the drawing room of Graceland except to say that it appears to have been lifted from some turn-of-the-century bordello down in the French Quarter of New Orleans.... The room is a gaudy melange of red velour and gilded tassels, Louis XV furniture and porcelain bric-a-brac, all informed by the kind of taste that delights in a ceramic temple d'amour housing a miniature Venus de Milo with an electrically simulated waterfall cascading over her naked shoulders.

Examine once again your collecting notes about your subject. If there are striking similarities or differences between the two parts or between various aspects of your subject, perhaps a comparison or contrast structure will organize your details.

● **DEFINITION**   Definition is the essence of observation. Defining a person, place, or object requires stating its exact meaning and describing its basic qualities. Literally, a definition sets the boundaries, indicating, for example, how an apple is distinct from an orange or how a canary is different from a sparrow. *Definition,* however, is a catchall term for a variety of strategies. It uses classification and comparison as well as description. It often describes a thing by negation—by saying what it is not. For example, Sidney Harris, a columnist for many years for the *Chicago Daily News,* once defined a "jerk" by referring to several types of people ("boob," "fool," "dope," "bore," "egotist," "nice person," "clever person") and then compared or contrasted these terms to show where "jerk" leaves off and "egotist" begins. In the following excerpt, Harris also defines by negation, saying that a jerk has no grace and is tactless. The result, when combined with a description of qualities he has observed in jerks, is definition.

Thinking it over, I decided that a jerk is basically a person without insight. He is not necessarily a fool or a dope, because some extremely clever persons can be jerks. In fact, it has little to do with intelligence as we commonly think of it; it is, rather, a kind of subtle but persuasive aroma emanating from the inner part of the personality.

I know a college president who can be described only as a jerk. He is not an unintelligent man, or unlearned, nor even unschooled in the social amenities. Yet he is a jerk *cum laude,* because of a fatal flaw in his nature—he is totally incapable of looking into the mirror of his soul and shuddering at what he sees there.

A jerk, then, is a man (or woman) who is utterly unable to see himself as he appears to others. He has no grace, he is tactless without meaning to be, he is a bore even to his best friends, he is an egotist without charm. All of us are egotists to some extent, but most of us—unlike the jerk—are perfectly and horribly aware of it when we make asses of ourselves. The jerk never knows.

At this stage in the writing process, you have already been defining your subject simply by describing it. But you may want to use a deliberately structured definition, as Harris does, to shape your observations.

● **SIMILE, METAPHOR, AND ANALOGY**   Simile, metaphor, and analogy create vivid word pictures or *images* by making *comparisons.* These images may take up only a sentence or two, or they may shape several paragraphs.

- A *simile* is a comparison using *like* or *as*: A is like B. "George eats his food like a vacuum cleaner."
- A *metaphor* is a direct or implied comparison suggesting that A is B. "At the dinner table, George is a vacuum cleaner."
- An *analogy* is an extended simile or metaphor that builds a point-by-point comparison into several sentences, a whole paragraph, or even a series of paragraphs. Writers use analogy to explain a difficult concept, idea, or process by comparing it with something more familiar or easier to understand. If the audience, for example, knows about engines but has never seen a human heart, a writer might use an analogy to explain that a heart is like a simple engine, complete with chambers or cylinders, intake and exhaust valves, and hoses to carry fuel and exhaust.

As an illustration of simile and metaphor, notice how Joseph Conrad, in the following brief passage from *Heart of Darkness,* begins with a simile and then continues to build on his images throughout the paragraph. Rather than creating a rigid structural shape for his details (as classification or comparison/contrast would do), the images combine and flow like the river he is describing.

> Going up that river was like travelling back to the earliest beginnings of the world, when vegetation rioted on the earth and the big trees were kings. An empty stream, a great silence, an impenetrable forest. The air was warm, thick, heavy, sluggish. There was no joy in the brilliance of sunshine. The long stretches of the waterway ran on, deserted, into the gloom of overshadowed distances. On silvery sand-banks hippos and alligators sunned themselves side by side. The broadening waters flowed through a mob of wooded islands; you lost your way on that river as you would in a desert, and butted all day long against shoals, trying to find the channel, till you thought yourself bewitched and cut off forever from everything you had known once—somewhere—far away—in another existence perhaps.

An analogy helps shape the following paragraph by Carl Sagan, author of *The Dragons of Eden* and *Cosmos.* To help us understand a difficult concept, the immense age of the Earth (and, by comparison, the relatively tiny span of human history), Sagan compares the lifetime of the universe to something simple and familiar: the calendar of a single year.

> The most instructive way I know to express this cosmic chronology is to imagine the fifteen-billion year lifetime of the universe . . . compressed into the span of a single year. . . . It is disconcerting to find that in such a cosmic year the Earth does not condense out of interstellar matter until early September; dinosaurs emerge on Christmas Eve; flowers arise on December 28th; and men and women originate at 10:30 P.M. on New Year's Eve. All of recorded history occupies the last ten seconds of December 31; and the time from the waning of the Middle Ages to the present occupies little more than one second.

Consider whether a good analogy would help you shape one or more paragraphs in your essay. Ask yourself, "What is the most difficult concept or idea I'm trying to describe?" Is there an extended point-by-point comparison—an analogy—that would clarify it?

● **TITLE, INTRODUCTION, AND CONCLUSION**   Depending on your purpose and audience, you may want a title for what you're writing. At the minimum, titles—like labels—should accurately indicate the contents in the package. In addition, however, good titles capture the reader's interest with some catchy phrasing or imaginative language—something to make the reader want to "buy" the package. Samuel H. Scudder's title is a good label (the essay is about looking at fish) and uses catchy phrasing: "Take This Fish and Look at It." If a title is appropriate for your observation, write out several possibilities in your journal.

The introduction should set up the context for the reader—*who, what, when, where,* and *why*—so that readers can orient themselves. Depending on your audience and purpose, introductions can be very brief, pushing the reader quickly into the scene, or they can take more time, easing readers into the setting. Stephen White, in his essay about Mesa Verde at the end of this chapter, begins mysteriously: "It is difficult for me to say exactly what it was that drew me to this solitary place." White doesn't tell his reader that he's talking about Mesa Verde until the second paragraph.

Conclusions should wrap up the observation, providing a sense of completeness. Conclusions vary, depending upon a writer's purpose and audience, but they tend to be of two types or have two components: a *summary* and a *reference* to the introduction. Scudder uses both components when he refers to his eight months of study and to Agassiz's "urgent exhortations" not to be content with hasty observations. The clincher to the conclusion is the parting quotation from Agassiz: "Facts are stupid things until brought into connection with some general law."

As you work on shaping strategies and drafting, make notes about possible titles, appropriate introductions, or effective conclusions for your written observations.

DRAFTING

● **REREAD JOURNAL ENTRIES AND NOTES**   Before you start drafting, review your material so you aren't writing cold. Stop and reread everything you've written on your subject. You're not trying to memorize particular sentences or phrases; you're just getting it all fresh in your mind, seeing what you still like and discarding details that are no longer relevant.

● **REOBSERVE YOUR SUBJECT**   If necessary, go back and observe your subject again. One more session may suggest an important detail or idea that will help you get started writing.

● **REEXAMINE PURPOSE, AUDIENCE, DOMINANT IDEA, AND SHAPE**
After all your writing and rereading, you may have some new ideas about your purpose, audience, or dominant idea. Take a minute to jot these down in your journal. Remember that your specific details should show the main point or dominant idea, whether you state it explicitly or not.

Next, if the shaping strategies suggested an order for your essay, use it to guide your draft. You may, however, have only your specific details or a general notion of the dominant idea you're trying to communicate to your reader. In that case, you may want to begin writing and work out a shape or outline as you write.

● **CREATE A DRAFT**   With the above notes as a guide, you are ready to start drafting. Work on establishing your ritual: Choose a comfortable, familiar place with the writing tools you like. Make sure you'll have no interruptions. Try to write nonstop. If you can't think of a word, substitute a dash. If you can't remember how to spell a word, don't stop to look it up now—keep writing. Write until you reach what feels like the end. If you do get stuck, reread your last few lines or some of your writing process materials. Then go back and pick up the thread. Don't stop to count words or pages. You should shoot for more material than you need because it's usually easier to cut material later, when you're revising, than to add more if you're short.

> 66 The idea is to get the pencil moving quickly. 99
> —BERNARD MALAMUD, NOVELIST

REVISING

● **GAINING DISTANCE AND OBJECTIVITY**   Revising, of course, has been going on since you put your first sentence down on paper. You've changed ideas, thought through your subject again, and observed your person, place, object, or image. After your rough draft is finished, your next step is to revise again to resee the whole thing. But before you do, you need to let it sit at least twenty-four hours, to get away from it for a while, to gain some distance and perspective. Relax. Congratulate yourself.

> 66 All the stuff you see back there on the floor is writing I did last week that I have to rewrite this week. 99
> —ERNEST J. GAINES, AUTHOR OF *THE AUTOBIOGRAPHY OF MISS JANE PITTMAN*

PEER RESPONSE

The instructions below will help you give and receive constructive advice about the rough draft of your observing essay. You may use these guidelines for an in-class workshop, a take-home review, or a computer response.

Writer: Before you exchange drafts with another reader, write out the following information about your rough draft.

1. What is the dominant impression that you want your description to make? What overall idea or impression do you want your reader to have?
2. What paragraph(s) contain(s) your best and most vivid description? What paragraph(s) still need(s) some revision?
3. Explain one or two things you would like your reader to comment on as he or she responds to your draft.

Reader: First, without making any marks, read the entire draft from start to finish. As you reread the draft, answer the following questions.

1. What *dominant impression* does the draft create? Does the dominant impression you received agree with the writer's own idea? If not, how might the writer better achieve that overall impression?
2. Look at the writer's responses to question 2. Does the writer, in fact, use vivid description in his or her best paragraph(s)? How might the paragraphs that the writer says need revision be improved? Review the six techniques for descriptive writing at the beginning of this chapter. Where or how might the writer improve the *sensory details, images,* descriptions of what is not there, changes in the subject, or *point of view?* Offer specific suggestions.
3. Reread the assignment for this essay. Explain how this essay should be revised to more clearly meet the assignment. Does the writer understand the *rhetorical situation?* What changes in purpose, audience, genre, or style would help the essay meet the assignment?
4. List the *two most important things* this writer should work on as he or she revises this draft. Explain why these are important.

About the time you try to relax, however, you may get a sudden temptation— even an overwhelming urge—to have someone else read it—immediately! Usually, it's better to resist that urge. Chances are, you want to have someone else read it either because you're bubbling with enthusiasm and you want to share it or because you're certain that it's all garbage and you want to hear the bad news right away. Most readers will not find it either as great as you hope *or* as awful as you fear. As a result, their offhand remarks may seem terribly insensitive or condescending. In a day or so, however, you'll be able to see your writing more objectively: Perhaps it's not great yet, but it's not hopeless, either. At that point, you're ready to get some feedback and start your revisions.

● **REREADING AND RESPONDING TO YOUR READERS**   When you've been away from the draft for a while, you are better able to see the whole piece of writing. Start by rereading your own draft and making marginal notes. Don't be distracted by spelling errors or typos; concentrate on the quality of the details and the flow of the sentences. Focus on the overall effect you're creating, see if your organization still makes sense, and check to make sure that all the details support the dominant idea. Now you're ready to get some peer feedback. Depending on the reactions of your readers, you may need to change the point of view, add a few specific examples or some comparisons or images, fix the organization of a paragraph, reorder some details, delete some sentences, or do several of the above. Be prepared, however, to rewrite several paragraphs to help your readers really see what you are describing.

GUIDELINES FOR REVISION

As you revise your essay, keep the following tips and checklist questions in mind.

- **Reexamine your purpose and audience.** Are you doing what you intended? If your purpose or audience has changed, what other changes do you need to make as you revise?
- **Pay attention to the advice your readers give you, but don't necessarily make all the changes they suggest.** Ask them *why* something should be changed. Ask them specifically *where* something should be changed.
- **Consider your genre.** Does your chosen genre still work for your purpose, audience, and context? Would including pictures, visuals, graphics, poetry, or quotations in a multigenre format be more effective?
- **Consider your point of view.** Would changing to another point of view clarify what you are describing?
- **Consider your vantage point.** Do you have a bird's-eye view, or are you observing from a low angle? Do you zoom in for a close-up of a person or object? Would a different vantage point fit your purpose and audience?
- **Make sure you are using sensory details where appropriate.** Remember, you must *show* your reader the details you observe. If necessary, *reobserve* your subject.
- **Do all your details and examples support your dominant idea?** Reread your draft and omit any irrelevant details.

- **What is *not* present in your subject that might be important to mention?**
- **What changes occur in the form or function of your subject?** Where can you describe those changes more vividly?
- **Make comparisons if they will help you or your reader understand your subject better.** Similes, metaphors, or analogies may describe your subject more vividly.
- **Does what you are observing belong to a class of similar objects?** Would classification organize your writing?
- **Be sure to cue or signal your reader with appropriate transition words.** Transitions will improve the coherence or flow of your writing.
  - **Spatial order:** on the left, on the right, next, above, below, higher, lower, farther, next, beyond
  - **Chronological order.** before, earlier, after, afterward, thereafter, then, from then on, the next day, shortly, by that time, immediately, slowly, while, meanwhile, until, now, soon, within an hour, first, later, finally, at last
  - **Comparison/contrast:** on one hand, on the other hand, also, similarly, in addition, likewise, however, but, yet, still, although, even so, nonetheless, in contrast
- **Revise sentences for clarity, conciseness, emphasis, and variety.**
- **When you have revised your essay, edit your writing for correct spelling and appropriate word choice, punctuation, usage, and grammar.**

> ❝I went for years not finishing anything. Because, of course, when you finish something you can be judged.❞
>
> —ERICA JONG,
> AUTHOR OF *FEAR OF FLYING*

POSTSCRIPT ON THE WRITING PROCESS

When you've finished writing this assignment, do one final journal entry. Briefly, answer the following questions.

1. What was the hardest part of this writing assignment for you?
2. Put brackets ([ ]) around the paragraph containing your most vivid sensory details. Explain what makes this paragraph so vivid.
3. What exercise, practice, strategy, or workshop was the "breakthrough" for you? What led you to your discovery or dominant idea?
4. State in one sentence your discovery or the dominant idea of your essay.
5. What did you learn about your writing ritual and process? What did you learn about observing? What did you learn from your choice of audience and genre?

Permanent Tracings

Jennifer Macke, a student in Professor Rachel Henne-Wu's class at Owens Community College in Findlay, Ohio, decided to write her observing essay about a tattoo parlor. She visited the Living Color Tattoo Parlor and took notes on the office, the clientele, the conversations, the artwork of the tattoos, and the owner of the establishment. Ms. Macke wrote that her preconceptions about tattoo parlors were that they were "smoke-filled, dimly lit places" where "undesirables gathered." Gradually, her impressions changed as she saw firsthand the high quality and the remarkable artistry of the tattoos. Reprinted below are some of her original notes, questions and answers, an outline, and the final version of her essay.

NOTES ON A VISIT

- A couple with a young school-aged daughter looks at the artwork on the walls for about 15 minutes before saying anything to the owner. They are looking for a design for the wife for her birthday. They appear to be a typical young couple with a limited amount of money. They ask how much a particular design will be and say they will have to save for it. "How much for this ankle bracelet?" he says. "It'll run you between $45 and $60, depending on how thick you want the rose vine," Gasket says.

- Two Latino men enter the waiting room. One peeks his head into the office and says, "I'm here early for my appointment because I'm not sure exactly what I want. Do you have any books or more pictures I can look through?" Gasket gives him six photo albums full of ideas (designs).

- Five young adult black men enter. They begin browsing through the photos on the wall. There are designs with prices below them so you know what it costs without asking. They too look through the photo albums the Latinos left on the floor. One of the black guys announces, "I'll go first 'cause I want to get it over with." One says, "I'm not going to do this. I can't stand the sound of that needle!" Gasket looks at me and says, "It's amazing how many people just think all you have to do is walk through the door like a walk-in barber shop. They don't know I'm booked for at least a week. During the summer, it's three weeks."

- The phone rings and since his daughter, who normally works there, is gone to visit her mother, he tells me to pick it up. The guy on the other end says, "My uncle wants to know if Jeff's cousin works here?" I relay the message to the owner and he replies, "Yes, that's me." Back on the phone, "He says he's the best in the business. Does he have any time today?" Gasket says, "Here we go again." I tell the guy it will be a week. He says, "OK, I'll call back then." I tell Gasket what he said and he comments, "He'll call back next week, and I'll have to tell him it'll be another week. You would not believe the intelligence level of some people."

- The next girl is going to have lips tattooed on her right hip. She is a petite nurse whom you would never guess would even consider such a thing. Her husband put lipstick on and kissed a napkin which she brought to use for the pattern. Gasket took a photocopy of this and made a transfer from it to use as the template. She dropped her shorts to expose where the art would be placed. She lay down on the table which Gasket explained he had gotten in trade for a tattoo. He also said the stirrups were still in the drawer. The girl smiled and talked the whole time he worked. At one point, he asked her, "Does it hurt?" She said, "No." He said, "I can go deeper!" She said, "Are you supposed to?" He said, laughing, "It's just a joke. If I see someone who's comfortable, I'll ask them this." It only took about 30 minutes to complete this one. You would swear someone just kissed her with bright red lipstick. It's amazing how realistic his work looks.

QUESTIONS AND ANSWERS

1. "Why do people get tattoos?"

   "A tattoo is a very personal thing. It's an expression of one's self."

2. "Does it hurt to get a tattoo?"

   "It all depends on the placement and the person. Guys tend to be bigger wimps. I'd rather do women any day. The most painful areas are the ankle and higher up on the belly. I've had the pain described as something annoying but not necessarily painful to such a point that they cannot stand it. I've never had anyone pass out, though."

3. "What kind of person gets a tattoo?"

   "There's not one particular type of person who gets a tattoo. I once had a call from some lawyers from Findlay. They wanted to know if they had five or so people who wanted a tattoo, would I come over? I said, yes, and I tattooed six lawyers at a party."

4. "What is the process of getting a tattoo?"

"Depending if it will be freehand or something the people bring in, it starts with drawing the art. It is drawn either on the person or on carbon paper backwards. The carbon design is transferred to the skin with Speed Stick deodorant. The outline is applied first. As the single needle picks up and sews into the skin, excess ink covers the work area."

As Gasket works, it's hard to see the actual area he's working on because of the excess ink. When asked how he can work with the excess ink obstructing the guidelines, he says he just knows where the line goes. (I wouldn't.) Once the outline is complete he changes to use a 3 or 4 needle set, depending on the coverage necessary. He colorizes the art, which brings it to life. After it's complete, he puts a thick coat of Bacitracin on and covers it with a gauze bandage. The gauze must remain on for one and a half to two hours.

5. "What is the most common place for a tattoo?"

"Placement runs in cycles, sometimes the upper arm, sometimes the ankle." While we were talking, a man came in with one on the back of his neck.

6. "How expensive are tattoos?"

The minimum is $30. Depending on how detailed and how big. Gasket has bartered for the tattoos, too.

7. "Do most people get more than one tattoo?"

"I've seen people go through life with only one or maybe two, but it's said when you get your third, you're hooked. You'll be back for more."

8. "Are there health department requirements?"

"At the beginning, the requirements (laws) weren't very strict. I knew I wanted to be supersterile, so I put my needles and equipment through a much stricter procedure. Since then, the health department has taken on my policy and requires everyone to process their stuff like me. They drop in to make sure the laws are being followed."

9. "How many times do you use your needles?"

"They are single-application needles, but they still need to be sterilized. People ask me if they can watch their needles being sterilized so they can make sure. I say fine, but it will be two and a half hours until I can work on you."

OUTLINE

Working Thesis: "Gasket's creative artistic
ability and perfectionist work ethic make his designs
worth sewing into your body for a lifetime."

    I. Describe the Tattoo Parlor

        A. Outer area (waiting room)

        B. Inner office

    II. Describe the owner

        A. The way he looks

        B. The way he feels about his work

    III. Describe the people

        A. People getting a tattoo

        B. People not getting a tattoo

FINAL VERSION

Permanent Tracings

At first glance, the Living Color Tattoo Parlor appears to be just another 1
typical tattoo establishment. You enter through a glass door only to find
a waiting room with the decor reminiscent of the 1970s. The dark pan-
eled walls display numerous types of artwork that range from pencil
sketching to color Polaroid snapshots of newly completed tattoos. The
gold and green davenport looks as if it came from a Saturday morning
garage sale. The inner office is celery green with a dental chair and an
obstetrics table that the owner bartered for a tattoo (the stirrups are still
in the drawer). A filing cabinet, desk, and copy machine make you feel as
if you're in a professional office. The sterilizer is in plain sight and is in
operation. Bottle after bottle of brightly colored inks are neatly arranged
on a tiered wooden stand. The sound of the oscillating fan that cools the
client interrupts the buzz of the needle sewing the paint into the client's
skin. A freeze-dried turtle is displayed on a table in the office.

    I still wondered, though. Could tattoos actually be a form of art?   2

    As soon as I could, I asked the owner, a man called Gasket, about his 3
occupation. "I was a suit for fifteen years and now I can work as much as
I want. There's always somebody wanting a tattoo or something pierced,"
Gasket said. He's often asked if he'll scratch out the name of a previous
girlfriend, and he always replies that he would never even consider it.
"That would be defacement," he said. "When I'm done, the design should
look better than when I started." Gasket is not his given name but one he

acquired because of his expert repair work on Harley Davidson motor-cycles. Gasket is the owner of this establishment, and to look at him, you would never guess he is a college-educated engineer. His long curly, gray-ing hair flows from under his Harley hat, and examples of his handiwork are visible under the rolled up sleeves of his black Harley T-shirt. The harshness of his heavily bearded face is softened by his slate-blue eyes, which mirror his gentle demeanor. If you look past his casual exterior, you will find a code of steel. "At the beginning, the laws weren't very strict. I knew I wanted to be supersterile, so I put my single-use needles and equipment through a much stricter procedure. Since then, the health department has taken on my policy and requires everyone to process their stuff like me," he said.

The appearance of the Living Color Tattoo Parlor may be typical, but *4* two things are distinctly different: the quality and the creativity of the tat-too designs. A young college couple from Toledo was asked why they would drive to Fremont for an appointment. They answered, "Gasket's the best! We wouldn't trust something that's going to be on our body for the rest of our lives to someone other than him."

"I already have two tattoos from you, and I love your work," a middle- *5* aged woman said. Displaying two greeting cards, she asked, "Is it possi-ble to get a combination of these two designs?"

"I can create anything you want," Gasket said. *6*

"I'll have to wait a couple of weeks because I'm not working much *7* and my other bills come first," she said.

"Yes, you have to get your priorities straight. When you're ready, I'm *8* here," he said.

Gasket is performing his tattoo magic on a young college female. He's *9* creating a rose with a heart stem wrapping around her belly button, which is pierced. The girl is nervously seated in the green dental chair, which is tilted back to flatten the skin surface. First, Gasket draws the sketch on her belly. He covers his hands with a thin layer of latex once the exact position and specific details are decided upon. A small device resembling a fountain pen with a brightly colored motor and a single needle moving at 1,000 rpm is used to apply the black outline first. As the needle moves up and down, it picks up a small amount of ink and deposits it just under the surface of the skin. When asked how he can work with the excess ink obstructing the guidelines, he simply said he just knows where the line goes. This is a diffi-cult task because unlike a paint-by-number design, the image not only has to be in his mind but he also has to have the artistic ability to convert the image to the skin. The girl asks a pain-filled question, "How much longer?"

"I can stop and let you take a break at any time," Gasket says. His soft *10* tone and slow-paced voice help soothe the girl. "The higher up on the belly, the more painful," he says. The process of colorizing the tattoo begins once the outline is complete. This is accomplished with a three- or four-needle set, depending on the amount of coverage desired. It takes about forty-five

...continued Permanent Tracings, **Jennifer Macke**

minutes to complete the multicolored masterpiece, which is literally sewn into her skin. Some of Gasket's designs can be compared to Picasso's brilliantly colored, dreamlike images. Upon completion, the girl is directed to a full-length mirror to inspect her permanently altered abs.

"It looks fantastic!" she exclaims. "I was a little vague on how I pictured 11 it would look, but it looks even better than I had imagined. I'm thrilled."

Once thought of as green-toned disfigurements that only drunken 12 sailors and lowlife people would don, tattoos are now high fashion. Now it is possible to see skin art on TV stars, sports superstars, and a multitude of individuals you might not suspect. The future of this trendy fashion has its roots firmly planted in today's society. Young people seem to be one of its biggest supporters.

"I'll go first 'cause I want to get it over with," one young black man 13 states to his four companions.

"I'm not going to do this. I can't stand the sound of that needle!" 14 another man proclaims.

"It's amazing how many people think all you have to do is just walk 15 through the door like a walk-in barber shop. They don't know I'm booked for at least a week. During the summer, it's three weeks," Gasket claims. He explains this to the young men, who make appointments. They leave, disappointed.

Gasket's tattoo designs can be compared to the famous fashion de- 16 signs by Bob Mackie. Like Mackie's one-of-a-kind designs, they are not mass-produced, but are hand-sewn for a specific individual. As I left, my first impression of the Living Color Tattoo Parlor was changed by the incredibly beautiful skin art and the comments of the satisfied clients. For many, Gasket's artistic ability and perfectionism make his designs worth sewing into your body for a lifetime.

 QUESTIONS FOR WRITING AND DISCUSSION

1. Review the techniques for writing observing papers at the beginning of the chapter. Which paragraph(s) in Macke's essay have the best sensory detail, images, comparisons, and other effective bits of description? Which paragraphs might use more descriptive detail?

2. Macke describes the office, the owner, the customers, the process of tattooing, and the prices of a tattoo. Should she also describe several of the tattoos? Should she describe the colors in a typical tattoo? If she did these descriptions, where might she put them in her essay?

3 Reread Macke's notes of her visit, including her questions and answers. What interesting ideas and descriptions in her notes might be included in her final draft? Why might Macke have left these details out? Assume that you are a peer reader for Macke's essay. Fill out the peer response questions printed earlier in this chapter so you can help her with a revision of her essay.

4 List the three things that you like best about Macke's essay. Which of her strategies might work for a revision of your own essay? Make a revision plan for your own essay, based on what you learned from reading "Permanent Tracings."

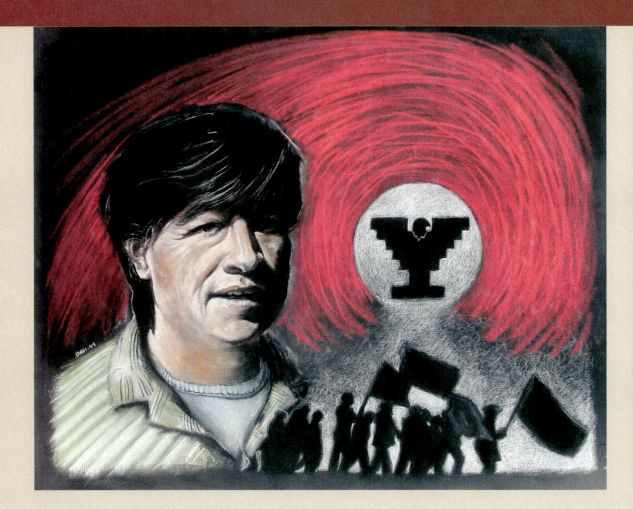

Described by Robert F. Kennedy as "one of the heroic figures of our time," César Chávez (1927–1993) spent his lifetime improving the conditions of agricultural workers in America. In 1994, President Clinton posthumously awarded Chávez the Presidential Medal of Freedom, the nation's highest and most prestigious civilian award. In his essay in this chapter, "César Chávez Saved My Life," Daniel Alejandrez remembers Chávez's influence on his own life.

Remembering

4

You and several coworkers have formed a committee to draft a report for your company's vice president in charge of personnel. You have grievances about workload, pay scale, daily procedures, and the attitudes of supervisors. Your report needs to recommend changes in current policies. The committee decides that each person will contribute part of the report by describing actual incidents that have had negative effects on efficiency and human relations. You decide to describe a day last June when your immediate supervisor expected you to learn a new word-processing system and at the same time meet a 3:00 P.M. deadline for a thirty-seven-page budget analysis.

This morning you accidentally ran into a certain person whom you knew several years ago, and for several hours you've been in a bad mood. You called your best friend, but no one answered the phone. You went to class and then for your usual jog, but you pooped out after only half a mile. You even watched a game show on television in the middle of the afternoon and ate half a bag of potato chips, but you still felt lousy. You yell at the television: "Why do I always react this way when I see that person?" But the television has no reply. So you grab some paper and begin scrawling out every memory you have of your experiences with the person you ran into this morning, hoping to understand your feelings.

> " For me the initial delight is in the surprise of remembering something I didn't know I knew. "
> —ROBERT FROST, POET

> " The fact is that there's no understanding the future without the present, and no understanding where we are now without a glance, at least, to where we have been. "
> —JOYCE MAYNARD, COLUMNIST AND AUTHOR OF *LOOKING BACKWARD: A CHRONICLE OF GROWING UP OLD IN THE SIXTIES*

THE HUMAN BRAIN IS A PACK RAT: NOTHING IS TOO SMALL, OBSCURE, OR MUNDANE FOR THE BRAIN'S COLLECTION. OFTEN THE BRAIN COLLECTS AND DISCARDS INFORMATION WITHOUT REGARD TO OUR WISHES. OUT OF THE COLLECTION MAY ARISE, WITH NO WARNING, the image of windblown whitecaps on a lake you visited more than five yeas ago, the recipe for Uncle Joe's incomparable chili, or even the right answer to an exam question that you've been staring at for the past fifteen minutes.

Remembering is sometimes easy, sometimes difficult. Often careful concentration yields nothing, while the most trivial occurrence—an old song on a car radio, the acrid smell of diesel exhaust, the face of a stranger—will trigger a flood of recollections. Someone tells a story and you immediately recall incidents, funny or traumatic, from your own life. Some memories, however, are nagging and troublesome, keeping you awake at night, daring you to deal with them. You pick at these memories. Why are they so important? You write about them, usually to probe that mystery of yesterday and today. Sights, sounds, or feelings from the present may draw you to the past, but the past leads, just as surely, back to the present.

Direct observations are important to learning and writing, but so are your memories, experiences, and stories. You may write an autobiographical account of part of your life, or you may recall a brief event, a person, or a place just as an example to illustrate a point. Whatever form your writing from memory takes, however, your initial purpose is to remember experiences so that you can understand yourself and your world. The point is not to write fiction, but to practice drawing on your memories and to write vividly enough about them so that you and others can discover and learn.

The value of remembering lies exactly here: Written memories have the power to teach you and, through the *empathy* of your readers, to inform or convince them as well. At first, you may be self-conscious about sharing your personal memories. But as you reveal these experiences, you realize that your story is worth telling—not because you're such an egotist, but because sharing experiences helps everyone learn.

Techniques for Writing About Memories

Writing vividly about memories includes all the skills of careful observing, but it adds several additional narrative strategies. Listed below are six techniques that writers use to compose effective remembering essays. As you read the essays that follow in this chapter, notice how each writer uses these techniques.

Then, when you write your own remembering essay, use these techniques in your own essay. Remember: Not all writing about memories uses all of these techniques, but one or two of them may transform a lifeless account into an effective narrative.

Techniques for Writing About Memories

Technique	Tips on How to Do It
Using *detailed observation* of people, places, and events	Writing vividly about memories requires many of the skills of careful observation. Use *sensory descriptions*, *comparisons*, and *images*. Include *actual dialogue* where appropriate.
Focusing on *occasion and cultural context*	Think about the personal occasion that motivated you to write about your experience. You may want to set your experiences in a larger cultural context.
Creating *specific scenes* set in time and space	Show your reader the actual events—don't just tell about them. Narrate or recreate specific incidents as they actually happened. Avoid summarizing events or presenting just the conclusions (for instance, "Those experiences really changed my life").
Noting *changes*, *contrasts*, or *conflicts*	Describe changes in people or places. Show contrasts between two different memories or between memories of expectations and realities. Narrate conflicts between people or ideas. Resolving (or sometimes not resolving) these changes, contrasts, or conflicts can often be the point of your memoir.
Making *connections* between *past* events, people, or places and the *present*	The main idea or focus of your narrative may grow out of the connections you make between the past and the present: what you felt then and how you feel now; what you thought you knew and what you know now.
Discovering and focusing on a *main idea*	Your narrative should not be a random account of your favorite memories. It should have a clear main point—something you learned or discovered or realized—without actually stating a "moral" to your story.

66 Time passes and the past becomes the present. . . . These presences of the past are there in the center of your life today. You thought . . . they had died, but they have just been waiting their chance. 99

—CARLOS FUENTES, MEXICAN ESSAYIST AND NOVELIST, AUTHOR OF *THE CRYSTAL FRONTIER*

All of these techniques are important, but you should also keep several other points in mind. Normally, you should write in the *first person,* using *I* or *we* throughout the narrative. Although you will usually write in *past tense,* sometimes you may wish to lend immediacy to the events by retelling them in the *present tense,* as if they are happening now. Finally, you may choose straightforward *chronological order,* or you may begin near the end and use a *flashback* to tell the beginning of the story.

The key to effective remembering, however, is to get beyond *generalities and conclusions* about your experiences ("I had a lot of fun—those days really changed my life"). Your goal is to *recall specific incidents set in time and place* that *show* how and why those days changed your life. The specific incidents should show your *main point* or *dominant idea.*

The following passage by Andrea Lee began as a journal entry during a year she spent in Moscow and Leningrad following her graduation from college. She then combined these firsthand observations with her memories and published them in a collection called *Russian Journal.* She uses first person and, frequently, present tense as she describes her reactions to the sights of Moscow. In these paragraphs, she weaves observations and memories together to show her main idea: The contrast between American and Soviet Union-style advertising helped her understand both the virtues and the faults of American commercialism. (The annotations in the margin illustrate how Lee uses all five remembering techniques.)

Specific scene

In Mayakovsky Square, not far from the Tchaikovsky Concert Hall, a big computerized electric sign sends various messages flashing out into the night. An outline of a taxi in green dots is accompanied by the words: "Take Taxis—All Streets Are Near." This is replaced by multicolored human figures and a sentence urging Soviet citizens to save in State banks. The bright patterns and messages come and go, making this one of the most sophisticated examples of advertising in Moscow. Even on chilly nights when I pass through the square, there is often a little group of Russians standing in front of the sign, watching in fascination for five and ten minutes as the colored dots go through their magical changes. The first few times I saw this, I chuckled and recalled an old joke about an American town so boring that people went out on weekends to watch the Esso sign.

Detailed observation

Connections past and present

Advertising, of course, is the glamorous offspring of capitalism and art: Why advertise in a country where there is only one brand, the State brand, of anything, and often not enough even of that? There is nothing here comparable to the glittering overlay of commercialism that Americans, at least, take for granted as part of our cities; nothing like the myriad small seductions of the marketplace, which have led us to expect to be enticed. The Soviet political propaganda posters that fill up a small part of the Moscow landscape with their uniformly cold red color schemes and monumental robot-faced figures are so unappealing that they are dismissable.

Contrast

Detailed observation

I realize now, looking back, that for at least my first month in Moscow, I was filled with an unconscious and devastating disappointment. Hardly realizing it, as I walked around the city, I was looking for the constant sensory distractions I was accustomed to in America. Like many others my age, I grew up reading billboards and singing advertising jingles; my idea of beauty was shaped—perniciously, I think—by the models with the painted eyes and pounds of shining hair whose beauty was accessible on every television set and street corner.

REMEMBERING PEOPLE

In the following passage from the introduction to *The Way to Rainy Mountain*, N. Scott Momaday remembers his grandmother. While details of place and event are also recreated, the primary focus is on the character of his grandmother as revealed in several *specific,* recurring actions. Momaday does not give us generalities about his feelings (for instance, "I miss my grandmother a lot, especially now that she's gone."). Instead, he begins with specific memories of scenes that *show* how he felt.

Now that I can have her only in memory, I see my grandmother in the several postures that were peculiar to her: standing at the wood stove on a winter morning and turning meat in a great iron skillet; sitting at the south window, bent above her beadwork, and afterwards, when her vision failed, looking down for a long time into the fold of her hands; going out upon a cane, very slowly as she did when the weight of age came upon her; praying. I remember her most often at prayer. She made long, rambling prayers out of suffering and hope, having seen many things. I was never sure that I had the right to hear, so exclusive were they of all mere custom and company. The last time I saw her she prayed standing by the side of her bed at night, naked to the waist, the light of a kerosene lamp moving upon her dark skin. Her long, black hair, always drawn and braided in the day, lay upon her shoulders and against her breasts like a shawl. I do not speak Kiowa, and I never understood her prayers, but there was something inherently sad in the sound, some merest hesitation upon the syllables of sorrow. She began in a high and descending pitch, exhausting her breath to silence; then again and again—and always the same intensity of effort, of something that is, and is not, like urgency in the human voice. Transported so in the dancing light among the shadows of her room, she seemed beyond the reach of time. But that was illusion; I think I knew then that I should not see her again.

Connections past and present

Contrast and change

Main idea

66 A writer is a reader moved to emulation. 99
—SAUL BELLOW, AUTHOR OF *HENDERSON THE RAIN KING*

66 There are two ways to live. One is as though nothing is a miracle, the other is as though everything is. 99
—ALBERT EINSTEIN, AUTHOR OF *WHAT I BELIEVE*

66 Some very small incident that takes place today may be the most important event that happens to you this year, but you don't know that when it happens. You don't know it until much later. 99
—TONI MORRISON, NOBEL PRIZE–WINNING AUTHOR OF *BELOVED* AND *SONG OF SOLOMON*

REMEMBERING PLACES

In the following passage from *Farewell to Manzanar,* Jeanne Wakatsuke Houston remembers the place in California where, as Japanese-Americans, her family was imprisoned during World War II. As you read, look for specific details and bits of description that convey her main idea.

In Spanish, Manzanar means "apple orchard." Great stretches of Owens Valley were once green with orchards and alfalfa fields. It has been a desert ever since its water started flowing south into Los Angeles, sometime during the twenties. But a few rows of untended pear and apple trees were still growing there when the camp opened, where a shallow water table had kept them alive. In the spring of 1943 we moved to block 28, right up next to one of the old pear orchards. That's where we stayed until the end of the war, and those trees stand in my memory for the turning of our life in camp, from the outrageous to the tolerable.

Papa pruned and cared for the nearest trees. Late that summer we picked the fruit green and stored it in a root cellar he had dug under our new barracks. At night the wind through the leaves would sound like the surf had sounded in Ocean Park, and while drifting off to sleep, I could almost imagine we were still living by the beach.

REMEMBERING EVENTS

In the following essay, called "The Boy's Desire," Richard Rodriguez recalls a particular event from his childhood that comes to mind when he remembers Christmas. In his memory, he sorts through the rooms in his house on 39th Street in Sacramento, recalling old toys: a secondhand bike, games with dice and spinning dials, a jigsaw puzzle, and a bride doll. In this passage, Rodriguez describes both the effort to remember and the memory itself—the one memory that still "holds color and size and shape." Was it all right, he wonders, that a boy should have wanted a doll for Christmas?

The fog comes to mind. It never rained on Christmas. It was never sharp blue and windy. When I remember Christmas in Sacramento, it is in gray: The valley fog would lift by late morning, the sun boiled haze for a few hours, then the tule fog would rise again when it was time to go into the house.

The haze through which memory must wander is thickened by that fog. The rooms of the house on 39th Street are still and dark in late afternoon, and I open the closet to search for old toys. One year there was a secondhand bike. I do not remember a color. Perhaps it had no color even then. Another year there were boxes of games that rattled their parts—dice and pegs and spinning dials. Or perhaps the rattle is of a jigsaw puzzle that compressed into an image . . . of what? of Paris? a litter of kittens? I cannot remember. Only one memory holds color and size and shape: brown hair, blue eyes, the sweet smell of styrene.

That Christmas I announced I wanted a bride doll. I must have been seven or eight—wise enough to know not to tell anyone at school, but young enough to whine out my petition from early November.

My father's reaction was unhampered by psychology. A shrug— "Una muñeca?"—a doll, why not? Because I knew it was my mother who would choose all the presents, it was she I badgered. I wanted a bride doll! "Is there something else you want?" she wondered. No! I'd make clear with my voice that nothing else would appease me. "We'll see," she'd say, and she never wrote it down on her list.

By early December, wrapped boxes started piling up in my parents' bedroom closet, above my father's important papers and the family album. When no one else was home, I'd drag a chair over and climb up to see . . . Looking for the one. About a week before Christmas, it was there. I was so certain it was mine that I punched my thumb through the wrapping paper and the cellophane window on the box and felt inside—lace, two tiny, thin legs. I got other presents that year, but it was the doll I kept by me. I remember my mother saying I'd have "to share her" with my younger sister—but Helen was four years old, oblivious. The doll was mine. My arms would hold her. She would sleep on my pillow.

And the sky did not fall. The order of the universe did not tremble. In fact, it was right for a change. My family accommodated itself to my request. My brother and sisters played round me with their own toys. I paraded my doll by the hands across the floor.

The other day, when I asked my brother and sisters about the doll, no one remembered. My mother remembers. "Yes," she smiled. "One year there was a doll."

The closet door closes. (The house on 39th Street has been razed for a hospital parking lot.) The fog rises. Distance tempts me to mock the boy and his desire. The fact remains: One Christmas in Sacramento I wanted a bride doll, and I got one.

WARMING UP   Journal Exercises

The following topics will help you practice writing about your memories. Read all of the following exercises, and then write on three that interest you the most. If another idea occurs to you, write a free entry about it.

1 Go through old family photographs and find one of yourself, taken at least five years ago. Describe the person in the photograph—what he or she did, thought, said, or hoped. How is that person like or unlike the person you are now?

2 Remember the first job you had. How did you get it, and what did you do? What mistakes did you make? What did you learn? Were there any humorous or serious misunderstandings between you and others?

3 What are your earliest memories? Choose one particular event. How old were you? What was the place? Who were the people around you? What happened? After you write down your earliest memories, call members of your family, if possible, and interview them for their memories of this incident. How does what you actually remember differ from what your family tells you? Revise your first memory to incorporate additional details provided by your family.

4 At some point in the past, you may have faced a conflict between what was expected of you—by parents, friends, family, coach, or employer— and your own personality or abilities. Describe one occasion when these expectations seemed unrealistic or unfair. Was the experience entirely negative or was it, in the long run, positive?

5 At least at one point in our lives, we have felt like an outsider. In a selection earlier in this chapter, for instance, Richard Rodriguez recalls feelings of being different, rejected, or outcast. Write about an incident when you felt alienated from your family, peers, or social group. Focus on a key scene or scenes that show what happened, why it was important, and how it affects you now.

PROFESSIONAL WRITING

César Chávez Saved My Life

Daniel "Nane" Alejandrez

Labor leader and civil rights worker César Chávez (1927–1993) founded the National Farm Workers Association and used the nonviolent principles of Mahatma Gandhi and Dr. Martin Luther King, Jr. to gain dignity, fair wages, and humane working conditions for farm workers. In addition to his post humously awarded Presidential Medal of Freedom and his induction into the California Hall of Fame, César Chávez has had his birthday, March 31st, recognized in eight states as an official holiday.

The author of the article, Daniel "Nane" Alejandrez, is the founder of Barrios Unidos and has spent his life fighting poverty, drugs, and gangs in Latino communities. In this essay, written in 2005 for Sojourners *magazine, Alejandrez remembers how the principles and the voice of César Chávez changed his life and inspired him to help others escape the cycle of drugs, violence, and incarceration.*

I'm the son of migrant farm workers, born out in a cotton field in *1* Merigold, Mississippi. My family's from Texas. A migrant child goes to five or six different schools in one year, and you try to assimilate to whatever's going on at that time. I grew up not having shoes or only having one pair of pants to wear to school all week. I always remembered my experience in Texas, where Mexicans and blacks couldn't go to certain restaurants. That leaves something in you.

I saw how my father would react when Immigration would come up *2* to the fields or the boss man talked to him. I would see my father bow his head. I didn't know why my father wasn't standing up to this man. As a child working in the rows behind him, I said to myself, "I'll never do that." A deep anger was developing in me.

But it was also developing in my father; the way that he dealt with *3* it was alcohol. He would become violent when he drank on the weekends. I realized later that the reason he would bow his head to the boss is that he had seven kids to feed. He took that humiliation in order to feed me.

I stabbed the first kid when I was 13 years old. I shot another guy *4* when I was 15. I almost killed a guy when I was 17. On and on and on. Then, in the late 1960s, I found myself as a young man in the Vietnam War. I saw more violence, inflicted more violence, and then tried to deal with the violence.

I came back from the war addicted to heroin, as many, many young *5* men did. I came back to the street war, in the drug culture. Suddenly there were farm workers—who lost jobs because of the bringing of machines into the fields—who turned into drug dealers; it's easier money.

But when I was still working in the fields, something happened. I was *6* 17 years old, out in the fields of central California, and suddenly I hear this voice coming out of the radio, talking about how we must better our conditions and better our lives in the migrant camps. It was like this voice was talking just to me.

The voice was César Chávez. He said, "You must organize. You must *7* seek justice. You must ask for better wages."

It's 1967. I'm busting my ass off pitching melons with six guys. Be- *8* cause we're the youngest, they put us on the hardest job, but we're getting paid $1.65 an hour. The guys working the harvesting machines are making $8 an hour. We said to ourselves, "Something's not right."

Having the words of César Chávez, I organized the young men and 9 called a strike. After lunch we just stopped working. We didn't go back on the fields. This was sort of a hard thing because my father was a foreman to this contractor, so I was going against him. He was concerned that we were rocking the boat—but I think he was proud of me. We shut down three of the melon machines, which forced the contractor to come, and then the landowner came. "What's going on?" he said. We said, "We're on strike, because we aren't getting our money." After about two hours, they said, "Okay, we're going to raise it to $1.95."

But it wasn't the $1.95—it was the fact that six young men were be- 10 ing abused, and that this little short Indian guy, César Chávez, had an influence. I kept his words.

When I wound up in Vietnam, I heard about Martin Luther King 11 and his stand against the war. Somebody also told me about Mahatma Gandhi. I didn't know who he was, only that he was a bald-headed dude that had done this kind of stuff.

In Vietnam I realized that there were people that I had never met 12 before, that had never done nothing to me, never called me a dirty Mexican or a greaser or nothing, and all of sudden I had to be an enemy to them.

I started looking at the words of César Chávez in terms of nonvio- 13 lence. I looked at the violence in the community, in the fields, yet Chávez was still calling for peace.

It has been an incredible journey since those days. For us this is a 14 spiritual movement. In Barrios Unidos, that's the primary thing—our spirit comes first. How do we take care of ourselves? Whatever people believe in, no matter what faith or religion, how do we communicate to the youngsters who are spiritually bankrupt? Many of us were addicted to drugs or alcohol, and we have to find a spiritual connection. Working with gang members, there's a lot of pain, so you have to find ways for healing. As peacemakers, we are wounded peacemakers.

This work has taken us into the prisons. Throughout the years, we've 15 been talking about the high rate of incarceration among our people, and the drug laws. Many people are doing huge amounts of time for nonviolent drug convictions; they did not need to be incarcerated—they need treatment. Currently in this country we deal with treatment by incarcerating people, which leads them to more violence and more negative ways of living.

As community-based organizations, we have had to prove to the cor- 16 rectional institutions that we're not in there to create any revolution. We're there to try to help. I'm asking how I can change the men that have been violent. How do I help change their attitude toward society and toward their own relatives? We see them as our relatives—these are our relatives that are incarcerated. How can we support them?

We go into the prison as a cultural and spiritual group helping men 17 in prison to understand their own culture and those of different cultures. They come from great warrior societies. But the warrior tradition doesn't just mean going to war, but also fighting for peace. The prisoners who help organize the Cinco de Mayo, Juneteenth, and Native powwow ceremonies within the prison system are a true testament of courage to change the madness of violence that has unnecessarily claimed many lives. By providing those ceremonies, we allow them to see who they really are. They weren't born gang members, or drug addicts, or thieves.

My best example of hope in the prisons is when we take the Aztec 18 dancers into the institutions. They do a whole indigenous ceremony. At the end, they invite people to what's called a friendship dance. It's a big figure-eight dance.

The first time that we were in prison in Tracy, California, out on the 19 yard, there were 2,000 men out there. The ceremony was led by Laura Castro, founder of the Xochut Aztec dance group, a very petite woman, very keen to her culture. She says to me, "What do you think, Nane? Do you think that these guys will come out and dance?" I'm looking at those guys—tattoos all over them and swastikas and black dudes that are really big. It's incredible to be in the prison yard. I say to her, "I don't know."

But what ties all those guys together is the drumbeat. Every culture 20 has some ceremonial drum you play. When the drumbeat started in the yard, the men just started coming. They divide themselves by race and then by gang. You got Norteños, Sureños, Hispanos, blacks, whites, Indians, and then "others" (mostly the Asian guys).

When the men were invited into the dance, those guys emptied out the 21 bleachers. They came. They held hands. This tiny woman, Laura, led them through the ceremony of the friendship dance. They went round and round. There were black, white, and brown holding hands, which doesn't happen in prison. And they were laughing. For a few seconds, maybe a minute, there was hope. We saw the smiles of men being children, remembering something about their culture. The COs [correctional officers] came out of the tower wondering what the hell was going on with these men dancing in prison, holding hands. It was an incredible sight. That day, the Creator was present. I knew that God's presence was there. Everyone was given a feeling that something had happened that wasn't our doing.

vo·cab·u·lar·y

In your journal, write the meanings of the italicized words in the following phrases.

- try to *assimilate* (**1**)
- took that *humiliation* (**3**)
- the high rate of *incarceration* (**15**)
- a whole *indigenous* ceremony (**18**)

QUESTIONS FOR WRITING AND DISCUSSION

1. The motto for César Chávez and his organization, The National Farm Workers Association, was "Si Se Puede," or "It Can Be Done." Although Alejandrez does not specifically refer to this motto, explain where this theme is most apparent in his essay.

2. One key strategy for writing successful narratives is setting and describing specific scenes. Alejandrez does an excellent job of setting two key scenes—one from his childhood and one from later in life. For each of these scenes, explain how Alejandrez (a) sets up the scene, (b) describes what happens using detailed observations, (c) uses dialogue to make the scene more vivid and dramatic, and (d) makes connections between the past and the present.

3. One key theme or motif in Alejandrez's essay is the idea of a "spiritual connection." Drawing on your description from question 2, explain how the idea of a spiritual connection is important in both of these key scenes. How does this theme connect to the nonviolent movements of Mahatma Gandhi and Martin Luther King, Jr.? How is this theme evoked in the final sentences of Alejandrez's essay? Explain.

4. Using Alejandrez's essay as a guide, write a remembering essay about a person in your life who became a role model or was influential at a key point in your life. Be sure to include key scenes showing how, when, and why this person was influential and then what you were able to accomplish because of that influence.

5. Go to the official Web sites for César Chávez and Barrios Unidos. What parallels are there between the lives of César Chávez and Daniel Alejandrez? How did both organizations use the nonviolent principles of Gandhi and Martin Luther King, Jr.? How are or were the goals of both organizations different? Explain.

Remembering: The Writing Process

> **Memory is more indelible than ink.**
>
> —ANITA LOOS,
> AUTHOR OF *KISS HOLLYWOOD GOODBYE*

ASSIGNMENT FOR REMEMBERING

Write an essay about an important person, place, and/or event in your life. Your purpose is to recall and then use specific examples and scenes that *recreate* this memory and *show why* it is important to you. If you don't have a specific audience and genre assigned, use the chart below to help you think about your possible audience and genre. You may be considering a personal audience of family and friends, but you may also want to think about a more public audience. Browsing through specialty magazines or Web sites (sports, nature, outdoors, genealogy, cooking, style) may give you an idea of how writers adapt an autobiographical narrative for a particular audience. Also, personal memoirs often have a place in academic writing in the humanities and social sciences.

Audience	Possible Genres for Writing About Memories
Personal Audience	Autobiographical essay, memoir, journal entry, social networking site entry, blog, photo essay, scrapbook, multigenre document.
Academic Audience	Essay for humanities or social science class, journal entry, forum entry on class site, multigenre document.
Public Audience	Column, memoir or essay in a magazine, newspaper, or newsletter; memoir or essay in a online site or blog; online memoir in a multigenre document.

CHOOSING A SUBJECT

If one of the journal entry exercises suggested a possible subject, try the collecting and shaping strategies below. If none of those exercises led to an interesting subject, consider the following ideas.

- Interview (in person or over the phone) a parent, a brother or sister, or a close friend. What events or experiences does your interviewee remember that were important to you?

- Look at a map of your town, city, state, or country and spend a few minutes doing an inventory of places you have been. Make a list of trips you have taken, with dates and years. Which of those places is the most memorable for you?

- Dig out a school yearbook or look through the pictures and comments on your friends Facebook profiles. Whom do you remember most clearly? What events do you recall most vividly?

- Go to the library and look through news magazines or newspapers from five to ten years ago. What were the most important events of those years? What do you remember about them? Where were you and what were you doing when these events occurred? Which events had the largest impact on your life?

- Choose an important moment in your life, but write from the *point of view* of another person—a friend, family member, or stranger who was present. Let this person narrate the events that happened to you.

Note: Avoid choosing overly emotional topics such as the recent death of a close friend or family member. If you are too close to your subject, responding to your reader's revision suggestions may be difficult. Ask yourself if you can emotionally distance yourself from that subject. If you received a C for that essay, would you feel devastated?

COLLECTING

Once you have chosen a subject for your essay, try the following collecting strategies.

● **BRAINSTORMING**   Brainstorming is merely jotting down anything and everything that comes to mind that is remotely connected to your subject: words, phrases, images, or complete thoughts. You can brainstorm by yourself or in groups, with everyone contributing ideas and one person recording them.

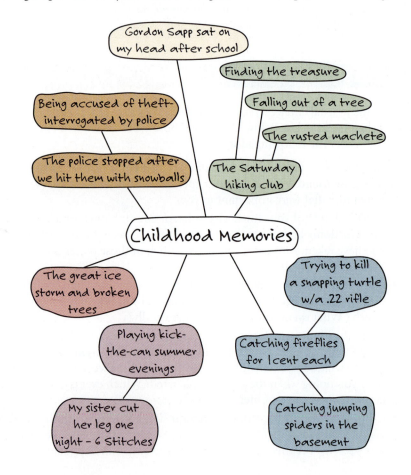

● **LOOPING**   Looping is a method of controlled freewriting that generates ideas and provides focus and direction. Begin by freewriting about your subject for eight to ten minutes. Then pause, reread what you have written, and *underline* the most interesting or important idea in what you've written so far. Then, using that sentence or idea as your starting point, write for eight to ten minutes more. Repeat this cycle, or "loop," one more time. Each loop should add ideas and details from some new angle or viewpoint, but overall you will be focusing on the most important ideas that you discover.

● **CLUSTERING**   Clustering is merely a visual scheme for brainstorming and free-associating about your topic. It can be especially effective for remembering because it helps you sketch relationships among your topics and subtopics. As you can see from the sample sketch, the sketch that you make of your ideas should help you see relationships between ideas or get a rough idea about an order or shape you may wish to use.

SHAPING

First, reconsider your purpose; perhaps it has become clearer or more definite since you recorded it in your journal entry. In your journal, jot down tentative answers for the following questions. If you don't have an answer, go on to the next question.

- **Subject:** What is your general subject?
- **Specific topic:** What aspect of your subject interests you?
- **Purpose:** Why is this topic interesting or important to you or your readers?
- **Main idea:** What might your main idea be?
- **Audience:** For whom are you writing? Why might your reader or readers be interested in this topic? (Review possible audiences suggested with the chapter assignment on pages 82–83.)
- **Genre:** What genre might help you communicate your purpose and main idea most effectively to your audience? (Review genre options suggested with the chapter assignment.)

As you think about ways to organize and shape your essay, reread your assignment and think about your purpose and possible audience. Consider several possible *genres* or combinations of genres that might work. Then, for particular parts or sections of your essay, review the strategies described below. *Chronological order* will shape a major part of your narrative, but think also about using *comparison/ contrast* for highlighting past and present or for contrasting two places, two events, or two key people. In addition, *similes*, *metaphors*, and *analogies* will make your writing more vivid, and paying attention to your *voice* and *tone* can help you achieve your purpose.

Most important, be sure to *narrow* and *focus* your subject. If you're going to write a three-page essay, don't try to cover everything in your life. Focus on one person, one episode, one turning point, one discovery, or one day, and do that in depth and detail.

● **GENRE**   As you collect ideas, draft sample passages, and discuss your assignment with your peers, think about appropriate genre possibilities. Start by reviewing the genre alternatives in the chapter assignment. You may choose to write in a traditional narrative format. However, you may want to use a multigenre or multimedia format with photographs, graphics, drawings, scrapbook materials, video, podcasts, and Web links. Check with your instructor to see if a multigenre approach meets the assignment.

● **CHRONOLOGICAL ORDER**   If you are writing about remembered events, you will probably use some form of chronological order. Try making a *chronological list of the major scenes or events.* Then go through the list, deciding what you will emphasize by telling about each item in detail and what you will pass over quickly. Normally, you will be using a straightforward chronological order, but you may wish to use a flashback, starting in the middle or near the end and then returning to tell the beginning. In his paragraph about a personal relationship, for example, student writer Gregory Hoffman begins the story at the most dramatic point, returns to tell how the relationship began, and then concludes the story.

> Her words hung in the air like iron ghosts. "I'm pregnant," she said as they walked through the park, the snow crackling beneath their feet. Carol was looking down at the ground when she told him, somewhat ashamed, embarrassed, and defiant all at once. Their relationship had only started in September, but both had felt the uneasiness surrounding them for the past months. She could remember the beginning so well and in such favor, now that the future seemed so uncertain. The all-night conversations by the bay window, the rehearsals at the university theater—where he would make her laugh during her only soliloquy, and most of all the Christmas they had spent together in Vermont. No one else had existed for her during those months. Yet now, she felt duped by her affections—as if she had become an absurd representation of a tragic television character. As they approached the lake, he put his arm around her, "Just do what you think is best, babe. I mean, I think you know how I feel." At that moment, she knew it was over. It was no longer "their" decision. His hand touched her cheek in a benedictorial fashion. The rest would only be form now. Exchanging records and clothes with an aside of brief conversation. She would see him again, in the market or at a movie, and they would remember. But like his affection in September, her memory of him would fade until he was too distant to see.

● **COMPARISON/CONTRAST**   Although you may be comparing or contrasting people, places, or events from the past, you will probably also be comparing or contrasting the past to the present. You may do that at the beginning, noting how something in the present reminds you of a past person, place, or event. You may do it at the end, as Andrea Lee does in *Russian Journal.* You may do it both at the beginning and at the end, as Richard Rodriguez does in "The Boy's Desire." Comparing or contrasting the past with the present will often clarify your dominant idea.

● **IMAGE**   Sometimes a single mental picture or recurring image will shape a paragraph or two in an essay. Consider how novelist George Orwell, in his essay "Shooting an Elephant," uses the image of a puppet or dummy to describe his feeling at a moment when he realized that, against his better judgment, he was going to have to shoot a marauding elephant in order to satisfy a crowd of two thousand Burmese who had gathered to watch him. The italicized words emphasize the recurring image.

> Suddenly I realized that I should have to shoot the elephant after all. The people expected it of me and I had got to do it; I could feel their *two thousand wills pressing me forward,* irresistibly. And it was at this moment, as I stood there with the rifle in my hands, that I first grasped the hollowness, the futility of the white man's dominion in the East. Here was I, the white man with his gun, standing in front of the unarmed native crowd—*seemingly the leading actor* of the piece; but in reality I was only an absurd *puppet pushed to and fro* by the will of those yellow faces behind. I perceived in this moment that when the white man turns tyrant it is his own freedom that he destroys. He becomes a sort of *hollow, posing dummy,* the *conventionalized figure* of a sahib. For it is the condition of his rule that he shall spend his life in trying to impress the "natives" and so in every crisis he has got to do what the "natives" expect of him. He *wears a mask,* and his face grows to fit it. I had got to shoot the elephant. I had committed myself to doing it when I sent for the rifle. *A sahib has got to act like a sahib;* he has got to appear resolute, to know his own mind and do definite things.

● **VOICE AND TONE**   When you have a personal conversation with someone, the way you look and sound—your body type, your voice, your facial expressions and gestures—communicates a sense of personality and attitude, which in turn affects how the other person reacts to what you say. In written language, although you don't have those gestures, expressions, or the actual sound of your voice, you can still create the sense that you are talking directly to your listener.

The term *voice* refers to a writer's personality as revealed through language. Writers may use emotional, colloquial, or conversational language to communicate a sense of personality. Or they may use abstract, impersonal language either to conceal their personalities or to create an air of scientific objectivity.

Tone is a writer's attitude toward the subject. The attitude may be positive or negative. It may be serious, humorous, honest, or ironic; it may be skeptical or accepting; it may be happy, frustrated, or angry. Often voice and tone overlap, and together they help us hear a writer talking to us. In the following passage, we hear student writer Kurt Weekly talking to us directly; we hear a clear, honest voice telling the story. His tone is not defensive or guilty: He openly admits he has a "problem."

> Oh no, not another trash day. Every time I see all those trash contain-ers, plastic garbage bags and junk lined up on the sidewalks, it drives me crazy. It all started when I was sixteen. I had just received my driver's li-cense and the most beautiful Ford pickup. It was Wednesday as I re-member and trash day. I don't know what happened. All of a sudden I was racing down the street swerving to the right, smashing into a large green Hefty trash bag filled with grass clippings. The bag exploded, and grass clippings and trash flew everywhere. It was beautiful and I was hooked. There was no stopping me.
>
> At first I would smash one or two cans on the way to school. Then I just couldn't get enough. I would start going out the night before trash day. I would go down the full length of the street and wipe out every garbage container in sight. I was the terror of the neighborhood. This was not a bad habit to be taken lightly. It was an obsession. I was in trou-ble. There was no way I could kick this on my own. I needed help.
>
> I received that help. One night after an evening of nonstop can smashing, the Arapahoe County Sheriff Department caught up with me. Not just one or a few but the whole department. They were willing to set me on the right path, and if that didn't work, they were going to send me to jail. It was a long, tough road to rehabilitation, but I did it. Not alone. I had the support of my family and the community.

● **PERSONA**   Related to voice and tone is the *persona*—the "mask" that a writer can put on. Sometimes in telling a story about yourself, you may want to speak in your own "natural" voice. At other times, however, you may change or exag-gerate certain characteristics in order to project a character different from your "real" self. Writers, for example, may project themselves as braver and more in-telligent than they really are. Or to create a humorous effect, they may create per-sonas who are more foolish or clumsy than they really are. This persona can shape a whole passage. In the following excerpt, James Thurber, a master of au-tobiographical humor, uses a persona—along with chronological narrative—to shape his account of a frustrating botany class.

> I passed all the other courses that I took at my university, but I could never pass botany. This was because all botany students had to spend several hours a week in a laboratory looking through a microscope at plant cells, and I could never see through a microscope. I never once saw a cell through a microscope. This used to enrage my instructor. He would wan-der around the laboratory pleased with the progress all the students were

making in drawing the involved and, so I am told, interesting structure of flower cells, until he came to me. I would just be standing there. "I can't see anything," I would say. He would begin patiently enough, explaining how anybody can see through a microscope, but he would always end up in a fury claiming that I could too see through a microscope but just pretended that I couldn't. "It takes away from the beauty of flowers anyway," I used to tell him. "We are not concerned with beauty in this course," he would say. "We are concerned solely with the mechanics of flowers." "Well," I'd say, "I can't see anything." "Try it just once again," he'd say, and I would put my eye to the microscope and see nothing at all, except now and again a nebulous milky substance—a phenomenon of maladjustment. You were supposed to see a vivid, restless clockwork of sharply defined plant cells. "I see what looks like a lot of milk," I would tell him. This, he claimed, was the result of my not having adjusted the microscope properly, so he would readjust it for me, or rather, for himself. And I would look again and see milk. I finally took a deferred pass, as they called it, and waited a year and tried again. (You had to pass one of the biological sciences or you couldn't graduate.) The professor had come back from vacation brown as a berry, bright-eyed, and eager to explain cell-structure again to his classes. "Well," he said to me, cheerily, when we met in the first laboratory hour of the semester, "we're going to see cells this time, aren't we?" "Yes, sir," I said. Students to the right of me and to the left of me and in front of me were seeing cells; what's more, they were quietly drawing pictures of them in their notebooks. Of course, I didn't see anything.

"We'll try it," the professor said to me, grimly, "with every adjustment of the microscope known to man. As God is my witness, I'll arrange this glass so that you see cells through it or I'll give up teaching. In twenty-two years of botany, I—" He cut off abruptly for he was beginning to quiver all over, like Lionel Barrymore, and he genuinely wished to hold onto his temper; his scenes with me had taken a great deal out of him.

So we tried it with every adjustment of the microscope known to man. With only one of them did I see anything but blackness or the familiar lacteal opacity, and that time I saw, to my pleasure and amazement, a variegated constellation of flecks, specks, and dots. These I hastily drew. The instructor, noting my activity, came back from an adjoining desk, a smile on his lips and his eyebrows high in hope. He looked at my cell drawing. "What's that?" he demanded, with a hint of a squeal in his voice. "That's what I saw," I said. "You didn't, you didn't, you didn't!" he screamed, losing control of his temper instantly, and he bent over and squinted into the microscope. His head snapped up. "That's your eye!" he shouted. "You've fixed the lens so that it reflects! You've drawn your eye!"

● **DIALOGUE**   Dialogue, which helps to *recreate* people and events rather than just tell about them, can become a dominant form and thereby shape your writing. Recreating an actual conversation, you could possibly write a whole scene using nothing but dialogue. More often, however, writers use dialogue occasionally for dramatic effect. In the account of his battle with the microscope, for instance, Thurber uses dialogue in the last two paragraphs to dramatize his conclusion:

> "We'll try it," the professor said to me, grimly, "with every adjustment of the microscope known to man. As God is my witness, I'll arrange this glass so that you see cells through it or I'll give up teaching. In twenty-two years of teaching botany, I—" . . . "What's that?" he demanded. . . . "That's what I saw," I said. "You didn't, you didn't, you didn't!" he screamed. . . . "You've fixed the lens so that it reflects! You've drawn your eye!"

● **TITLE, INTRODUCTION, AND CONCLUSION**   In your journal, sketch out several possible titles you might use. You may want a title that is merely an accurate label, such as *Russian Journal* or "The Boy's Desire," but you may prefer something less direct that gets your reader's attention. For example, for his essay about his hat that appears at the end of this chapter, student writer Todd Petry uses the title "The Wind Catcher."

Introductions or beginning paragraphs take several shapes. Some writers plunge the reader immediately into the action—as Gregory Hoffman does—and then later fill in the scene and context. Others are more like Kurt Weekly, announcing the subject—trash cans—and then taking the reader from the present to the past and the beginning of the story: "It all started when I was sixteen. . . ." At some point, however, readers do need to know the context—the *who, what, when,* and *where* of your account.

Conclusions are also of several types. In some, writers will return to the present and discuss what they have learned, as Andrea Lee does in *Russian Journal.* Many writers will try to tie the conclusion back to the beginning, as Richard Rodriguez does at the end of "The Boy's Desire": "The closet door closes . . . the fog rises." In your journal, experiment with several possibilities until you find one that works for your subject.

DRAFTING

When you have experimented with the above shaping strategies, reconsider your purpose, audience, and main idea. Have they changed? In your journal, reexamine the notes you made before trying the shaping activities. If necessary, revise your statements about purpose, audience, or main idea based on what you have actually written.

Working from your journal material and from your collecting and shaping activities, draft your essay. It is important *not* to splice different parts together or just recopy and connect segments, for they may not fit or flow together. Instead, reread what you have written, and then start afresh. Concentrate on what you want to say and write as quickly as possible.

To avoid interruptions, choose a quiet place to work. Follow your own writing rituals. Try to write nonstop. If you cannot think of the right word, put a line or a dash, but keep on writing. When necessary, go back and reread what you have previously written.

REVISING

Revising begins, of course, when you get your first idea and start collecting and shaping. It continues as you redraft certain sections of your essay and rework your organization. In many classes, you will give and receive advice from the other writers in your class. Use the guidelines below to give constructive advice about a remembering essay draft.

> 66 The difference between the right word and the nearly right word is the same as that between lightning and the lightning bug. 99
>
> —MARK TWAIN,
> AUTHOR OF *THE ADVENTURES OF HUCKLEBERRY FINN*

GUIDELINES FOR REVISION

- **Reexamine your purpose and audience.** Are you doing what you intended?
- **Reconsider the genre you selected.** Is it working for your purpose and audience? Can you add multigenre elements to make your narrative more effective?
- **Revise to make the main idea of your account clearer.** You don't need a "moral" to the story or a bald statement saying, "This is why this person was important." Your reader, however, should know clearly why you wanted to write about the memory that you chose.
- **Revise to clarify the important relationships in your story.** Consider relationships between past and present, between you and the people in your story, between one place and another place, between one event and another event.
- **Close and detailed observation is crucial.** *Show,* don't just tell. Can you use any of the collecting and shaping strategies for observing discussed in Chapter 3?
- **Revise to show crucial changes, contrasts, or conflicts more clearly.** Walker's essay, for instance, illustrates how *conflict and change* are central to an effective remembering essay. See if this strategy will work in your essay.
- **Have you used a straight chronological order?** If it works, keep it. If not, would another order be better? Should you begin in the middle and do a flashback? Do you want to move back and forth from present to past or stay in the past until the end?

    If you are using a chronological order, cue your reader by occasionally using transitional words to signal changes: *then, when, first, next, last, before, after, while, as, sooner, later, initially, finally, yesterday, today.*

PEER RESPONSE

The instructions below will help you give and receive constructive advice about the rough draft of your remembering essay. You may use these guidelines for an in-class workshop, a take-home review, or a computer e-mail response.

Writer: Before you exchange drafts with another reader, write out the following information about your own rough draft.

1. State the main idea that you hope your essay conveys.
2. Describe the best *one* or *two* key scenes that your narrative creates.
3. Explain one or two problems that you are having with this draft that you want your reader to focus on.

Reader: Without making any comments, read the *entire* draft from start to finish. As you *reread* the draft, answer the following questions.

1. Locate one or two of the *key scenes* in the narrative. Are they clearly set at an identified time and place? Does the writer use vivid description of the place or the people? Does the writer use dialogue? Does the writer include his or her reflections? Which of these areas need the most attention during the writer's revision? Explain.
2. Write out a *time line* for the key events in the narrative. What happened first, second, third, and so forth? Are there places in the narrative where the time line could be clearer? Explain.
3. When you finished reading the draft, *what characters or incidents were you still curious about?* Where did you want more information? What characters or incidents did you want to know more about?
4. What *overall idea* does the narrative convey to you? How does your notion of the main idea compare to the writer's answer to question 1? Explain how the writer might revise the essay to make the main idea clearer.
5. Answer the *writer's questions* in question 3.

After you have some feedback from other readers, you need to distance yourself and objectively reread what you have written. Review the advice you received from your peer readers. Remember, you will get both good and bad advice, so *you* must decide what you think is important or not important. If you are uncertain about advice you received from one of your peers, ask for a third or fourth opinion. In addition, most writing centers will have tutors available who can help you sort through the advice you have received on your draft and figure out a revision plan. Especially for this remembering essay, make sure your memories are recreated on paper. Don't be satisfied with suggesting incidents that merely trigger your own memories: You must *show* people and events vividly for your reader.

- **Be clear about point of view.** Are you looking back on the past from a viewpoint in the present? Are you using the point of view of yourself as a child or at some earlier point in your life? Are you using the point of view of another person or object in your story?

- **What are the key images in your account?** Should you add or delete an image to show the experience more vividly?

- **What voice are you using?** Does it support your purpose? If you are using a persona, is it appropriate for your audience and purpose?

- **Revise sentences to improve clarity, conciseness, emphasis, and variety.**

- **Check your dialogue for proper punctuation and indentation.** See the essay by Alice Walker in this chapter for a model.

- **When you are relatively satisfied with your draft, edit for correct spelling, appropriate word choice, punctuation, and grammar.**

POSTSCRIPT ON THE WRITING PROCESS

After you finish writing, revising, and editing your essay, you will want to breathe a sigh of relief and turn it in. But before you do, think about the problems that you solved as you wrote this essay. *Remember:* Your major goal for this course is to learn to write and revise more effectively. To do that, you need to discover and adapt your writing processes so you can anticipate and solve the problems you face as a writer. Take a few minutes to answer the following questions. Be sure to hand in this postscript with your essay.

1. Review your writing process. Which collecting, shaping, and revising strategies helped you remember and describe incidents most quickly and clearly? What problems were you unable to solve?

2. Reread your essay. With a small asterisk [*], identify in the margin of your essay sentences where you used sensory details, dialogue, or images to show or recreate the experience for your reader.

3. If you received feedback from your peers, identify one piece of advice that you followed and one bit of advice that you ignored. Explain your decisions.

4. Rereading your essay, what do you like best about it? What parts of your essay need work? What would you change if you had another day to work on this assignment?

STUDENT WRITING

TODD PETRY

The Wind Catcher

Todd Petry decided to write about his cowboy hat, observing it in the present and thinking about some of the memories that it brought back. His notes, his first short draft paragraphs, and his revised version demonstrate how observing and remembering work together naturally: The details stimulate memories, and memories lead to more specific details.

NOTES AND DETAILS

DETAILS	MORE SPECIFIC DETAILS
Gray	Dirty, dust coated, rain stained cowdung color
Resistol	The name is stained and blurred
Size 7 3/8	
Diamond shape	Used to be diamond shape, now battered, looks abandoned
4" brim	Front tipped down, curled up in back
1" sweat band	blackish
5 yrs. old	still remember the day I bought it
4x beaver	
What it is not:	it is unlike a hat fresh out of the box
What it compares to:	point of crown like the north star like a pancake with wilted edges battered like General Custer's hat
What I remember:	the day I bought the hat a day at Pray Mesa

FIRST DRAFT

The Wind Catcher

The other day while I was relaxing in my favorite chair and listening to Ian *1*
Tyson, I happened to notice my work cowboy hat hanging on the wall.
Now I look at that old hat no less than a dozen times a day without too
much thought, but on that particular day, my eyes remained fixed on it
and my mind went to remembering.

I still remember I had $100 cash in my pocket the day I went hat *2*
shopping. The local tack, feed, and western wear CO-OP was my first
and only stop. Finding a hat to meet my general specifications was no
big deal. I wanted a gray Resistol, size 7 3/8, with a 4-inch brim and
diamond-shaped crown. From there on, though, my wants became very
particular. I took 30 minutes to find the one that had the right fit, and five
times that long to come to terms with the hat shaper. Boy, but I was one
proud young fellow the next day when I went to school sporting my new
piece of head gear. I've had that wind catcher five years through rough
times, but in a way, it really looks better now, without any shape, dirty,
and covered with dust and cowdung.

REVISED VERSION

The Wind Catcher

The other day, while I was relaxing in my favorite chair and listening to *1*
Ian Tyson, I happened to notice my work cowboy hat hanging on the
wall. Now, I look at that old hat no less than a dozen times a day without
too much thought, but on that particular day, my eyes remained fixed on
it and my mind went to remembering.

I was fifteen years old and had $100 cash in my pocket the day I went *2*
hat shopping five years ago. The local tack, feed, and western wear CO-OP
was my first and only stop. Finding a hat to meet my general specifications
was no big deal. I wanted a gray 4X Resistol, size 7 3/8, with a four-inch brim
and diamond-shaped crown. I wanted no flashy feathers or gaudy hat-
bands, which in my mind were only for pilgrims. From there on, though,
my wants became very particular. I took thirty minutes to find the one that
had the right fit, and five times that long to come to terms with the hat
shaper. Boy, but I was one proud young fellow the next day when I went to
school sporting my new piece of head gear.

About that time, Ian Tyson startled me out of my state of reminis- *3*
cence by singing "Rose in the Rockies," with that voice of his sounding
like ten cow elk cooing to their young in the springtime. As I sat there
listening to the music and looking at that old hat, I had to chuckle to
myself because that wind catcher had sure seen better days. I mean it
looked rode hard and put up wet. The gray, which was once as sharp

...*continued* The Wind Catcher, **Todd Petry**

and crisp as a mountain lake, was now faded and dull where the sun had beat down. Where the crown and brim met, the paleness was suddenly transformed into a gritty black which ran the entire circumference of the hat. This black was unlike any paint or color commercially available, being made up of head sweat, dirt, alfalfa dust, and powdered cow manure. Water blemishes from too much rain and snow mottled the brim, adding to the colors' turbidity. Inside the crown and wherever the slope was less than ninety degrees, dust had collected to hide the natural color even more.

After a while, my attention lost interest in the various colors and began 4 to work its way over the hat's shape, which I was once so critical of. General Custer's hat itself could not have looked worse. All signs of uniformity and definite shape had disappeared. The diamond-shaped crown, which was once round and smooth, now bowed out on the sides and had edges as blunt as an orange crate. The point, which once looked like the North Star indicating the direction, now was twisted off balance from excessive right hand use. Remembering last spring, how I threw that hat in the face of an irate mother cow during calving, I had to chuckle again. Throwing that hat kept my horse and me out of trouble but made the "off-balance look" rather permanent. As I looked at the brim, I was reminded of a three-day-old pancake with all its edges wilted. The back of that brim curled upward like a snake ready to strike, and the front had become so narrow and dipped, it looked like something a dentist would use on your teeth.

For probably half an hour, I sat looking at the wear and tear on that 5 ancient hat. Awhile back, I remember, I decided to try to make my old hat socially presentable by having it cleaned and blocked, removing those curls and dips and other signs of use. However, when a hat shop refused to even attempt the task, I figured I'd just leave well enough alone. As I scanned my eyes over the hat, I noticed several other alterations from its original form, such as the absent hat band, which was torn off in the brush on Pray Mesa, and the black thread that drew together the edges of a hole in the crown. However, try as I might, I could not for the life of me see where any character had been lost in the brush, or any flair had been covered with cowdung.

 QUESTIONS FOR WRITING AND DISCUSSION

1. Close observation often leads to specific memories. In the opening paragraph of his revised version, Todd Petry says that "on that particular

day, my eyes remained fixed on it and my mind went to remembering." He then recalls the time when he was fifteen years old and bought his hat. Identify two other places where observation leads Petry to remember specific scenes from the past.

2 Petry chose "The Wind Catcher" as the title for his essay. Reread the essay and then brainstorm a list of five other titles that might be appropriate for this short essay. Which title do you like best?

3 Where does Petry most clearly express the main idea of his essay? Write out the main idea in your own words.

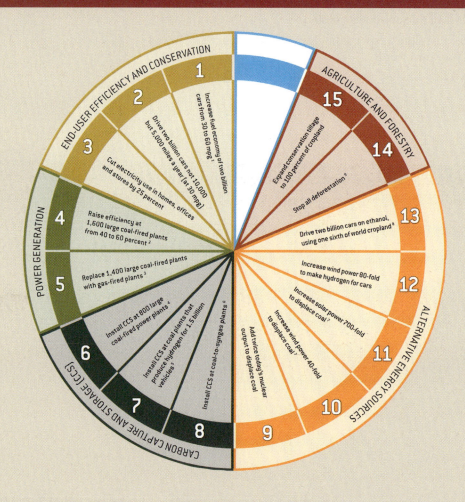

15 Ways to Make a Wedge
Illustration by Janet Chao

END-USER EFFICIENCY AND CONSERVATION

1 — Increase fuel economy of two billion cars from 30 to 60 mpg [1]

2 — Drive two billion cars not 10,000 but 5,000 miles a year (at 30 mpg) [1]

3 — Cut electricity use in homes, offices and stores by 25 percent

POWER GENERATION

4 — Raise efficiency at 1,600 large coal-fired plants from 40 to 60 percent [2]

5 — Replace 1,400 large coal-fired plants with gas-fired plants [3]

CARBON CAPTURE AND STORAGE (CCS)

6 — Install CCS at 800 large coal-fired power plants [4]

7 — Install CCS at coal plants that produce hydrogen for 1.5 billion vehicles [5]

8 — Install CCS at coal-to-syngas plants [6]

ALTERNATIVE ENERGY SOURCES

9 — Add twice today's nuclear output to displace coal [7]

10 — Increase wind power 40-fold to displace coal [7]

11 — Increase solar power 700-fold to displace coal [7]

12 — Increase wind power 80-fold to make hydrogen for cars

13 — Drive two billion cars on ethanol, using one sixth of world cropland [8]

AGRICULTURE AND FORESTRY

14 — Stop all deforestation [9]

15 — Expand conservation tillage to 100 percent of cropland

This illustration, "15 Ways to Make a Wedge," by Janet Chao, first appeared in "A Plan to Keep Carbon on Track," by Robert H. Socolow and Stephen W. Pacala, in the September 2006 issue of *Scientific American*. According to the caption, "An overall carbon strategy for the next half a century produces seven wedges' worth of emissions reductions. Here are 15 technologies from which those seven can be chosen [taking care to avoid double-counting]. Each of these measures, when phased in over 50 years, prevents the release of 25 billion tons of carbon. Leaving one wedge blank symbolizes that this list is by no means exhaustive." After reading the articles on climate change in this chapter, see discussion question 2 on page 125.

Reading

5

After discussing in class how to write letters to the editor, you decide to respond to Margaret Atwood's "Letter to America." Atwood, the award-winning Canadian author of *Surfacing* and *The Handmaid's Tale*, addresses America personally, arguing that what was great about America in previous centuries—its great writers like Twain and Dickinson, its great films, and its history and Constitution—is now being lost through its deteriorating economy and foreign policy. In your response, you acknowledge areas where you agree with Atwood, but then argue that not everything in America's past was as rosy as Atwood portrays. Moreover, even current events show flaws but also continued signs of greatness. America, you conclude, "is still that city upon a hill."

As an assignment in class, you are reading and critiquing an article by Deborah Tannen on how men and women respond differently during class conversations. As you read the article, you have trouble locating the main focus of the article, and then you are disturbed by some unsupported assertions that she makes about typical behavior of men and women. Do men really like to argue and dominate class discussions? Do women always benefit from smaller, more intimate group discussions? You reread the article and make notes in the margin. After discussing your reactions with other readers, you decide to argue that readers should expect clearer organization and fewer unsupported assertions about the gender-based differences between men and women.

> " If we think of it, all that a University, or final highest School can do for us, is still but what the first School began doing— teach us to read. "
>
> —THOMAS CARLYLE, AUTHOR OF *ON HEROES AND HERO WORSHIP*

> " Reading is not a passive process by which we soak up words and information from the page, but an active process by which we predict, sample, and confirm or correct our hypotheses about the written text. "
>
> —CONSTANCE WEAVER, AUTHOR OF *READING PROCESS AND PRACTICE*

A T FIRST GLANCE, A CHAPTER ON READING IN A TEXTBOOK ON WRITING MAY CATCH YOU BY SURPRISE. THIS CHAPTER, HOWEVER, IS NOT ABOUT LEARNING YOUR ABC'S OR ABOUT READING *THE CAT IN THE HAT*. IT IS ABOUT LEARNING TO READ TEXTS ACTIVELY AND critically. It is about learning how to summarize and respond to what you read. It is about using reading—along with observing and remembering—as a source for your writing.

At the beginning of this chapter, we need to define two key terms: *texts* and *reading*. Normally, when you think about a text, you may think of a textbook. A text, however, can be any graphic matter—a textbook, an essay, a poem, a newspaper editorial, a photograph, or an advertisement. Some people expand the definition of texts to include any thing or phenomenon in the world. In this widest sense, the layout of a restaurant, the behavior of children on a playground, or clouds in the sky could be "texts" that can be read.

Similarly, the term *reading* has both narrow and broad senses. In a narrow sense, reading is simply understanding words on a page. But reading has a variety of wider meanings as well. Reading can mean analyzing, as when an architect "reads" blueprints and knows how to construct a roof. Reading can also mean interpreting, as when a sailor "reads" the sky and knows that the day will bring winds and rough weather. Reading can also mean examining texts or cultural artifacts and perceiving messages of racism, gender bias, or cultural exploitation. All of these "readings" require close, critical reading of the text and an ability to engage, analyze, probe, respond to, and interpret the text.

In this chapter, you will practice active, critical reading and responding to academic and cultural texts. (In Chapter 6, you will focus specifically on analyzing and responding to images, photographs, advertisements, and other visual texts.) Implied in active, critical reading are both writing about the texts and discussing the texts with other readers. Writing requires reading with your pen in your hand to annotate the texts you read with comments, questions, and observations. You can also write double-entry logs that will help you become an active, critical reader. You may consider reading a solitary activity, but texts appear in social contexts and should be read in social contexts. Active reading, therefore, also involves sharing ideas in small groups, engaging in a class conversation, posting e-mail responses, or writing for an online discussion forum.

This chapter provides guidelines for critical reading, tips for summarizing ideas accurately, and techniques for responding to academic essays, editorials, and other texts you will encounter in college, on the job, and in your community.

Techniques for Analyzing and Responding to Texts

Analysis of texts requires several different techniques to ensure both comprehension and intelligent response. Although the strategies below are listed in a typical order for any reading assignment, remember that the analytical reading process is just like the writing process. You may need to circle back and reread, summarize a second time, research key terms or topics, or double check on the context or author's background as you work.

Techniques for Analyzing and Responding to Texts

Technique	Tips on How to Do It
Using active and responsive reading, writing, and discussing strategies	Preview the author's background and the writing context. Prewrite about your own experiences with the subject. Read initially for information but then reread, make annotations, ask questions, research on the internet, or do a double-entry log. Discuss the text with other readers in class or online.
Summarizing the main ideas or features of the text	A summary should accurately and objectively represent the key ideas. Cite the author and title, accurately represent the main ideas, directly quote key phrases or sentences, and describe the main ideas or features of the text.
Responding to or critiquing the ideas in the text	Responses may *agree or disagree* with the argument in the text; they may *analyze* the argument, organization, or quality of evidence in the text; and/or they may *reflect* on assumptions or implications.
Supporting the response with evidence	Evidence should cite examples of strengths or weaknesses in the argument, cite evidence from other texts or outside reading, and/or use examples from personal experience.
Combining summary and response into a coherent essay	Usually the summary appears first, followed by the reader's response, but be sure to integrate the two parts. Your response should focus quickly on your main idea. Use a transition between the summary and response or integrate the summary and response throughout.

66 Reading involves a fair measure of push and shove. You make your mark on a book and it makes its mark on you. Reading is not simply a matter of hanging back and waiting for a piece, or its author, to tell you what the writing has to say. 99

—DAVID BARTHOLOMAE AND ANTHONY PETROSKY, AUTHORS OF *WAYS OF READING*

As you work on these techniques, don't simply read the text, listen to a class discussion, and write out your critique. Instead, annotate the text by circling key ideas and writing your questions and responses in the margin. Continue reading and discussing your ideas after you have written out a draft. Use the interactive powers of reading, writing, and discussing to help you throughout your writing process.

CRITICAL READING STRATEGIES

Critical reading does not mean that you always criticize something or find fault. *Critical reading simply means questioning what you read.* You may end up liking or praising certain features of a text, but you begin by asking questions, by resisting the text, and by demanding that the text be clear, logical, reliable, thoughtful, and honest.

You begin your critical reading by asking questions about every element in the rhetorical situation. Who is the *author,* and what is his or her background or potential bias? What was the *occasion,* and who was the intended *audience?* Is the writer's *purpose* achieved for that occasion and audience? Did the writer understand and fairly represent other writers' positions on this topic? Did the writer understand the *genre* and use it to achieve the purpose? How did the *cultural context* affect the author and the text? How did the context affect you as a reader?

You continue your critical reading by asking about the writer's claim or argument, the representation of the background information, the organization, the logical use of evidence, and the effectiveness of the style, tone, and word choice. You may find these elements effective or ineffective, but you start your critical reading by reading and then rereading, by probing key passages, by looking for gaps or ideas not included, by discussing the text with other readers, by assessing your position as a reader, and by continually making notes and asking questions.

● **DOUBLE-ENTRY LOG**   One of the most effective strategies to promote critical reading is a double-entry log. Draw a line down the middle of a page in your notebook. On the left-hand side, keep a running summary of the main ideas and features that you notice in the text. On the right-hand side, write your questions and reactions.

Author and Title: _____

Summary	Response
Main ideas, key features	Your reactions, comments, and questions

● **CRITICAL REREADING GUIDE**   If your double-entry log did not yield some good ideas, try the ideas and suggestions in this rereading guide. First, read the essay in its entirety. Then, let the following set of questions guide your

Summary and Analysis of Text	Critical Response
I. Purpose • Describe the author's overall *purpose* (to inform, explain, explore, evaluate, argue, negotiate, or other purpose). • How does the author/text want to affect or change the reader?	• Is the overall purpose clear or muddled? • Was the actual purpose different from the stated purpose? • How did the text actually affect you?
II. Audience/Reader • Who is the *intended* audience? • What *assumptions* does the author make about the reader's knowledge or beliefs? • From what *point of view* or *context* is the author writing?	• Are you part of the intended audience? • Does the author misjudge the reader's knowledge or beliefs? • Examine your own personal or cultural bias or point of view. How does that hinder you from being a critical reader of this text?
III. Occasion, Genre, Context • What was the *occasion* for this text? • What *genre* is this text? • What is the *cultural* or *historical context* for this text?	• What conversation was taking place on this topic? • Does the author's chosen genre help achieve the purpose for the audience? • What passages show the cultural forces at work on the author and the text?
IV. Thesis and Main Ideas • What key *question* or *problem* does the author/ text address? • What is the author's *thesis*? • What *main ideas* support the thesis? • What are the key passages or key moments in the text?	• Where is the thesis stated? • Are the main ideas related to the thesis? • Where do you agree or disagree? • Does the essay have contradictions or errors in logic? • What ideas or arguments does the essay omit or ignore? • What experience or prior knowledge do you have about the topic? • What are the implications or consequences of the essay's ideas?

Continued

Summary and Analysis of Text	Critical Response
V. Organization and Evidence <ul><li>Where does the author *preview* the essay's organization?</li><li>How does the author *signal* new sections of the essay?</li><li>What kinds of *evidence* does the author use (personal experience, descriptions, statistics, interviews, other authorities, analytical reasoning, or other)?</li></ul>	<ul><li>At what point could you accurately predict the organization of the essay?</li><li>At what points were you confused about the organization?</li><li>What evidence was most or least effective?</li><li>Where did the author rely on assertions rather than on evidence?</li><li>Which of your own personal experiences did you recall as you read the essay?</li></ul>
VI. Language and Style <ul><li>What is the author's *tone* (casual, humorous, ironic, angry, preachy, academic, or other)?</li><li>Are *sentences* and *vocabulary* easy, average, or difficult?</li><li>What key *words* or *images* recur throughout the text?</li></ul>	<ul><li>Did the tone support or distract from the author's purpose or meaning?</li><li>Did the sentences and vocabulary support or distract from the purpose or meaning?</li><li>Did recurring words or images relate to or support the purpose or meaning?</li></ul>

rereading. The questions on the left-hand side will help you summarize and analyze the text; the questions on the right-hand side will start your critical reading and help focus your response.

Remember that not all these questions will be relevant to any given essay or text, but one or two of these questions may suggest a direction or give a *focus* to your overall response. When one of these questions suggests a focus for your response to the essay, *go back to the text, to other texts, and to your experience* to gather *evidence* and *examples* to support your response.

GUIDELINES FOR CLASS DISCUSSION

Class discussions are an important part of the reading, writing, and discussing process. Often, however, class discussions are not productive because not everyone knows the purpose of the discussion or how to discuss openly and fairly. Follow-ing is a suggested list of goals for class discussion. Read them carefully. Make notes about any suggestions, revisions, or additions for your class. Your class can then review these goals and agree to adopt, modify, or revise them for your own class discussions for the remainder of the semester.

Discussion Goals

1. To understand and accurately represent the views of the author(s) of an essay. The first discussion goal should be to summarize the author's views fairly.

2. To understand how the views and arguments of individual authors relate to each other. Comparing and contrasting different authors' views help clarify each author's argument.

3. To encourage all members of the class to articulate their understanding of each essay and their response to the ideas in each essay. Class discussions should promote multiple responses rather than focus on a single "right" interpretation or response.

4. To hear class members' responses in an open forum. All points of view must be recognized. *Discussions in class should focus on ideas and arguments, not on individual class members.* Class members may attack ideas but not people.

5. To relate class discussions to the assigned reading/writing task. What effective writing strategies are illustrated in the essay the class is discussing? How can class members use any of these strategies in writing their own essays?

Summarizing and Responding to an Essay

Following is an essay by Barbara Ehrenreich, "Teach Diversity—with a Smile." First, write for five minutes on the suggested Prereading Journal Entry that pre-cedes the essay. The purpose of the journal entry is to allow you to collect your thoughts about the subject *before* you read Ehrenreich's essay. You will be a much more responsive reader if you reflect on your experiences and articulate your opinions *before* you are influenced by the author and her text. If possible, discuss your experiences and opinions with your classmates after you write your entry but before you read the essay. Next, read the introductory note about Barbara Ehrenreich to understand her background and the context for the essay. Finally, practice active reading techniques as you read. Read first for information and enjoyment. Then, reread with a pen in your hand. Either write your comments and questions directly in the text or do a double-entry log, summarizing the main ideas on one side of a piece of paper and writing your questions and reactions on the other.

PREREADING JOURNAL ENTRY

Describe the ethnic groups of people who live in your neighborhood or who attended your previous school. List all the groups you can recall. Then choose one of the following terms and briefly explain what it means: *diversity, multiculturalism*, or *political correctness*. Finally, describe one personal experience that taught you something about diversity or political correctness. What was the experience and how did you react?

PROFESSIONAL WRITING

Teach Diversity—with a Smile

Barbara Ehrenreich

Barbara Ehrenreich was born in Butte, Montana, in 1941 and received a B.A. degree from Reed College and a Ph.D. from Rockefeller University. She has been a health policy adviser and a professor of health sciences, but since 1974, she has spent most of her time writing books and articles about socialist and feminist issues. She has received a Ford Foundation Award and a Guggenheim Fellowship for her writings, which include The Worst Years of Our Lives: Irreverent Notes from a Decade of Greed *(1990),* The Snarling Citizen: Essays *(1995),* Nickel and Dimed: On (Not) Getting by in America *(2001), and* This Land Is Their Land: Reports from a Divided Nation *(2008). Her articles and essays have appeared in* Esquire, Mother Jones, Ms., New Republic, The New York Times Magazine, *and* Time. *The following essay on cultural diversity appeared in* Time *magazine.*

Something had to replace the threat of communism, and at last a work-   1
able substitute is at hand. "Multiculturalism," as the new menace is known, has been denounced in the media recently as the new McCarthyism, the

new fundamentalism, even the new totalitarianism—take your choice. According to its critics, who include a flock of tenured conservative scholars, multiculturalism aims to toss out what it sees as the Eurocentric bias in education and replace Plato with Ntozake Shange and traditional math with the Yoruba number system. And that's just the beginning. The Jacobins of the multiculturalist movement, who are described derisively as P.C., or politically correct, are said to have launched a campus reign of terror against those who slip and innocently say "freshman" instead of "freshperson," "Indian" instead of "Native American" or, may the Goddess forgive them, "disabled" instead of "differently abled."

So you can see what is at stake here: freedom of speech, freedom of 2 thought, Western civilization and a great many professorial egos. But before we get carried away by the mounting backlash against multiculturalism, we ought to reflect for a moment on the system that the P.C. people aim to replace. I know all about it; in fact it's just about all I do know, since I—along with so many educated white people of my generation— was a victim of monoculturalism.

American history, as it was taught to us, began with Columbus's "dis- 3 covery" of an apparently unnamed, unpeopled America, and moved on to the Pilgrims serving pumpkin pie to a handful of grateful red-skinned folks. College expanded our horizons with courses called Humanities or sometimes Civ, which introduced us to a line of thought that started with Homer, worked its way through Rabelais and reached a poignant climax in the pensées of Matthew Arnold. Graduate students wrote dissertations on what long-dead men had thought of Chaucer's verse or Shakespeare's dramas; foreign languages meant French or German. If there had been high technology in ancient China, kingdoms in black Africa or women anywhere, at any time, doing anything worth noticing, we did not know it, nor did anyone think to tell us.

Our families and neighborhoods reinforced the dogma of mono- 4 culturalism. In our heads, most of us '50s teenagers carried around a social map that was about as useful as the chart that guided Columbus to the "Indies." There were "Negroes," "whites" and "Orientals," the latter meaning Chinese and "Japs." Of religions, only three were known—Protestant, Catholic and Jewish—and not much was known about the last two types. The only remaining human categories were husbands and wives, and that was all the diversity the monocultural world could handle. Gays, lesbians, Buddhists, Muslims, Malaysians, Mormons, etc. were simply off the map.

So I applaud—with one hand, anyway—the multiculturalist goal of 5 preparing us all for a wider world. The other hand is tapping its fingers impatiently, because the critics are right about one thing: when advocates of multiculturalism adopt the haughty stance of political correctness, they quickly descend to silliness or worse. It's obnoxious, for example, to rely on university administrations to enforce P.C. standards of verbal inoffensiveness. Racist, sexist and homophobic thoughts cannot, alas, be abolished by fiat but only by the time-honored methods of persuasion, education and exposure to the other guy's—or, excuse me, woman's—point of view.

And it's silly to mistake verbal purification for genuine social re- 6 form. Even after all women are "Ms." and all people are "he or she," women will still earn only 65¢ for every dollar earned by men. Minorities by any other name, such as "people of color," will still bear a hugely disproportionate burden of poverty and discrimination. Disabilities are not just "different abilities" when there are not enough ramps for wheelchairs, signers for the deaf or special classes for the "specially" endowed. With all due respect for the new politesse, actions still speak louder than fashionable phrases.

But the worst thing about the P.C. people is that they are such 7 poor advocates for the multicultural cause. No one was ever won over to a broader, more inclusive view of life by being bullied or relentlessly "corrected." Tell a 19-year-old white male that he can't say "girl" when he means "teen-age woman," and he will most likely snicker. This may be the reason why, despite the conservative alarms, P.C.-ness remains a relatively tiny trend. Most campuses have more serious and ancient problems: faculties still top-heavy with white males of the monocultural persuasion; fraternities that harass minorities and women; date rape; alcohol abuse; and tuition that excludes all but the upper fringe of the middle class.

So both sides would be well advised to lighten up. The conservatives 8 ought to realize that criticisms of the great books approach to learning do not amount to totalitarianism. And the advocates of multiculturalism need to regain the sense of humor that enabled their predecessors in the struggle to coin the term P.C. years ago—not in arrogance but in self-mockery.

Beyond that, both sides should realize that the beneficiaries of 9 multiculturalism are not only the "oppressed peoples" on the standard P.C. list (minorities, gays, etc.). The "unenlightened"—the victims of monoculturalism—are oppressed too, or at least deprived. Our educations, whether at Yale or at State U, were narrow and parochial and left us ill-equipped to navigate a society that truly is multicultural and is becoming more so every day. The culture that we studied was, in fact, *one* culture and, from a world perspective, all too limited and ingrown. Diversity is challenging, but those of us who have seen the alternative know it is also richer, livelier and ultimately more fun.

SUMMARIZING

The purpose of a summary is to give a reader a condensed and objective account of the main ideas and features of a text. Usually, a summary has between one and three paragraphs or one hundred to three hundred words, depending on the length and complexity of the original essay and the intended audience and purpose. Typically, a summary will do the following:

- **Cite the author and title of the text.** In some cases, the place of publication or the context for the essay may also be included.
- **Indicate the main ideas of the text.** Accurately representing the main ideas (while omitting the less important details) is the major goal of a summary.
- **Use direct quotation of key words, phrases, or sentences.** *Quote* the text directly for a few key ideas; *paraphrase* the other important ideas (that is, express the ideas in your own words).
- **Include author tags.** ("According to Ehrenreich" or "as Ehrenreich explains") to remind the reader that you are summarizing the author and the text, not giving your own ideas. ***Note:*** Instead of repeating "Ehrenreich says," choose verbs that more accurately represent the purpose or tone of the original passage: "Ehrenreich argues," "Ehrenreich explains," "Ehrenreich warns," "Ehrenreich asks," "Ehrenreich advises."
- **Avoid summarizing specific examples or data.** unless they help illustrate the thesis or main idea of the text.
- **Report the main ideas as objectively as possible.** Represent the author and text as accurately and faithfully as possible. Do not include your reactions; save them for your response.

> 66 Inferences about the writer's intentions appear to be an essential building block—one that readers actively use to construct a meaningful text. 99
>
> —LINDA FLOWER,
> AUTHOR OF "THE
> CONSTRUCTION OF PURPOSE"

SUMMARY OF "TEACH DIVERSITY— WITH A SMILE"

Following is a summary of Ehrenreich's essay. Do *not* read this summary, however, until you have tried to write your own. After you have made notes and written a draft for your own summary, you will more clearly understand the key features of a summary. ***Note:*** There are many ways to write a good summary. If your summary conveys the main ideas and has the features described previously, it may be just as good as the following example. (Key features of a summary are annotated in the margin.)

In "Teach Diversity—with a Smile," journalist Barbara Ehrenreich explains the current conflict between people who would like to replace our Eurocentric bias in education with a multicultural approach and those critics and conservative scholars who are leading the backlash against

Title and author

Main idea paraphrase

Context for essay

Author tag

Direct quotations

Main idea paraphrase

Author tag
Main idea paraphrase

multiculturalism and "political correctness." Writing for [readers of *Time* magazine] Ehrenreich uses her own experience growing up in the 1950s to explain that her narrow education left her a "victim of monocultural-ism," ill-equipped to cope with America's growing cultural diversity. Ehrenreich applauds multiculturalism's goal of preparing people for a culturally diverse world, but she is impatient at the "haughty stance" of the P.C. people because they mistake "verbal purification for genuine social reform" and they arrogantly bully people and "correct" their language. Since actions speak louder than words, Ehrenreich argues, the multiculturalists should focus more on genuine social reform—paying equal salaries to men and women, creating access for people with disabil-ities, and reducing date rape and alcohol abuse. The solution to the problem, according to Ehrenreich, is for both sides to "lighten up." The conservatives should recognize that criticizing the great books of Western civilization is not totalitarian, and the multiculturalists should be less arrogant and regain their sense of humor.

> 66 Reading the world always precedes read-ing the word, and read-ing the word implies continually reading the world. 99
> —PAULO FREIRE
> AUTHOR OF *LITERACY: READING THE WORD AND THE WORLD*

RESPONDING

A response requires your reaction and interpretation. Your own perspective—your experiences, beliefs, and attitudes—will guide your particular response. Your response may be totally different from another reader's response, but that does not necessarily make yours better or worse. Good responses say what you think, but then they *show why* you think so. They show the relationships between your opinions and the text, between the text and your experience, and between this text and other texts.

Depending on its purpose and intended audience, a response to a text can take several directions. Responses may focus on one or more of the following strategies. Consider your purpose and audience or check your assignment to see which type(s) you should emphasize.

TYPES OF RESPONSES

- **Analyzing the effectiveness of the text.** In this case, the response analyzes key features such as the clarity of the main idea, the rhetorical situation, the organization of the argument, the logical reasoning of an argument, the quality of the supporting evidence, and/or the effectiveness of the author's style, tone, and voice.
- **Agreeing and/or disagreeing with the ideas in the text.** Often responders react to the ideas or the argument of the essay. In this case, the responders show why they agree and/or disagree with what the author/text says.
- **Interpreting and reflecting on the text.** The responder explains key passages or examines the underlying assumptions or the implications

of the ideas. Often, the responder reflects on how his or her own experiences, attitudes, and observations relate to the text.

Analyzing, agreeing/disagreeing, and interpreting are all slightly different directions that a response may take. But regardless of the direction, responses must be supported by evidence, examples, facts, and details. A responder cannot simply offer an opinion or agree or disagree. Good responses draw on several kinds of supporting evidence.

KINDS OF EVIDENCE

- **Personal experience.** Responders may use *examples* from their personal experiences to show why they interpreted the text as they did, why they agreed or disagreed, or why they reacted to the ideas as they did.
- **Evidence from the text.** Responders should cite *specific phrases or sentences* from the text to support their explanation of a section, their analysis of the effectiveness of a passage, or their agreement or disagreement with a key point.
- **Evidence from other texts.** If appropriate, responders may bring in ideas and information from other relevant essays, articles, books, or graphic material.

Not all responses use all three kinds of supporting evidence, but all responses *must* have sufficient examples to support the responder's ideas, reactions, and opinions. Responders should not merely state their opinions. They must give evidence to *show* how and why they read the text as they did.

One final—and crucial—point about responses: A response should make a coherent, overall main point. It should not be just a laundry list of reactions, likes, and dislikes. Sometimes the main point is that the text is not convincing because it lacks evidence. Sometimes the overall point is that the text makes an original statement even though it is difficult to read. Perhaps the basic point is that the author/text stimulates the reader to reflect on his or her experience. Every response should focus on a coherent main idea.

RESPONSE TO "TEACH DIVERSITY— WITH A SMILE"

Following is one possible response to Ehrenreich's essay. Before you read this response, however, write out your own reactions. You need to decide what you think before other responses influence your reading. There are, of course, many different but legitimate responses to any given essay. As you read this response, note the marginal annotations indicating the different types of responses and the different kinds of evidence this writer uses.

*Analyzing effectiveness
of text
Responder's main point*

What I like best about Barbara Ehrenreich's article is her effective use of personal experience to clarify the issues on both sides of the multiculturalism debate. However, her conclusion, that we should "lighten up" and accept diversity because it's "more fun," weakens her argument by ignoring the social inequalities at the heart of the debate. The issue in this debate, I believe, is not just enjoying diversity, which is easy to do, but changing cultural conditions, which is much more difficult.

Ehrenreich effectively uses her own experiences—and her common sense—to let us see both the virtues and the excesses of multiculturalism.

Evidence from text

When she explains that her monocultural education gave her a social map that was "about as useful as the chart that guided Columbus to the 'Indies,'" she helps us understand how vital multicultural studies are in a society that is more like a glass mosaic than a melting pot. Interestingly, even her vocabulary reveals—perhaps unconsciously—her Western bias:

Evidence from text

Jacobins, pensées, fiat, and *politesse* are all words that reveal her Eurocentric education. When Ehrenreich shifts to discussing the P.C. movement, her commonsense approach to the silliness of excessive social correctness ("the other guy's—or, excuse me, woman's—point of view") makes us as readers more willing to accept her compromise position.

Reflecting on the text

My own experience with multiculturalism certainly parallels Ehrenreich's impatience with the "haughty stance" of the P.C. people. Of course, we should avoid racist and sexist terms and use our increased

Personal experience

sensitivity to language to reduce discrimination. But my own backlash began several years ago when a friend said I shouldn't use the word *girl.* I said, "You mean, not ever? Not even for a ten-year-old female child?" She replied that the word had been so abused by people referring to a "woman" as a "girl" that the word *girl* now carried too many sexist connotations. Although I understood my friend's point, it seems that *girl* should still be a perfectly good word for a female child under the age of

Evidence from other

twelve. Which reminds me of a book I saw recently, *The Official Politically Correct Dictionary.* It is loaded with examples of political correctness out of control: Don't say *bald,* say *hair disadvantaged.* Don't use the word *pet,* say *nonhuman companion.* Don't call someone *old,* say that they are *chronologically gifted.*

*Analyzing effectiveness
of text*

Ehrenreich does recommend keeping a sense of humor about the P.C. movement, but the conclusion to her essay weakens her argument. Instead of focusing on her earlier point that "it's silly to mistake verbal purification for genuine social reform," she advises both sides to lighten up and have fun with the diversity around us. Instead, I wanted her to conclude by reinforcing her point that "actions still speak louder than fashionable phrases." Changing the realities of illiteracy, poverty, alcohol abuse, and sexual harassment should be the focus of the multiculturalists. Of course, changing language is crucial to changing the world, but the language revolution has already happened—or at least

Responder's main point

begun. Ehrenreich's article would be more effective, I believe, if she concluded her essay with a call for both sides to help change cultural conditions rather than with a reference to the silly debate about what to call a teenage woman.

WARMING UP   Journal Exercises

The following topics will help you practice your reading and responding.

1 **Community Service Learning Project.** Go to your agency or organization and collect texts, images, and brochures that advertise the organization or explain its mission. Choose one or two documents and write a summary and response addressed both to your classmates and to the organization itself. Consider the rhetorical context of these documents (author, purpose, audience, occasion, genre, and cultural context) as you explain why they are or are not effective or appropriate and/or how you interpret the assumptions and implications contained in these texts or images. Your goal is to provide constructive suggestions about ways to revise or improve these texts.

2 Study the print by Maurits Escher reproduced here. How many different ways of perceiving this picture can you see? Describe each perspective. How is "reading" this picture similar to reading a printed text? How is it different?

3 **Writing Across the Curriculum.** Because previewing material is an important part of active reading, most recent psychology and social science textbooks use previewing or prereading strategies at the beginning

Day and Night by M. C. Escher. © 1997 Cordon Art-Baarn-Holland.
All rights reserved.

of each new chapter. Find one chapter in a textbook that uses these previewing techniques. How does the author preview the material? Does the preview help you understand the material in the chapter?

4 Reading the following paragraph illustrates how our prior experience can combine with our predictions to make meaning. The following passage describes a common procedure in our lives. Read the passage. Can you identify the procedure?

> The procedure is actually quite simple. First, you arrange things into different groups. Of course, one pile may be sufficient depending on how much there is to do. If you have to go somewhere else because of lack of facilities, that is the next step; otherwise you are pretty well set. It is important not to overdo things. That is, it is better to do too few things at once than too many. In the short run this may not seem important, but complications can easily arise. A mistake can be expensive as well. At first, the whole procedure will seem complicated. Soon, however, it will become just another facet of life. It is difficult to foresee any end to the necessity for this task in the immediate future, but then one can never tell. After the procedure is completed, one arranges the materials into different groups again. Then they can be put into their appropriate places. Eventually, they will be used once more, and the whole cycle will then have to be repeated. However, that is part of life.

As you read, record your guesses. What words helped to orient you? Where did you make wrong guesses? Discuss your reactions in class.

5 Reprinted below is a letter written by Margaret Atwood, which appeared in *The Nation*. The editors of *The Nation* had asked several foreign writers and political commentators to "share their reflections" about the debate concerning America's foreign policy. An award-winning Canadian novelist, Margaret Atwood has written many volumes of poetry and short fiction as well as over a dozen novels, including *Surfacing* (1973), *The Handmaid's Tale* (1986), and *Oryx and Crake* (2003). Read her "Letter to America," and then write your own summary and response to her ideas.

LETTER TO AMERICA
Margaret Atwood

Dear America

This is a difficult letter to write, because I'm no longer sure who you are. Some of you may be having the same trouble.

I thought I knew you: We'd become well acquainted over the past fifty-five years. You were the Mickey Mouse and Donald Duck comic books I read in the late 1940s. You were the radio shows—*Jack Benny, Our Miss Brooks.* You were the music I sang and danced to: the Andrews Sisters, Ella Fitzgerald, the Platters, Elvis. You were a ton of fun.

You wrote some of my favorite books. You created Huckleberry Finn, and Hawkeye, and Beth and Jo in *Little Women,* courageous in their different ways. Later, you were my beloved Thoreau, father of environmentalism, witness to individual conscience; and Walt Whitman, singer of the great Republic; and Emily Dickinson, keeper of the private soul. You were Hammett and Chandler, heroic walkers of mean streets; even later, you were the amazing trio, Hemingway, Fitzgerald and Faulkner, who traced the dark labyrinths of your hidden heart. You were Sinclair Lewis and Arthur Miller, who, with their own American idealism, went after the sham in you, because they thought you could do better.

You were Marlon Brando in *On the Waterfront,* you were Humphrey Bogart in *Key Largo,* you were Lillian Gish in *Night of the Hunter.* You stood up for freedom, honesty and justice; you protected the innocent. I believed most of that. I think you did, too. It seemed true at the time.

You put God on the money, though, even then. You had a way of thinking that the things of Caesar were the same as the things of God: That gave you self-confidence. You have always wanted to be a city upon a hill, a light to all nations, and for a while you were. Give me your tired, your poor, you sang, and for a while you meant it.

We've always been close, you and us. History, that old entangler, has twisted us together since the early seventeenth century. Some of us used to be you; some of us want to be you; some of you used to be us. You are not only our neighbors: In many cases—mine, for instance—you are also our blood relations, our colleagues and our personal friends. But although we've had a ringside seat, we've never understood you completely, up here north of the 49th parallel. We're like Romanized Gauls—look like Romans, dress like Romans, but aren't Romans—peering over the wall at the real Romans. What are they doing? Why? What are they doing now? Why is the haruspex eyeballing the sheep's liver? Why is the soothsayer wholesaling the Bewares?

Perhaps that's been my difficulty in writing you this letter. I'm not sure I know what's really going on. Anyway, you have a huge posse of experienced entrail-sifters who do nothing but analyze your every vein and lobe. What can I tell you about yourself that you don't already know?

This might be the reason for my hesitation: embarrassment, brought on by a becoming modesty. But it is more likely to be embarrassment of another sort. When my grandmother—from a New England background—was confronted with an unsavory topic, she would change the subject and gaze out the window. And that is my own inclination: Keep your mouth shut, mind your own business.

But I'll take the plunge, because your business is no longer merely your business. To paraphrase Marley's Ghost, who figured it out too late, mankind is your business. And vice versa: When the Jolly Green Giant goes on the rampage, many lesser plants and animals get trampled underfoot. As for us, you're our biggest trading partner: We know perfectly well that if you go down the plug-hole, we're going with you. We have every reason to wish you well.

I won't go into the reasons why I think your recent Iraqi adventures have been—taking the long view—an ill-advised tactical error. By the time you read this, Baghdad may or may not be a pancake, and many more sheep entrails will have been examined. Let's talk, then, not about what you're doing to other people but about what you're doing to yourselves.

You're gutting the Constitution. Already your home can be entered without your knowledge or permission, you can be snatched away and incarcerated without cause, your mail can be spied on, your private records searched. Why isn't this a recipe for widespread business theft, political intimidation and fraud? I know you've been told that all this is for your own safety and protection, but think about it for a minute. Anyway, when did you get so scared? You didn't used to be easily frightened.

You're running up a record level of debt. Keep spending at this rate and pretty soon you won't be able to afford any big military adventures. Either that or you'll go the way of the USSR: lots of tanks, but no air conditioning. That will make folks very cross. They'll be even crosser when they can't take a shower because your shortsighted bulldozing of environmental protections has dirtied most of the water and dried up the rest. Then things will get hot and dirty indeed.

You're torching the American economy. How soon before the answer to that will be not to produce anything yourselves but to grab stuff other people produce, at gunboat-diplomacy prices? Is the world going to consist of a few mega-rich King Midases, with the rest being serfs, both inside and outside your country? Will the biggest business sector in the United States be the prison system? Let's hope not.

If you proceed much further down the slippery slope, people around the world will stop admiring the good things about you. They'll decide that your city upon the hill is a slum and your democracy is a sham, and therefore you have no business trying to impose your sullied vision on them. They'll think you've abandoned the rule of law. They'll think you've fouled your own nest.

The British used to have a myth about King Arthur. He wasn't dead, but sleeping in a cave, it was said: and in the country's hour of greatest peril, he would return. You too have great spirits of the past you may call upon: men and women of courage, of conscience, of prescience. Summon them now, to stand with you, to inspire you, to defend the best in you. You need them.

Casebook on Responses to Climate Change

The importance of critical reading, interpretation, and response is dramatically illustrated today in our public discussion about climate change. The central scientific document is still the report of the 2007 Intergovernmental Panel on Climate Change. The next IPCC report is due in 2014, but in the meantime, scientific articles on the increase of greenhouse gases, the melting of glaciers, and the changes to animal habitat continue to support earlier IPCC findings. With the Obama administration, the focus has shifted to mitigating the effects of greenhouse gases through alternative energies, cap-and-trade policies, and more efficient houses, factories, and automobiles.

This casebook begins with "The Rise of Renewable Energy," by Daniel M. Kammen, which briefly explains the effects of climate change and discusses how best to reduce greenhouse gases. The next document, "Take the Campus Carbon Challenge: 50 Things You Can Do" from an Oregon State Web site at http://oregonstate.edu/~johnsonc/50%20 Things.html, typifies the efforts made by schools, colleges, local communities, and state governments to involve citizens in a cooperative effort to use alternative energies, reduce our carbon footprint, and be more efficient in our use of traditional carbon-based energies.

Critical reading and response requires asking questions of any document we read or graphic that we see. For example, does the graphic at the beginning of this chapter, "15 Ways to Make a Wedge," help us think more constructively about the problem? As you read the following articles, consider these questions: Is there still a "debate" about whether climate change is happening or whether it is significantly caused by the activities of human beings? How can we reduce greenhouse gases without further harming the economy? What changes in our personal lives will bring about the best results?

But critical readers must also ask questions about themselves as readers. Are we climate change skeptics or believers? What arguments or evidence are we most likely to believe? Who seems to be an authority—and why? Finally, what media—scientific journals, popular magazines, Web sites, blogs, or videos—seem most convincing for us?

As you read the following articles and documents, write your questions in the margin. What bits of evidence are most or least persuasive? What topics, questions, or arguments are not addressed? Your purpose in reading these articles is not just to confirm your current belief, but to consider how your position is changing—and why.

PROFESSIONAL WRITING

The Rise of Renewable Energy

Daniel M. Kammen

No plan to substantially reduce greenhouse gas emissions can succeed *1* through increases in energy efficiency alone. Because economic growth continues to boost the demand for energy—more coal for powering new factories, more oil for fueling new cars, more natural gas for heating new homes—carbon emissions will keep climbing despite the introduction of more energy-efficient vehicles, buildings and appliances. To counter the alarming trend of global warming, the U.S. and other countries must make a major commitment to developing renewable energy sources that generate little or no carbon.

Renewable energy technologies were suddenly and briefly fashionable *2* three decades ago in response to the oil embargoes of the 1970s, but the interest and support were not sustained. In recent years, however, dramatic improvements in the performance and affordability of solar cells, wind turbines and biofuels—ethanol and other fuels derived from plants—have paved the way for mass commercialization. In addition to their environmental benefits, renewable sources promise to enhance America's energy security by reducing the country's reliance on fossil fuels from other nations. What is more, high and wildly fluctuating prices for oil and natural gas have made renewable alternatives more appealing.

We are now in an era where the opportunities for renewable en- *3* ergy are unprecedented, making this the ideal time to advance clean power for decades to come. But the endeavor will require a long-term investment of scientific, economic and political resources. Policymakers and ordinary citizens must demand action and challenge one another to hasten the transition.

LET THE SUN SHINE

Solar cells, also known as photovoltaics, use semiconductor materials to 4
convert sunlight into electric current. They now provide just a tiny slice
of the world's electricity: their global generating capacity of 5,000
megawatts (MW) is only 0.15 percent of the total generating capacity
from all sources. Yet sunlight could potentially supply 5,000 times as
much energy as the world currently consumes. And thanks to technology
improvements, cost declines and favorable policies in many states and
nations, the annual production of photovoltaics has increased by more
than 25 percent a year for the past decade and by a remarkable 45 percent in 2005. The cells manufactured last year added 1,727 MW to worldwide generating capacity, with 833 MW made in Japan, 353 MW in
Germany and 153 MW in the U.S.

  Solar photovoltaics are particularly easy to use because they can be 5
installed in so many places—on the roofs or walls of homes and office
buildings, in vast arrays in the desert, even sewn into clothing to power
portable electronic devices. The state of California has joined Japan and
Germany in leading a global push for solar installations; the "Million Solar Roof" commitment is intended to create 3,000 MW of new generating capacity in the state by 2018. Studies done by my research group,
the Renewable and Appropriate Energy Laboratory at the University of
California, Berkeley, show that annual production of solar photovoltaics
in the U.S. alone could grow to 10,000 MW in just 20 years if current
trends continue.

  The biggest challenge will be lowering the price of the photo- 6
voltaics, which are now relatively expensive to manufacture. Electricity
produced by crystalline cells has a total cost of 20 to 25 cents per kilowatt-
hour, compared with four to six cents for coal-fired electricity, five to
seven cents for power produced by burning natural gas, and six to nine
cents for biomass power plants. (The cost of nuclear power is harder
to pin down because experts disagree on which expenses to include in
the analysis; the estimated range is two to 12 cents per kilowatt-hour.)
Fortunately, the prices of solar cells have fallen consistently over the
past decade, largely because of improvements in manufacturing
processes. In Japan, where 290 MW of solar generating capacity were
added in 2005 and an even larger amount was exported, the cost
of photovoltaics has declined 8 percent a year; in California, where
50 MW of solar power were installed in 2005, costs have dropped
5 percent annually.

BLOWING IN THE WIND

Wind power has been growing at a pace rivaling that of the solar indus- 7
try. The worldwide generating capacity of wind turbines has increased
more than 25 percent a year, on average, for the past decade, reaching

nearly 60,000 MW in 2005. The growth has been nothing short of explosive in Europe—between 1994 and 2005, the installed wind power capacity in European Union nations jumped from 1,700 to 40,000 MW. Germany alone has more than 18,000 MW of capacity thanks to an aggressive construction program. The northern German state of Schleswig-Holstein currently meets one quarter of its annual electricity demand with more than 2,400 wind turbines, and in certain months wind power provides more than half the state's electricity. In addition, Spain has 10,000 MW of wind capacity, Denmark has 3,000 MW, and Great Britain, the Netherlands, Italy and Portugal each have more than 1,000 MW.

In the U.S. the wind power industry has accelerated dramatically in 8 the past five years, with total generating capacity leaping 36 percent to 9,100 MW in 2005. Although wind turbines now produce only 0.5 percent of the nation's electricity, the potential for expansion is enormous, especially in the windy Great Plains states. (North Dakota, for example, has greater wind energy resources than Germany, but only 98 MW of generating capacity is installed there.) If the U.S. constructed enough wind farms to fully tap these resources, the turbines could generate as much as 11 trillion kilowatt-hours of electricity, or nearly three times the total amount produced from all energy sources in the nation last year. The wind industry has developed increasingly large and efficient turbines, each capable of yielding 4 to 6 MW. And in many locations, wind power is the cheapest form of new electricity, with costs ranging from four to seven cents per kilowatt-hour.

The growth of new wind farms in the U.S. has been spurred by a pro- 9 duction tax credit that provides a modest subsidy equivalent to 1.9 cents per kilowatt-hour, enabling wind turbines to compete with coal-fired plants. Unfortunately, Congress has repeatedly threatened to eliminate the tax credit. Instead of instituting a long-term subsidy for wind power, the lawmakers have extended the tax credit on a year-to-year basis, and the continual uncertainty has slowed investment in wind farms. Congress is also threatening to derail a proposed 130-turbine farm off the coast of Massachusetts that would provide 468 MW of generating capacity, enough to power most to Cape Cod, Martha's Vineyard and Nantucket.

The reservations about wind power come partly from utility compa- 10 nies that are reluctant to embrace the new technology and partly from so-called NIMBY-ism. ("NIMBY" is an acronym for Not in My Backyard.) Although local concerns over how wind turbines will affect landscape views may have some merit, they must be balanced against the social costs of the alternatives. Because society's energy needs are growing relentlessly, rejecting wind farms often means requiring the construction or expansion of fossil fuel-burning power plants that will have far more devastating environmental effects.

GREEN FUELS

Researchers are also pressing ahead with the development of biofuels that 11 could replace at least a portion of the oil currently consumed by motor vehicles. The most common biofuel by far in the U.S. is ethanol, which is typically made from corn and blended with gasoline. The manufacturers of ethanol benefit from a substantial tax credit: with the help of the $2-billion annual subsidy, they sold more than 16 billion liters of ethanol in 2005 (almost 3 percent of all automobile fuel by volume), and production is expected to rise 50 percent by 2007. Some policymakers have questioned the wisdom of the subsidy, pointing to studies showing that it takes more energy to harvest the corn and refine the ethanol than the fuel can deliver to combustion engines. In a recent analysis, though, my colleagues and I discovered that some of these studies did not properly account for the energy content of the by-products manufactured along with the ethanol. When all the inputs and outputs were correctly factored in, we found that ethanol has a positive net energy of almost five megajoules per liter.

We also found, however, that ethanol's impact on greenhouse gas 12 emissions is more ambiguous. Our best estimates indicate that substituting corn-based ethanol for gasoline reduces greenhouse gas emissions by 18 percent, but the analysis is hampered by large uncertainties regarding certain agricultural practices, particularly the environmental costs of fertilizers. If we use different assumptions about these practices, the results of switching to ethanol range from a 36 percent drop in emissions to a 29 percent increase. Although corn-based ethanol may help the U.S. reduce its reliance on foreign oil, it will probably not do much to slow global warming unless the production of the biofuel becomes cleaner.

But the calculations change substantially when the ethanol is made 13 from cellulosic sources: woody plants such as switch-grass or poplar. Whereas most makers of corn-based ethanol burn fossil fuels to provide the heat for fermentation, the producers of cellulosic ethanol burn lignin—an unfermentable part of the organic material—to heat the plant sugars. Burning lignin does not add any greenhouse gases to the atmosphere, because the emissions are offset by the carbon dioxide absorbed during the growth of the plants used to make the ethanol. As a result, substituting cellulosic ethanol for gasoline can slash greenhouse gas emissions by 90 percent or more.

Another promising biofuel is so-called green diesel. Researchers 14 have produced this fuel by first gasifying biomass—heating organic materials enough that they release hydrogen and carbon monoxide—and then converting these compounds into long-chain hydrocarbons using the Fischer-Tropsch process. (During World War II, German engineers employed these chemical reactions to make synthetic motor fuels out to coal.) The result would be an economically competitive liquid fuel for motor vehicles that would add virtually no greenhouse gases to the atmosphere. Oil giant Royal Dutch/Shell is currently investigating the technology.

THE NEED FOR R&D

Each of these renewable sources is now at or near a tipping point, the cru- 15 cial stage when investment and innovation, as well as market access, could enable these attractive but generally marginal providers to become major contributors to regional and global energy supplies. At the same time, aggressive policies designed to open markets for renewables are taking hold at city, state and federal levels around the world. Governments have adopted these policies for a wide variety of reasons: to promote market diversity or energy security, to bolster industries and jobs, and to protect the environment on both the local and global scales. In the U.S. more than 20 states have adopted standards setting a minimum for the fraction of electricity that must be supplied with renewable sources. Germany plans to generate 20 percent of its electricity from renewables by 2020, and Sweden intends to give up fossil fuels entirely.

But perhaps the most important step toward creating a sustainable 16 energy economy is to institute market-bases schemes to make the prices of carbon fuels reflect their social cost. The use of coal, oil and natural gas imposes a huge collective toll on society, in the form of health care expenditures for ailments caused by air pollution, military spending to secure oil supplies, environmental damage from mining operations, and the potentially devastating economic impacts of global warming. A fee on carbon emissions would provide a simple, logical and transparent method to reward renewable, clean energy sources over those that harm the economy and the environment. The tax revenues could pay for some of the social costs of carbon emissions, and a portion could be designated to compensate low-income families who spend a larger share of their income on energy. Furthermore, the carbon fee could be combined with a cap-and-trade program that would set limits on carbon emissions but also allow the cleanest energy suppliers to sell permits to their dirtier competitors. The federal government has used such programs with great success to curb other pollutants, and several northeastern states are already experimenting with greenhouse gas emissions trading.

Best of all, these steps would give energy companies an enormous fi- 17 nancial incentive to advance the development and commercialization of renewable energy sources. In essence, the U.S. has the opportunity to foster an entirely new industry. The threat of climate change can be a rallying cry for a clean-technology revolution that would strengthen the country's manufacturing base, create thousands of jobs and alleviate our international trade deficits—instead of importing foreign oil, we can export high-efficiency vehicles, appliances, wind turbines and photo-voltaics. This transformation can turn the nations' energy sector into something that was once deemed impossible: a vibrant, environmentally sustainable engine of growth.

PROFESSIONAL WRITING

50 Things You Can Do[1]

Take the Campus Carbon Challenge. Pledge to try 5 carbon-reducing ac-   *1*
tions in February. Choose from our list of 50 or make up one of your own.

On the Go

1. Carpool instead of going it alone (at least 1 day a week)

   Burning just one gallon of gasoline produces about 20 pounds of carbon emissions. Find out more about carbon emissions from Terrapass, then check out local Ride Shares to find out if someone is going your way.

2. Take the bus instead of driving (at least 1 day a week)

   According to Public Transportation, the typical public transit rider uses half the gas consumed by car commuters. On average, public transportation saves 4 million gallons of gas in the United States every day. That is the equivalent of 300,000 fill-ups! Check out the Corvallis bus schedule, then sit back, relax, and enjoy the ride for free with a valid Oregon State University ID.

[1]This excerpt from the Oregon State University web page shows only the first nine suggestions.

...continued The Rise of Renewable Energy, **Daniel M. Kammen**

3. Bike instead of driving (at least 1 day a week)

   Biking is 50 times more energy efficient than driving. If you are new to cycling, Commuting by Bike has a Biking 101 class to get you started, and Corvallis has extensive bike paths to get you where you need to go. If you don't have a bike yet, there are usually cycles for sale at OSU's Wednesday Salvage Sale or on Craigslist.

4. Work or study from home instead of commuting (at least 1 day a week)

   According to a recent study, 3.9 million people in the U.S. work from home at least one day a week. By avoiding the average 22-mile commute to the office, and taking into account the increased use of home power, telecommuting saves about 840 million gallons of gas, which is equivalent to taking two million cars off the road for a year.

5. Consolidate errands instead of making multiple car trips (at least twice this month)

   Fewer trips means fewer emissions. Visit Sustainable Choices to find out more. Then call a friend to see if he or she needs to run similar errands, toss your reusable bags in the car, and hit the road.

6. Inflate your tires (check your air pressure of your tires to make sure they are properly inflated)

   According to Click and Clack, "The softer your tires are, the greater the friction between the road and the rubber, and the harder your engine will have to work to move the car." Inflating your tires to recommended pressure levels can increase gas mileage by about 1–4%. Good for your wallet and the environment.

7. Lighten your load (every 100 lbs. in your car increases gas consumption by 1–2%)

   Every extra 100 pounds in your car increases gas consumption by 1–2%. So clean out your trunk, then find out more about getting better fuel economy from Click and Clack.

8. Slow down (go the speed limit and get better gas mileage)

   According to Click and Clack, for every ten miles per hour you floor it, you lose as much as 15% in fuel economy.

At Home

9. Light up with compact fluorescents (change at least half the light bulbs in your house)

Compact fluorescents (CFLs) use one quarter of the electricity and last years longer than incandescent bulbs. According to Energy Star, if every American home replaced just one light bulb with a CFL bulb, "we would save enough energy to light more than 3 million homes for a year, more than $600 million in annual energy costs, and prevent greenhouse gases equivalent to the emissions of more than 800,000 cars." When your CFLs finally do burn out, remember to recycle them because they contain mercury.

vo·cab·u·lar·y

In your journal, write the meanings of the italicized words in the following phrases.

"The Rise of Renewable Energy"

- the oil *embargoes* (**2**)
- wisdom of the *subsidy* (**11**)
- is more *ambiguous* (**12**)
- heat for *fermentation* (**13**)
- *sustainable* energy economy (**16**)

"Take the Campus Carbon Challenge"

- that is the *equivalent* (**2**)
- *telecommuting* saves (**4**)
- longer than *incandescent* bulbs (**9**)

? QUESTIONS FOR WRITING AND DISCUSSION

1. Of the alternative energies that Daniel Kammen cites in "The Rise of Renewable Energy," which do you have some personal knowledge about? Are solar cells, wind turbines, or green fuels used in your community or state? Which are developing and growing the fastest?

2. Analyze the full-page visual, "15 Ways to Make a Wedge" that appears at the beginning of this chapter. Read the caption under the graphic. Which of these wedges or reductions of carbon emissions does Kammen discuss? How would the cap-and-trade proposals or the "market-based schemes" that Kammen discusses in paragraph 16 help promote the carbon savings depicted in these wedges? What makes this graphic effective (or ineffective) at showing workable solutions for reducing carbon emissions?

3 Use your library's databases or reliable Web sites, such as the Environmental Protection Agency (http://www.epa.gov) or RealClimate (http://www.realclimate.org/), to research the latest information about climate change, its recent effects, or new ways to reduce carbon emissions. How has the conversation or the focus of the conversation changed since the last IPCC report? Write your own summary and response to one of the articles that you discover in your research.

Reading and Writing Processes

ASSIGNMENT FOR READING/WRITING

Write an essay that summarizes and then responds to one or more essays, articles, or advertisements. As you review your particular assignment, make sure you understand what text or texts you should respond to, how long your summary and response should be, and what type(s) of responses you should focus on.

Your purpose for this assignment is to represent the text(s) accurately and faithfully in your summary and to explain and support your response. Taken together, your summary and response should be a coherent essay, with a main idea and connections between summary and response. Assume that your audience is other members of the class, including the instructor, with whom you are sharing your reading.

Your instructor's assignment should indicate which of the possible audiences and genres suggested below you should use.

Audience	Possible Genres for Reading/Writing Assignments
Personal Audience	Class or laboratory notes, journal entry, blog, scrapbook, multigenre document
Academic Audience	Academic summary, summary and response, synopsis, critique, review, journal entry, forum entry on class site, multigenre document
Public Audience	Column, editorial, letter to the editor, article in a magazine, newspaper, online site, newsletter, or multigenre document

CHOOSING A SUBJECT

Suggested processes, activities, and strategies for reading and writing will be illustrated in response to the following essay by Dudley Erskine Devlin.

Teaching Tolerance in America

Dudley Erskine Devlin

Dudley Erskine Devlin was born in Syracuse, New York, and attended the University of Kansas. Originally trained as a scientist, he currently teaches English at Colorado State University and writes columns and editorials on contemporary problems. The targets for his editorials are often the large and complicated issues of the day, such as education, violence, health care, and the media. "My first goal as a writer," Devlin said in a recent interview, "is to provoke response. If just one reader is angry enough to write me a letter of response, then my time is not wasted." As you read Devlin's essay, note places where you agree or disagree with his ideas. How would you respond to Devlin's argument?

In the past few years, American high schools have struggled with a variety of forces that have threatened to tear them apart: reduced funding, increased class sizes, fewer music and art classes, violence in schools, and racial and class divisions among students. Although educational reform in America tends to focus on curriculum issues, class sizes, and security issues, one lesson seems increasingly hard to teach—helping students appreciate and welcome differences in culture, racial heritage, and personal identity. Despite the emphasis on increasing respect and tolerance in schools, teenagers still bring the social and racial divisions found in society at large back into the halls of high schools across America. Social cliques based on race, gender, athletic prowess, income, social class, dress, and even body piercings still define the culture at most schools. [1]

America, we fervently believe, is still the land of opportunity, the land where we can be judged on our merits and achievements, not on stereotypes or preconceptions or prejudices. Yet the social clique is based on the notion that one group imagines it is superior to another and thus can ridicule, taunt, or even bully another group. And nowhere does the social clique have more devastating and long-lasting effects than in our high schools. [2]

High school cliques, which reproduce the class divisions found in society, originate from three distinct sources: racial differences, gender differences, and social differences. Racial problems in high schools need no explanation. Every high school in America has racial problems that have led to continuing conflicts. A reporter visiting one typical suburban high school found that each ethnic group—Hispanics, whites, blacks, Asians—had a place where they gathered between classes and after school. Although individual members in an ethnic group gain security from being in the group, they make outsiders—people who do not belong to their racial group—feel insecure and often threatened. As one student put it, "The problem is that [3] some people think they are better than others. So they make disparaging remarks about one another, creating tension and conflict in the school."

The ongoing gender problems in America's high schools are mentioned—if at all—on the back pages of newspapers, as if the sexist treatment of girls is a normal and inconsequential behavior. Nan Stein, author of *Classrooms and Courtrooms: Facing Sexual Harassment in K-12 Schools,* recounts numerous incidents where school administrations overlook student-on-student sexual harassment. In a recent interview with *Harvard Educational Letter,* Stein recalled a case in which "15 boys harassed this one girl verbally, mooing like cows whenever they saw her and talking about the size of her breasts. They did this outside of school, in school, on the way to school. Other kids heard it and saw it. Teachers and custodians told the administrator, who kept saying, 'It's not a big deal.'" When the case involves males of status, the chances are even more likely that school administrators will look the other way. Ignoring the flagrant behavior of the popular students happens at every school in America—despite a recent Supreme Court ruling that now holds schools liable in such cases of sexual harassment. 4

Finally, the differences in social classes among the various cliques—most notably between the jocks and the geeks, between the powerful and the weak—is a continuing source of conflict. As one student put it, "If you're not a jock in this school . . . you're not part of it." The outsiders, geeks, and gays are ridiculed by everyone and harassed, bullied, and picked on by the jocks and by other members of the elite social class. Bullying is sometimes connected to cliques and gangs, and it affects both boys and girls. Allan Beane, author of *The Bully-Free Classroom,* writes that he has "heard from so many adults who are still very angry and hurt from when they were mistreated in school." Frequently school bullies are boys—and the ridicule and intimidation they inflict has played a role, Beane says, in "almost all of the school shootings that have outraged the nation in the past two years." Hara Marano, an editor for *Psychology Today,* points out that girls, too, engage in physical aggression even though they are "more apt to be masters of indirect bullying, spreading lies and rumors and destroying reputations." The result is that about one in seven schoolchildren is either a bully or a victim of bullying. 5

How do we solve these problems? First we need to eliminate those liberal solutions that simply aren't working—thus releasing funds for more effective deterrents. Many schools, for example, have introduced diversity issues into English and social studies classes, and some schools even have sensitivity training classes that seek to "instill respect for others and training students how to speak up when they hear insulting or intimidating comments." However, most students react negatively to such classes. In a recent report, one student said that he really didn't like having notions of tolerance and acceptance drilled into him: "It's like shoving something down our throats." . . . 6

There are, however, some real and sensible solutions that could solve ₇ the intolerance problem in our high schools. For years, parents and educators have recommended that schools adopt uniforms, so that every student wears the same clothing to school. Already, many schools ban specific colors or types of hats, shirts, or jewelry. We need uniforms not just to eliminate gangs, but to reduce the visual cues that enable one group to maintain social power. And we need to enforce those dress rules with a zero tolerance policy. Second, schools need to make single-sex classes a standard practice. Not only do boys and girls learn better in single-sex environments, but the segregated classes will reduce the differences and thus reduce conflicts. Finally, schools need to improve security—both to protect students from the outside and to protect students from each other. Schools need more video cameras, drug sniffing dogs, and spot checks of cars and lockers. Governor Jesse Ventura had an excellent idea when he suggested that every school needs to have teachers with paramilitary and anti-riot training. Last but not least, students need to wear picture ID tags hung on ribbons around their necks—so videotapes can easily identify any troublemakers.

The class system that is created and perpetuated by student cliques is ₈ the most important problem in our high schools today. In any high school on any day, we see the strong picking on the weak, the bullies intimidating the outcasts, and the jocks and the social elite dominating everyone else. Only when we apply our zero tolerance policy to the dress code, the gender makeup of our classes, and the security of our schools will students learn how to treat all people and social classes with acceptance and tolerance.

COLLECTING

Once a text has been selected or assigned for your summary and response, try the following reading, writing, and discussing activities.

PREREADING JOURNAL ENTRY

In your journal, write what you already know about the subject of the essay. The following questions will help you to recall your prior experiences and think about your own opinions before you read the essay. The purpose of this entry is to think about your own experiences and opinions *before* you are influenced by the arguments of the essay.

- What classes or programs at your high school were designed to improve tolerance of social differences among students? Did they increase or decrease tolerance for social, sexual, or racial difference among students at your school?

- Were cliques a big problem at your school? Did your high school have bullies who picked on other students? Were the jocks or the upper-class students given preferential treatment?
- What measures to increase security, reduce potential violence, and increase tolerance has your high school taken in the last few years? Were these changes necessary? Did they improve the quality of your education? Did they make you feel more secure at school?

● TEXT ANNOTATION   Most experts on reading and writing agree that you will learn more and remember more if you actually write out your comments, questions, and reactions in the margins of the text you are reading. Writing your responses helps you begin a conversation with the text. Reproduced below are one reader's marginal responses to paragraph 7 of Devlin's essay.

Why not have them optional for some subjects?

Second, schools need to make single-sex classes a standard practice. Not only do

boys and girls learn better in single-sex environments, but the segregated classes

In the real world men and women work together, so why not start now?

will reduce the differences and thus reduce conflicts. Finally, schools need to

A few cameras will provide security, but spot checks invade our privacy.

improve security—both to protect students from the outside and to protect

students from each other. Schools need more video cameras, drug sniffing dogs,

and spot checks of cars and lockers. Governor Jesse Ventura had an excellent idea

What? Schools are not wrestling arenas and we don't have riots.

when he suggested that every school needs to have teachers with paramilitary and

anti-riot training. Last but not least, students need to wear picture ID tags hung

Students should not be treated like jail inmates!

on ribbons around their necks—so videotapes can easily identify any trouble-

makers.

● READING LOG   A reading log, like text annotation, encourages you to interact with the author/text and write your comments and questions as you read. While text annotation helps you identify specific places in the text for commentary, a reading log encourages you to write out longer, more thoughtful responses. In a reading log, you can keep a record of your thoughts *while you read and reread* the text. Often, reading-log entries help you focus on a key idea to develop later in your response.

Below is one reader's response to Devlin's ideas about single-sex classes and bullying.

> I attended a private elementary school and junior high where a school uniform was required and some of the classes were single-sex. Personally, I can say that the uniform did not make a bit of difference where bullying was an issue. Kids still made fun of other kids no matter what they were wearing. The real reason that kids make fun of others is because of social differences and because they themselves do not want to be picked on, so they deflect the attention onto others.
>
> It is true that bullying is carried on with people throughout life, which is why there should be no tolerance at all for teasing. For example, I was talking with a very good friend of mine who told me that he is still haunted by memories of when children would call him a "fag" on the playground. This has affected him for a long time, and he is still fearful of admitting his homosexuality because he feels as if he is letting the bullies win and proving that they were right.

SHAPING

Summaries and responses have several possible shapes, depending on the writer's purpose and intended audience. Keep in mind, however, that in a summary/response essay or critique, *the summary and the response should be unified by the writer's overall response.* The summary and the response may be organized or drafted separately, but they are still parts of one essay, focused on the writer's most important or overall response.

SUMMARY SHAPING

Summaries should convey the main ideas, the essential argument, or the key features of a text. The purpose should be to represent the author's/text's ideas as accurately and as faithfully as possible. Summaries rely on description, paraphrase, and direct quotation. Below are definitions and examples for each of these terms.

● **DESCRIPTION**   The summary should *describe* the main features of an essay, including the author and title, the context or place of publication of the essay (if appropriate), the essay's thesis or main argument, and any key text features, such as sections, chapters, or important graphic material.

> In the article "Teaching Tolerance in America," Dudley Erskine Devlin reports some disturbing issues concerning America's high schools. Devlin states that intimidation, through dress, social cliques, gender, and race, is

causing tension and danger in high schools today. According to Devlin, sexual harassment is allowed and condoned, and in some cases jocks bully geeks and racial and social groups intimidate one another. As a solution, Devlin suggests that schools enforce strict, zero-tolerance dress codes, segregate the sexes in classes, increase security through surveillance cameras and drug-sniffing dogs, and require students to wear photo IDs.

● **PARAPHRASE**   A paraphrase restates a passage or text in different words. The purpose of a paraphrase is to recast the author's/text's words in your own language. A good paraphrase retains the original meaning without plagiarizing from the original text.

ORIGINAL: High school cliques, which reproduce the class divisions found in society, originate from three distinct sources: racial differences, gender differences, and social differences.

PARAPHRASE: Peer groups in high school mirror society's class distinctions, which stem from differences in race, gender, and social status.

PLAGIARISM: Peer groups in high school *reproduce the class divisions found in society* and come *from three distinct sources: race, gender, and social differences.* [This is plagiarism because the writer uses exact phrases (see italics) from the original without using quotation marks.]

● **DIRECT QUOTATION**   Often, summaries directly quote a few key phrases or sentences from the source. *Remember: Any words or phrases within the quotation marks must be accurate, word-for-word transcriptions of the original.* Guidelines for direct quotation and examples are as follows. Use direct quotations sparingly to convey the key points in the essay:

> Devlin focuses on what he believes is the school system's largest problem today, the issue of "helping students appreciate and welcome differences in culture, racial heritage, and personal identity."

Use direct quotations when the author's phrasing is more memorable, more concise, or more accurate than your paraphrase might be:

> Devlin claims that teenagers "still bring the social and racial divisions found in society at large back into the halls of high schools across America."

Use direct quotations for key words or phrases that indicate the author's attitude, tone, or stance:

> According to Devlin, we should "eliminate those liberal solutions that simply aren't working" in order to fund his solutions.

Don't quote long sentences. Condense the original sentence to the most important phrases. Use just a short phrase from a sentence or use an ellipsis (three spaced points . . .) to indicate words that you have omitted.

ORIGINAL: Although educational reform in America tends to focus on curriculum issues, class sizes, and security issues, one lesson seems increasingly hard to teach—helping students appreciate and welcome differences in culture, racial heritage, and personal identity.

CONDENSED QUOTATION: Educational reform, according to Devlin, should focus less on curriculum issues and class sizes and more on helping students "appreciate . . . differences in culture, racial heritage, and personal identity."

● **AVOIDING PLAGIARISM**   As you work with your sources, paraphrasing key ideas and quoting key phrases or sentences, keep in mind that in order to avoid plagiarizing, you need to document any ideas, facts, statistics, or actual language you use in your text and in a Works Cited or References page. *Plagiarism* is knowingly and deliberately using the language, ideas, or visual materials of another person or source without acknowledging that person or source. Use the following guidelines to avoid plagiarism.

- Do not use language, ideas, or graphics from any essay, text, or visual image that you find online, in the library, or from commercial sources without acknowledging the source.
- Do not use language, ideas, or visual images from any other student's essay without acknowledging the source.

Students who deliberately plagiarize typically fail the course and face disciplinary action by the university.

Sometimes, however, students plagiarize out of carelessness or inadequately citing words, specific languages, ideas, or visual images. You can avoid this inadvertent plagiarism by learning how to quote accurately from your sources, how to paraphrase using your own words, and how to cite your sources accurately. In this chapter, you will learn how to quote accurately, to paraphrase without plagiarizing, and to use author tags to indicate your sources. In addition, Chapter 7, "Investigating," and Chapter 11, "Writing a Research Paper," have examples illustrating how to do in-text citation and how to do a Works Cited page.

The best way to avoid inadvertent plagiarism is to ask your instructor how to document a source you are using. Your instructor will help you with conventions of direct quotation, paraphrasing, and in-text reference or citation.

SAMPLE SUMMARIES

Following are summaries of Devlin's essay written by two different readers. Notice that while both convey the main ideas of the essay by using description, paraphrase, and direct quotation, they are not identical. Check each summary to see how well it meets these guidelines:

- Cite the author and title of the text.
- Indicate the main ideas of the text.
- Use direct quotation of key words, phrases, or sentences.

- Include author tags.
- Do not summarize most examples or data.
- Be as accurate, fair, and objective as possible.

Summary 1

Dudley Erskine Devlin's essay "Teaching Tolerance in America" addresses several hot topics concerning the American public school system. Devlin focuses on what he believes is the school system's largest problem today, the issue of "helping students appreciate and welcome differences in culture, racial heritage, and personal identity." According to Devlin, the root of the problem lies within the social clique, particularly the social cliques found inside the halls of your local high school. According to Devlin, these cliques originate from three different sources: social, racial, and gender differences. Devlin suggests that we solve the problems these cliques create by eliminating "those liberal solutions that simply aren't working—thus releasing funds for more effective deterrents." Devlin's solutions to eradicate the intolerance are to impose dress codes or uniforms, to create single-sex classrooms, and to markedly increase security at every high school.

Summary 2

The idea of social reform in education has been a pressing issue given the increase in youth violence in high schools across America. In Dudley Erskine Devlin's article "Teaching Tolerance in America," he outlines some of the problems in schools caused by members of cliques and bullies who feed on the "racial differences, gender differences, and social differences" found in society at large. Devlin's argument then moves on to attack the "liberal solutions" (such as introducing diversity issues in classes) and proposes to replace them with "more effective deterrents" such as instituting single-sex classes, school uniforms, picture IDs, and heightened security measures. This zero-tolerance policy, Devlin believes, will teach students how to accept diversity and "appreciate and welcome differences in culture, racial heritage, and personal identity."

RESPONSE SHAPING

Strategies for organizing a response depend on the purpose of the response. Typically, responses include one or more of the following three purposes:

- Analyzing the effectiveness of the text.
- Agreeing and/or disagreeing with the ideas in the text.
- Interpreting and reflecting on the text.

As the following explanations illustrate, each of these types of responses requires supporting evidence from the text, from other texts, and/or from the writer's own experience.

● **ANALYZING**   Analysis requires dividing a whole into its parts in order to better understand the whole. In order to analyze a text for its effectiveness, start by examining key parts or features of the text, such as the purpose, the intended audience, the thesis and main ideas, the organization and evidence, and the language and style. Notice how the following paragraph analyzes Devlin's illogical argument.

> Devlin's essay has some clear problems with the logic of his argument. The title of his essay is "Teaching Tolerance in America," but his solutions contradict his stated purpose. Devlin's proposal to tighten security in our high schools is not going to teach tolerance in high schools across America. As a teenager in a post-Columbine era, I can tell you that ID card checks, patrolling security officers, and hall monitors do not create an atmosphere conducive to teaching tolerance. Students who are treated like prisoners in a maximum security ward do not feel increased warm wishes to faculty and administrators nor are they more likely to tolerate differences in their classmates. Being watched like a hawk by a hall monitor does nothing to make a person more socially outgoing or more tolerant of difference. These security measures will increase fear during the school hours and not encourage tolerance once students leave the school grounds. In short, Devlin's solutions do not, in fact, solve the problems with tolerance created by racial, gender, or social differences.

● **AGREEING/DISAGREEING**   Often, a response to a text focuses on agreeing and/or disagreeing with its major ideas. Responses may agree completely, disagree completely, or agree with some points but disagree with others. Responses that agree with some ideas but disagree with others are often more effective because they show that the responder sees both strengths and weaknesses in an argument. In the following paragraphs, notice how the responder agrees and disagrees and then supports each judgment with evidence.

> About Devlin's recommendation that schools can "reduce conflicts" and teach tolerance by creating single-sex classrooms, I have mixed feelings. From my own personal experience, I agree that single-sex classes can have benefits. Perhaps I am biased, but attending an all-girls high school was very beneficial for me and many of my classmates. Although I have always been a very outgoing individual, I watched many of my friends grow from timid, shy freshmen to independent, strong women. Furthermore, I was never sexually harassed by a classmate, nor did I hear of any of the kinds of harassment Devlin mentions. On the other hand, however, I must disagree with Devlin that single-sex classes are a long-term solution. In the real world, women and men

constantly interact, so they need to learn how to positively interact as girls and boys in school. Students need to be comfortable and learn to work with the opposite sex in preparation for college and the workplace. Although my high school gave me academic confidence, it did not really prepare me for the diverse world I met once I went to college. Single-sex classrooms may just postpone learning about tolerance and difference rather than actually teaching it.

● **INTERPRETING AND REFLECTING** Many responses contain interpretations of passages that might be read from different points of view or reflections on the assumptions or implications of an idea. An interpretation says, "Here is what the text says, but let me explain what it means, what assumptions the argument carries, or what the implications might be." Here is a paragraph from an interpretive response to Devlin's essay.

> If we stop a moment and reflect on the purpose of schools, we realize that schools should be a place where learning and growth can take place. All of Devlin's solutions, however, are designed to increase security and control rather than actually teach tolerance. Perhaps Devlin has modeled his "final solution" on prisons, where students as inmates would have no rights, no privacy, no room to express either tolerance or hatred. Rather than place students in a maximum security prison, we should return to the more liberal approach of teaching tolerance and understanding—the very solution that Devlin initially rejects. While the simple method of teaching about cultural, social, and ethnic differences does not guarantee a conflict-free school environment, it does ensure that students have the opportunity to embrace rather than just accept differences. The forced tolerance that Devlin recommends through dress codes and maximum security measures ultimately discourages students from using their schools to actively examine and freely embrace the differences among their peers.

OUTLINES FOR SUMMARY/ RESPONSE ESSAYS

Three common outlines for summary/response essays follow. Select or modify one of these outlines to fit your audience, purpose, and kind of response. Typically, a summary/response takes the following form

   I. Introduction to text(s)

  II. Summary of text(s)

III. Response(s)
    A. Point 1
    B. Point 2
    C. Point 3, etc.
IV. Conclusion

A second kind of outline focuses initially on key ideas or issues and then examines the text or texts for their contribution to these key ideas. This outline begins with the issues, then summarizes the text(s), and then moves to the reader's responses

  I. Introduction to key issues
 II. Summary of relevant text(s)
III. Response(s)
    A. Point 1
    B. Point 2
    C. Point 3, etc.
 IV. Conclusion

A third outline integrates the summary and the response. It begins by introducing the issue and/or the text, gives a brief overall idea of the text, but then summarizes and responds point by point.

  I. Introduction to issues and/or text(s)
 II. Summary of text's Point 1/response to Point 1
III. Summary of text's Point 2/response to Point 2
 IV. Summary of text's Point 3/response to Point 3, etc.
  V. Conclusion

DRAFTING

If you have been reading actively, you have been writing throughout the reading/writing/discussing process. At some point, however, you will gather your best ideas, have a rough direction or outline in mind, and begin writing a draft. Some writers like to have their examples and evidence ready when they begin drafting. Many writers have outlines in their heads or on paper. Perhaps you like to put your rough outline on the computer and then just expand each section as you write. Finally, most writers like to skim the text and *reread their notes* immediately before they start their drafts, just to make sure everything is fresh in their minds.

Once you start drafting, keep interruptions to a minimum. Because focus and concentration are important to good writing, try to keep writing as long as possible. If you come to a spot where you need an example that you don't have at your fingertips, just put in parentheses—(put the example about cosmetics and animal abuse here)—and keep on writing. Concentrate on making all your separate responses add up to a focused, overall response.

REVISING

Revision means, literally, *reseeing*. Revising requires rereading the text and rewriting your summary and response. While revision begins as you read and reread the text, it continues until—and sometimes after—you turn in a paper or send it to its intended audience.

A major step in your revision is receiving responses from peer readers and deciding on a revision plan, based on the feedback. Use the following guidelines as you read your peers' papers and respond to their advice.

GUIDELINES FOR REVISION

- **Review the purpose and audience for your assignment.** Is your draft addressed to the appropriate audience? Does it fulfill its intended purpose?
- **Reconsider the genre you selected.** Is the genre you selected (essay, letter, letter to the editor) still working for your audience and purpose? Are there multigenre elements you could add to make your summary and response more effective?
- **Continue to use your active reading/writing/discussing activities as you revise your draft.** If you are uncertain about parts of your summary or response, reread the text, check your notes, or discuss your draft with a classmate.
- **Reread your summary for key features.** Make sure your summary indicates author and title, cites main ideas, uses an occasional direct quotation, and includes author tags. Check your summary for accuracy and objectivity.
- **Check paraphrases and direct quotations.** If you are paraphrasing (without quotation marks), you should put the author's ideas into your own language. If you are quoting directly, make sure the words within the quotation marks are accurate, word-for-word transcriptions.
- **Review the purpose of your response.** Are you analyzing, agreeing/ disagreeing, interpreting, or some combination of all three? Do your types of responses fit the assignment or address your intended audience and satisfy your purpose?
- **Amplify your supporting evidence.** Summary/response drafts often need additional, relevant evidence. Be sure you use sufficient personal experience, evidence from the text, or examples from other texts to support your response.

PEER RESPONSE

The instructions below will help you give and receive constructive advice about the rough draft of your summary/response essay. You may use these guidelines for an in-class workshop, a take-home review, or a computer e-mail response.

Writer: Before you exchange drafts with another reader, write out the following information about your own rough draft.

1. On your draft, *label* the parts that are summary and the parts that are your own response.
2. *Underline* the sentence(s) that signal to the reader that you are shifting from objective summary to personal response.
3. Indicate your purpose, intended audience, and any special genre features such as graphs or images.
4. Explain *one or two problems* that you are having with this draft that you want your reader to comment on.

Reader: Without making any comments, read the *entire* draft from start to finish. As you *reread* the draft, answer the following questions.

1. Review the guidelines for writing summaries. Has the writer remained *objective* in his or her summary? Does the summary *omit* any key ideas? Does the writer use *author tags* frequently and accurately? Can you clearly understand the main ideas of the article? Is the summary written in language appropriate for the intended audience? Do any added images or graphic material support the writer's purpose?
2. Review the guidelines for writing responses. What type(s) of response is the writer using? In the margin, label the types. What kinds of evidence does the writer use in support of his or her response? In the margin, label the kinds of supporting evidence. Is this response addressed appropriately to the audience?
3. In your own words, state the main idea or the focus that organizes the writer's response.
4. Write out your own reactions to the writer's response. Where do you disagree with the writer's analysis or interpretation? Explain.
5. Answer the writer's questions in number 4, above.

- **Focus on a clear, overall response.** Your responses should all add up to a focused, overall reaction. Delete or revise any passages that do not maintain your focus.
- **Revise sentences to improve clarity, conciseness, emphasis, and variety.** (See Handbook.)
- **Edit your final version.** Use the spell check on your computer. Have a friend help proofread. Check the Handbook for suspected problems in usage, grammar, and punctuation.

POSTSCRIPT ON THE WRITING PROCESS

1. As you finish your essay, what questions do you still have about how to summarize? What questions do you have about writing a good response?
2. Which paragraphs in your response contain your most effective supporting evidence? What kinds of evidence (analysis of the text, evidence from other texts, or personal experience) did you use?
3. What sentences in your response contain your overall reaction to the text?
4. If you had one more day to work on your essay, what would you change? Why?
5. Review the guidelines for critical reading at the beginning of this chapter. Which of those strategies was most successful for you? What did you learn about active, critical reading that you applied to the writing of your response? Cite one passage that illustrates what you learned about critical reading.

STUDENT WRITING

DEAN C. SWIFT

Letter to Margaret Atwood

After reading Margaret Atwood's "Letter to America," which is reprinted earlier in this chapter, Dean Swift decided to write a letter of response to Ms. Atwood. In his letter, he focuses particularly on Ms. Atwood's rosy picture of America's past and her claim that America is no longer a "city on a hill," but instead a country where a war with Iraq, problems with erosion of constitutional rights, and looming economic problems have threatened America's standing in the world. In his letter of response, Swift argues that the America in the past faced significant problems with civil rights, with assassinations of our great leaders, and with a severe economic depression. Before you read Swift's response, however, be sure to read Atwood's letter and form your own opinion.

1763 Fox Wood Ct.
Rockford, IL 61106
March 11, 2004

Ms. Margaret Atwood
C/o Editors, *The Nation*
33 Irving Place
New York, New York 10003

Dear Ms. Atwood

I am writing in response to your "Letter to America." Although I do not agree totally with everything you say in the letter, I do agree that you can get a much better sense of your country through the eyes of another. There are many things we do not see or realize as Americans until we look at America from the outside. We get tunnel vision. Yet when reading your letter and hearing your description of the America you "once knew," I believe you also have tunnel vision. Throughout the letter you seem to compare the negative things about America today to all the positive things of the past. You fail to mention any negative aspects of America during those days. Maybe you should take a look at someone else's view on America today versus America in the past. 1

You started your letter by relating the America you once knew to its popular culture. For one thing, I don't really think that is an appropriate subject on which to judge a country. There are more important aspects to our history than what the hit movies and songs were. But on that subject, of course it has changed—that was fifty years ago! You can't expect all the music and books to be the same; we are a completely different generation. Now we have our Dave Mathews Band and our Jennifer Lopez—we go to the movies to see *Lord of the Rings*. What is wrong with that? You've drawn us a picture that the America you once knew was flawless. Why don't you try to tell that to the African Americans living in this country back at that time? Would they really believe that America was so much better back then? I'll guarantee that if you were to ask Rosa Parks today whether America has changed for the better or worse, she would go on for hours on how great this country has become. African Americans have been used as slaves, abused, discriminated against, and even tortured to death for hundreds of 2

...*continued* Letter to Margaret Atwood, **Dean C. Swift**

years until the later 1950s and '60s. Violent race riots and disturbing demonstrations took place during the Civil Rights Movement. Didn't it bother you that women didn't have equal rights until 1964? How was that such a perfect country when people were being discriminated against and in some cases beaten, simply because of their race or gender?

Our economy now and the debt we have gotten ourselves into is frustrating 3 to everyone, but what about the economy in the past? Were there no problems with it in the 1930s during the Great Depression? I understand that you feel there are many corrupt things in our country today, but it is no more corrupt than it was in the past. Our country has been going to war as far back as our history dates. What about all the assassinations that took place back then? Your generation lost some great people. Throughout America's history, these tragedies have taken place: the assassination of President Lincoln and President Kennedy, Martin Luther King, Jr., Senator Robert Kennedy—yet these disturbing events don't seem to have left an impression on you.

On the subject of gutting the constitution, it's hard to draw a clear line as to 4 where I stand on that issue. On the one hand, according to our amendments, it is wrong for the government to be able to do such things as tap phone lines, enter a home without a warrant, and incarcerate suspects without cause. These are our rights as Americans. But is this invasion of our privacy really wrong? Why should this bother us unless we are on the guilty side or under suspicion of a crime? I know I don't have anything to hide myself. Although everyone in the U.S. should be entitled to certain privacy rights, isn't it in our best interest—for safety purposes—to sacrifice some rights in order to gain better knowledge and leads on subjects such as terrorism, gang violence, drug deals, and other serious matters? From my point of view, I believe that the Patriot Act is good for our country, and for our own safety. If you have nothing to hide, then why worry—if you are guilty or have information on something serious, then it should be in our best interest to apprehend the suspects or information by any means possible.

You say that our "city upon a hill" is slipping to the slums, but I say you are 5 far from the truth. Though we have fallen in some ways, we have also risen in many. Look at all the technological and medical advances we have made. Our efforts to improve equal rights among all people have clearly improved since your time. We are still a great country. To be sure, there are flaws along the way, but that doesn't change for any country, at any time in history. I felt you were a little narrow minded in your judgment about how America has changed since the time period you grew up in. From generation to generation, people will always have different views on other time periods. I think you should try to open your mind and see that there were many flaws in your time also, and that although there are still many today, we have changed many things for the better. America is still that city upon a hill.

Sincerely,

Dean C. Swift

? QUESTIONS FOR WRITING AND DISCUSSION

1. Reread Margaret Atwood's "Letter to America" reprinted earlier in this chapter. Write your own summary of her main ideas. Then reread Dean Swift's essay. Which of her points or arguments does he mention and respond to? Which ones does he ignore? Would he have a more effective letter if he responded to all of her points? Why or why not?

2. Dean Swift chose to use the genre of a letter to respond to Atwood's own letter. How are the stylistic conventions of a letter different from the conventions of an academic essay? How would Swift's response be different if he were writing a letter to the editor of *The Nation*? Does Swift use the more informal conventions of a letter to make his point in a more effective or personal way? Explain.

3. Responses typically analyze the logic and presentation of the argument, agree or disagree with the main ideas, and/or offer an interpretation or an examination of assumptions and implications behind an argument. Which of these does Swift do most effectively? Where could he add more supporting analysis, evidence, or interpretation? Should he use more of his own personal experience? Explain, referring to specific paragraphs in his essay.

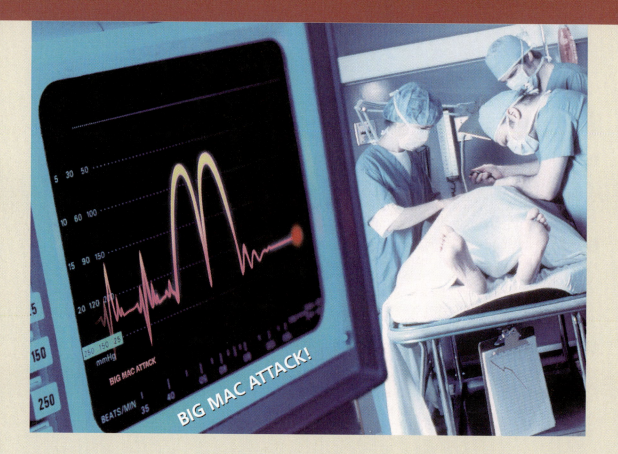

The above spoof ad appears on the Adbusters Web site. After analyzing the composition, images, and contexts for this advertisement, read and respond to Journal Exercise 3 on page 164.

Analyzing and Designing Visuals

6

For one of your composition class projects, you work with the managers of a local adult fitness center in writing a brochure that they can use to promote their fitness, healthy diet, and weight loss programs. First you research information about healthy approaches to weight loss programs. Then you prepare a draft with information organized into key topics from your research and, working with the adult center, decide how to best select, organize, and present this information for their adult clients. As you revise, you focus on giving good, concise advice for adults, presented in an easy-to-read, visually appealing document. Your final product is a four-color brochure with your information, advice, photographs, and graphs that the center will print and distribute.

The editor of your college newspaper asks you to write an article calling attention to upcoming events celebrating César Chávez Day on March 31. You interview organizers of the day's activities to gather basic information. After researching César Chávez's life, however, you decide to write your article primarily to let readers know about his life and accomplishments. You plan to have a calendar of the day's events accompany your biographical information. Your final article features your profile, two pictures of César Chávez, and a sidebar of the campus and community activities.

> " Graphic design creates visual logic and seeks an optimal balance between visual sensation and graphic information. Without the visual impact of shape, color, and contrast, pages are graphically boring and will not motivate the viewer. "
>
> —PATRICK LYNCH AND SARAH HORTON, *WEB STYLE GUIDE*

> " Now we make our networks, and our networks make us. "
>
> —WILLIAM MITCHELL, *CITY OF BITS*

COMMUNICATION IN THE 21ST CENTURY IS, INCREASINGLY, MULTIMEDIA COMMUNICATION. WRITTEN TEXTS ARE INTERWOVEN WITH PICTURES, NEWS PHOTOGRAPHS, GRAPHIC DESIGNS, WORKS OF ART, CHARTS, AND DIAGRAMS. IN ADDITION, WEB SITES AND ELECTRONIC communication contain sound and video, with music, podcasts, and video clips often only a mouse click away. High-tech cell phones now offer true multimedia communication, with e-mail, text messaging, photographs, news updates, video and text files, and music.

Even though our digital-age technology is new, our means for analyzing and designing visuals remains very traditional. In every case, we analyze and design by asking basic rhetorical questions. What is the purpose of this image or bit of media? Who is the intended audience? In what social, political, or cultural context does this visual appear? Who is the author or group of authors? What appeals to logic, emotion, or character do these hybrid or multimedia texts make?

This chapter begins by providing the rhetorical questions you need to analyze visuals and hybrid texts. After you understand how to analyze visuals, you can practice composing and designing hybrid texts of your own. This chapter focuses primarily on visuals as one key element of a multimedia text, but the rhetorical principles will help you analyze other kinds of media as well. The diagram below will help you analyze visuals, their contexts, and their meanings.

The chapter begins with you as the reader, viewer, or member of the audience. You will examine the visual and its relationship to any accompanying text. Then you will consider how the visual and the text interact with the cultural, political, or social context in which the image appears. The context is both immediate (the magazine, newspaper, essay, Web site, or blog in which the image appears) and more general (the cultural context of the image, the

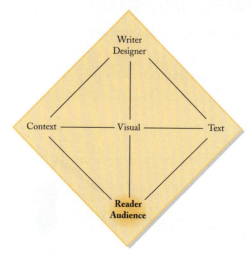

written or spoken conversation that is occurring about this image). Finally, throughout the process of analyzing, you will estimate the rhetorical effect: What is the purpose and audience for this image and its text? What appeals to logic and reason, to emotion and feelings, to reliability and character is the writer making? How effective are those appeals?

After you practice analyzing the rhetorical effect of visuals, you will be better prepared to switch roles from reader or audience to writer or designer of visuals for your own documents. In the second half of this chapter, you will practice several possible visual or design choices. You will analyze which visuals help support your purpose for your specific audience, and how effectively the visuals add to your audience appeals.

Techniques for Analyzing Visuals

As you analyze images and visuals—as well as any accompanying text or surrounding context—always consider the rhetorical situation, the purpose of the visual, and the intended audience for the visual or hybrid text. The techniques explained here help you **analyze**—that is, look at each part of the visual separately—but the ultimate goal is to **synthesize**, to put the pieces together in an explanation that shows how the parts work together (or do not work together) to achieve a rhetorical purpose for an intended audience. Your conclusion about the visual's significance or meaning becomes your **claim**. These techniques shouldn't necessarily be followed in lock-step order. If you begin by analyzing the genre of a visual, for example, you may more quickly see how the text and the visual work together. Similarly, returning to analyze the visual *after* you know more about the context can be very important.

Techniques for Analyzing Visuals	
Technique	Tips on How to Do It
Analyzing the composition of the visual itself	Describe the *layout, balance, color, key figures, symbols,* and *cultural references*. What message or messages is/are being conveyed? Based on your analysis, what is the purpose and who is the audience? What claim can you make about the significance or meaning of the visual? *Continued*

Technique	Tips on How to Do It
Analyzing the visual in combination with any accompanying text	Does the *accompanying text or caption* work to complement the meaning of the visual? How does the text add to or distract from the visual? What do the words help you notice in the visual? (What do the words distract you from noticing?) Do the words and the visual work together to achieve the same purpose for the intended audience?
Analyzing the visual and the text in context	In what magazine, essay, newspaper, or Web site does the visual appear? What does this *context* tell you about its purpose and audience? In what larger cultural, political, or social context does the visual appear? How does analyzing the visual, the accompanying text, and the larger context help you arrive at a thesis or claim?
Analyzing the genre of the visual	Visual genres include advertisements, photographs, art, graphics, posters, brochures, and charts. Compare the visual you are analyzing with other similar ones. What features do they share? How is your example different? How do those similarities/differences affect the overall meaning and purpose of the visual or its effect on the audience?
Analyzing the rhetorical appeals of a visual	What appeals to reason and logic, to emotion, or to character and credibility does the visual make? Does the writer or designer use multiple appeals (to reason and to emotion, for example)? How effective are these appeals in achieving the writer's purpose for the intended audience? How does your analysis of these appeals lead to your thesis or claim?

ANALYZING VISUALS

When we analyze stand-alone visuals and images, we need to pay particular attention to the details of composition, focus, narrative, and genre. We rely primarily on this analysis to reach conclusions about the purpose, intended audience, and effectiveness of the visual. These conclusions will become your claim or thesis for your analysis. Use the following sets of questions to guide your analysis. Depending on the particular image, of course, some questions will be more important than others.

● COMPOSITION

- Who or what is pictured in the main figure?
- How are key images arranged or organized on the page?
- What is the relationship between the main figure and the background?
- What is excluded from the main figure or background?
- When and where was the image or photograph made?
- What use of color, contrasts of light and shade, or repeated figures are present?
- How do these composition details come together to create a purpose or message for the intended audience/viewer?

● FOCAL POINT

- What point or image first draws your attention?
- Is this focal point centered or offset?
- Do background figures or diagonal lines draw your attention to or away from the focal point?
- How does the focus (or lack of focus) contribute to the purpose or message of the image?

● NARRATIVE

- What story or narrative does the image or visual suggest?
- Do certain objects or figures act as symbols or metaphors?
- How do these story elements support (or not support) the purpose or message for the intended audience?

● THEMES

- Who has the power in this visual? Who does not? Who is included or excluded?
- What sexist, racist, or body image stereotypes exist? Are these stereotypes promoted and reproduced or are they resisted or challenged? Explain.
- What is this image trying to sell? Does the image make a commodity out of social or cultural values, including holidays (Christmas or Independence Day), ideals (patriotism, charity, or religion), or personal values (integrity or status)?

Now practice applying these questions to two photographs taken by Dorothea Lange. One of America's most famous documentary photographers of migrant workers and sharecroppers, Lange took the following images during the Great Depression of the 1930s, near Berkeley, California.

In the first picture, the composition focuses on several main figures—the two women and the three children. The makeshift tarp helps to frame these figures,

and the diagonal lines from the chair and the woman on the left bring the viewer's focus to the children standing in the center and then to the mother holding her child on the right. The half-opened suitcase of clothes appears in the foreground. The background helps establish the rural, agricultural setting.

In contrast, the second picture has much a much stronger **composition**. The main figure is the woman, with her two children, looking away from the camera. The background—the tent—does not distract from this central, pyramid-like image. The children's faces are also turned away from the camera, leaving the **focal point** on the mother. The picture is in black and white, which helps focus the viewer's attention on the figures of the mother and the children. Even the angle of the mother's arm, and her chin in her hand, lead the eye to the woman's face. Her expression is determined, but without much hope. All of these compositional features support the purpose and message of the photograph: A migrant mother is caring for her family, as best as she can, in the most primitive of environments.

As viewers, we can construct our own **narrative** based on the information in the picture. This woman is caring for her children in a migrant worker environment. She has no apparent support. This shelter appears to be where she is living, both during the day and at night. She may have other family members working in the area, but we can only guess at their whereabouts.

Our own conjectural narrative is, in fact, not very different from the description that Dorothea Lange herself gives of the day when she took these photographs:

> "I saw and approached the hungry and desperate mother, as if drawn by a magnet. I do not remember how I explained my presence or my camera to her, but I do remember she asked me no questions. I made five exposures, working closer and closer from the same direction. I did not ask her name or her history. She told me her age, that she was thirty-two. She said that they had been living on frozen vegetables from the surrounding fields, and birds that the children killed. She had just sold the tires from her car to buy food. There she sat in that lean-to tent with her children huddled around her, and seemed to know that my pictures might help her, and so she helped me. There was a sort of equality about it." (*Popular Photography,* Feb., 1960)

We can put all these analytical pieces together to better understand the purpose and meaning of this photograph. For its **theme**, the photograph brings something hidden (the human story of poverty and exploitation) out into the open and gives it dignity. Lange's purpose was to call attention to the predicament of migrant workers in order to gather support for governmental reform. Her purpose was thus persuasive: she hoped to change public awareness as a first step to improving governmental assistance programs.

ANALYZING VISUALS WITH TEXT

Analyzing visuals with accompanying words or text requires considering how the composition of the image and the written text function together. Text serves to call attention to and support the message of the visual. Often, words serve as a focusing device, calling our attention to key features, guiding us to "read" the visual in a certain way. (Of course, a text that encourages us to see one meaning in the visual may keep us from seeing other possible meanings or messages in that visual.) Ideally, image and text should not just duplicate each other; they should each contribute something unique so that the combined effect is more powerful, appealing, or persuasive than either the text or the image taken separately.

In the following recruiting poster for the American Red Cross, the text is spare, simple, and direct: "Join." Notice how the composition of the picture supports this appeal. The foreground figure contrasts clearly with the less distinct background, a representation of a flood-ravaged town. And the figures in the background—a rundown house and a Red Cross nurse who is caring for children—seem to hover in the middle distance, perhaps connected, perhaps not, to the flooded town. The nurse in the foreground extends her hand to the viewer, inviting her or him to join. Thematically, women rather than men are featured in the foreground and background in this stereotypical service role. The patriotic red, white, and blue colors of the nurse's blouse and cape are repeated as a

66 There can be no words without images. 99

—ARISTOTLE,
AUTHOR OF *RHETORIC*

66 My eyes make pictures when they are shut. 99

—SAMUEL TAYLOR COLERIDGE,
AUTHOR OF *"THE RIME OF THE ANCIENT MARINER"*

motif in the red of the cross, the blue of the word *join*, and the white of the immediate foreground. The focus on the foreground figure, the color, the center focal point, and the balance of the background figures on the right and left function with the text and the implied narrative (Join the Red Cross and serve your country!) to achieve this visual's persuasive purpose.

In the next image with accompanying text, photographer Jim Goldberg effectively illustrates how visual and text should combine to create a more powerful message than either word or image alone. The photograph, taken in San Francisco in 1982, shows the lady of the house, Mrs. Stone, standing in her modern kitchen with her servant, Vickie Figueroa, standing in the background. The diagonal lines of the white counter and window to the right send us first to the figure of Mrs. Stone, and then to Ms. Figueroa in the background. This foreground/background juxtaposition sets up a power relationship, confirmed by Mrs. Stone's hands grasping (and owning) the counter while Ms. Figueroa's hands are tucked behind her. The contrast between the pointed and poignant writing and the rather conventional kitchen scene gives the visual a special, combined power. The language in Ms. Figueroa's note supports the power relationship of the image: "I am used to standing behind Mrs. Stone." Finally, Goldberg's choice to present the text in what is apparently Ms. Figueroa's own handwriting, complete with crossed out letters, uneven lines, and signature,

My dream was to became a shool teacher.
Mrs Stone is rich.
I have talents but not opportunity.
I ~~teno~~ am used to standing behind
Mrs Stone.
  I have been a servant for 40 years.
        Vickie Figueroa.

Jim Goldberg, USA, San Francisco, 1982

gives her lost dream of becoming a school teacher remarkable power. If Goldberg had simply put her note in typeface, much of the authenticity and power of the visual would be lost.

ANALYZING VISUALS IN CONTEXT

Often, the key to analyzing a visual lies in understanding and explaining the context of the image. The context is the publication or medium in which the image appeared, but taken more widely, the context is the surrounding political, social, and cultural context of the times. The following image of Michael J. Fox does not, in itself, appear to be unusual. But this still photograph actually represents a frame in a video in which Fox is speaking in support of a political candidate who supports stem cell research. On the video, Fox shows visible tremors, a symptom of his battle with Parkinson's disease. As a result of the controversy created by Rush Limbaugh's criticism of the video—followed by Limbaugh's apology—this image became a focal point in a larger cultural and political battle over governmental support for stem cell research.

In the following short commentary in *Newsweek*, one of hundreds of articles and editorials appearing in the media at the time, Jonathan Alter explains how the video image impacted the political debate on stem cell research.

Progress or Not

Jonathan Alter

Oct. 25, 2006—"The ad was in extremely poor taste," said a spokesman for Michael Steele, Republican candidate for the Senate in Maryland, referring to a TV spot made for his opponent, Rep. Ben Cardin.

That will be the line of Republicans under assault from what could become one of the most powerful political advertisements ever made. The new ad features an ailing Michael J. Fox talking about politicians who oppose embryonic stem-cell research. This is not just another celebrity ad, like those cut by the late Christopher Reeve. It's a celebrity shot to the solar plexus of the GOP. Whatever happens in the campaign, the ad is already a classic and will be mentioned in the same breath as LBJ's famous 1964 "Daisy" ad and other unforgettable political moments on television.

Rush Limbaugh helped cement the ad's place in history with his astonishingly insensitive remark that Fox "was either off his medication or was acting." Limbaugh quickly apologized but the damage to his own reputation was already done.

Fox, star of megahit TV shows and movies like "Family Ties" and *Back to the Future,* was for years one of the most popular actors in the United States. He still works, but is clearly debilitated by Parkinson's. Throughout the ad, he sways back and forth, showing signs of advanced disease.

In the version cut for Democrat Claire McCaskill, who is running against Sen. Jim Talent in Missouri, the actor, wearing a blue blazer and open-collared shirt, says, "Senator Talent even wanted to criminalize the science that gives us a chance for hope." This is in apparent reference to Talent's early support for Sen. Sam Brownback's view that embryonic stem-cell research should be illegal. Then comes the clincher: "They say all politics is local, but it's not always the case. What you do in Missouri matters to millions of Americans—Americans like me."

Sometimes, the accompanying text for a visual carries a message that in the larger social context creates controversy and anger. Consider the following two photographs showing people wading through the floodwaters in New Orleans following hurricane Katrina in 2005. The first, taken by Associated Press photographer Dave Martin, has a caption stating that the young man, an African American, was "looting a grocery store." The second, taken by photographer

Chris Graythen for Getty Images, has a caption stating that two white residents are wading through the floodwaters after "finding bread and soda from a local grocery store." Several Internet sites and bloggers picked up these photographs and highlighted the key words with a red box in order to illustrate racial bias in media coverage of Hurricane Katrina.

The controversy created by these images was reported one week later by Tania Ralli in a *New York Times* article titled "Who's a Looter?" Read her account of the circumstances surrounding this media event. When you finish reading her article, you may want to Google the photographers, Dave Martin and Chris Graythen, to read more about their accounts of the events and the story surrounding their photographs. This controversy shows the dramatic power of images, but it also emphasizes the power of our reading or interpretation of these images. A picture may be worth a thousand words, but sometimes a single word is more powerful than a dramatic picture.

> 66 In any hypertext, the text originates in an interaction that neither the author nor the reader can completely predict or control. 99
>
> —JAY DAVID BOULTER, "LITERATURE IN THE ELECTRONIC WRITING SPACE"

A young man walks through chest deep flood water after looting a grocery store in New Orleans on Tuesday, Aug. 30, 2005. Flood waters continue to rise in New Orleans after Hurricane Katrina did extensive damage. Associated Press

Two residents wade through chest-deep water after finding bread and soda from a local grocery store after Hurricane Katrina came through the area in New Orleans, Louisiana. (AFP/Getty Images/Chris Graythen) AFP/Getty Images Tue Aug 30, 3:47 AM ET

Who's a Looter?

Tania Ralli

Two news photographs ricocheted through the Internet last week and set off a debate about race and the news media in the aftermath of Hurricane Katrina.

The first photo, taken by Dave Martin, an Associated Press photographer in New Orleans, shows a young black man wading through water that has risen to his chest. He is clutching a case of soda and pulling a floating bag. The caption provided by The A.P. says he has just been "looting a grocery store."

The second photo, also from New Orleans, was taken by Chris Graythen for Getty Images and distributed by Agence France-Presse. It shows a white couple up to their chests in the same murky water. The woman is holding some bags of food. This caption says they are shown "after finding bread and soda from a local grocery store."

Both photos turned up Tuesday on Yahoo News, which posts automatic feeds of articles and photos from wire services. Soon after, a user of the photo-sharing site Flickr juxtaposed the images and captions on a single page, which attracted links from many blogs. The left-leaning blog Daily Kos linked to the page with the comment, "It's not looting if you're white."

The contrast of the two photo captions, which to many indicated a double standard at work, generated widespread anger toward the news media that quickly spread beyond the Web.

On Friday night, the rapper Kanye West ignored the teleprompter during NBC's live broadcast of "A Concert for Hurricane Relief," using the opportunity to lambast President Bush and criticize the press. "I hate the way they portray us in the media," he said. "You see a black family, it says they're looting. You see a white family, it says they're looking for food."

Many bloggers were quick to point out that the photos came from two different agencies, and so could not reflect the prejudice of a single media outlet. A writer on the blog BoingBoing wrote: "Perhaps there's more factual substantiation behind each copywriter's choice of words than we know. But to some, the difference in tone suggests racial bias, implicit or otherwise."

According to the agencies, each photographer captioned his own photograph. Jack Stokes, a spokesman for The A.P., said that photographers are told to describe what they have seen when they write a caption.

Mr. Stokes said The A.P. had guidelines in place before Hurricane Katrina struck to distinguish between "looting" and "carrying." If a photographer sees a person enter a business and emerge with goods, it is described as looting. Otherwise The A.P. calls it carrying.

Mr. Stokes said that Mr. Martin had seen the man in his photograph wade into a grocery store and come out with the sodas and bag, so by A.P.'s definition, the man had looted.

The photographer for Getty Images, Mr. Graythen, said in an e-mail message that he had also stuck to what he had seen to write his caption, and had actually given the wording a great deal of thought. Mr. Graythen described seeing the couple near a corner store from an elevated expressway. The door to the shop was open, and things had floated out to the street. He was not able to talk to the couple, "so I had to draw my own conclusions," he said.

In the extreme conditions of New Orleans, Mr. Graythen said, taking necessities like food and water to survive could not be considered stealing. He said that had he seen people coming out of stores with computers and DVD players, he would have considered that looting.

"If you're taking something that runs solely from a wall outlet that requires power from the electric company—when we are not going to have power for weeks, even months—that's inexcusable," he said.

Since the photo was published last Tuesday Mr. Graythen has received more than 500 e-mail messages, most of them supportive, he said.

Within three hours of the photo's publication online, editors at Agence France-Presse rewrote Mr. Graythen's caption. But the original caption remained online as part of a Yahoo News slide show. Under pressure to keep up with the news, and lacking the time for a discussion about word choice, Olivier Calas, the agency's director of multimedia, asked Yahoo! to remove the photo last Thursday.

Now, in its place, when readers seek the picture of the couple, a statement from Neil Budde, the general manager of Yahoo! News, appears in its place. The statement emphasizes that Yahoo! News did not write the photo captions and that it did not edit the captions, so that the photos can be made available as quickly as possible.

Mr. Calas said Agence France-Presse was bombarded with e-mail messages complaining about the caption. He said the caption was unclear and should have been reworded earlier. "This was a consequence of a series of negligences, not ill intent," he said.

For Mr. Graythen, whose parents and grandparents lost their homes in the disaster, the fate of the survivors was the most important thing. In his e-mail message he wrote: "Now is no time to pass judgment on those trying to stay alive. Now is no time to argue semantics about finding versus looting. Now is no time to argue if this is a white versus black issue."

ANALYZING THE GENRE OF THE VISUAL

Visuals, like other texts, are of certain kinds or types that we call *genres*. Common visual genres are advertisements, works of art, photographs, charts, and other kinds of graphics. We can learn more about the purpose, audience, and context by understanding how a visual that we are analyzing is similar to (and different from) other visuals belonging to its genre. The World War II posters on the next

Rosie the Riveter

"She's a WOW"

"Patriotism Means Silence"

page, for example, illustrate a visual genre from the 1940s. The purpose of these posters was to recruit men and women to the war effort. The posters featured here were intended to appeal to women to help with war-related tasks or even to join the Women's Army Corps.

The first poster is possibly the most famous example of this genre: Rosie the Riveter. The focus is on Rosie's strong right arm, with her sleeves rolled up, ready for work. The strong diagonal of her arm points back to Rosie's face and to the text at the top of the poster. The purpose of this poster was to encourage women to participate in the war effort, both by direct exhortation ("We Can Do It!") and by offering an image of an attractive, capable, and courageous woman. The Rosie the Riveter poster helped revolutionize gender images during the war.

The second poster, "She's a WOW," presents a similarly strong image designed to recruit women for ordnance work. Like Rosie, she is capable, attractive, and ready for work, with her hair wrapped in a red and white bandana. Although she is in the foreground against the background image of the soldier, the text keeps her in a supportive role: "The Girl He Left Behind Is Still Behind Him." She is not looking out at the viewer, as Rosie is, but back at the soldier. Still, her color image, accented in red and white, is larger than the soldier's background picture.

The war poster genre continues in contemporary satiric posters questioning our Homeland Security laws. The poster on the left suggests that patriotism requires being silent and refraining from speaking out against these laws or against other government policies. It uses a popular and patriotic image to imply that the Homeland Security Office is trying to silence freedom of speech.

We understand this message partly from the words and partly from the genre of the patriotic wartime poster.

RHETORICAL APPEALS TO THE AUDIENCE

All of the features of visuals analyzed earlier—the composition of the visual, the accompanying text, the context, and the genre—contribute to the overall rhetorical purpose and the effect on its audience or viewer. Visuals, like written texts, also make specific rhetorical appeals to reason and logic (logos), to emotion (pathos), and to character and credibility (ethos).

● **APPEAL TO REASON**   Usually charts, graphs, and diagrams contain appeals to reason, logic, facts, and other kinds of data. The following visual diagram, which accompanied a newspaper story about alternative sources of energy, illustrates the appeal to reason (*logos*). Using a sequence of logical steps, it explains in text and in image how wind could be used to generate hydrogen to power electric grids as well as automobiles. Its purpose is apparently to inform or explain, but because the information for the graphic is provided by an energy company, its more subtle purpose is to improve public relations by persuading customers that Xcel Energy is doing its part in the search for alternative energies.

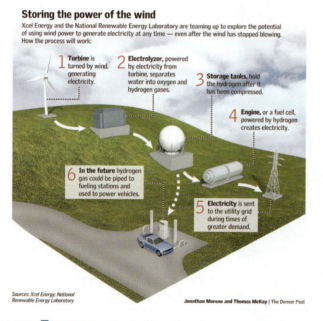

Storing the power of the wind
Xcel Energy and the National Renewable Energy Laboratory are teaming up to explore the potential of using wind power to generate electricity at any time — even after the wind has stopped blowing. How the process will work:

1 **Turbine** is turned by wind, generating electricity.

2 **Electrolyzer,** powered by electricity from turbine, separates water into oxygen and hydrogen gases.

3 **Storage tanks,** hold the hydrogen after it has been compressed.

4 **Engine,** or a fuel cell, powered by hydrogen creates electricity.

6 **In the future** hydrogen gas could be piped to fueling stations and used to power vehicles.

5 **Electricity** is sent to the utility grid during times of greater demand.

Sources: Xcel Energy, National Renewable Energy Laboratory

Jonathan Moreno and Thomas McKay | The Denver Post

● **APPEAL TO EMOTION**   Typically, advertisements use strong appeals to emotion (*pathos*), simply because emotions are so effective in persuading viewers to buy a product. Emotional appeals include positive feelings (beauty, sex, status, image, and sometimes even humor) as well as negative emotions (fear, anxiety, insecurity, and pity). These appeals come from the composition of the image, the text, the context, and even the genre of the visual. Magazines are a good source for advertisements relying primarily on emotional appeals.

● **APPEAL TO CHARACTER AND CREDIBILITY**   Often visuals use a strong appeal to character and credibility (*ethos*) to convince, move, or persuade viewers. This appeal is not to the character of any person pictured in the visual, but to the character and credibility of the designer or creator of the image. If viewers sense that the visual conveys a sense of integrity and authenticity, that the maker of the image is sincere and is not relying on cheap emotional appeals, or that the visual communicates a sense of humanity and goodwill, the appeal to character is successful. Look again at Dorothea Lange's images of a migrant mother on page 176. These pictures have an emotional appeal, to be sure, but they are composed with an integrity and credibility that give them a strong character appeal, too. Lange's pictures give the mother and her children dignity at the same time that they call attention to their plight.

● **COMBINED APPEALS IN AN AD**   Often visuals and their texts will combine appeals to logic, emotion, and character. Consider the following spoof-ad posted on Adbusters of the popular ads for Absolut, a brand of vodka. Emotional appeals

Adbusters

emerge from the blood-colored reds and dramatic blacks, the long shadows and spilt liquids, the white chalk outline of the body (the bottle), the police officer taking notes, and the red taillights of the car. The bold caption, "Absolute End," (notice how the spelling has been changed from *Absolut* to *Absolute*) and the statistics cited below the picture appeal to logic, connecting the 100,000 alcohol ads teenagers see with the fact that 50% of automobile fatalities are linked to alcohol. This visual also generates an ethos or character appeal because the creator of the ad is apparently someone we can trust, someone of good character whose goal is to prevent the needless and tragic fatalities associated with drinking and driving.

As you practice analysis of a variety of visuals, remember three important points. First, not all types of analysis will be important for a particular visual or hybrid text. Focus on the kinds of analysis that work best for your project. Second, techniques for analysis should be repeated or combined until you discover the key features of the visual. Start with the visual, work through accompanying text, consider the context and the genre, and analyze the rhetorical appeals, but come back to the visual after you know more about the context and have thought about appeals. Third, remember that the ultimate goal of your analysis will be **synthesis**. You examine the parts and pieces of a multimedia text in order to support your synthesis of these parts into a meaningful whole. Your explanation of the meaning and significance of the visual or the rhetorical purpose and effectiveness of the visual in its context becomes your thesis or **claim**.

Techniques for Designing Visuals

When you practiced analyzing visuals, you were the reader or audience in the diagram shown here, judging the visual with its accompanying text, in its context, and considering how the creator of the image worked to achieve a particular purpose for the intended audience.

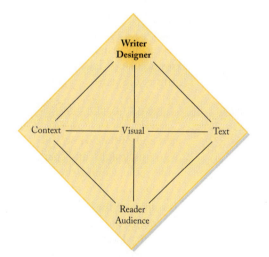

   Now you need to switch roles. After you have practiced analyzing a variety of visuals for their overall rhetorical effect, you are better prepared to add or design visuals for your own essay, article, pamphlet, or Web site. As the primary designer or creator, you will likely be using visuals and diagrams, but you should also consider the layout of your text as a visual element: typeface, size of font, margins, color, and use of white space all have visual appeal for your readers.
   Visuals, illustrations, graphics, photographs, and document design are all elements of your writing that have a rhetorical effect. Use the following techniques as you consider visuals and text layout possibilities for your essay, article, brochure, or other document.

> 66 Effective visual presentation . . . [requires] minimizing the possibility of competition between picture and text and ensuring that the pictures used are relevant to the material presented. 99
> —JENNIFER WILEY,
> "COGNITIVE AND EDUCATIONAL IMPLICATIONS OF VISUAL RICH MEDIA"

Techniques for Designing Visuals

Technique	Tips on How to Do It
Designing for your audience and purpose	Your *purpose* and *audience* should guide your selection of an appropriate genre, the most effective visual(s), and a clear document design. *Example:* The image taken by Jim Goldberg on page 153 places Vickie Figueroa in the background in order to support his purpose, that Vickie's dreams are subordinate to Mrs. Stone's power.
Choosing and understanding your genre	Collect and study several *examples of your genre,* whether it is an article, brochure, poster, or Web site. Does your genre use many visuals and only a few words? Does it use mostly text with a few visuals or diagrams? Take notes on the layout typically used, and then choose the best features and creatively modify them for your own purposes. *Examples:* Examine more posters like "Rosie the Riveter" by searching Google Images for World War II posters. Take notes on the common features of the genre.
Selecting or designing visuals for your document	Choose or design visual elements with *strong compositional features:* key figures, strong diagonals, appropriate color, and balance. Make your diagrams, graphs, and charts clear and easy to understand. Choose the most striking illustrations but use them sparingly. Avoid clutter. *Examples:* In the World War II posters on page 158, notice the strong central figures, bright colors (red, white, blue, yellow), strong diagonals, and large, bold font. Look again at the "Absolute End" visual on page 160 or the American Red Cross image on page 152 for examples of strong compositional features.
Designing your written text to support your purpose	Choose *typeface, font, white space,* and *margins* with an eye to your purpose and audience. Balance chunks of text with visuals on the page. Use bold type and white space to create emphasis. Make your visuals or illustrations compatible with your text. *Examples:* The World War II posters and the American Red Cross poster are excellent examples of bold type and effective use of white space.

WARMING UP   Journal Exercises

The following exercises will help you practice analyzing and designing visuals. Respond to these exercises individually, in groups, or on your class Web site.

1 Go to the Web site of a newspaper or news organization. Choose a section that you like to read, such as world news, business, sports, fashion, dining, home and garden, books, movies, or music. Find an interesting article and see what visuals or graphics accompany the article. Copy the article into a Word file. Then design an additional graph or select an additional or alternative image that would be appropriate for that article. Practice designing a simple bar graph or pie graph if the article has statistics. For alternative visuals, search Google Images for appropriate art or photos. After you have designed your graph or selected your image, explain why your choice or design fits the subject, purpose, and audience of the original article.

2 In a visual that contains text or a caption, the image and the words should complement each other, working toward a single meaning. *The New Yorker* regularly sponsors a cartoon caption contest. Drawings are initially published without captions, and readers are invited to contribute their

"Well, then, it's unanimous." Anne Whiteside, San Francisco, Calif. (The winning caption.)

"So that settles it. This year, instead of cooking the books, we'll bake them in a light, flaky pastry." Michael Hirson, Washington, D.C.

"Who else found Gary's report a little too angry, white, and male?" Grant Ruple, Morristown, N.J.

World War II Kiss

Gordon Parks, *American Gothic*

best lines during the next two weeks. Study the cartoon on page 163. By yourself or in a group, suggest possible captions. Once you have a caption or two, explain why your entry complements the drawing. (Below the cartoon are the three finalist suggestions, printed upside down. Don't read them until you've made your own suggestions.)

3 Analyze the spoof-ad that appears on the opening page of this chapter. First, examine the visual for composition, focus, narrative, theme, and rhetorical appeals. After you have written your analysis, search the Internet and your library databases for a short, full-text news article, report, editorial, or op-ed column that discusses the dietary or health problems associated with fast foods. Download a full-text version of this article into a Word file, and then download and insert this image in an appropriate place in that article. Write a paragraph explaining why this McDonald's spoof-ad is (or perhaps is not) appropriate to the purpose and audience of that article.

4 Study the two famous photographs presented on this page. Choose one and write your own analysis of that image. First, analyze the image. Then write a narrative of what you imagine happened before, during, and after the moment recorded in this image. Finally, *research* these two photographs and their photographers on the internet and add a final paragraph explaining how the information you discovered confirms or revises your analysis and your narrative.

⑤ Find three advertisements that advertise the same product (or same kind of product, such as cars, jeans, or perfume) in different magazines directed at different audiences. For example, you might find similar ads in *Time, Wired,* and *Seventeen.* Analyze each ad for its compositional features, and then describe how the ad changes in its composition, focus, narrative, theme, or appeals based on different target audiences. Which of these ads is most effective for its target audience? Why?

⑥ Choose an essay that you have already written for this course or for a previous writing course. Revise and format it on your computer for a more public audience, choosing the genre of a short newspaper article, brochure, flyer, or poster. Practice using the layout features (sidebars, inserted visuals, double columns, pulled quotations, drop caps, tables, and color) appropriate for that genre. As a postscript for your revision, explain why you made the choices you did during your revision.

⑦ Analyze the following cartoon, which appeared in *The New Yorker.* What are the main compositional features? Is this cartoon humorous, serious, or both? If you were looking for a visual to use in an article about possible cell phone legislation, would this image be effective? Research your library's databases for recent newspaper articles or editorials about cell phone use and abuse. Find a short article or editorial, copy it into your computer Word file, and insert this image at an appropriate place. Then write a paragraph explaining why this

"I was distracted for a moment. Go on."

THERE'S ANOTHER LANGUAGE INSIDE YOU. GIVE IT A VOICE.

Do you want to communicate a new voice to the world, to express another side of you? With Rosetta Stone® you can. In any language.

- We teach language naturally, pairing words spoken by native speakers with vivid, real-life imagery in context, activating your mind's inherent ability to learn a language.
- Speech recognition coaches you to the right pronunciation, so you'll be speaking quickly and correctly. In no time at all, you'll find that the new language you tried on is a perfect fit.

Rosetta Stone. The fastest way to learn a language. Guaranteed.

Over 30 languages available.

SAVE 10%

Level 1	$233
Level 1&2	$377
Level 1,2&3	$494

100% six-month money-back guarantee.

PICK UP A NEW LANGUAGE TODAY!
(866) 833-8301 RosettaStone.com/sas029a
Use promo code sas029a when ordering. Offer expires June 30, 2009.

RosettaStone

The woman in this advertisement appears to be a successful and affluent professional based upon her attire. Many of the members of the audience for this publication are likely to be part of this elite class, since 82% of readers have a college degree. There is also an intellectual appeal in the picture: this woman is seeking to broaden her horizons even though she is already successful. Since 51% of readers for *Scientific American Mind* are women, a large number of audience members may be able to identify with her or aspire to her status and success.

The Rosetta Stone program is relatively expensive and must therefore seek to target an affluent audience. *Scientific American Mind* is a good publication to appeal to this audience because the average household income is $119,000, and average household net worth is $827,000.

The bright yellow of the Rosetta Stone logo also frames the picture and serves as a backdrop for the saying "There's another language inside you. Give it a voice." This effectively unifies the elements of the advertisement. The bright yellow is an active appeal to initiative, which is likely to draw the attention of this magazine's audience. *Scientific American Mind*'s web site says in its mission statement that it is "aimed at inquisitive adults who are passionate about knowing more about how the mind works." These same individuals who want to know more about the mind are likely to be interested in learning about other cultures and languages.

Analysis of Rosetta Stone ad by Sarah Kay Hurst

image complements the message of the article. On Google Images, find another image about cell phone use that would be effective for your article or editorial. Which of the two images (the cartoon shown here or the visual you found) would be more effective? Explain.

8. Choose an advertisement in a magazine and analyze it for how it works in the context of that particular magazine. First, research the magazine to profile its readers (typical income, class, occupations, or interests). Then examine several advertisements from this magazine to see which ads make the most effective appeals to this group of readers. Choose one particular ad and annotate it for appeals to audience as well as use of key images, color, graphics, balance, layout, diagonals, and accompanying text. Use the analysis of a Rosetta Stone advertisement in *Scientific American Mind* by student writer Sarah Kay Hurst as an example (see page 166).

Processes for Analyzing and Designing Visuals

ASSIGNMENT FOR ANALYZING VISUALS

Choose an audience and genre and analyze the effectiveness of a visual by itself or a visual with accompanying text and/or social context. For example, you might analyze an advertising campaign, political document with photographs, prize-winning or historical photograph, fine art, Internet visual, or other scientific, cultural, or social text that uses images and visuals.

Your purpose for this assignment is to analyze the visual for its composition, focus, narrative, themes, and/or rhetorical appeals in order to show how—and how effectively—it works with any accompanying text in its social context for the intended purpose and audience.

Audience	Possible Genres for Analyzing Visuals
Personal Audience	Class notes, journal entry, blog, scrapbook, social networking page.
Academic Audience	Academic analysis, media critique, review, journal entry, forum entry on class site, multi-genre document.
Public Audience	Column, editorial, article, or critique in a magazine, newspaper, online site, newsletter, or multi-genre document.

ASSIGNMENT FOR DESIGNING VISUALS

Choose a piece of writing that you are currently working on or have already written for this class or another class you are taking. Your assignment is to add visual elements (pictures, art, charts, graphic material) to your writing that will help illustrate the subject for your particular audience. Start by explaining the audience, purpose, genre, and context for this particular piece of writing. Then look for opportunities to provide visual elements that will help achieve your purpose for your audience. Select or design the visuals you will be using and insert them into your document. When you finish this assignment, write a postscript explaining the process you went through of selecting, designing, and integrating the material into your piece of writing. Illustrate your choices by referring to graphs or visuals that you decided **not** to use because they were not effective or appropriate for your audience or purpose.

Audience	Possible Visual Genres
Personal Audience	Photographs, art, digitized scrapbook images, collage, video, comics.
Academic Audience	Graphs, charts, diagrams, flow charts, organizational diagrams, photographs, digital images, art, video.
Public Audience	Graphs, charts, diagrams, flow charts, organizational diagrams, photographs, digital images, art, comics, graphic novel, video.

CHOOSING A SUBJECT

Unless you have a particular assignment, choose a contemporary image that you find incorporated in your reading for your other classes, reading and research that you do for your job, news items, Internet sites, billboards, or any other place where visuals appear in a clear rhetorical context. Video clips from the Internet can work if they are short and if you are submitting your document online or in a digital environment. You may wish to choose a visual and compare it to other examples from that genre. You may wish to consider several similar images used for different gender, racial, or cultural contexts. Your assignment may even be to analyze a variety of possible visuals you could choose for an essay you are writing and to show why the ones you select are best suited to your purpose, audience, and genre. *Remember that when you download images from the Internet, you must give credit to the photographer, artist, or designer of the visual.*

COLLECTING

Many images are available on the Internet through Google or Yahoo! searches, or on popular image sites such as Corbis. Once you locate several appropriate visuals, begin by analyzing and taking notes on them, looking for key parts of the composition, focus, narrative, themes, and rhetorical appeals. However, you should also collect and analyze any accompanying texts or evidence that illustrates the social or historical context. Collecting visuals belonging to the same genre (historical photographs, advertising campaigns, political photographs, or Internet images) will also provide evidence helpful for your analysis. Researching the background, context, origin, or maker/designer of the image can be important, as is finding other commentaries and analyses of your particular type or genre of visuals. Use your *critical reading skills* to understand key points in these commentaries. Be sure to use your *observing* skills to help your analysis. Try closing your eyes and drawing the visual for yourself—what details did you remember and reproduce and what details did you forget? If you have any particular *memories* of this image or of the first time you saw this visual, you may want to add those to your account.

SHAPING

How you organize your analysis depends on the assignment, purpose, audience, and genre for your analysis. Three effective strategies for organizing are explained and illustrated here.

● **ANALYSIS FOCUSED ON THE VISUAL**   Often the specific details of the visual are the primary focus of the analysis. This is often the case with detailed or complex images whose meaning or significance may not be immediately obvious. The analysis focuses on composition, arrangement, focus, foreground and background images, images in the center and on the margin, symbols, cultural references, and key features of the genre. Only after analyzing these details will the commentary explain how these details are related to the cultural or historical context and thus contribute to the overall meaning.

The following analysis, by Charles Rosen and Henri Zerner, appeared in the *New York Review of Books*, and is of a painting by Norman Rockwell that appeared on the cover of *The Saturday Evening Post* in 1960. The authors devote over half of their essay to an analysis of the picture before they interpret the significance of Rockwell's self-portrait. Before you read Rosen's and Zerner's analysis, however, study the painting presented on page 169. What are the important details in the picture? What is the overall meaning or significance, based on your analysis?

Triple Self-Portrait
Charles Rosen and Henri Zerner

Claim: The portrait is a clever and witty comment on his own art.

Triple Self-Portrait of 1960 is clever and witty. It is not simply a portrait of the artist by himself but represents the process of painting a self-portrait, and in the bargain Rockwell takes the opportunity to comment on his brand of "realism" and his relation to the history of art. A sheet of preparatory drawings in different poses is tacked onto the left of the canvas. The artist represents himself from the back; the canvas he works on already has a fully worked-out black-and-white drawing of his face with the pipe in his mouth, based on the central drawing of the sketch sheet. The artist gazes at his own reflection in a mirror propped up on a chair. The reflection we see in the mirror is similar to, but not identical with, the portrait sketched on the canvas. The artist wears glasses, and the glare of the lenses completely obliterates his gaze, while the portrait he works on is without glasses and a little younger-looking, certainly less tense than the reflection. Rockwell seems to confess that the reality of his depicted world, compelling as it may be, is in fact a make-believe.

Layout and composition of portrait

Description of details

More description of details

Tacked on the upper right corner of the canvas is a series of reproductions of historical self-portraits: Dürer, Rembrandt, Van Gogh, and Picasso—grand company to measure oneself against, although the humorous tone of the image preserves it from megalomania. But there is a problem: "If Rockwell nodded humbly in Picasso's direction," as Robert Rosenblum suggests, how humbly was it? It is "most surprising," Rosenblum observes, that Rockwell chose "a particularly difficult Picasso that mixes in idealized self-portrait in profile with an id-like female monster attacking from within" rather than something easily recognizable. This was a cover for *The Saturday Evening Post*. The strength of Rockwell is that he knew his public, and knew that such subtleties would be entirely lost on its readers, that most of them would not recognize the Picasso as a self-portrait at all but would consider it as pretentious humbug compared to Rockwell's honest picture and those of the illustrious predecessors he claims. Nor does he seem to have been particularly anxious to change their minds, whatever he himself may have thought.

Interpreting the meaning and significance of the painting

● **ANALYSIS FOCUSED ON THE SOCIAL CONTEXT**   Often the visual or image is not detailed or complex, but the social, political, or historical context is complex, involved, or highly controversial. The following analysis, "Out of the Picture on the Abortion Ban," by Ellen Goodman, appeared in the *Boston Globe*. In this case, the photograph is not particularly complex or difficult, but it reveals much about the political and social context. The photograph is described at the beginning and then referred to at the end, providing a framework for Goodman's comment about the abortion debate.

Out of the Picture on the Abortion Ban
Ellen Goodman

Maybe this picture isn't worth a thousand words. That honor probably belongs to the flight deck portrait of the president under the sign, "Mission Accomplished." Maybe the presidential photo op now flying around the Internet and soon to be available on your local T-shirt is only worth 750 words.

Early reference to another frequently appearing photograph

The picture shows the president surrounded by an all-male chorus line of legislators as he signs the first ban on an abortion procedure. It's a single-sex class photo of men making laws governing something they will never have: a womb.

Short description and analysis of the photograph

This was not just a strategic misstep, a rare Karl Rove lapse. It perfectly reflected the truth of the so-called partial-birth abortion law. What's wrong with this picture? The legislators had indeed erased women. They used the law as if it were Photoshop software, to crop out real women with real problems.

Indeed, just days after the shutter snapped, three separate courts ordered a temporary halt to the ban on these very grounds: It doesn't have any exemption for the health of a woman.

*Analysis: What is missing from the photograph
Analysis: How the photograph connects to abortion*

This is what brings me back, kicking and screaming, to the subject of abortion. I don't want to write about this. Like most Americans, I want the abortion debate to end. I want abortion to be safe and rare. That's safe and rare. And early.

Over the years, I've rejoiced at sonograms and picked names for what we call a baby when it's wanted and a fetus when it isn't. I'm aware that medicine has put the moment of viability on a collision course with the moment of legal abortion. And I am also aware that not every pregnancy goes well, that sometimes families face terrible, traumatic choices.

Social and political contexts

Sixty-eight percent of Americans have been convinced by a public relations coup that this new law bans only a fringe and outrageous procedure. But the refusal to include an exception for the health of a pregnant woman takes this from the fringe to the heart of the debate. It's a deliberate, willful first strike at some of the most vulnerable women, those who need medical help the most.

The moment the anti-abortion leaders invented the term "partial-birth abortion," they made women invisible. The cartoon figures shown at congressional debates were, literally, drawings of a headless womb holding a perfect Gerber baby of some six or more months.

Social and political contexts

As Priscilla Smith, legal director of the Center for Reproductive Rights, said, "they turned the argument from the right of a woman to have an abortion to the reasons women have abortions." And then they declared those reasons to be frivolous.

The headless womb belonged to a generic woman who, as one opponent said, would get an abortion to fit into a prom dress. She would carry a pregnancy for months and then casually flip a coin between birth and an abortion "inches from life."

Reference to the abortion ban being signed in the photograph

Time and again, abortion-rights supporters said they too would vote for the ban if opponents recognized that some pregnancies go terribly awry for the fetus or the woman and that some doctors found this procedure safest. But anti-abortion forces simply declared—against the evidence of the AMA or the American College of Obstetrics and Gynecology—that it was never medically necessary.

Some years ago, when President Clinton vetoed a similar bill, he was surrounded by women. These women had been through pregnancies that came with words like hydrocephalus and polyhydramnia, and came with risks like hysterectomies. But the men around Bush see a health exception as a giant loophole. They believe a woman would leap through this loophole to get to the prom.

Reminder that another president had not signed a similar bill

Behind this is simply a mistrust of women as moral decision-makers. A mistrust so profound that their health is now in the hands of the courts. Not long ago, the Supreme Court ruled by exactly one vote that a law similar to this one violated the Constitution.

This should be a wake-up call to young women, because it's their health at risk, their role as moral decision-makers disparaged.

The most reliable supporters of abortion rights today are women over 50. It is, ironically, post-menopausal women who still lead the struggle to keep abortion legal for younger women. Everyone will tell you that the younger generation simply doesn't remember a time when abortion was illegal. They can't believe that it will ever be illegal again. How many believe they could be among those who need it?

Days before signing this ban, the president tried to reassure voters that it wasn't the time to "totally ban abortions." But young women should put this picture up on their desktops. The folks in that photo op don't trust you. They don't even see you.

Final reference to the omission of women in the photograph and in the making of laws directly affecting women

• **ANALYSIS FOCUSED ON THE STORY** In this organizational pattern, the visual or photograph receives some analysis and commentary, but most of the analysis is of the history of the photograph and the life story of the key figures in the photograph. A narrative or story can often be very effective as a means of understanding the significance or true meaning behind a picture. The following example, "Coming Home," by Carolyn Kleiner Butler, was published in *Smithsonian* in 2003. Her article appeared at a time when many families in the United States had loved ones serving in Iraq or Afghanistan. Butler chooses to analyze a famous Vietnam era photograph by Sal Veder, which he titled *Burst of Joy* and which won a Pulitzer Prize in 1974. Usually an analysis of an image focuses on what the image reveals and what it represents. In this case, however, Butler emphasizes how the reality behind the photograph contrasts sharply with the reality in the photograph. In other words, Butler contrasts the happy story of what the image reveals with the reality that it conceals.

Coming Home

Carolyn Kleiner Butler

To a war-weary nation, a U.S. POW's return from captivity in Vietnam in 1973 looked like the happiest of reunions.

SITTING IN THE BACK SEAT of a station wagon on the tarmac at Travis Air Force Base, in California, clad in her favorite fuchsia miniskirt,

The story just before the photograph was taken

15-year-old Lorrie Stirm felt that she was in a dream. It was March 17, 1973, and it had been six long years since she had last seen her father, Lt. Col. Robert L. Stirm, an Air Force fighter pilot who was shot down over Hanoi in 1967 and had been missing or imprisoned ever since. She simply couldn't believe they were about to be reunited. The teenager waited while her father stood in front of a jubilant crowd and made a brief speech on behalf of himself and other POW's who had arrived from Vietnam as part of "Operation Homecoming."

Lorrie's memories of her feelings when her dad returned

The minutes crept by like hours, she recalls, and then, all at once, the car door opened. "I just wanted to get to Dad as fast as I could," Lorrie says. She tore down the runway toward him with open arms, her spirits—and feet—flying. Her mother, Loretta, and three younger siblings—Robert Jr., Roger and Cindy—were only steps behind. "We didn't know if he would ever come home," Lorrie says. "That moment was all our prayers answered, all our wishes come true."

Shift to the photographer's story

Associated Press photographer Slava "Sal" Veder, who'd been standing in a crowded bullpen with dozens of other journalists, noticed the sprinting family and started taking pictures. "You could feel the energy and the raw emotion in the air," says Veder, then 46, who had spent much of the Vietnam era covering antiwar demonstrations in San Francisco and Berkeley. The day was overcast, meaning no shadows and near-perfect light. He rushed to a makeshift darkroom in a ladies' bathroom on the base (United Press International had commandeered the men's).

A hero's welcome: Lorrie, Robert Jr., Cindy, Loretta and Roger Stirm greet Lt. Col. Robert Stirm after his six years as a prisoner of war.

In less than half an hour, Veder and his AP colleague Walt Zeboski had developed six remarkable images of that singular moment. Veder's pick, which he instantly titled *Burst of Joy*, was sent out over the news-service wires, published in newspapers around the nation and went on to win a Pulitzer Prize in 1974.

The photographer's recollection of the emotions of that day

It remains the quintessential homecoming photograph of the time. Stirm, 39, who had endured gunshot wounds, torture, illness, starvation and despair in North Vietnamese prison camps, including the infamous Hanoi Hilton, is pictured in a crisp new uniform. Because his back is to the camera, as Veder points out, the officer seems anonymous, an everyman who represented not only the hundreds of POW's released that spring but all the troops in Vietnam who would return home to the mothers, fathers, wives, daughters and sons they'd left behind. "It's a hero's welcome for guys who weren't always seen or treated as heroes," says Donald Goldstein, a retired Air Force lieutenant colonel and a coauthor of *The Vietnam War: The Stories and The Photographs*, of the Stirm family reunion picture. "After years of fighting a war we couldn't win, a war that tore us apart, it was finally over, and the country could start healing."

The story from the soldier's or father's point of view

But there was more to the story than was captured on film. Three days before Stirm landed at Travis, a chaplain had handed him a Dear John letter from his wife. "I can't help but feel ambivalent about it," Stirm says today of the photograph. "I was very pleased to see my children—I loved them all and still do, and I know they had a difficult time—but there was a lot to deal with." Lorrie says, "So much had happened—there was so much that my dad missed out on—and it took a while to let him back into our lives and accept his authority." Her parents were divorced within a year of his return. Her mother remarried in 1974 and lives in Texas with her husband. Robert retired from the Air Force as a colonel in 1977 and worked as a corporate pilot and businessman. He married and was divorced again. Now 72 and retired, he lives in Foster City, California.

Events behind the moment of this photograph

As for the rest of the family, Robert Jr. is a dentist in Walnut Creek, California; he and his wife have four children, the oldest of whom is a marine. Roger, a major in the Air Force, lives outside Seattle. Cindy Pierson, a waitress, resides in Walnut Creek with her husband and has a daughter in college. And Lorrie Stirm Kitching, now 47, is an executive administrator and mother of two sons. She lives in Mountain View, California, with her husband. All four of Robert Stirm Sr.'s children have a copy of *Burst of Joy* hanging in a place of honor on their walls. But he says he can't bring himself to display the picture.

How the lives of all the family members have changed

Three decades after the Stirm reunion, the scene, having appeared in countless books, anthologies and exhibitions, remains part of the nation's collective consciousness, often serving as an uplifting postscript to Vietnam. That the moment was considerably more fraught than we first assumed makes it all the more poignant and reminds us that not all war casualties occur on the battlefield.

Concluding comments leading up to Butler's thesis: Pictures do not always tell the complete story, and not all casualties occur on the battlefield.

"We have this very nice picture of a very happy moment," Lorrie says, "but every time I look at it, I remember the families that weren't reunited, and the ones that aren't being reunited today—many, many families—and I think, I'm one of the lucky ones."

DRAFTING

Before you begin drafting, collect all your notes, your visuals, and your research. Based on your materials, determine what you want the *focus* of your analysis to be—the visual itself, its relationship to any accompanying text or context, its relation to other images in its genre, or the rhetorical appeals that the visual makes. Depending on the assignment, your visuals, and your own purpose, narrow the strategies to the few that are most helpful in understanding the rhetoric of the visual.

If you are designing your own document, write out your accompanying text in a draft, and then experiment with the overall placement of text, images, and graphs. Cut out and arrange/rearrange the chunks of your text and visuals on a blank page until you find a combination of text, image, and use of white space that has the best effect for your purpose and audience.

Finally, obtain feedback or peer response to help you as you move from drafting to revising.

REVISING

As you revise your visual analysis or visual design project, consider your peer-response feedback. Some of it will be helpful, but some may not help you achieve your purpose. You must decide which changes to make.

GUIDELINES FOR REVISION

- **Review the purpose and audience for your assignment.** Does your draft analyze the key parts of the visual? If you are designing a document, give a draft to someone who is your intended audience or who might understand the needs of your intended audience. What suggestions does that person have?
- **Reexamine the visual.** What else do you notice about its composition, focus, narrative, or themes?
- **Reconsider relationships between the image and its text and context.** Much of the meaning and impact of the visual depends on the accompanying text and on the social, political, and cultural context. Look again at these possible relationships.
- **Reconsider the genre of your visual or your document.** If you are analyzing a visual, have you collected other examples of visuals in that

PEER RESPONSE

The instructions that follow will help you give and receive constructive advice about the rough draft of your visual analysis or design document. Use these guidelines for an in-class workshop, a take-home review, or an electronic class forum response.

Writer: Before you exchange drafts, write out your responses to the following questions.

1. **Purpose** Briefly describe the purpose and intended audience of your essay or document. What is the main point you are trying to communicate?
2. **Revision Plans** Point out one part of your essay that is successful at achieving your purpose. Describe the parts of your essay that do not seem to be working or are not yet completed.
3. **Questions** Write out one or two specific questions that you still have about your visual analysis or your design. Where exactly would you like help on this project?

Reader: First, read the entire draft or document from start to finish without making any comments. Then as you reread the draft, answer the following questions.

1. **Techniques for analyzing visuals** Where in the draft do you see the writer using the techniques for analyzing visuals discussed in this chapter? Which techniques should be more developed to help achieve the writer's purpose? Explain.
2. **Context** Where do you see the writer analyzing or using the social, political, or cultural context of the visuals? What other aspects of context might the writer consider?
3. **Responses to visuals** Write out your response to these visuals. What key elements of these visuals do you see that the writer does not comment on? Where would you disagree with the writer's analysis? Explain.
4. **Response to design** Analyze the writer's document design. Is it too busy, cluttered, or crowded? Does the document need more text and fewer visuals? Does it need to cut text and increase white space? What might the audience for this document say about its attractiveness, simplicity of message, or overall effectiveness?
5. **Response to the assignment** The visual analysis or document design needs to respond to the assignment. Where does this draft respond to the assignment? Where doesn't it respond to the assignment? Explain.
6. **Answer the writer's questions** Briefly respond to the writer's questions listed above.

genre? How are these examples similar to or different from your visual? If you are designing a document, have you checked other documents belonging to this genre? How does yours compare to them? How could you use their ideas to improve your document?

- **Check your visual or your document for its rhetorical appeals.** Make sure your draft comments on or makes use of appropriate rhetorical appeals to logic, to character, and to emotion. Are these appeals effective for the purpose and audience of the visual or the document?

- **Organize your analysis.** Check your draft to make sure the parts of your analysis add up to or contribute to your overall thesis or claim.

- **Revise and edit sentences to improve clarity, conciseness, and emphasis.** Check your handbook for suspected problems with usage, grammar, and punctuation. Be sure to spell check your final version.

POSTSCRIPT ON THE WRITING PROCESS

1. Describe the process you used to analyze your visual in its context or to design your own document. What did you do first? How did your research help? What advice did you get from your peers? What major change(s) did you make for your final version?

2. Write out the sentence or sentences that contain your thesis or main claim of your visual analysis. If you are designing a document, explain where you put the focus and how you related both your text and your images to that focus or main idea.

3. Explain the two or three most important things you learned about visual analysis or document design as you wrote your analysis or worked through your project.

4. What parts of your analysis or document still need revision? If you had one more day to work on the project, what changes would you make? Explain.

STUDENT WRITING

KARYN M. LEWIS

Some Don't Like Their Blues at All

Karyn Lewis decided to write an analysis of an advertisement for Fila jeans that she found in a magazine. She chose this particular advertise-ment because it created an image for the product that was based on stereotyped portrayals of gender roles. Instead of using its power to break down gender stereotypes, Fila deliberately used common stereotypes (men are strong and hard; women are weak and soft) to help sell their clothing. Lewis's analysis explains how Fila's images perpetuate the myth that men are "creatures of iron," while women are soft and "silly bits of fluff," leaving viewers of the advertisement without positive gender role models.

He strides toward us in navy and white, his body muscled and heavy-set, one 1 arm holding his casually flung jeans jacket over his shoulder. A man in his prime, with just the right combination of macho and sartorial flair.

He is also black.   2

She is curled and giggling upon a chair, her hair loose and flowing 3 around her shoulders, leaning forward innocently—the very picture of a blossoming, navy flower.

She is white.   4

They are each pictured on a magazine page of their own, situated op- 5 posite each other in a complementary two-page spread. They are stationed in front of a muted photograph which serves as a background for each one. They both merit their own captions: bold indigo letters presiding over them in the outer corners of each page.

His says: SOME LIKE THEIR BLUES HARD.   6

Hers says: SOME LIKE THEIR BLUES SOFT.   7

His background depicts a thrusting struggle between a quarterback 8 and a leaping defender, a scene of arrested violence and high tension.

Her background is a lounging, bikini-clad goddess, who looks at the 9 camera with intriguing, calm passion. She raises her hand to rest behind her head in a languid gesture as she tries to incite passion within the viewer.

At the bottom of the page blazes the proud emblem of the company 10 that came up with this ad: FILA JEANS.

This advertisement blatantly uses stereotypes of men and women to 11 sell its product. It caters to our need to fit into the roles that society has deemed right for the individual sexes ever since patriarchal rule rose up and replaced the primitive worship of a mother goddess and the reverence for women. These stereotypes handed down to us throughout the centuries spell out to us that men are violence and power incarnate, and that the manly attitude has no room for weakness or softness of nature. And we find our role model of women in the compliant and eager female who obeys her man in all things, who must not say no to a male, and who is not very bright—someone who flutters her eyelashes, giggles a lot, and uses tears to get her way.

This ad tells us, by offering the image of a hard, masculine male, who 12 is deified in violence, that he is the role model men should aspire to, and that for women, their ideal is weak but sexual, innocent and at the same time old enough to have sex. In viewing this ad, we see our aspirations clothed in Fila jeans, and to be like them, we must buy the clothes pictured here. This ad also suggests that a man can become hard and powerful (or at least look it) dressed in these jeans; a woman can become sexually intense and desirable dressed in Fila's clothing.

The words of the captions tantalize with their sexual innuendo. The 13 phrase "Some like their blues hard" hints at male sexual prowess. Most men and women in this country are obsessed with males' need to prove their virility, and Fila plays on this obsession. Females too have their own stereotype of what constitutes their sexuality. "Some like their blues soft" exemplifies this ideal: A woman should be soft and yielding. Her soft, sensuous body parts, which so excite her partners, have been transformed into her personal qualities. By using the term *soft,* Fila immediately links the girl with her sexuality and sexual organs.

We are shown by the models' postures that men and women are 14 (according to Fila) fundamentally different and total antonyms of one another. He is standing and walking with purpose; she sits, laughing trivially at the camera. Even the background hints at separation of the sexes.

The football players on the man's page are arranged in a diagonal 15 line which starts at the upper left-hand corner and runs to the opposite corner, which is the center of the ad. On her page, the enchanting nymph in the bathing suit runs on a diagonal; beginning where his ends, and traveling up to the upper right-hand corner of her page. These two photos in effect create a *V,* which both links the two models and suggests movement away from one another. Another good example of their autonomy from one another is their skin color. He is a black man, she's white. Black is the opposite color of white on an artist's color wheel and palette and symbolizes dynamically opposed forces: good and evil, night and day, man and woman. This ad hits us with the idea that men and women are not parallel in nature to one another but are fundamentally different in all things. It alienates the sexes from each other. Opposites may attract, but there is no room for understanding a nature completely alien to your own.

So in viewing this ad, and reading its captions, the consumer is left 16 with the view that a woman must be "soft" and sensual, a male's sexual dream, and must somehow still retain her innocence after having sex. She must be weak, the opposite of the violence which contrasts with her on the opposite page. The men looking at this ad read the message that they are supposed to be well-dressed and powerful and possess a strength that borders on violence. As we are told by the caption, men should be "hard." Furthermore, men and women are opposite creatures, as different as two sides of a coin.

This ad is supposed to cause us to want to meet these requirements, *17* but it fills me with a deep-rooted disgust that we perpetuate the myth that men are unyielding creatures of iron and women are silly bits of fluff. The ad generates no good role models to aspire to, where men and women are equal beings, and both can show compassion and still be strong. Fila may like their blues hard and soft, but I don't like their blues at all.

? QUESTIONS FOR WRITING AND DISCUSSION

1 Fila did not grant permission to reproduce their advertisement for this text. However, Lewis does an excellent job of describing the layout, balance, color, key figures, diagonals, and background. In the margin of this essay, indicate those sentences where Lewis describes the advertisement, enabling us to clearly visualize it.

2 Parts of Lewis's essay describe and analyze the text that accompanies the advertisement, but she spends most of her time discussing the social, cultural, and gendered contexts of the advertisement. In the margin of the essay, indicate places where she analyzes the accompanying *text* and where she analyzes the *context* of the advertisement. Where in her analysis do you see her showing how text and context relate to each other? Explain.

3 Examine how Lewis *organizes* her analysis of the Fila advertisement. How does her organization reflect her thesis that the two figures, hers and his, are opposites? In other words, where and how does she use sentences and paragraphs to show that these two figures are "fundamentally different and total antonyms of each other"?

4 The genre of the Fila promotion is the clothing or fashion advertisement. Find at least three other advertisements for clothing or fashion. Use Lewis's strategy and analyze how the images, text, and context function together. How are the overall messages in these advertisements similar to or different from the messages that Lewis finds? Explain.

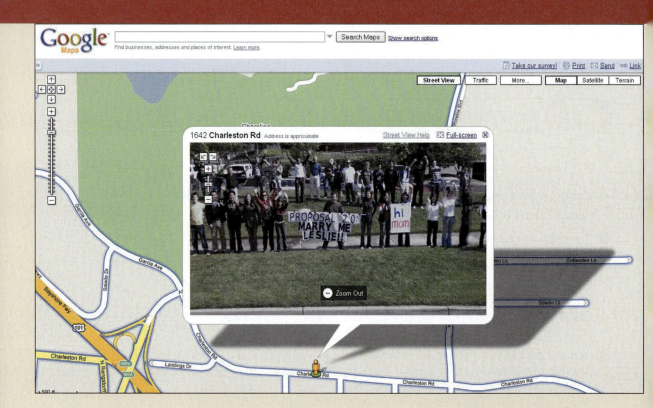

Examine the image above, captured from Google Street Views. Although many Google street views show people unaware that the Google camera car is passing, these people knew the camera car was coming and prepared to have their picture taken. After studying this image, answer Journal question 6 on page 193.

Explaining

7

You have decided to quit your present job, so you write a note to your boss giving thirty days' notice. During your last few weeks at work, your boss asks you to write a three-page job description to help orient the person who will replace you. The job description should include a list of your current duties as well as advice to your replacement on how to execute them most efficiently. To write the description, you record your daily activities, look back through your calendar, comb through your records, and brainstorm a list of everything you do. As you write up the description, you include specific examples and illustrations of your typical responsibilities.

As a gymnast and dancer, you gradually become obsessed with losing weight. You start skipping meals, purging the little food you do eat, and lying about your eating habits to your parents. Before long, you weigh less than seventy pounds, and your physician diagnoses your condition: anorexia nervosa. With advice from your physician and counseling from a psychologist, you gradually begin to control your disorder. To explain to others what anorexia is, how it is caused, and what its effects are, you write an essay in which you explain your ordeal, alerting other readers to the potential dangers of uncontrolled dieting.

> " Become aware of the two-sided nature of your mental make-up: one thinks in terms of the connectedness of things, the other thinks in terms of parts and sequences. "
> —GABRIELE LUSSER RICO, AUTHOR OF *WRITING THE NATURAL WAY*

> " What [a writer] knows is almost always a matter of the relationships he establishes, between example and generalization, between one part of a narrative and the next, between the idea and the counter idea that the writer sees is also relevant. "
> —ROGER SALE, AUTHOR OF *ON WRITING*

E XPLAINING AND DEMONSTRATING RELATIONSHIPS IS A FREQUENT PUR- POSE FOR WRITING. EXPLAINING GOES BEYOND INVESTIGATING THE FACTS AND REPORTING INFORMATION; IT ANALYZES THE COMPONENT PARTS OF A SUBJECT AND THEN SHOWS HOW THE PARTS FIT in relation to one another. Its goal is to clarify for a particular group of readers *what* something is, *how* it happened or should happen, and/or *why* it happens.

Explaining begins with assessing the rhetorical situation: the writer, the oc- casion, the intended purpose and audience, the genre, and the cultural context. As you begin thinking about a subject, topic, or issue to explain, keep in mind your own interests, the expectations of your audience, the possible genre you might choose to help achieve your purpose (essay, article, pamphlet, multigenre essay, Web site), and finally the cultural or social context in which you are writ- ing or in which your writing might be read.

Explaining any idea, concept, process, or effect requires analysis. Analysis starts with dividing a thing or phenomenon into its various parts. Then, once you explain the various parts, you put them back together (synthesis) to explain their relationship or how they work together.

Explaining how to learn to play the piano, for example, begins with an analysis of the parts of the learning process: playing scales, learning chords, get- ting instruction from a teacher, sight reading, and performing in recitals. Ex- plaining why two automobiles collided at an intersection begins with an analysis of the contributing factors: the nature of the intersection, the number of cars in- volved, the condition of the drivers, and the condition of each vehicle. Then you bring the parts together and show their *relationships:* you show how practicing scales on the piano fits into the process of learning to play the piano; you demonstrate why one small factor—such as a faulty turn signal—combined with other factors to cause an automobile accident.

The emphasis you give to the *analysis* of the object or phenomenon and the time you spend explaining *relationships* of the parts depends on your purpose, subject, and audience. If you want to explain how a flower reproduces, for ex- ample, you may begin by identifying the important parts, such as the pistil and stamen, that most readers need to know about before they can understand the reproductive process. However, if you are explaining the process to a botany ma- jor who already knows the parts of a flower, you might spend more time discussing the key operations in pollination or the reasons why some flowers cross-pollinate and others do not. In any effective explanation, analyzing parts and showing relationships must work together for that particular group of readers.

Because its purpose is to teach the reader, *expository writing,* or writing to explain, should be as clear as possible. Explanations, however, are more than organized pieces of information. Expository writing contains informa- tion that is focused by your point of view, by your experience, and by your reasoning powers. Thus, your explanation of a thing or phenomenon makes a point or has a thesis: This is the *right* way to define *happiness.* This is how one *should* bake lasagne or do a calculus problem. These are the *most important* reasons why the senator from New York was elected. To make your explanation clear, you show what you mean by using specific support: facts, data, examples, illustrations, statistics, comparisons, analogies, and images. Your thesis is a *general* assertion about the relationships of the *specific* parts. The support helps your reader identify the parts and see the relationships. Expository writing teaches the reader by alternating between generalizations and specific examples.

Techniques for Explaining

Explaining requires first that you assess your rhetorical situation. Your purpose must work for a particular audience, genre, and context. You may revise some of these aspects of the rhetorical situation as you draw on your own observations and memories about your topic. As you research your topic, conduct an interview, or do a survey, keep thinking about issues of audience, genre, and context. Below are techniques for writing clear explanations.

> 66 The main thing I try to do is write as clearly as I can. 99
> —E. B. WHITE, JOURNALIST AND COAUTHOR OF *ELEMENTS OF STYLE*

Techniques for Explaining

Technique	Tips on How to Do It
Considering (and reconsidering) your purpose, audience, genre, and social context	As you change your *audience* or your *genre*, you must change how you explain something as well as how much and what kind of evidence you use.
Getting the reader's attention and stating the thesis	Devise an accurate but interesting *title*. Use an attention-getting *lead-in*. State the *thesis* clearly.
Defining key terms and describing *what* something is	Analyze and define by *describing, comparing, classifying* and/or *giving examples.*
Identifying the steps in a process and showing *how* each step relates to the overall process	Describe *how* something should be done or *how* something typically happens. *Continued*

Technique	Tips on How to Do It
Describing causes and effects and showing *why* certain causes lead to specific effects	Analyze how several causes lead to a *single effect*, or show how a single cause leads to *multiple effects*.
Supporting explanations with specific evidence	Use descriptions, examples, comparisons, analogies, images, facts, data, or statistics to *show* what, how, or why.

In *Spirit of the Valley: Androgyny and Chinese Thought,* psychologist Sukie Colgrave illustrates many of these techniques as she explains an important concept from psychology: the phenomenon of *projection.* Colgrave explains how we "project" attributes missing in our own personality onto another person—especially someone we love:

Explaining what: Definition example

Explaining why: Effects of projection

Explaining how: The process of freeing ourselves from dependency

A one-sided development of either the masculine or feminine principles has [an] unfortunate consequence for our psychological and intellectual health: it encourages the phenomenon termed "projection." This is the process by which we project onto other people, things, or ideologies, those aspects of ourselves which we have not, for whatever reason, acknowledged or developed. The most familiar example of this is the obsession which usually accompanies being "in love." A person whose feminine side is unrealised will often "fall in love" with the feminine which she or he "sees" in another person, and similarly with the masculine. The experience of being "in love" is one of powerful dependency. As long as the projection appears to fit its object nothing awakens the person to the reality of the projection. But sooner or later the lover usually becomes aware of certain discrepancies between her or his desires and the person chosen to satisfy them. Resentment, disappointment, anger and rejection rapidly follow, and often the relationship disintegrates. . . . But if we can explore our own psyches we may discover what it is we were demanding from our lover and start to develop it in ourselves. The moment this happens we begin to see other people a little more clearly. We are freed from some of our needs to make others what we want them to be, and can begin to love them more for what they are.

EXPLAINING *WHAT:* DEFINITION

Explaining *what* something is or means requires showing the relationship between it and the *class* of beings, objects, or concepts to which it belongs. *Formal definition,* which is often essential in explaining, has three parts: the thing or term to be defined, the class, and the distinguishing characteristics of the thing or term. The thing being defined can be concrete, such as a turkey, or abstract, such as democracy.

Thing or Term	Class	Distinguishing Characteristics
A turkey is a	bird	that has brownish plumage and a bare, wattled head and neck; it is widely domesticated for food.
Democracy is	government	by the people, exercised directly or through elected representatives.

Frequently, writers use *extended definitions* when they need to give more than a mere formal definition. An extended definition may explain the word's etymology or historical roots, describe sensory characteristics of something (how it looks, feels, sounds, tastes, smells), identify its parts, indicate how something is used, explain what it is not, provide an example of it, and/or note similarities or differences between this term and other words or things.

The following extended definition of democracy, written for an audience of college students to appear in a textbook, begins with the etymology of the word and then explains—using analysis, comparison, example, and description—what democracy is and what it is not:

Since democracy is government of the people, by the people, and for the people, a democratic form of government is not fixed or static. Democracy is dynamic; it adapts to the wishes and needs of the people. The term *democracy* derives from the Greek word *demos,* meaning "the common people," and *-kratia,* meaning "strength or power" used to govern or rule. Democracy is based on the notion that a majority of people creates laws and then everyone agrees to abide by those laws in the interest of the common good. In a democracy, people are not ruled by a king, a dictator, or a small group of powerful individuals. Instead, people elect officials who use the power temporarily granted to them to govern the society. For example, the people may agree that their government should raise money for defense, so the officials levy taxes to support an army. If enough people decide, however, that taxes for defense are too high, then they request that their elected officials change the laws or they elect new officials. The essence of democracy lies in its responsiveness: Democracy is a form of government in which laws and lawmakers change as the will of the majority changes.

Formal definition
Description: What democracy is
Etymology: Analysis of the word's roots

Comparison: What democracy is not

Example

Formal definition

Figurative expressions—vivid word pictures using similes, metaphors, or analogies—can also explain what something is. During World War II, for example, the Writer's War Board asked E. B. White (author of *Charlotte's Web* and many *New Yorker* magazine essays, as well as other works) to provide an explanation of democracy. Instead of giving a formal definition or etymology, White responded with a series of imaginative comparisons showing the *relationship* between various parts of American culture and the concept of democracy.

> Surely the Board knows what democracy is. It is the line that forms on the right. It is the don't in Don't Shove. It is the hole in the stuffed shirt through which the sawdust slowly trickles; it is the dent in the high hat. Democracy is the recurrent suspicion that more than half of the people are right more than half of the time. It is the feeling of privacy in the voting booths, the feeling of communion in the libraries, the feeling of vitality everywhere. Democracy is the score at the beginning of the ninth. It is an idea which hasn't been disproved yet, a song the words of which have not gone bad. It's the mustard on the hot dog and the cream in the rationed coffee. Democracy is a request from a War Board, in the middle of a morning in the middle of a war, wanting to know what democracy is.

EXPLAINING *HOW:* PROCESS ANALYSIS

Explaining *how* something should be done or how something happens is usually called *process analysis.* One kind of process analysis is the "how-to" explanation: how to cook a turkey, how to tune an engine, how to get a job. Such recipes or directions are *prescriptive:* You typically explain how something *should* be done. In a second kind of process analysis, you explain how something happens or is typically done—without being directive or prescriptive. In a *descriptive* process analysis, you explain how some natural or social process typically happens: how cells split during mitosis, how hailstones form in a cloud, how students react to the pressure of examinations, or how political candidates create their public images. In both prescriptive and descriptive explanations, however, you are analyzing a *process*—dividing the sequence into its parts or steps—and then showing how the parts contribute to the whole process.

Cookbooks, automobile-repair manuals, instructions for assembling toys or appliances, and self-improvement books are all examples of *prescriptive* process analysis. Writers of recipes, for example, begin with analyses of the ingredients and the steps in preparing the food. Then they carefully explain how the steps are related, how to avoid problems, and how to serve mouth-watering concoctions. Farley Mowat, naturalist and author of *Never Cry Wolf,* gives his readers the following detailed—and humorous—recipe for creamed mouse. Mowat became interested in this recipe when he decided to test the nutritional content of the wolf's diet. "In the event that any of my readers may be interested in personally exploiting this hitherto overlooked source of excellent animal protein," Mowat writes, "I give the recipe in full."

Souris à la Crème

Ingredients:

One dozen fat mice	Salt and pepper	One cup white flour
Cloves	One piece sowbelly	Ethyl alcohol

Skin and gut the mice, but do not remove the heads; wash, then place in a pot with enough alcohol to cover the carcasses. Allow to marinate for about two hours. Cut sowbelly into small cubes and fry slowly until most of the fat has been rendered. Now remove the carcasses from the alcohol and roll them in a mixture of salt, pepper and flour; then place in frying pan and sauté for about five minutes (being careful not to allow the pan to get too hot, or the delicate meat will dry out and become tough and stringy). Now add a cup of alcohol and six or eight cloves. Cover the pan and allow to simmer slowly for fifteen minutes. The cream sauce can be made according to any standard recipe. When the sauce is ready, drench the carcasses with it, cover and allow to rest in a warm place for ten minutes before serving.

Explaining *how* something happens or is typically done involves a *descriptive* process analysis. It requires showing the chronological relationship between one idea, event, or phenomenon and the next—and it depends on close observation. In *The Lives of a Cell,* biologist and physician Lewis Thomas explains that ants are like humans: while they are individuals, they can also act together to create a social organism. Although exactly how ants communicate remains a mystery, Thomas explains how they combine to form a thinking, working organism.

[Ants] seem to live two kinds of lives: they are individuals, going about the day's business without much evidence of thought for tomorrow, and they are at the same time component parts, cellular elements, in the huge, writhing, ruminating organism of the Hill, the nest, the hive. . . .

A solitary ant, afield, cannot be considered to have much of anything on his mind; indeed, with only a few neurons strung together by fibers, he can't be imagined to have a mind at all, much less a thought. He is more like a ganglion on legs. Four ants together, or ten, encircling a dead moth on a path, begin to look more like an idea. They fumble and shove, gradually moving the food toward the Hill, but as though by blind chance. It is only when you watch the dense mass of thousands of ants, crowded together around the Hill, blackening the ground, that you begin to see the whole beast, and now you observe it thinking, planning, calculating. It is an intelligence, a kind of live computer, with crawling bits for its wits.

At a stage in the construction, twigs of a certain size are needed, and all the members forage obsessively for twigs of just this size. Later, when outer walls are to be finished, thatched, the size must change, and as though given new orders by telephone, all the workers shift the search to the new twigs. If you disturb the arrangement of a part of the Hill, hundreds of ants will set it vibrating, shifting, until it is put right again. Distant sources of food are somehow sensed, and long lines, like tentacles, reach out over the ground, up over walls, behind boulders, to fetch it in.

EXPLAINING *WHY:* CAUSAL ANALYSIS

"Why?" may be the question most commonly asked by human beings. We are fascinated by the reasons for everything that we experience in life. We ask questions about natural phenomena: Why is the sky blue? Why does a teakettle whistle? Why do some materials act as superconductors? We also find human attitudes and behavior intriguing: Why is chocolate so popular? Why do some people hit small leather balls with big sticks and then run around a field stomping on little white pillows? Why are America's family farms economically depressed? Why did the United States go to war in Iraq? Why is the Internet so popular?

Explaining *why* something occurs can be the most fascinating—and difficult— kind of expository writing. Answering the question "why" usually requires analyzing *cause-and-effect relationships.* The causes, however, may be too complex or intangible to identify precisely. We are on comparatively secure ground when we ask *why* about physical phenomena that can be weighed, measured, and replicated under laboratory conditions. Under those conditions, we can determine cause and effect with precision.

Fire, for example, has three *necessary* and *sufficient* causes: combustible material, oxygen, and ignition temperature. Without each of these causes, fire will not occur (each cause is "necessary"); taken together, these three causes are enough to cause fire (all three together are "sufficient"). In this case, the cause-and-effect relationship can be illustrated by an equation:

Cause 1	+	Cause 2	+	Cause 3	=	Effect
(combustible material)		(oxygen)		(ignition temperature)		(fire)

Analyzing both necessary and sufficient causes is essential to explaining an effect. You may say, for example, that wind shear (an abrupt downdraft in a storm) "caused" an airplane crash. In fact, wind shear may have *contributed* (been necessary) to the crash but was not by itself the total (sufficient) cause of the crash: an airplane with enough power may be able to overcome wind shear forces in certain circumstances. An explanation of the crash is not complete until you analyze the full range of necessary *and* sufficient causes, which may include wind shear, lack of power, mechanical failure, and even pilot error.

Sometimes, explanations for physical phenomena are beyond our analytical powers. Astrophysicists, for example, have good theoretical reasons for believing that black holes cause gigantic gravitational whirlpools in outer space, but they have difficulty explaining why black holes exist—or whether they exist at all.

In the realm of human cause and effect, determining causes and effects can be as tricky as explaining why black holes exist. Why, for example, do some children learn math easily while others fail? What effect does failing at math have on a child? What are necessary and sufficient causes for divorce? What are the effects of divorce on parents and children? Although you may not be able to explain all the causes or effects of something, you should not be satisfied until you have considered a wide range of possible causes and effects. Even then, you need to qualify or modify your statements, using such words as *might, usually, often, seldom, many,* or *most,* and then giving as much support and evidence as you can.

In the following paragraphs, Jonathan Kozol, a critic of America's educational system and author of *Illiterate America*, explains the multiple effects of a single cause: illiteracy. Kozol supports his explanation by citing specific ways that illiteracy affects the lives of people:

> Illiterates cannot read the menu in a restaurant.
>
> They cannot read the cost of items on the menu in the window of the restaurant before they enter.
>
> Illiterates cannot read the letters that their children bring home from their teachers. They cannot study school department circulars that tell them of the courses that their children must be taking if they hope to pass the SAT exams. They cannot help with homework. They cannot write a letter to the teacher. They are afraid to visit in the classroom. They do not want to humiliate their child or themselves. . . .
>
> Many illiterates cannot read the admonition on a pack of cigarettes. Neither the Surgeon General's warning nor its reproduction on the package can alert them to the risks. Although most people learn by word of mouth that smoking is related to a number of grave physical disorders, they do not get the chance to read the detailed stories which can document this danger with the vividness that turns concern into determination to resist. They can see the handsome cowboy or the slim Virginia lady lighting up a filter cigarette; they cannot heed the words that tell them that this product is (not "may be") dangerous to their health. Sixty million men and women are condemned to be the unalerted, high-risk candidates for cancer. . . .
>
> Illiterates cannot travel freely. When they attempt to do so, they encounter risks that few of us can dream of. They cannot read traffic signs and, while they often learn to recognize and to decipher symbols, they cannot manage street names which they haven't seen before. The same is true for bus and subway stops. While ingenuity can

sometimes help a man or woman to discern directions from familiar landmarks, buildings, cemeteries, churches, and the like, most illiterates are virtually immobilized. They seldom wander past the streets and neighborhoods they know. Geographical paralysis becomes a bitter metaphor for their entire existence. They are immobilized in almost every sense we can imagine. They can't move up. They can't move out. They cannot see beyond.

WARMING UP   Journal Exercises

The following exercises will help you practice writing explanations. Read all of the following exercises and then write on the three that interest you most. If another idea occurs to you, write about it.

1. **Writing Across the Curriculum.** Write a one-paragraph explanation of an idea, term, or concept that you have discussed in a class that you are currently taking. From biology, for example, you might define *photosynthesis* or *gene splicing*. From psychology, you might define *psychosis* or *projection*. From computer studies, you might define *cyberspace* or *morphing*. First, identify someone who might need to know about this subject. Then give a definition and an illustration. Finally, describe how the term was discovered or invented, what its effects or applications are, and/or how it works.

2. Imitating E. B. White's short "definition" of democracy, use imaginative comparisons to write a short definition—serious or humorous— of one of the following words: *freedom, adolescence, mathematics, politicians, parents, misery, higher education, luck,* or a word of your own choice.

3. Novelist Ernest Hemingway once defined courage as "grace under pressure." Using this definition, explain how you or someone you know showed this kind of courage in a difficult situation.

4. When asked what jazz is, Louis Armstrong replied, "Man, if you gotta ask you'll never know." If you know quite a bit about jazz, explain what Armstrong meant. Or choose a familiar subject to which the same remark might apply. What can be "explained" about that subject, and what cannot?

5. Choose a skill that you've acquired (for example, playing a musical instrument, operating a machine, playing a sport, drawing, counseling others, driving in rush-hour traffic, dieting) and explain to a novice how he or she can acquire that skill. Reread what you've written. Then write another version addressed to an expert. What parts can you leave out? What must you add?

6 Examine the illustration of Google Street Views shown on the opening page of this chapter. Do some research online about what Google Street Views are, how these images are captured, and how to access them online. Then consider the possible effects. Although Google says that they blur the faces of people so that they are not identifiable, is this always true? Are there examples of images that are clear invasions of privacy? Google has already captured images of apparent crimes—does that mean that these images could protect public safety or help send alleged criminals to jail? For a private, public, or academic audience, write your own blog or essay explaining the real or possible good or bad effects of Google Street Views.

PROFESSIONAL WRITING

How to Take Control of Your Credit Cards

Suze Orman

The author of several best selling books, including The Nine Steps to Financial Freedom *(1997),* The Money Book for the Young, Fabulous & Broke *(2005), and* Women and Money: Owning the Power to Control Your Destiny *(2007), Suze Orman was born in 1951 in Chicago, earned a degree in social work from the University of Illinois, and started her career not as a financial expert but as a waitress in Berkeley, California. After working at a restaurant for seven years, she talked her way into a job as a financial advisor with Merrill Lynch. She then started her own business and published her first book* You've Earned It, Don't Lose It. *Six of her most recent books have been* New York Times *bestsellers. Now that she is young(ish), fabulous, and very wealthy, Suze Orman has her own CNBC TV show, and she appears on* Oprah, *the* Today Show, The View, *and* Larry King. *She is also the winner of 2 Emmy Awards for her PBS specials and has been the recipient of the most GRACIE Awards in the history of the AWRT (American Women in Radio and Television). "How to Take Control of Your Credit Cards" appeared originally as one of her regular columns for Money Matters on Yahoo! Finance.*

I'm all for taking credit where credit is due, but when it comes to 1 credit cards, way too many of you are overdoing it. For Americans who don't pay their entire credit card bill each month, the average balance is close to $4,000. And when we zoom in on higher-income folks—those with annual incomes between $75,000 and $100,000—the average balance clocks in at nearly $8,000. If you're paying, say, 18 percent interest on an $8,000 balance, and you make only the 2 percent minimum payment due each month, you are going to end up paying more than $22,000 in interest over the course of the 54 years it will take to get the balance down to zero.

That's absolute insanity.   *2*

And absolutely unnecessary.   *3*

If you have the desire to take control of your credit card mess, you can. *4* It's just a matter of choice. I am not saying it will be easy, but there are plenty of strategies that can put you on a path out of credit card hell. And as I explain later, even those of you who can't seem to turn the corner and become credit responsible on your own, can get plenty of help from qualified credit counseling services.

How to Be a Credit Card Shark

If you overspend just because you like to buy buy buy on credit, then *5* you are what I call Broke by Choice. You are willfully making your own mess. I am not going to lecture you about how damaging this is; I'm hoping the fact that you're reading this article means you are ready to make a change.

But I also realize that some of you are Broke by Circumstance. I ac- *6* tually tell young adults in the dues-paying stage of their careers to lean on their credit cards if they don't yet make enough to always keep up with their bills. But the key is that if you rely on your credit cards to make ends meet, you must limit the plastic spending to true necessities, not indulgences. Buying groceries is a necessity. Buying dinner for you and your pals at a swank restaurant is an indulgence you can't afford if it will become part of your unpaid credit card balance.

But whether you are broke by choice or by circumstance, the strat- *7* egy for getting out of credit card debt is the same: to outmaneuver the card companies with a strategy that assures you pay the lowest possible interest rate, for the shortest possible time, while avoiding all of the many snares and traps the card companies lay out for you.

Here's how to be a Credit Card Shark.   *8*

Take an Interest in Your Rate

The average interest rate charged on credit cards is 15 percent, with *9* plenty of folks paying 18 percent, 20 percent, or even more. If you carry a balance on any credit cards, your primary focus should be to get that rate down as low as possible.

Now then. If you have a FICO score of at least 720, and you make at *10* least the minimum payment due each month, on time, you should be able to negotiate with your current credit card issuer to lower your rate. Call 'em up and let them know you plan to transfer your entire balance to another card with a lower rate—more on this in a sec—if they don't get your rate down.

If your card issuer doesn't step up to the plate and give you a better *11* deal, then do indeed start shopping around for a new card with a sweet intro offer. For those of you with strong FICO scores, a zero-rate deal ought to be possible. You can search for top card deals at the Yahoo! Finance Credit Card Center.

Don't forget, though, that the key with balance transfer offers is to *12* find out what your rate will be when the intro period expires in six months to a year. If your zero rate will skyrocket to 20 percent, that's a crappy deal, unless you are absolutely 100 percent sure you will get the balance paid off before the rate changes. (And if you got yourself into card hell in the first place, I wouldn't be betting on you having the ability to wipe out your problem in just six months. . . .)

Once you are approved for the new low- or zero-rate card, move as *13* much of your high-rate balances onto this new card. But don't—I repeat, do NOT—use the new card for new purchases. Hidden in the fine print on these deals are provisions stating, first, that any new purchases you make on the card will come with a high interest rate, and second, that you'll be paying that high interest on the entirety of your new purchase charges until you pay off every last cent of the balance transfer amount. This, to put it mildly, could really screw up your zero-rate deal. So please, use the new card only to park your old high-rate debt, and not to shop with.

Another careless mistake you can make is to cancel your old cards. *14* Don't do that either. Those cards hold some valuable "history" that's used to compute your FICO credit score. If you cancel the cards, you cancel your history, and your FICO score can take a hit. If you are worried about the temptation of using the cards, just get out your scissors and give them a good trim. That way you can't use 'em, but your history stays on your record.

Coddle Your New Card

When you do a balance transfer, you need to protect your low rate as *15* if it were an endangered species—because if the credit card issuer has anything to say about it, it will be. Look, you don't really think the card company is excited about charging you no interest, do you? How the heck do they make money off of that? They only offer up the great deal to lure you over to their card. Then they start working overtime trying to get you to screw up so they have an excuse to change your zero interest rate, often to as much as 20 percent or more.

And the big screw-up they are hoping you don't know about is *16* buried down in the fine print of your card agreement: make one late payment and you can kiss your zero deal good-bye. Even worse is that card companies are now scouring all your credit cards—remember, they can check your credit reports—to see if you have been late on any card, not just their card. So even if you always pay the zero-rate card on time, if you are late on any other card, your zero deal can be in jeopardy.

That's why I want you to make sure every credit card bill is paid ahead *17* of schedule. Don't mail it in on the day it is due; that's late. Mail it in at least five days early. Better yet, convert your card to online bill pay so you can zap your payments over in time every month. And remember, it's only the minimum monthly payment that needs to be paid. That's not asking a lot.

Dealing with High-Rate Debt

Okay, I realize not everyone is going to qualify for these low-rate bal- *18* ance transfer deals, so let's run through how to take control of your cards if you are stuck with higher rates.

I want you to line up all your cards in descending order of their in- *19* terest rates. Notice I said the card with the highest interest rate comes first. Not the one with the biggest balance.

Your strategy is to make the minimum monthly payment on every *20* card, on time, every month. But your card with the highest interest rate gets some special treatment. I want you to pay more than the minimum amount due on this card. The more you can pay, the better; but everyone should put in, at the minimum, an extra $20 each month. Push yourself hard to make that extra payment as large as possible. It can save you thousands of dollars in interest charges over time.

Keep this up every month until your card with the highest rate is paid *21* off. Then turn your attention to the card with the next highest rate. In addition to the usual monthly minimum payment due on that second card, I want you to add in the entire amount you were previously paying on the first card (the one that's now paid off). So let's say you were paying a total of $200 a month on your original highest-rate card, and making a $75 monthly minimum on the second card. Well, now you are going to fork over $275 a month to the second card. And, of course, you'll continue to make the minimum monthly payment due on any other cards. Once your second card is paid off, move on to the third. If your monthly payment on that second card was $275, then that's what you should add to the minimum payment due on your third card. Get the idea? Rinse and repeat as often as needed, until you have all your debt paid off. For some of you this may take a year, for others it may take many years. That's okay. Just get yourself moving in the right direction and you'll be amazed how gratifying it is to find yourself taking control of your money rather than letting it control you.

And be sure to keep an eye on your FICO credit score. As you pay *22* down your card balances—and build a record of paying on time—your score is indeed going to rise. Eventually your score may be high enough to finally qualify for a low-rate balance transfer offer.

Is Credit Counseling Right for You?

There is plenty of help available if you can't seem to get a solid grip 23 on dealing with your credit card debt. But not all the help is good. Given that so many Americans are drowning in card debt, it's really no surprise that some enterprising—and underhanded—folks have figured out a way to make money off of this epidemic by charging high fees for counseling and advice.

So you need to make sure you choose an honest and fair credit coun- 24 seling service. Start by getting references from the National Foundation for Credit Counseling.

Next, make an appointment to talk with a counselor face-to-face. A 25 good counselor will question you thoroughly and in detail about your financial situation before proposing anything. If you are simply told right off the bat that you need a Debt Management Plan, you should run out the door PDQ. That firm is not interested in truly helping you. They just want to hit you up with a bunch of fees.

A good counselor is also going to require that you attend education 26 classes. This is not punishment! On the contrary, it's the best help you can get. Quite often, you can make the changes necessary to take control of your credit card spending just by learning a few good habits.

vo·cab·u·lar·y

In your journal, write the meaning of the italicized words in the following phrases.

- true necessities, not *indulgences* (**6**)
- to *outmaneuver* the card companies (**7**)
- you have a *FICO* score (**10**)
- deal can be in *jeopardy* (**16**)
- make money off this *epidemic* (**23**)

? QUESTIONS FOR WRITING AND DISCUSSION

1 Writers of effective explaining essays focus their thesis for a specific audience. Describe the audience Orman addresses in her essay. Which sentences help you identify this audience? Which sentences in Orman's essay most clearly express her thesis?

2 Explaining essays typically use definition of terms, explanation of processes, and analyses of causes and effects. Identify at least one example of each of the following strategies in Orman's essay: definition, process analysis, and causal analysis. In each case, decide if the information Orman gives is clear to you. Where do you need additional information or clarification?

3 Two strategies that Orman uses to connect with her readers is addressing them in the second person, "you," and using informal language such as "you

and your pals," "call 'em up," "more on this in a sec," and "sweet intro offer." Find other examples of informal language in her essay. Does this language work for her audience? Does it make the essay more lively and readable for you? Is this language appropriate in an essay about finances? Explain.

4 Appeals to the audience often involve more than simply using informal language. Effective appeals connect to the readers' sense of identity and their personal and social values. Read the following introduction to Chapter I in Orman's book, *Women and Money: Owning the Power to Control Your Destiny.* Cite specific sentences from the following paragraph to explain how Orman identifies with her readers while at the same time suggesting that they need to make changes in their lives.

> I never thought I'd write a book about money just for women. I never thought it was necessary. So then why am I doing just that in my eighth book? And why now? Let me explain. All my previous books were written with the belief that gender is not a factor on any level in mastering the nuts and bolts of smart financial management. Women can invest, save, and handle debt just as well and skillfully as any man. I still believe that—why would anyone think differently? So imagine my surprise when I learned that some of the people closest to me in my life were in the dark about their own finances. Clueless. Or, in some cases, willfully resisting doing what they knew needed to be done.

5 Find one of the offers for credit cards that you, a friend, or a family member has recently received. Study the fine print. Then, in your own words, explain what the fine print means in language that another member of your class can understand. Is Orman right about the "many snares and traps" that the card companies set for their customers?

6 Write a profile of Suze Orman that recounts key events in her life and explains why she has been so successful as a writer, motivator, and financial advisor. Check your online library databases as well as online reviews and Web sites. Write your profile so that it could appear in a local newspaper, on a Web site, or as a promotion for one of Suze Orman's latest books.

Explaining: The Writing Process

ASSIGNMENT FOR EXPLAINING

After assessing your rhetorical situation, *explain* what something means or is, *how* it should be done or *how* it occurs, and/or *why* something occurs. Your purpose is to explain something as clearly as possible for your audience by analyzing, showing relationships, and demonstrating with examples, facts, illustrations, data, or other information.

With a topic in mind, use the grid below to think about a possible audience and genre that would meet your assignment. Once you've chosen an audience, think about how much they already know about the subject. Are they experts, novices, or somewhere in between? What can you assume that they already know? What points or information are they least likely to know?

Audience	Possible Genres for Explaining
Personal Audience	Class notes, annotations in a textbook, journal entry, blog, scrapbook, social networking page
Academic Audience	Expository essay, academic analysis and synthesis, journal entry, forum entry on class site, multigenre document
Public Audience	Column, editorial, letter, or article, or in a magazine, newspaper, online site, newsletter, or multigenre document

CHOOSING A SUBJECT

If one of your journal entries suggested a possible subject, go on to the collecting and shaping strategies. If you still need an interesting subject, consider the following suggestions.

- Reread your authority list or the most interesting journal entries from previous chapters. Do they contain ideas that you might define or explain, processes suitable for how-to explanations, or causes or effects that you could analyze and explain for a certain audience?

- **Writing Across the Curriculum.** Reread your notes from another class in which you have an upcoming examination. Select some topic, idea, principle, process, famous person, or event from the text or your notes. Investigate other texts, popular magazines, or journals for information on that topic. If appropriate, interview someone or conduct a survey. Explain this principle or process to a member of your writing class.

- **Community Service Learning.** If you are doing a community-service-learning project, consider a writing project explaining the agency's mission to the public or to a potential donor. You might also write an article for a local or campus newspaper explaining some aspect of their service or a recent contribution the agency has made to the community.

- Consider writing an artistic, cultural, historical, or social explanation of a particular visual image or a set of visual images. One excellent Web site for famous photographs is the Pulitzer site at

> 66 You can write about anything, and if you write well enough, even the reader with no intrinsic interest in the subject will become involved. 99
>
> —TRACY KIDDER, NOVELIST

http://www.gallerym.com/pulitzerphotos.htm. Decide on a particular
audience, genre, and context appropriate for the photograph.

- Choose a current controversy to explain. Instead of arguing for one side or
  the other, however, explain the different points of view in this controversy.
  Who are the leading figures or groups representing each of several different
  positions? Choose a particular audience, genre, and context, and explain
  what each of these people or groups have to gain or lose and how their
  personal investments in the topic determine their position.

COLLECTING

● **QUESTIONS**   Once you have a tentative subject and audience in mind,
consider which of the following will be your primary focus (all three may be
relevant).

- *What* something means or is
- *How* something occurs or is done (or should be done)
- *Why* something occurs or what its effects are

Focus on Definition.   To explain *what* something is, jot down answers to
each of the following questions. The more you can write on each question, the
more details you'll have for your topic.

- What are its class and distinguishing characteristics?
- What is its etymology?
- How can you describe it?
- What examples can you give?
- What are its parts or its functions?
- What is it similar to? What is it *not*?
- What figurative comparisons apply?
- How can it be classified?
- Which of the above is most useful to your audience?

Focus on Process Analysis.   To explain *how* something occurs or is done,
answer the following questions.

- What are the component parts or steps in the whole process?
- What is the exact sequence of steps or events?
- Are several of the steps or events related?
- If steps or events were omitted, would the outcome change?
- Which steps or events are most crucial?
- Which steps or events does your audience most need to know?

Focus on Causal Analysis.   To explain *why* something occurs or what its effects are, consider the following issues.

- Which are the necessary or sufficient causes?
- Which causes are remote in time, and which are immediate?
- What is the order or sequence of the causes? Do the causes occur simultaneously?
- What are the effects? Do they occur in a sequence or simultaneously?
- Do the causes and effects occur in a "chain reaction"?
- Is there an action or situation that would have prevented the effect?
- Are there comparable things or events that have similar causes or effects?
- Which causes or effects need special clarification for your audience?

● **BRANCHING**   Often, *branching* can help you visually analyze your subject. Start with your topic and then subdivide each idea into its component parts. The resulting analysis will not only help generate ideas but may also suggest ways to shape an essay.

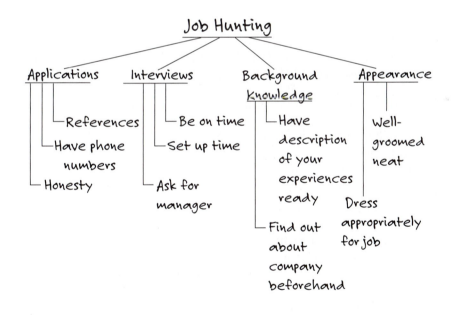

● **OBSERVING**   If you can observe your subject, try drawing it, describing it, or taking careful notes. Which senses can you use to describe it—sight, sound, touch, smell, taste? If it is a scientific experiment that you can reproduce or a social situation you can reconstruct, go through it again and observe carefully. As you observe it, put yourself in your readers' shoes: What do you need to explain it to them?

● **REMEMBERING**   Your own experience and memory are essential for explaining. *Freewriting, looping,* and *clustering* may all generate detailed information, good examples, and interesting perspectives that will make your explanation clearer and move vivid. (See Chapter 4 for an explanation of looping and clustering.)

● **READING**   When you find written texts about your subject, be sure to use your active reading strategies. You may need only a few sources if you reread them carefully. Write out a short summary for each source. Respond to each source by analyzing its effectiveness, agreeing or disagreeing with its ideas, or interpreting the text. The quality of your understanding is more important than the sheer number of sources you cite.

● **INVESTIGATING**   Use sources available in the library, textbooks containing relevant information, or interviews with teachers, participants, or experts. Interview your classmates about their own subjects for this assignment: Someone else's subject may trigger an idea that you can write about or may suggest a fresh approach to the subject that you have already chosen.

> 66 Readers may be strangers who have no immediate reason to care about your writing. They want order, clarity, and stimulation. 99
>
> —ELIZABETH COWAN NEELD,
> TEACHER AND AUTHOR

SHAPING

As you collect information and generate ideas from your collecting activities, be sure to *narrow* and *focus* your subject into a topic suitable for a short essay. You will not be able to cover everything you've read, thought, or experienced about your subject. Choose the most interesting ideas—for you and for your audience—and shape, order, and clarify those ideas.

● **AUDIENCE AND GENRE**   As you consider ways to organize and shape your explaining essay, think about a possible audience and genre. An essay directed at a general audience composed of peers like your classmates is just one possibility. A letter to the editor, a pamphlet for a community agency, a job analysis for your employer, an article for a local or school newspaper, a posting or response to a listserve, or an essay for students in your major are other possibilities. Once you have a tentative audience and genre, you'll have a better idea about how to organize your explanation. Reread your assignment for specific suggestions and guidelines about audience and genre.

● **DEFINITION AND CLASSIFICATION**   An essay explaining *what* something means or is can be shaped by using a variety of definition strategies or by classifying the subject.

Definition itself is not a single organizing strategy; it supports a variety of strategies that may be useful in shaping your essay: description, analysis of

Research Tips

Review your audience, purpose, and possible focus. Which of the following three research strategies would help you gather information on your topic?

1. Direct *observation* (see Chapter 3)
2. Use of *memories* and personal experience (see Chapter 4)
3. *Library/internet research* (see Chapter 11)

As you do your research, keep the following tips in mind:

- Save all your *links* or *Word files* or make *photocopies* or *printouts* of all the sources that you plan to cite in your essay.
- Be sure to *write all relevant bibliographic information*, such as author, date, publisher, place of publication, journal title, and volume and issue numbers. in your Word files or on the photocopies or printouts. Note the Web site sponsor and your access date for Web sources.
- When you cite sources in the text, be sure to *introduce* your sources. Make sure your direct quotations are *accurate* word-for-word transcriptions.

For more details on these suggestions, see Chapter 11.

parts or function, comparison/contrast, development by examples, or figures of speech such as simile, metaphor, and analogy.

Classification, on the other hand, is a single strategy that can organize a paragraph or even a whole essay quickly. Observers of human behavior, for example, love to use classification. Grocery shoppers might be classified by types: racers (the ones who seem to have just won forty-five seconds of free shopping and run down the aisles filling their carts as fast as possible), talkers (the ones whose phone must be out of order because they stand in the aisles gossiping forever), penny-pinchers (who always have their calculators out and read the unit price labels for everything), party shoppers (who camp out in the junk food aisles, filling their carts with potato chips, dip, candy, peanuts, and drink mixers), and dawdlers (who leave their carts crosswise in the aisles while they read twenty-nine different soup can labels). You can write a sentence or two about each type or devote a whole paragraph to explaining a single type.

● **EXAMPLE**   Development by example can effectively illustrate what something is or means, but it can also help explain how or why something happens. Usually, an example describes a specific incident, located at a certain place and occurring at a particular time, that *shows* or *demonstrates* the main idea. In the following paragraph from *Mediaspeak,* Donna Woolfolk Cross explains what effects soap operas can have on addicted viewers. This paragraph is developed by several examples—some described in detail, others referred to briefly.

> Dedicated watchers of soap operas often confuse fact with fiction. . . . Stars of soap operas tell hair-raising stories of their encounters with fans suffering from this affliction. Susan Lucci, who plays the promiscuous Erica Kane on "All My Children," tells of a time she was riding in a parade: "We were in a crowd of about 250,000 traveling in an antique open car moving ver-r-ry slowly. At that time in the series I was involved with a character named Nick. Some man broke through, came right up to the car and said to me, 'Why don't you give me a little bit of what you've been giving Nick?'" The man hung onto the car, menacingly, until she was rescued by the police. Another time, when she was in church, the reverent silence was broken by a woman's astonished remark, "Oh, my god, Erica prays!" Margaret Mason, who plays the villainous Lisa Anderson in "Days of Our Lives," was accosted by a woman who poured a carton of milk all over her in the supermarket. And once a woman actually tried to force her car off the Ventura Freeway.

● **VOICE AND TONE**   Writers also use voice and tone to shape and control whole passages, often in combination with other shaping strategies. In the following paragraph, Toni Bambara, author of *The Salt Eaters* and numerous short stories, explains *what* being a writer is all about. This paragraph is shaped both by a single extended example and by Bambara's voice talking directly to the reader.

> When I replay the tapes on file in my head, tapes of speeches I've given at writing conferences over the years, I invariably hear myself saying—"A writer, like any other cultural worker, like any other member of the community, ought to try to put her/his skills in the service of the community." Some years ago when I returned south, my picture in the paper prompted several neighbors to come visit. "You a writer? What all you write?" Before I could begin the catalogue, one old gent interrupted with—"Ya know Miz Mary down the block? She need a writer to help her send off a letter to her grandson overseas." So I began a career as the neighborhood scribe—letters to relatives, snarling letters to the traffic chief about the promised stop sign, nasty letters to the utilities, angry letters to the principal about that confederate flag hanging in front of the school, contracts to transfer a truck from seller to buyer, etc. While my efforts have been graciously appreciated in the form of sweet potato dumplings, herb teas,

hair braiding, and the like, there is still much room for improvement—
"For a writer, honey, you've got a mighty bad hand. Didn't they teach
penmanship at that college?" Another example, I guess, of words
setting things in motion. What goes around, comes around, as the
elders say.

● **CHRONOLOGICAL ORDER AND PROCESS ANALYSIS**   Writers use
chronological order in expository writing to help explain how to do something or how something is typically done. In her essay "Anorexia Nervosa,"
student writer Nancie Brosseau uses transitional words to signal the various
stages of anorexia. In the following sentences, taken from the third paragraph
of her essay, the *italicized* words mark the chronological stages of her
anorexia.

> Several serious health problems bombarded me, and it's a wonder
> I'm still alive. . . . *As my weight plummeted,* my circulation grew
> *increasingly worse.* . . . My hair *started* to fall out, and my whole
> body took on a very skeletal appearance. . . . I would force myself to
> vomit *as soon as possible* if I was forced to eat. The enamel on my
> teeth *started to be eaten away* by the acid in the vomit, and my lips
> cracked and bled regularly. I *stopped* menstruating completely be-
> cause I was not producing enough estrogen. . . . *One time,* while ex-
> ecuting a chain of back handsprings, I broke all five fingers on one
> hand and three on the other because my bones had become so brit-
> tle. . . . I chose to see a psychologist, and she helped me sort out the
> emotional aspects of anorexia, *which in turn* solved the physical
> problems.

● **CAUSAL ANALYSIS**   In order to explain *why* something happens or
what the effects of something are, writers often use one of the following three
patterns of cause and effect to shape their material:

> Cause 1 + Cause 2 + Cause 3 . . . + Cause $n \rightarrow$ Effect

In the case of fire, for example, we know that three causes lead to a single
effect. These causes do not occur in any special sequence; they must all be
present at the same time. For historical events, however, we usually list causes
in chronological order.

Sometimes one cause has several effects. In that case, we reverse the pattern:

> Cause $\rightarrow$ Effect 1 + Effect 2 + Effect 3 . . . + Effect n

For example, an explanation of the collapse of the economy following the
stock market crash of 1929 might follow this pattern. The crash (itself a
symptom of other causes) led to a depreciated economy, widespread unemployment, bankruptcy for thousands of businesses, foreclosures on farms,

and so forth. An essay on the effects of the crash might devote one or two paragraphs to each effect.

In the third pattern, causes and effects form a pattern of chain reactions. One cause leads to an effect that then becomes the cause of another effect, and so on:

Cause 1 → Effect 1 (Cause 2) → Effect 2 (Cause 3) → Effect 3

We could analyze events in the Middle East during and after the Iraq War as a series of actions and reactions in which each effect becomes the cause of the next effect in the chain of car bombings, air raids, terrorist hijackings, and kidnappings. An essay on the chain reaction of events in the Middle East might have a paragraph or two on each of the links in this chain.

● **INTRODUCTION AND LEAD-IN**   Often, the first sentences of the introductory paragraph of an essay are the hardest to write. You want to get your reader's attention and focus on the main idea of your essay, but you don't want to begin, boringly, with your thesis statement. Below are several kinds of opening sentences designed to grab your reader's interest. Consider your topic—see if one of these strategies will work for you.

A Personal Example

I knew my dieting had gotten out of hand, but when I could actually see the movement of my heart beating beneath my clothes, I knew I was in trouble.

—"Anorexia Nervosa," Nancie Brosseau

A Description of a Person or Place

He strides toward us in navy and white, his body muscled and heavyset, one arm holding his casually flung jeans jacket over his shoulder. A man in his prime, with just the right combination of macho and sartorial flair.

—"Some Don't Like Their Blues at All," Karyn M. Lewis

It's still there, the Chinese school on Yale Street where my brother and I used to go. Despite the new coat of paint and the high wire fence, the school I knew ten years ago remains remarkably, stoically the same.

—"The Struggle to Be an All-American Girl," Elizabeth Wong

An Example from a Case Study

Susan Smith has everything going for her. A self-described workaholic, she runs a Cambridge, Massachusetts, real estate consulting company with her husband Charles and still finds time to cuddle and nurture their two young kids, David, 7, and Stacey, 6. What few people know is that Susan, 44, needs a little chemical help to be a supermom: She has been taking the antidepressant Prozac for five years.

—"The Personality Pill," Anastasia Toufexis

A Startling Statement, Fact, or Statistic

Embalming is indeed a most extraordinary procedure, and one must wonder at the docility of Americans who each year pay hundreds of millions of dollars for its perpetuation, blissfully ignorant of what it is all about, what is done, how it is done.

—"To Dispel Fears of Live Burial," Jessica Mitford

A Statement from a Book

The American novelist John Barth, in his early novel *The Floating Opera,* remarks that ordinary, day-to-day life often presents us with embarrassingly obvious, totally unsubtle patterns of symbolism and meaning—life in the midst of death, innocence vindicated, youth versus age, etc.

—"I'm O.K., but You're Not," Robert Zoellner

A Striking Question or Questions

Do non-human animals have rights? Should we humans feel morally bound to exercise consideration for the lives and well-being of individual members of other animal species? If so, how much consideration, and by what logic?

—"Animal Rights and Beyond," David Quammen

A Common Error or Mistaken Judgment

There was a time when, in my search for essences, I concluded that the canyonland country has no heart. I was wrong. The canyonlands did have a heart, a living heart, and that heart was Glen Canyon and the golden, flowing Colorado River.

—"The Damnation of a Canyon," Edward Abbey

Combined Strategies

Last December a man named Robert Lee Willie, who had been convicted of raping and murdering an 18-year-old woman, was executed in the Louisiana state prison. In a statement issued several minutes before his death, Mr. Willie said: "Killing people is wrong. . . . It makes no

difference whether it's citizens, countries, or governments. Killing is
wrong."

—"Death and Justice," Edward Koch

● **LEAD-IN, THESIS, AND ESSAY MAP**   The introduction to an explaining essay—whether one paragraph or several—usually contains the following features.

- **Lead-in:** Some example, description, startling statement, statistic,
  short narrative, allusion, or quotation to get the reader's interest *and*
  focus on the topic the writer will explain.
- **Thesis:** Statement of the main idea; a "promise" to the reader that the
  essay fulfills.
- **Essay map:** A sentence, or part of a sentence, that *lists* (in the order in
  which the essay discusses them) the main subtopics for the essay.

In an essay about anorexia nervosa, student Nancie Brosseau's introductory paragraph has all three features.

Lead-in: Startling
statement

I knew my dieting had gotten out of hand, but when I could actually
see the movement of my heart beating beneath my clothes, I knew I
was in trouble. At first, the family doctor reassured my parents that
my rapid weight loss was a "temporary phase among teenage girls."

Description

However, when I, at fourteen years old and five feet tall, weighed in
at sixty-three pounds, my doctor changed his diagnosis from "tem-

Statistics
Thesis and
essay map

porary phase" to "anorexia nervosa." Anorexia nervosa is the process
of self-starvation that affects over 100,000 young girls each year.
Almost 6,000 of these girls die every year. Anorexia nervosa is a self-
mutilating disease that affects its victim both physically and emotionally.

The essay map is contained in the phrase "both physically and emotionally":
The first half of the essay discusses the physical effects of anorexia nervosa; the
second half explains the emotional effects. Like a road map, the essay map
helps the reader anticipate what topics the writer will explain.

● **PARAGRAPH TRANSITIONS AND HOOKS**   Transition words and paragraph hooks are audience cues that help the reader shift from one paragraph
to the next. These connections between paragraphs help the reader see the relationships of the various parts. Transition words—*first, second, next, another, last, finally,* and so forth—signal your reader that a new idea or a new
part of the idea is coming up. In addition to transition words, writers often
tie paragraphs together by using a key word or idea from a previous paragraph in the first sentence of the following paragraph to "hook" the paragraphs

together. The following paragraphs from Suze Orman's "How to Take Control of Your Credit Cards" illustrate how transition words and paragraph hooks work together to create smooth connections between paragraphs.

If you overspend just because you like to buy buy buy on credit, then you are what I call Broke by Choice. You are willfully making your own mess. I am not going to lecture you about how damaging this is; I'm hoping the fact that you're reading this article means you are ready to make a change.

But I also realize that some of you are Broke by Circumstance. I actually tell young adults in the dues-paying stage of their careers to lean on their credit cards if they don't yet make enough to always keep up with their bills. But the key is that if you rely on your credit cards to make ends meet, you must limit the plastic spending to true necessities, not indulgences. Buying groceries is a necessity. Buying dinner for you and your pals at a swank restaurant is an indulgence you can't afford if it will become part of your unpaid credit card balance.

But whether you are broke by choice or by circumstance, the strategy for getting out of credit card debt is the same: to out maneuver the card companies with a strategy that assures you pay the lowest possible interest rate. . . .

Transition: but, also

Hooks: you

Paragraph hooks: broke by choice, broke by circumstance

● **BODY PARAGRAPHS**   Body paragraphs in expository writing are the main paragraphs in an essay, excluding any introductory, concluding, or transition paragraphs. They often contain the following features.

- **Topic sentence:** To promote clarity and precision, writers often use topic sentences to announce the main ideas of paragraphs. The main idea should be clearly related to the writer's thesis. A topic sentence usually occurs early in the paragraph (first or second sentence) or at the end of the paragraph.

- **Unity:** To avoid confusing readers, writers focus on a single idea for each paragraph. Writing unified paragraphs helps writers—and their readers—concentrate on one point at a time.

- **Coherence:** To make their writing flow smoothly from one sentence to the next, writers supplement their shaping strategies with coherence devices: repeated key words, pronouns referring to key nouns, and transition words.

The following body paragraph from Suze Orman's "How to Take Control of Your Credit Cards" illustrates these features. The first sentence of this paragraph is the *topic sentence*. It announces that the focus of this paragraph will be on how to use a low-rate or a zero-rate credit card. This paragraph has *unity* because every sentence in the paragraph relates to how to use the new low- or zero-rate card. The paragraph achieves *coherence* through the use of transitions and repeated key words.

Topic sentence

Transitions: but, first, second

Repeated key words: new card, deals, new purchases

Once you are approved for the new low- or zero-rate card, move as much of your high-rate balances onto this new card. But don't— I repeat, do NOT—use the new card for new purchases. Hidden in the fine print on these deals are provisions stating, first, that any new purchases you make on the card will come with a high interest rate, and second, that you'll be paying that high interest on the entirety of your new purchase charges until you pay off every last cent of the balance transfer amount. This, to put it mildly, could really screw up your zero-rate deal. So please, use the new card only to park your old high-rate debt, and not to shop with.

DRAFTING

Before you begin drafting, reconsider your purpose and audience. What you explain depends on what your audience needs to know or what would demonstrate or show your point most effectively.

As you work from an outline or from an organizing strategy, remember that all three questions—*what, how,* and *why*—are interrelated. If you are writing about causes, for example, an explanation of *what* the topic is and *how* the causes function may also be necessary to explain your subject clearly. As you write, balance your sense of plan and organization with a willingness to pursue ideas that you discover as you write. While you need to have a plan, you should be ready to change course if you discover a more interesting idea or angle.

REVISING

As you revise your explaining essay, concentrate on making yourself perfectly clear, on illustrating with examples where your reader might be confused, and on signaling the relationship of the parts of your essay to your reader.

PEER RESPONSE

The instructions that follow will help you give and receive constructive advice about the rough draft of your explaining essay. You may use these guidelines for an in-class workshop, a take-home review, or a computer e-mail response.

Writer: Before you exchange drafts with another reader, write out the following on your essay draft.

1. **Purpose** Briefly describe your purpose, genre, and intended audience.
2. **Revision plans** What do you still intend to work on as you revise your draft?
3. **Questions** Write out one or two questions that you still have about your draft. What questions would you like your reader to answer?

Reader: First, read the entire draft from start to finish. As you reread the draft, answer the following questions.

1. **Clarity** What passages were clearest? Where were you most confused? Refer to specific sentences or passages to support your response. How and where could the writer make the draft clearer?
2. **Evidence** Where does the writer have good supporting evidence (specific examples, facts, visuals, statistics, interview results, or citations from sources)? Where does the writer need additional evidence? Refer to specific sentences or passages to support your response.
3. **Organization** Summarize or briefly outline the main ideas of the essay. Where was the organization most clear? Where were you confused? Refer to specific passages as you suggest ways to improve the draft.
4. **Purpose** Underline sentences that express the purpose or contain the thesis of the essay. Does your understanding of the essay's purpose match the writer's statement about purpose? Explain. How might the writer clarify the thesis for the intended audience?
5. **Reader's response** Overall, describe what you liked best about the draft. Then identify one major area that the writer should focus on during the revision. Does your suggestion match the writer's revision plans? Explain. Answer the writer's own question or questions about the draft.

GUIDELINES FOR REVISION

- **Review your purpose, audience, and genre.** Is your purpose clear to your target audience? Should you modify your chosen genre to appeal to your audience?

- **Review possibilities for visuals or graphics.** What additions or changes to images might be appropriate for your purpose, genre, or audience?

- **Compare your thesis sentence with what you say in your conclusion.** You may have a clearer statement of your thesis near the end of your paper. Revise your original thesis sentence to make it clearer, more focused, or more in line with what your essay actually says.

- **Explaining means *showing* and *demonstrating* relationships.** Be sure to follow general statements with *specific examples, details, facts, statistics, memories, dialogues,* or other *illustrations.*

- **In a formal definition, be sure to include the class of objects or concepts to which the term belongs.** Avoid ungrammatical writing, such as "Photosynthesis is *when* plants absorb oxygen" or "The lymphatic system is *where* the body removes bacteria and transports fatty cells."

- **Avoid introducing definitions with "Webster says . . . ."** Instead, read definitions from several dictionaries and give the best or most appropriate definition.

- **Remember that you can modify the dictionary definition of a term or concept to fit your particular context.** For example, to you, *heroism* may mean having the courage to *say* what you believe, not just to endanger your life through selfless actions.

- **Don't mix categories when you are classifying objects or ideas.** If you are classifying houses *by floor design* (ranch, bilevel, split-level, two-story), don't bring in other categories, such as passive-solar, which could be incorporated into any of those designs.

- **In explaining *how* something occurs or should be done, be sure to indicate to your audience which steps are *most important*.**

- **In cause-and-effect explanations, avoid post hoc fallacies.** This term comes from the Latin phrase *post hoc, ergo propter hoc:* "After this, therefore because of this." For example, just because Event B occurred after Event A, it does not follow, necessarily, that A caused B. If, for example, statistics show that traffic fatalities in your state actually declined after the speed limit on interstate highways was increased, you should not conclude that higher speeds actually caused the reduction in fatalities. Other causes—increased radar patrols, stiffer drunk-driving penalties, or more rigorous vehicle-maintenance laws—may have been responsible for the reduction.

• **As you revise to sharpen your meaning or make your organization clearer, use appropriate transitional words and phrases to signal the *relationships among the various parts of your subject*.**

—*To signal relation in time:* before, meanwhile, later, soon, at last, earlier, thereafter, afterward, by that time, from then on, first, next, now, presently, shortly, immediately, finally

—*To signal similarity:* likewise, similarly, once again, once more

—*To signal difference:* but, yet, however, although, whereas, though, even so, nonetheless, still, on the other hand, on the contrary

—*To signal consequences:* as a result, consequently, therefore, hence, for this reason

POSTSCRIPT ON THE WRITING PROCESS

Before you hand in your essay, reflect on your writing and learning process. In your journal, spend a few minutes answering the following questions.

1. Describe the purpose and intended audience for your essay.

2. What was the best workshop advice that you received? What did you revise in your draft because of that advice? What piece of advice did you ignore? Why?

3. What caused you the most difficulty with this essay? How did you solve the problem—or attempt to solve it? With what parts are you still least satisfied?

4. What are the best parts of your paper? Refer to specific paragraphs—what do you like most about them?

5. If you added visual images or special document-design features to your essay, explain how they supported your purpose or rhetorical goals.

6. What was the most important thing you learned about writing or your writing process as you wrote this paper?

STUDENT WRITING
CHRIS BLAKELY

White Lies: White-Collar Crime in America

Chris Blakely decided to write his essay on white-collar crime after the recent collapse of financial institutions such as AIG and the wave of collapsed pyramid schemes such as the one perpetrated by Bernie Madoff that cost investors $65 billion. After gathering information about the nature of white-collar crime and its devastating effects on workers and investors, Blakely decided to focus on two examples: the Enron collapse and the Adelphia Communications scandal. His purpose was to explain what white-collar crime is and how its effects can, in fact, be more devastating than those of street crime. As his essay overview explains, he also wrote a graphic novel to help make his point more visually and memorably for his audience. Some sample pages from his graphic novel appear on the next page.

ESSAY OVERVIEW

In this paper, I planned to analyze the state of white collar crime 1 and how it is perceived by the general public and the justice system. I found in my early research that white-collar criminals are perceived as less of a threat than street criminals (Holtfreter). This helped me to realize that public perception needs to change—and helping to change that perception was the main goal of my paper. I first needed to define white-collar crime, which I limited to cases where an employee of a public company engaged in illegal activity that seems to benefit that person and the company, but in the end harms the company, its employees, and its stockholders. I found examples of crime on a large scale, such as the Enron, Tyco, and WorldCom scandals, to show how damaging white-collar crime can be at its highest levels.

Understanding this type of crime first became important to me 2 when I found that, "according to the Federal Bureau of Investigation, white-collar crime is estimated to cost the United States more than $300 billion annually" (Cornell Law Index). Despite a recent rise in white-collar crime awareness, I was outraged that the justice system had not shifted its efforts to reduce white-collar crime. How are white-collar criminals getting away with $300 billion dollars every year? What happens to the employees when companies go bankrupt as a result of this crime? It is necessary to understand all types of crime so that society can treat all criminals in a fair and just manner.

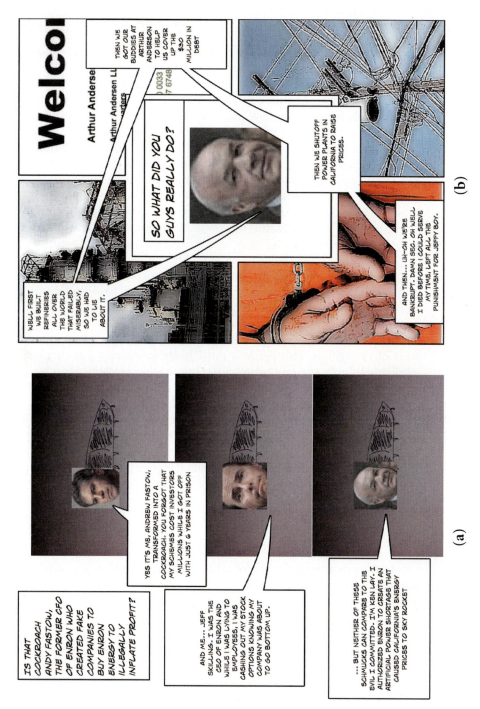

I also wanted to understand why people didn't take white-collar *3* crime seriously, so the second part of my paper used studies, mainly one by Florida State University, which look at public perception of white-collar crime. I wanted to show how white-collar crime can be just as damaging to the general public as street crime. This part helped to validate my thesis and show that this paper is exigent.

One major audience for this paper is business students. It will be *4* their decisions that shape the business world, and the ethical decisions they make could reduce white-collar crime. It will be their bosses, coworkers, and corporations committing white-collar crime—and maybe asking them to participate. If they have a better understanding of the term, as well as a sense of how damaging it can be, businesses may act more ethically.

Considering the audience of students, I then created a short *5* graphic novel about a CEO who is tempted to commit white-collar crime, but is dissuaded after meeting characters like Jeff Skilling, Dennis Kozlowski, and Karl Marx. My graphic novel, "Hope for America," looks at the illegal activity orchestrated by the CEOs of Enron. I wanted readers to be intrigued but not overwhelmed by the magnitude of the crimes. This genre is more likely to interest students by presenting the facts about white-collar crime in an accessible and humorous manner. I imagine that clips of the novel could be published in magazines that accept reader submitted cartoons. I felt that the graphic novel, which I created by learning and using the program "Comic Life," would be a great medium for presenting the information because it can be informal and is driven by visuals. It is also a much faster way for the audience to understand my point than reading a research paper—and maybe can interest them in later reading more details.

FINAL DRAFT OF ESSAY

In the prosperous days before the current economic crisis, stories *1* about misdoings among corporate executives got little more than a nod and a wink; businesspeople, it seemed, were expected to cut corners and bend the rules in seeking the profits expected of their shareholders. After all, were these "real" crimes?

But times have changed. In the face of growing unemployment, *2* numerous bankruptcies, and shrinking retirement funds, suddenly the public (and the justice system) has turned their attention—and sometimes their rage—toward the white-collar criminal. Joe Nacchio, CEO of Qwest Communication has been sentenced to six years in federal prison; Bernie Madoff, who pled guilty to defrauding clients out of some sixty-five billion dollars, has faced not only criminal penalties but also death threats; and bonuses paid to executives at the American International Group (AIG) has caused public outrage by citizens and legislators. But while these and countless other abuses have finally caught the public and governmental eye, white-collar crime is no new phenomenon. We are, in short, now paying the price for not paying attention to the long history of this phenomenon. And if we do not come to understand the problem, the outrage will not solve it. A look back at the all-but forgotten Aldephia Communications scandal and the Enron debacle before that demonstrates how, despite the spectacular headlines, we have largely ignored this building storm until it was too late.

On March 27, 2002, John Rigas and his executive board at Adelphia prepared for a routine financial check by the Securities and Exchange Commission. The investigation disclosed that the Rigas family had illegally co-borrowed $2.3 billion from the company. To cover the loans, it was estimated that Adelphia would have to borrow $1 billion. In response, investors pushed Adelphia's stock down 30% the very next day. Adelphia's shares were temporarily taken off the market and by summer the company filed for bankruptcy. On July 24, 2002 Rigas and his sons were arrested in New York City. Rigas's son, Tim, was sentenced to twenty years, while his father was given fifteen years for securities fraud (Cauley). After his trial, John Rigas maintained that, "It was a case of being in the wrong place at the wrong time. If this happened a year before, there would have been no headlines" (Cauley). In other words, Rigas felt that few would have noticed his actions if he had been caught before the Enron and the other corporate scandals of 2001 were exposed. And perhaps he was right.

The manner in which Rigas broke the law, and to the extent which he abused his power, was and is astounding. At one point Rigas was embezzling one million dollars every month (Meier). Rigas built a private golf course in his backyard, bought the Buffalo Sabres hockey team, and maintained his three private jets (Huffington 1). But the spectacular nature of this greed hides the damage that those crimes have caused to the people surrounding Adelphia. At its peak Adelphia was the largest cable company in America (Cauley). After Rigas's actions were exposed, share values dropped from eighty-seven dollars to twelve cents, costing investors and employees millions of dollars (Huffington 41). While some employees were re-hired when Adelphia was bought-up by several companies, most employees lost their jobs and all the securities that they had invested in company stock. Despite all the financial damage that the Rigas family caused, they were able to avoid jail for five years. It wasn't until 2004 that the Rigases were convicted of fraud, and because they hired a team of elite lawyers, they did not have to report to prison until the summer of 2007 (Cauley).

...continued White Lies: White-Collar Crime in America, **Chris Blakely**

The Adelphia story would be a tragedy in its own right, but when 5
it is looked at in conjunction with companies like Enron, WorldCom,
Tyco, Global Crossing, Qwest, Xerox, and several other Fortune 500
companies that went bankrupt after white-collar crime was exposed, a
pattern of corruption that has existed for many years emerges. In the
film *Enron: The Smartest Guys in the Room,* Bethany Mclean, a coauthor of the book of the same title, shows a significant problem with
how white-collar crime is perceived: "The Enron story is so fascinating because people perceive it as a story that's about numbers, that it's
some how about all these complicated transactions. In reality it's a
story about people, and it's really a human tragedy" (Gibney). Mclean
here demonstrates that the complicated transactions that surround
the case distract people from the heart of the matter: the human
tragedy.

By explaining the human costs behind these white-collar crimes, I 6
hope to show why the public must pay attention to this public scourge.
First, I want to show how the sentencing of these criminals, as compared to the sentencing of street criminals, sends the wrong message
about the serious nature of white-collar crime. Second, I hope to
demonstrate that public perception of white-collar crime is flawed
and out of sync with the personal tragedies that crime causes.

The term white-collar crime was originally coined by Edward 7
Sutherland in 1939. Sutherland defined white-collar crime as "crime
committed by a person of high social status and respectability, in the
course of their occupation." Recently, sociologists and criminologists
have debated what crimes are actually considered white-collar. Often,
the term refers to a crime committed in the course of a person's occupation—no matter the social class. But, as Sutherland suggests, true
white-collar crime is that which has a great impact upon society.

White-collar crime is often very difficult to detect. The crimes 8
take place in private offices where there are rarely eye-witnesses. The
government has to base their prosecution on complex paper trails instead of concrete evidence (Strader 1-4). Also, white-collar criminals
of high social status are able to hire better-trained, more experienced
lawyers. This makes convicting white-collar criminals much more difficult than street criminals.

Because white-collar crimes are often not given due attention, it is 9
difficult for the majority of Americans to understand their financial
complexity. Understanding the methods used to commit the crimes,
however, is not nearly as important as recognizing the damage that is
done to countless employees who lose everything that they worked
years to accomplish. Americans need to realize that their ignorance of

the effects of white collar crime has allowed the American justice system to be unfairly lax in the way it treats white-collar criminals.

If we compare white collar crime to a typical armed robbery, we *10* can see the inequality of the current justice system. For example, just compare the sentencing of John Rigas to that of three Kentuckians who robbed a small grocery store. In November, 2007, Morgan Wallace, 30, entered the grocery store with a handgun and demanded money. Geneva S. Goodin and Megan Johnston assisted in the escape before the three were apprehended on a highway near the scene of the crime. All three were held in a detention center after the robbery. On April 11, 2008, Wallace and Goodin were sentenced to ten years in prison while Johnston was sentenced to five years (McCreary County Voice). Unlike Rigas, Wallace, Goodin, and Johnston were not able to obtain bail money so that they could go to their homes before their trial. The three robbers were arrested, tried, and convicted within five to six months. That period is a stark contrast to the five years of freedom that Rigas was allowed, before a judge requested he begin his jail time (Cauley). There is also a clear disparity in the punishment that was handed out in relation to the damage of the crimes to society. The amount that the Kentuckians made off with was not disclosed, but it is certainly a miniscule amount compared with the $2.3 billion that Rigas gained, followed by the millions of dollars that were lost to shareholders. However, Wallace's term is only five years shorter than that of John Rigas, and there was no stipulation that the sentence could be as short as two years (as with Rigas' case), if Wallace's health declined.

Wallace and his accomplices are clearly criminals. That is not *11* the point. What *is* important here is the clear bias between the ways that these two cases were tried. If the two cases are looked at separately, there is little ground to claim injustice in either case. If the two cases are compared, however, the injustice is clear. Wallace's armed robbery did not kill anyone and it robbed a store owner of a very small amount of money compared to the 2.3 billion that Rigas took from his employees.

The Rigas case is important in its own right, but it is impossible to *12* explain the devastation caused by white-collar crime without also examining the Enron scandal. In January 2001, Enron was the seventh largest corporation in America. Enron had built oil-extracting stations all over the world, but most of them were performing terribly. However, instead of accurately releasing the correct financial statistics, Enron's executives included prospective profits in its bottom-line. Enron, and its accounting firm, Arthur Anderson, were able to hide the fact that they were $30 million in debt. Enron's CFO Andy Fastow created fake partnerships that would buy energy from Enron, in order to increase Enron's value. However, Fastow was merely working under Kenneth Lay, the founder of the company, and Jeffrey Skilling, the CEO. When investors started to question Enron's finances, Enron was not able to provide legitimate documentation for their profits. The final straw was when Enron began shutting down power plants in California in order to create artificial power shortages to increase the price of energy. The SEC began to inquire into Enron. In response, Enron began to release massive restatements, and Arthur Anderson began to shred the documents concerning Enron. Six weeks after the investigations began, Enron filed for bankruptcy (Gibney). Ken Lay passed away before he could be sentenced. Jeff Skilling was sentenced to twenty-four years and $60 million in fines; however, he was allowed to keep his $5 million mansion and $50 million in stocks and bonds. Andy Fastow was sentenced to just six years in prison. The term was reduced because of his cooperation with the government (MSNBC).

The difference between Enron and other corporate scandals is that no other company has ever been so high and fallen with such damaging consequences. While Adelphia was partially bought up by Time Warner (Cauley), Enron completely collapsed. The stock value went from $90.75 at its peak to just $.08 after the company filed for bankruptcy. Five thousand employees lost their jobs, along with $800 million in pension funds. The total market loss for the company was $68 million (Huffington 12). These numbers do not include the money that was lost by California residents during the artificial power outages or the prospective earnings that thousands of Enron employees lost when they were fired. Despite efforts to re-coop money lost by employees, most of the damage was irreversible. It is also important to remember that not all of the damage was financial. Enron employees and investors were personally affected. After losing their jobs, they were forced to deal with the stress that surrounds finding a new job, and making ends meet while providing for a family. The employees went from having a secure future in a successful company to being unemployed with most of their stock and their retirement funds erased. Enron was white-collar crime at its worst.   13

These personal tragedies are often lost in the extravagant numbers and complex business practices. As a result of the fraud committed by a small group of men, thousands of people lost their livelihood. This problem cannot be considered an isolated incident. Doing that would ignore the damage that white-collar crime has already done, as well as be ignorant of future corporate fraud. As Ben Lerach, the chief attorney for Enron employees stated, "It's the same old adage; if it looks to good to be true, then it is. Enron was making millions of dollars out of nowhere, and no one inside the company was there to stand up and question where this money was coming from" (Gibney). But is the public aware?   14

Following these high profile white-collar crimes, researchers took *15* specific interest in how white-collar crime is perceived by the general public. Researchers at the College of Criminology at Florida State University published a study in February 2008 that addressed this topic. In preliminary research it was found that white-collar crime costs the United States about $250 billion per year, whereas personal, or "street crimes," and household crimes account for only $17.6 billion lost. Despite this large disparity, the focus of criminal justice authorities and criminologists has been on explaining and preventing personal crime. Previous research found that authorities focus on street crime because the public perceives it as more of a threat. In a study of 402 participants nation-wide, researchers found that in a case where a white-collar criminal stole $1,000 and a street criminal stole $1,000 about two-thirds of the participants believed that the street criminal was more likely to be caught. Two-thirds also believed that the street criminal should be given a harsher punishment than the white-collar criminal. In contrast, two-thirds of participants believed that the government should devote more resources to catching white-collar criminals (Holtfreter). This research shows that while Americans see white-collar crime as a problem, they are still more threatened by street crime and believe it should be dealt with more harshly. If Americans feel more threatened by street crime, authorities will respond by devoting their efforts to stopping it.

A study by researchers at Cal State and the University of Florida *16* published in February 2007 provides more data on the topic. Researchers used data from a national phone poll of 1,106 participants and found that three-quarters of the sample believed that street criminals were more likely to be caught and more likely to receive a harsher punishment. The sample was split in who *should* receive a harsher punishment. This study suggests that while the public may believe all criminals should receive the same punishment, it is clear that Americans believe white-collar criminals will receive less of a punishment (Schoepfer).

Interesting conclusions can be drawn from both of these studies. *17* From the Florida State study, participants believed that in a case where a white-collar and a street criminal commit crimes of equal financial damage, the street criminal should receive a harsher punishment. This may be because street crime is usually a crime where the victim is personally involved in a confrontation, whereas white-collar crime is a more indirect form of victimization. However, it is obvious, due to the large gap in total damages, that white-collar criminals are acting more frequently and doing more financial damage than street criminals. The second study shows that the public acknowledges a disparity in the sentencing of white-collar and street criminals, yet no major reforms have attempted

...continued White Lies: White-Collar Crime in America, **Chris Blakely**

to change this pattern. These studies show that public perception is inaccurate as based on the threat that each type of crime poses financially.

The American business model is an institution that has shown sustainability and reliability for the past two hundred years. However, it is through this institution that Americans are stealing nearly fifteen times more money than through conventional street crimes. The devastating effects of white-collar crime need to be discussed by all Americans and addressed in a systematic way. The current outrage is not sufficient for a long-term fix. People lock their doors when they leave their house, but they see no problem in putting ninety percent of their 401k stock options into one company. White-collar crime has produced real damage and without change in public opinion, there are no signs that it will decline. Understanding white-collar crime now can prevent or reduce the damage that white-collar crime inflicts on America.

18

Works Cited

Cauley, Leslie. "John Rigas Tells His Side of the Adelphia Story." *USA Today*. Gannett, 10 Apr. 2008. Web. 12 Apr. 2009.

Enron: The Smartest Guys in the Room. Dir. Alex Gibney. Perf. Peter Coyote. Jigsaw, 2005. Film.

"Former Enron CEO Skilling Gets 24 Years." *Associated Press*. Associated Press, 23 Oct. 2006. Web. 11 Apr. 2009.

Holtfreter, Kristy., et al. "Public Perception of White-Collar Crime." *Journal of Criminal Justice* 36:1 (2008): 50–60. Print.

Meier, Barry. "Founder of Adelphia Is Found Guilty of Conspiracy." *New York Times*. New York Times, 8 July 2004. Web.13 Apr. 2009.

Schoepfer, Andrea., et al. "Do Perceptions of Punishment Vary Between White Collar and Street Crimes?" *Journal of Criminal Justice* 35:2 (2007): 151–163. Print.

Strader, Kelly. "Understanding White Collar Crime." *Understanding White Collar Crime*. New York: Mathew Bender, 2002. 1–13. Print.

"Three Plead Guilty in Store Robbery." *McCreary County Voice*. McCreary County Voice, 11 Apr. 2008. Web. 13 Apr. 2009.

 ## QUESTIONS FOR WRITING AND DISCUSSION

1 In his essay overview, Blakely says his purpose is to change public perception about the effects of white-collar crime. Cite at least two specific sentences from his essay where Blakely states this purpose.

2 Explaining essays typically use definition, process analysis, and cause and effect reasoning to demonstrate the main points. Reread Blakely's essay. Then cite examples of all of the above strategies from his paper. Which of these strategies is most closely related to his purpose or thesis? Explain.

3 As he explains the effects of white-collar crime on society, Blakely makes a comparison between a "street crime" and white-collar crime. What two crimes is he comparing? How does Blakely say they are similar and different? Are there other differences that Blakely doesn't explain that may account for the public's fear of street crime but their complacency about white-collar crime?

4 In an explaining essay, transitions from paragraph to paragraph help to clarify the subject for the audience. Review the section on "Paragraph Transitions and Hooks" in this chapter (page 208). Then find two places where Blakely makes clear and smooth transitions from one paragraph to the next. Identify the transition words and hooks he uses to connect these paragraphs.

5 Review the selections from Blakely's graphic novel. How do the scenes he depicts relate to the subject and purpose of his essay? Do the cartoon-like pictures and captions make white-collar crime seem too humorous? How do Blakely's images and captions convey the seriousness of these crimes? Explain, citing specific images and dialogue.

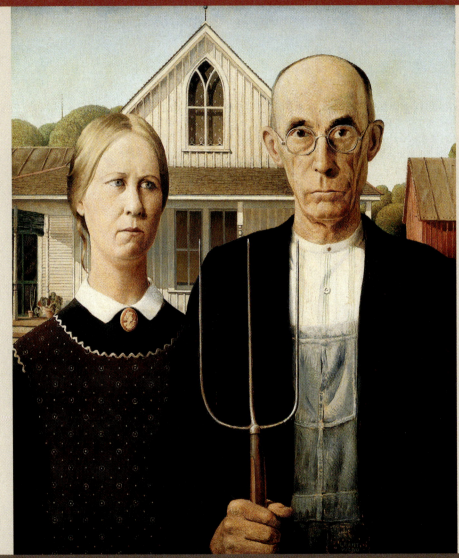

Study the details in "American Gothic" by Grant Wood and then read the review of
"American Gothic" by Paul Richard on page 231 of this chapter.

Evaluating

8

During your fall semester library-orientation tour, you discover a small office tucked away in the corner of the library building: the interlibrary loan office. Because you occasionally need to see articles and books that your library does not have, you decide to investigate the interlibrary loan service and evaluate the helpfulness of the staff as well as the convenience, speed, and cost of obtaining materials. As part of your evaluation, you interview the office coordinator as well as several teachers and students who have used the service. Their responses—combined with your own observations—indicate that although an interlibrary loan can sometimes take a couple of weeks, the loan office gets high marks for its service. The staff is always helpful and patient, the service is easily accessible through electronic mail, and the cost of books and articles is surprisingly low.

In an e-mail to your parents, you explain that you are considering transferring to a different school for the following year. You have some misgivings about your decision to change, but after listing your criteria and ranking them in order from most to least important, you are convinced that you're making the right choice. In the message, you explain your decision, based on your criteria, and ask that your parents continue to support your education.

> " When we evaluate, we have in mind ... an ideal of what a good thing—pianist, painting, or professor—should be and do, and we apply that ideal to the individual instance before us. "
> —JEANNE FAHNESTOCK AND MARIE SECOR, AUTHORS OF *A RHETORIC OF ARGUMENT*

> " Purpose and craftsmanship—ends and means—these are the keys to your judgment. "
> —MARYA MANNES, JOURNALIST AND SOCIAL COMMENTATOR

Hardly a day passes that we do not express our likes or dislikes. We constantly pass judgment on people, places, objects, events, ideas, and policies. "Sue is a wonderful person." "The food in this cafeteria is horrible." "That movie we saw Saturday night ought to get an Oscar nomination for best picture." "The bailout for America's banks and auto industry was a horrible waste of taxpayers' money." In addition to our own reactions, we are constantly exposed to the opinions of our friends, family members, teachers, and business associates. The media also barrage us with claims about products, famous personalities, and candidates for political office.

A claim or opinion, however, is not an *evaluation*. Your reaction to a person, a sports event, a meal, a movie, or a public policy becomes an evaluation *only* when you support your value judgment with clear standards and specific evidence. Your goal in evaluating something is not only to express your viewpoint, but also to *persuade* others to accept your judgment. You convince your readers by indicating the standards for your judgment and then supporting it with evidence: "The food in this cafeteria is horrible [your claim]. I know that not all cafeteria food tastes great, but it should at least be sanitary [one standard of judgment]. Yesterday, I had to dig a piece of green mold out of the meat loaf, and just as I stuck my fork into the green salad, a large black roach ran out [evidence]."

Most people interested in a subject agree that certain standards are important, for example, that a cafeteria be clean and pest-free. The standards that you share with your audience are the *criteria* for your evaluation. You convince your readers that something is good or bad, ugly or beautiful, tasty or nauseating by analyzing your subject in terms of your criteria. For each separate criterion, you support your judgment with specific *evidence:* descriptions, statistics, testimony, or examples from your personal experience. If your readers agree that your standards or criteria are appropriate, and if you supply detailed evidence, your readers should be convinced. They will take your evaluation seriously—and think twice about eating at that roach-infested cafeteria.

Techniques for Writing Evaluations

The most common genre for evaluations is the review. Most frequently, we read reviews of films, books, restaurants, commercial products, public performances, and works of art. Reviews vary widely depending on the topic, the place of publication, and the social context. Some reviews seem to be little more than thinly disguised promotions, while other reviews are thorough, complex, and highly critical. For any substantive evaluation, the review must set standards of judgment, rely on fair criteria, balance positive and negative evaluations, and provide sufficient evidence to persuade its readers. Use the following techniques as you write your evaluation.

> 66 It is as hard to find a neutral critic as it is a neutral country in a time of war. 99
>
> —KATHERINE ANNE PORTER,
> NOVELIST AND SHORT STORY WRITER

Techniques for Evaluating

Technique	Tips on How to Do It
Assessing the *rhetorical situation*	What is the occasion and context for your review? Find examples of the genre you propose to write— where are these reviews or critiques typically published? Who is the audience, and what do they already believe or know about the topic?
Stating an *overall claim* about your subject	The overall claim is your *thesis* for your evaluation. It sums up both the positive and negative judgments you make for each criterion.
Clarifying the *criteria* for your evaluation	A criterion is a standard of judgment that most people who are knowledgeable about your subject agree is important. A criterion serves as a yardstick against which you measure your specific subject.
Stating a *judgment* for each criterion	The overall claim is based on your *judgment* of each separate criterion. Avoid being too critical or too enthusiastic by including both positive and negative judgments.
Supporting each judgment with *evidence*	Support should include *detailed observations, facts, examples, testimonials, quotations from experts,* or *statistics.*
Balancing your evaluation with both *positive* and *negative* judgments about your subject	Evaluations that are all positive are merely advertisements; evaluations that are entirely negative may seem too harsh or mean-spirited.

In the following evaluation of a Chinese restaurant in Washington, D.C., journalist and critic Phyllis C. Richman illustrates the main features of an evaluation.

Hunan Dynasty

215 Pennsylvania Ave. SE. 546–6161

Open daily 11 A.M. TO 3 P.M. for lunch, 3 P.M. TO 10 P.M. for dinner, until 11 P.M. on Friday and Saturday.

Reservations suggested for large parties.

Information and description

Prices for lunch: appetizers $2 to $4.50, entrees $4.75 to $6.50. For dinner: appetizers $1 to $13.95 (combination platter), entrees $6.75 to $18.

Complete dinner with wine or beer, tax, and tip about $20 a person.

Description

Chinese restaurants in America were once places one went just to eat. Now one goes to dine. There are now waiters in black tie, cloths on the tables and space between those tables, art on the walls and decoratively carved vegetables on the plate—elegance has become routine in Chinese restaurants. What's more, in Chinese restaurants the ingredients are fresh (have you ever found frozen broccoli in a Chinese kitchen?), and the cooking almost never sinks below decent. . . . And it is usually moderately priced. In other words, if you're among unfamiliar restaurants and looking for good value, Chinese restaurants now are routinely better than ever.

Overall claim

The Hunan Dynasty is an example of what makes Chinese restaurants such reliable choices. A great restaurant? It is not. A good value? Definitely. A restaurant to fit nearly any diner's need? Probably.

Criterion #1: Nice setting
Judgment: Attractive
Evidence
Criterion #2: Good service
Judgment: Often expert
Evidence

First, it is attractive. There are no silk tassels, blaring red lacquer or Formica tables; instead there are white tablecloths and subtle glass etchings. It is a dining room—or dining rooms, for the vastness has been carved into smaller spaces—of gracefulness and lavish space.

Second, service is a strong priority. The waiters look and act polished, and serve with flourishes from the carving of a Peking duck to the portioning of dishes among the diners. I have found some glitches—a forgotten appetizer, a recommendation of two dishes that turned out nearly identical—but most often the service has been expert. . . .

Criterion #3: Good main dishes
Judgment: Good but not memorable
Evidence

As for the main dishes, don't take the "hot and spicy" asterisks too seriously, for this kitchen is not out to offer you a test of fire. The peppers are there, but not in great number. And, like the appetizers, the main dishes are generally good but not often memorable. Fried dishes—and an inordinate number of them seem to be fried—are crunchy and not greasy. Vegetables are bright and crisp. Eggplant with hot garlic sauce is properly unctuous; Peking duck is as fat-free and crackly-skinned as you could hope (though pancakes were rubbery). And seafoods—shrimp, scallops, lobster—are tenderly cooked, though they are not the most full-flavored examples of those ingredients.

I have found only one dismal main dish in a fairly broad sampling: lemon chicken had no redeeming feature in its doughy, greasy, overcooked and underseasoned presentation. Otherwise, not much goes wrong. Crispy shrimp with walnuts might be preferable stir-fried rather than batter-fried, but the tomato-red sauce and crunchy walnuts made a good dish. Orange beef could use more seasoning but the coating was nicely crusty and the meat tender. . . .

Criterion #3 cont.
Judgment: Sometimes
bad
Evidence

So with the opening of the Hunan Dynasty, Washington did not add a stellar Chinese restaurant to its repertoire, but that is not necessarily what the city needed anyway. Hunan Dynasty is a top-flight neighborhood restaurant—with good food, caring service and very fair prices—that is attractive enough to set a mood for celebration and easygoing enough for an uncomplicated dinner with the family after work.

Overall claim restated

EVALUATING COMMERCIAL PRODUCTS OR SERVICES

Writers frequently evaluate commercial products or services. Consumer magazines test and rate every imaginable product or service—from cars and dishwashers to peanut butter and brokerage houses. Guidebooks evaluate tourist spots, restaurants, colleges, and hunting lodges. Specialty magazines, such as *Modern Photography, Road and Track, Skiing,* and *Wired,* often rate products and services of interest to their readers. To qualify as evaluation—and not just advertising—the authors and the publishers must maintain an independent status, uninfluenced by the manufacturers of the products or services they are judging.

Consider, first, the following "evaluation" of a wine, found on a bottle of Cabernet Sauvignon:

This Cabernet Sauvignon is a dry, robust, and complex wine whose hearty character is balanced by an unusual softness.

This "evaluative" language is so vague and esoteric that it may mean very little to the average consumer who just wants some wine with dinner. *Dry:* How can a liquid be dry? *Robust:* Does this refer to physique? *Soft:* Wine is not a pillow, though it might put you to sleep. *Complex:* Are they describing a wine or conducting a psychological analysis? While an independent evaluator may legitimately use these terms for knowledgeable wine drinkers, this particular description suggests that the wine is absolutely everything the buyer would like it to be—dry yet robust, hearty but at the same time soft. Apparently, the writer's purpose here is not to evaluate a product but to flatter readers who imagine themselves connoisseurs of wine.

Now consider the following evaluation of two popular cell phones, Apple's iPhone and the Palm Pre. In this comparative evaluation, the editors at *Consumer Reports* judge the two cell phones in terms of their display functions, cameras, Web search capabilities, and voice qualities. After providing evidence to support their judgments for each of these criteria, the editors conclude with their overall assessment.

Cell-phone Face-off

Apple's iPhone 3G S ($200, two-year contract, AT&T) is a slight update on its previous version and now sits atop our smart-phone Ratings. The new Palm Pre ($200, two-year contract, Sprint) ranked close, turning in a fine performance. Here are the details:

Display. The iPhone offers superb multimedia functionality via a 3.5-inch touch screen. That provides access to most controls and allows you to move or enlarge photos and Web pages with your fingertips. The Pre lets you shuffle multiple applications on its 3.1-inch touch screen like a deck of cards without losing your place. Flick the application off the page to close it.

Camera. The Pre's 3.1-megapixel camera has a flash and produces decent 8 × 10 prints. The iPhone's 3.1-megapixel camera, which also made fine 8 × 10 prints, has auto-focus and can shoot videos.

Search. Type a name or word on the Pre's slide-out keyboard and it will check your contacts and applications for that term, listing them for quick access. It also offers a useful Web search option. On the iPhone, typing a name or word on its virtual keyboard will provide an extensive internal search of your contacts, e-mail messages, applications, and music.

Voice. The phones have very good voice quality when talking, fair when listening.

Bottom line. The iPhone 3G S has a slight edge overall and is the best for multimedia. The Pre is better if you do a lot of messaging and prefer a real keyboard.

EVALUATING WORKS OF ART

Evaluations of commercial products and services tend to emphasize usefulness, practicality, convenience, and cost. Evaluations of works of art, on the other hand, focus on form, color, texture, design, balance, image, or theme. Even the phrase "appreciating a work of art" suggests that we are making a value judgment, though usually not one based on money. Through evaluation, writers teach us to appreciate all kinds of art: paintings, sculpture, photographs, buildings, antique cars or furniture, novels, short stories, essays, poems, and tapestries. A Dior fashion, a quilt, a silverware pattern, even an old pair of jeans might be evaluated primarily on aesthetic rather than practical grounds.

In the following selection, Paul Richard, art critic for *The Washington Post*, evaluates the painting, "American Gothic," by Grant Wood. (This painting is reproduced on the opening page of this chapter.) Although the painting was completed in 1930, the occasion for Richard's review was a 2006 Grant Wood exhibition at the Renwick Gallery of the Smithsonian American Art Museum. Richard's overall claim is that "American Gothic" is a famous and even iconic example of American art—as well known as Andy Warhol's Campbell soup can or Norman Rockwell's Thanksgiving turkey. The fact that "American Gothic" has so often been the subject of parody (search Google Images, "American Gothic Parodies") is further evidence of the painting's iconic status.

PROFESSIONAL WRITING

"American Gothic," Pitchfork Perfect

Paul Richard

Is "American Gothic" America's best-known painting? Certainly it's one 1 of them. Grant Wood's dual portrait—with its churchy evocations, its stiffness and its pitchfork—pierced us long ago, and got stuck into our minds. Now, finally, it's here.

"American Gothic," which hasn't been in Washington in 40 years, 2 goes on view today at the Renwick Gallery of the Smithsonian American Art Museum. By all means, take it in—although, of course, you have already.

It should have gone all fuzzy—it's been parodied so often, and 3 parsed so many ways—but the 1930 canvas at the Renwick is as sharp as ever. Its details are finer than its travesties suggest, its image more absorbing. It's also smaller than one might have imagined, at only two feet wide. Wood painted it in his home town of Cedar Rapids, Iowa, showed it only once and then sold it, with relief, to the Art Institute of Chicago—for $300.

The picture with a pitchfork is an American unforgettable. Few 4 paintings, very few, have its recognizability. Maybe Whistler's mother. Maybe Warhol's soup can. Maybe Rockwell's Thanksgiving turkey. They're national emblems, all of them, visual manifestations of the American dream.

Whistler's figure, stiff and dark, looks half-enthroned and half- 5 embalmed; what she evokes is Mom. Family and food are the twin themes of the Rockwell. And with his Campbell's can, fluorescent-lit, Warhol nails shopping.

"American Gothic," too, hits the psychic bull's-eye. Wood's sly paint- 6 ing gives us the bedrock Christian values, the sober rural rectitude and the gnawing fear of sex that have made this country great.

The dangers of the dirty deed might not be depicted, but they're 7 present nonetheless. The sinful is suggested by the serpent made of hair that slithers up the woman's neck to whisper in her ear, by the lightning rod atop the house and, of course, by the Devil's pitchfork. Wood's painting has a wink in it. No wonder it has been so frequently cartooned.

"The couple in front of the house have become preppies, yuppies, 8 hippies," writes critic Robert Hughes, "Weathermen, pot growers, Ku Kluxers, jocks, operagoers, the Johnsons, the Reagans, the Carters, the Fords, the Nixons, the Clintons, and George Wallace with an elderly black lady."

But cartoons tend toward the slapdash, and Wood's calculated im- 9 age is not at all haphazard. Nothing's out of place. The bright tines of the fork have been echoed one, two, three, by, at the left, the distant steeple, the window's pointed arch and the sharp roof at the right. The pitchfork rhymes as well with the seams of the man's overalls. When Wood painted "American Gothic," he fit its symmetries together as if he were making a watch.

Often, for self-portraits, the painter posed in overalls. But don't fall 10 for the costume. Grant Wood (1891–1942) was no hick. He'd been four times to Europe. He taught in universities. He'd studied art in Paris, Germany and Italy, and it's clear he'd learned a lot. He was an exceptionally skillful painter, although not for long. Most of his best pictures—a dozen are included in "Grant Wood's Studio: Birthplace of 'American Gothic,'" the Renwick's exhibition—were painted in the five years after 1930. He had other things to do.

He was, this show reminds us, a carpenter, a carver, a skilled interior 11 decorator. He could make a metal lampshade, or devise a chandelier, or embellish a posh room with faux rococo decorations. He could design a woman's necklace or a stained-glass window. He hammered teapots out of copper. Examples are on view.

They're here for a reason. And two works of art are key to Jane C. 12 Milosch's exhibition. One is Wood's strict picture; the other is the vaguely medieval studio in which he made that painting—a charming, hand-built place acquired by the Cedar Rapids Museum of Art in 2002. They have a lot in common. The painting and the studio demonstrate the principles—the insistence on the local, the display of traditional craftsmanship—of the decorative movement known as American Arts and Crafts.

The picture takes its title from an architectural fashion. In its higher 13
manifestations, American Gothic gave us the Washington Cathedral and
the colleges at Yale. Far out in the sticks (in, for instance, rural Iowa), the
style left its mark on the factory-made windows, porch columns and pattern books that in the 19th century were shipped in by train.

"American Gothic's" farmhouse, with its pointed gable window, is 14
another local artifact. Wood discovered that wooden building in nearby
Eldon, Iowa. It's still there. His figures were local, too. The bald man is his
dentist, B.H. McKeeby. The woman is Wood's sister, Nan. (She was 30 at
the time, McKeeby, 62.) Their eyes are cold, their mouths are prim. They
wear period clothes. He stares the viewer down, she averts her gaze. They
understand their roles.

Modern art, this isn't. Wood's painting is behind its times, rather 15
than ahead of them. What gives the work its punch is its slippery ambi-
guities. These haven't aged at all.

Try asking it a question. Is the woman the farmer's wife, or might 16
she be (nudge, nudge) the famous farmer's daughter of countless
naughty jokes?

What does this painting mean to do, celebrate or satirize? Do its fig- 17
ures dwell in paradise, where the pioneering Protestant verities still hold,
or is their rural neighborhood not so far from Hell? . . .

I don't know whether Wood expected "American Gothic" to become 18
an American icon, but he wouldn't have been surprised. In the early
1930s, mythic American icons were very much on his mind.

Had you asked him to identify America's best-known paintings, you 19
can bet he would have named two pictures of George Washington:
Gilbert Stuart's likeness, the so-called Atheneum Portrait of 1796, the
one that's on the dollar; and "Washington Crossing the Delaware"
(1851), Emanuel Leutze's famous river scene with ice floes. In fact, both
of these chestnuts can be found in Wood's own art. . . .

What is remarkable about "American Gothic" is its famousness. 20
What is equally remarkable is that the picture's fame was not achieved by
accident. The Renwick's show suggests that's what Grant Wood had in
mind.

EVALUATING PERFORMANCES

Evaluating live, recorded, or filmed performances of people in sports, dance,
drama, debate, public meetings or lectures, and music may involve practical criteria, such as the prices of tickets to sports events or rock concerts. However,
there are also aesthetic criteria that apply to people and their performances. In
film evaluations, for example, the usual criteria are good acting and directing,

an entertaining or believable story or plot, memorable characters, dramatic special effects, and so forth.

In the following review of *Slumdog Millionaire*, Manohla Dargis, writing for *The New York Times*, evaluates key elements of this Academy Award winning film: the director, the actors, the story, and the cinematography. As is typical of the film review genre, Dargis is writing for readers who have seen the film but also for those still deciding whether to watch it. To appeal to both sets of readers, Dargis weaves her evaluation into a summary of the film that gives a sense of the story and its context without revealing too much about the twists and turns of the plot. Dargis' overall judgment is that the film has a "resolutely upbeat pitch and seductive visual style" even though it feels "blithely glib" and calculated in places.

PROFESSIONAL WRITING

"Slumdog Millionaire"

Manohla Dargis

A gaudy, gorgeous rush of color, sound and motion, "Slumdog Millionaire," the latest from the British shape-shifter Danny Boyle, doesn't travel through the lower depths, it giddily bounces from one horror to the next. A modern fairy tale about a pauper angling to become a prince, this sensory blowout largely takes place amid the squalor of Mumbai, India, where lost children and dogs sift through trash so fetid you swear you can smell the discarded mango as well as its peel, or could if the film weren't already hurtling through another picturesque gutter. *1*

Mr. Boyle, who first stormed the British movie scene in the mid-1990s with flashy entertainments like "Shallow Grave" and "Trainspotting," has a flair for the outré. Few other directors could turn a heroin addict rummaging inside a rank toilet bowl into a surrealistic underwater reverie, as he does in "Trainspotting," and fewer still could do so while holding onto the character's basic humanity. The addict, played by Ewan McGregor, emerges from his repulsive splish-splashing with a near-beatific smile (having successfully retrieved some pills), a terrible if darkly funny image that turns out to have been representative not just of Mr. Boyle's bent humor but also of his worldview: better to swim than to sink. *2*

Swimming comes naturally to Jamal (the British actor Dev Patel in his feature-film debut), who earns a living as a chai-wallah serving fragrant tea to call-center workers in Mumbai and who, after a series of alternating exhilarating and unnerving adventures, has landed in the hot seat on the television game show "Who Wants to Be a Millionaire." Yet while the story opens with Jamal on the verge of grabbing the big prize, *3*

Simon Beaufoy's cleverly kinked screenplay, adapted from a novel by Vikas Swarup, embraces a fluid view of time and space, effortlessly shuttling between the young contestant's past and his present, his childhood spaces and grown-up times. Here, narrative doesn't begin and end: it flows and eddies—just like life.

By all rights the texture of Jamal's life should have been brutally 4 coarsened by tragedy and poverty by the time he makes a grab for the television jackpot. But because "Slumdog Millionaire" is self-consciously (perhaps commercially) framed as a contemporary fairy tale cum love story, or because Mr. Boyle leans toward the sanguine, this proves to be one of the most upbeat stories about living in hell imaginable. It's a life that begins in a vast, vibrant, sun-soaked, jam-packed ghetto, a kaleidoscopic city of flimsy shacks and struggling humanity and takes an abrupt, cruel turn when Jamal (Ayush Mahesh Khedekar), then an exuberant 7, and his cagier brother, Salim (Azharuddin Mohammed Ismail), witness the murder of their mother (Sanchita Choudhary) by marauding fanatics armed with anti-Muslim epithets and clubs.

Cast into the larger, uncaring world along with another new or- 5 phan, a shy beauty named Latika (Rubina Ali plays the child, Freida Pinto the teenager), the three children make their way from one refuge to another before falling prey to a villain whose exploitation pushes the story to the edge of the unspeakable. Although there's something undeniably fascinating, or at least watchable, about this ghastly interlude—the young actors are very appealing and sympathetic, and the images are invariably pleasing even when they shouldn't be—it's unsettling to watch these young characters and, by extension, the young nonprofessionals playing them enact such a pantomime. It doesn't help even if you remember that Jamal makes it out alive long enough to have his 15 televised minutes.

It's hard to hold onto any reservations in the face of Mr. Boyle's res- 6 olutely upbeat pitch and seductive visual style. Beautifully shot with great sensitivity to color by the cinematographer Anthony Dod Mantle, in both film and digital video, "Slumdog Millionaire" makes for a better viewing experience than it does for a reflective one. It's an undeniably attractive package, a seamless mixture of thrills and tears, armchair tourism (the Taj Mahal makes a guest appearance during a sprightly interlude) and crackerjack professionalism. Both the reliably great Irrfan Khan ("A Mighty Heart"), as a sadistic detective, and the Bollywood star Anil Kapoor, as the preening game-show host, run circles around the young Mr. Patel, an agreeable enough if vague centerpiece to all this coordinated, insistently happy chaos.

In the end, what gives me reluctant pause about this bright, cheery, 7 hard-to-resist movie is that its joyfulness feels more like a filmmaker's calculation than an honest cry from the heart about the human spirit (or,

...*continued* "Slumdog Millionaire," **Manohla Dargis**

better yet, a moral tale). In the past Mr. Boyle has managed to wring giggles out of murder ("Shallow Grave") and addiction ("Trainspotting"), and invest even the apocalypse with a certain joie de vivre (the excellent zombie flick "28 Days Later"). He's a blithely glib entertainer who can dazzle you with technique and, on occasion, blindside you with emotion, as he does in his underrated children's movie, "Millions." He plucked my heartstrings in "Slumdog Millionaire" with well-practiced dexterity, coaxing laughter and sobs out of each sweet, sour and false note.

WARMING UP   Journal Exercises

The following exercises will help you practice writing evaluations. Read all of the following exercises and then write on the three that interest you most. If another idea occurs to you, write about it.

1. **Writing Across the Curriculum.** Choose the best of the courses that you are currently taking. To persuade a friend to take it, evaluate the course, the teacher, or both. What criteria and evidence would you select to persuade your friend?

2. Evaluate an object related to one of your hobbies or special interests—stereo or video equipment, water or snow skis, a cooking appliance or utensil, diving or hiking equipment, photography or art equipment, ranching or farming apparatus, fishing rods or reels, some part of a car, or computers. Write an evaluation of that object following the format used by *Consumer Reports*.

3. Evaluate a TV show that you find particularly irritating, boring, or insipid, but that you find yourself watching occasionally anyway. Watch the show, taking notes about scenes, characters, dialogue, and plot. Write a critique of the show for other students in this class.

4. To gather some information for yourself about a possible job or career, interview a person in your prospective field about his or her job or profession. Focus your questions on the person's opinions and judgments about this career. What criteria does this person use to judge it? What other jobs serve as a good basis for comparison? What details from this person's daily routine support his or her judgments?

5. At your place of work, evaluate one of your products or services. Write down the criteria and evidence that your business might use to determine whether it is a "good" product or service. Then list the criteria and evidence that your customers or patrons probably use. Are these two sets of criteria and evidence identical? Explain.

6 Choose a piece of modern art (painting, drawing, poster, sculpture, ceramics, and so forth). Describe and evaluate it for an audience that is indifferent or possibly even hostile to contemporary art. Explain why your readers should appreciate this particular art object.

PROFESSIONAL WRITING

Today's Special

David Sedaris

It is his birthday, and Hugh and I are seated in a New York restaurant, *1* awaiting the arrival of our fifteen-word entrées. He looks very nice, dressed in the suit and sweater that have always belonged to him. As for me, I own only my shoes, pants, shirt, and tie. My jacket belongs to the restaurant and was offered as a loan by the maître d', who apparently thought I would feel more comfortable dressed to lead a high-school marching band.

I'm worrying the thick gold braids decorating my sleeves when the *2* waiter presents us with what he calls "a little something to amuse the palette." Roughly the size and color of a Band-Aid, the amusement floats on a shallow, muddy puddle of sauce and is topped with a sprig of greenery.

"And this would be . . . what, exactly?" Hugh asks. *3*

"This," the waiter announces, "is our raw Atlantic sword-fish served in *4* a dark chocolate gravy and garnished with fresh mint."

"Not again," I say. "Can't you guys come up with something a little less *5* conventional?"

"Love your jacket," the waiter whispers. *6*

As a rule, I'm no great fan of eating out in New York restaurants. It's *7* hard to love a place that's outlawed smoking but finds it perfectly acceptable to serve raw fish in a bath of chocolate. There are no normal restaurants left, at least in our neighborhood. The diners have all been taken over by precious little bistros boasting a menu of indigenous American cuisine. They call these meals "traditional," yet they're rarely the American dishes I remember. The patty melt has been pushed aside in favor of the herb-encrusted medallions of baby artichoke hearts, which never leave me thinking, Oh, right, those! I wonder if they're as good as the ones my mom used to make.

Part of the problem is that we live in the wrong part of town. SoHo is *8* not a macaroni salad kind of place. This is where the world's brightest young talents come to braise carmelized racks of corn-fed songbirds or offer up their famous knuckle of flash-seared crappie served with a collar of chided ginger and cornered by a tribe of kiln-roasted Chilean

...continued Today's Special, **David Sedaris**

toadstools, teased with a warm spray of clarified musk oil. Even when they promise something simple, they've got to tart it up—the meatloaf has been poached in sea water, or there are figs in the tuna salad. If cooking is an art, I think we're in our Dada phase.

I've never thought of myself as a particularly finicky eater, but it's 9 hard to be a good sport when each dish seems to include no fewer than a dozen ingredients, one of which I'm bound to dislike. I'd order the skirt steak with a medley of suffocated peaches, but I'm put off by the aspirin sauce. The sea scallops look good until I'm told they're served in a broth of malt liquor and mummified litchi nuts. What I really want is a cigarette, and I'm always searching the menu in the hope that some courageous young chef has finally recognized tobacco as a vegetable. Bake it, steam it, grill it, or stuff it into littleneck clams, I just need something familiar that I can hold on to.

When the waiter brings our entrées, I have no idea which plate might 10 be mine. In yesterday's restaurants it was possible both to visualize and to recognize your meal. There were always subtle differences, but for the most part, a lamb chop tended to maintain its basic shape. That is to say that it looked choplike. It had a handle made of bone and a teardrop of meat hugged by a thin rind of fat. Apparently, though, that was too predictable. Order the modern lamb chop, and it's likely to look no different than your companion's order of shackled pompano. The current food is always arranged into a senseless, vertical tower. No longer content to recline, it now reaches for the sky, much like the high-rise buildings lining our city streets. It's as if the plates were valuable parcels of land and the chef had purchased one small lot and unlimited air rights. Hugh's saffron linguini resembles a miniature turban, topped with architectural spires of shrimp. It stands there in the center while the rest of the vast, empty plate looks as though it's been leased out as a possible parking lot. I had ordered the steak, which, bowing to the same minimalist fashion, is served without the bone, the thin slices of beef stacked to resemble a funeral pyre. The potatoes I'd been expecting have apparently either been clarified to an essence or were used to stoke the grill.

"Maybe," Hugh says, "they're inside your tower of meat."   11

This is what we have been reduced to. Hugh blows the yucca pollen off 12 his blackened shrimp while I push back the sleeves of my borrowed sport coat and search the meat tower for my promised potatoes.

"There they are, right there." Hugh uses his fork to point out what 13 could easily be mistaken for five cavity-riddled molars. The dark spots must be my vegetable.

Because I am both a glutton and a masochist, my standard com- 14 plaint, "That was so bad," is always followed by "And there was so little of it!"

Our plates are cleared, and we are presented with dessert menus. I *15* learn that spiced ham is no longer considered just a luncheon meat and that even back issues of *Smithsonian* can be turned into sorbets.

"I just couldn't," I say to the waiter when he recommends the white *16* chocolate and wild loganberry couscous.

"If we're counting calories, I could have the chef serve it without the *17* crème fraîche."

"No," I say. "Really, I just couldn't." *18*

We ask for the check, explaining that we have a movie to catch. It's *19* only a ten-minute walk to the theater, but I'm antsy because I'd like to get something to eat before the show. They'll have loads of food at the concession stand, but I don't believe in mixing meat with my movies. Luckily there's a hot dog cart not too far out of our way.

Friends always say, "How can you eat those? I read in the paper that *20* they're made from hog's lips."

"And . . . ?" *21*

"And hearts and eyelids." *22*

That, to my mind, is only three ingredients and constitutes a refreshing *23* change of pace. I order mine with nothing but mustard, and am thrilled to watch the vendor present my hot dog in a horizontal position. So simple and timeless that I can recognize it, immediately, as food.

vo•cab•u•lar•y

In your journal, write the meaning of the italicized words in the following phrases.

- *garnished* with fresh mint (**4**)
- we're in the *Dada* phase (**8**)
- *mummified* litchi nuts (**9**)
- same *minimalist* fashion (**10**)

- a *glutton* and a *masochist* (**14**)
- turned into *sorbets* (**15**)
- without the crème *fraîche* (**17**)

? QUESTIONS FOR WRITING AND DISCUSSION

❶ In his essay, David Sedaris claims to enjoy simple food like potatoes and hot dogs, yet he knows and uses the vocabulary of a sophisticated gourmand. List the words and phrases Sedaris uses to describe the cuisine of this particular restaurant. Does he use this vocabulary to praise the cooking of this restaurant or to ridicule it? Explain.

❷ As a humorist, Sedaris looks for the amusing and absurd in people, places, and events. As a restaurant critic, however, Sedaris uses evaluation to make a serious point. He doesn't explicitly state his overall claim about this particular restaurant, but his opinion is evident throughout. What exactly does Sedaris like and dislike? Write your own three-column log for this essay. List the *criteria* (such as ambiance, food taste, service, presentation, etc.) that Sedaris uses in this review, the *evidence* he gives, and his *judgment* for each of the criteria. State in your own words Sedaris' overall judgment or claim.

3 In his review, Sedaris uses several descriptive and narrative strategies to convey the scene and describe the action. Review the techniques for observing and remembering in Chapters 3 and 4. Where in his essay does Sedaris give vivid and detailed descriptions or use images, similes, and metaphors? Where does Sedaris use narrative techniques such as scene setting, dialogue, and characterization? Support your response by citing specific sentences, phrases, or images.

4 Visit a local restaurant—preferably one you are already familiar with—for the purpose of writing a review. If you wish, bring some of your friends. Take notes during the meal so you won't miss any names of foods or service details. Then write two versions of your review. For the first one, follow the informative model of the Hunan Dynasty review at the beginning of this chapter. Organize your comments clearly by the criteria you choose. For your second version, write in a narrative fashion as Sedaris does, including scene description, key events, characters, and dialogue. When you finish, evaluate your reviews. Which do you like best? What magazine, newspaper, or Web site would be the best choice for each of your versions?

Evaluating: The Writing Process

66 I love criticism so long as it's unqualified praise. 99

—NOEL COWARD,
PLAYWRIGHT, SONGWRITER,
NOVELIST, DIRECTOR, AND
PERFORMER

ASSIGNMENT FOR EVALUATING

With a specific audience and genre in mind, evaluate a product or service, a work of art, or a performance. Choose a subject that is reobservable—that you can revisit or review as you write your essay. Select criteria appropriate for your subject, genre, and audience. Collect evidence to support your judgment for each criterion. *Remember: In order to remain objective and credible, your review or critique should contain both positive and negative judgments.*

As the grid below indicates, the review is the most common genre for evaluating, but "reviews" cover a wide range of documents. Some film reviews, for example, are academic and critical whereas others merely indicate the major plot line without much critical evaluation. As you choose your topic, be sure to reread your assignment and consider the requirements or expectations of your audience. Are they expecting merely to be informed or entertained, or do they want the thorough and critical evaluation described in this chapter?

Audience	Possible Genres for Evaluating
Personal Audience	Class notes, journal entry, blog, scrapbook, or social networking page
Academic Audience	Academic critique, media critique, review, journal entry, forum entry on class site, multigenre document
Public Audience	Column, editorial, article, or critique in a magazine, newspaper, newsletter, online site, or multigenre document

CHOOSING A SUBJECT

If you have already settled on a possible subject, try the following collecting and shaping strategies. If you have not found a subject, consider these ideas.

- Evaluating requires some expertise about a particular person, performance, place, object, or service. You generate expertise not only through experience but also through writing, reading, and rewriting. Reread your journal entries on observing and investigating. Did you observe or investigate some person, place, or thing that you could write about again, this time for the purpose of evaluating it?

- Comparing and contrasting lead naturally to evaluation. For example, compare two places you've lived, two friends, or two jobs. Compare two newspapers for their coverage of international news, local features, sports, or business. Compare two famous people from the same profession. Compare your expectations about a person, place, or event with the reality. The purpose of your comparison is to determine, for a specific audience, which is "better," based on the criteria you select and the evidence you find.

- Evaluating a possible career choice can help you choose courses, think about possible summer jobs, and prepare for job interviews. Begin by describing several jobs that fit your particular career goals. Then go to several of the following Web sites and gather information.

http://www.monster.com   http://www.bestjobsusa.com
http://www.careers.com   money.cnn.com/services/careerbuilder
http://careers.yahoo.com   http://www.getthatgig.com

Choose the career criteria that are most important for you, such as job satisfaction, location, benefits, salary, education requirements, and so forth. Decide which criteria are most important for **you.** Is job satisfaction more important than pay or location? Choose your criteria and rank them in order of importance. Then write an evaluation of one or two jobs that you find described on the Internet or in your local newspaper.

- **Community Service Learning.** Community service-learning projects often require an assessment at the end of the period of service. These reflective evaluations start with the goals of the agency, the goals of your class project, and your goals as a learner as the major criteria. Then you gather evidence to see how well the actual experiences and projects met these overall project goals. Sometimes participants use short evaluation questionnaires to get feedback at the midpoint and then again at the end of the project. If you are participating in a community service-learning project, check with your teacher or coordinator about how to write this assessment.

COLLECTING

Once you have a tentative subject and audience in mind, ask the following questions to focus your collecting activities

- Can you *narrow, restrict,* or *define* your subject to focus your paper?
- What *criteria* will you use to evaluate your subject?
- What *evidence* might you gather? As you collect evidence, focus on three questions:

    What *comparisons* can you make between your subject and similar subjects?

    What are the *uses* or *consequences* of this subject?

    What *experiments* or *authorities* might you cite for support?
- What initial *judgments* are you going to make?

● **OBSERVING**   Observation and description of your subject are crucial to a clear evaluation. In most cases, your audience will need to know *what* your subject is before they can understand your evaluation.

- Examine a place or object repeatedly, looking at it from different points of view. Take notes. Describe it. Draw it, if appropriate. Analyze its component parts. List its uses. To which senses does it appeal—sight, sound, touch, smell, taste? If you are comparing your subject to other similar subjects, observe them carefully. Remember: The second or third time you observe your subject, you will see even more key details.
- If you are evaluating a person, collect information about this person's life, interests, abilities, accomplishments, and plans for the future. If you are

able to observe the person directly, describe his or her physical features, write down what he or she says, and describe the person's environment.

- If you are evaluating a performance or an event, a tape recording or videotape can be extremely useful. If possible, choose a concert, film, or play on tape so that you can stop and review it if and when necessary. If a tape recording or videotape is not available, attend the performance or event twice.

Making notes in a *three-column log* is an excellent collecting strategy for evaluations. Using the following example from Phyllis Richman's evaluation of the Hunan Dynasty restaurant, list the criteria, evidence, and judgments for your subject.

Subject: Hunan Dynasty Restaurant

Criteria	Evidence	Judgment
Attractive setting	No blaring red-lacquer tables	Graceful
	White tablecloths	
	Subtle glass etchings	
Good service	Waiters serve with flourishes	Often expert
	Some glitches, such as forgotten appetizer	

● **REMEMBERING**   You are already an authority on many subjects, and your personal experiences may help you evaluate your subject. Try *freewriting, looping, branching,* or *clustering* your subject to help you remember relevant events, impressions, and information. In evaluating appliances for consumer magazines, for example, reporters often use products over a period of months, recording data, impressions, and experiences. Those experiences and memories are then used to support criteria and judgments. Evaluating a film often requires remembering similar films that you have liked or disliked. An evaluation of a great athlete may include your memories of previous performances. A vivid narrative of those memories can help convince an audience that a performance is good or bad.

● **READING**   Some of the ideas and evidence for your evaluation may come from reading descriptions of your subject, other evaluations of your subject, or the testimony of experts. Be sure you read these texts critically: Who is the intended audience for the text? What evidence does the text give? What is the author's bias? What are other points of view? Read your potential sources critically.

● **INVESTIGATING**   All evaluations involve some degree of formal or informal investigation as you probe the characteristics of your subject and seek evidence to support your judgments.

Use the Library or the Internet   Check the library and Internet resources for information on your subject, for ideas about how to design and conduct an evaluation of that subject, for possible criteria, for data in evaluations already performed, and for a sense of different possible audiences. In its evaluation of chocolate chip cookies, for example, *Consumer Reports* suggests criteria and outlines procedures. The magazine rated some two dozen popular store-bought brands, as well as four "boutique" or freshly baked varieties, on "strength of chocolate flavor and aroma, cookie and chip texture, and freedom from sensory defects." When the magazine's evaluators faced a problem sampling the fresh cookies in the lab, they decided to move the lab: "We ended up loading a station wagon with scoresheet, pencils, clipboards, water containers, cups, napkins . . . and setting off on a tasting safari to shopping malls."

Gather Field Data   You may want to supplement your personal evaluation with a sample of other people's opinions by using *questionnaires* or *interviews*. If you are rating a film, for example, you might give people leaving the theater a very brief *questionnaire*, asking for their responses on key criteria relating to the movie that they just saw. If you are rating a class, you might want to *interview* several students in the class to support your claim that the class was either effective or ineffective. The interviews might also give you some specific examples: descriptions of experiences that you can then use as evidence to support your own judgments.

SHAPING

While the shaping strategies that you have used in previous essays may be helpful, the strategies that follow are particularly appropriate for shaping evaluations.

● **AUDIENCE AND GENRE**   As you consider ways to organize and shape your explaining essay, think about your probable audience and genre. Reviews vary greatly in length, critical depth, complexity, and reader appeal. Think about your own purpose and goal; find several magazines, newspapers, or Web sites that publish the kind of review you would like to write, and use the best ones as genre models—not as blueprints—to guide your own writing.

● **ANALYSIS BY CRITERIA**   Often, evaluations are organized by criteria. You decide which criteria are appropriate for the subject and audience, and then you use those criteria to outline the essay. Your first few paragraphs of introduction establish your thesis or overall claim and then give background information: what the subject is, why you are evaluating it, what the competition is, and how you gathered your data. Then you order the criteria according to some plan: chronological order, spatial order, order of importance, or another logical sequence. Phyllis Richman's evaluation of the Hunan Dynasty restaurant follows the criteria pattern:

  • **Introductory paragraphs:** *information* about the restaurant (location, hours, prices), general *description* of Chinese restaurants today, and *overall claim:* The Hunan Dynasty is reliable, a good value, and versatile.

- **Criterion #1/judgment:** Good restaurants should have an attractive setting and atmosphere/Hunan Dynasty is attractive.
- **Criterion #2/judgment:** Good restaurants should give strong priority to service/Hunan Dynasty has, despite an occasional glitch, expert service.
- **Criterion #3/judgment:** Restaurants that serve moderately priced food should have quality main dishes/Main dishes at Hunan Dynasty are generally good but not often memorable. (*Note:* The most important criterion—the quality of the main dishes—is saved for last.)
- **Concluding paragraphs:** Hunan Dynasty is a top-flight neighborhood restaurant.

● **COMPARISON AND CONTRAST**   Many evaluations compare two subjects in order to demonstrate why one is preferable to another. Books, films, restaurants, courses, music, writers, scientists, historical events, sports—all can be evaluated by means of comparison and contrast. In evaluating two Asian restaurants, for example, student writer Chris Cameron uses a comparison-and-contrast structure to shape her essay. In the following body paragraph from her essay, Cameron compares two restaurants, the Unicorn and the Yakitori, on the basis of her first criterion—an atmosphere that seems authentically Asian.

Of the two restaurants, we preferred the authentic atmosphere of the Unicorn to the cultural confusion at the Yakitori. On first impression, the Yakitori looked like a converted truck stop, sparsely decorated with a few bamboo slats and Japanese print fabric hanging in slices as Bruce Springsteen wailed loudly in the ears of the customers. The feeling at the Unicorn was quite the opposite as we entered a room that seemed transported from Chinatown. The whole room had a red tint from the light shining through the flowered curtains, and the place looked truly authentic, from the Chinese patterned rug on the wall to the elaborate dragon on the ceiling. Soft oriental music played as the customers sipped tea from small porcelain cups and ate fortune cookies.

Cameron used the following *alternating* comparison-and-contrast shape for her whole essay.

- Introductory paragraph(s)
- **Thesis:** Although several friends recommended the Yakitori, we preferred the Unicorn for its more authentic atmosphere, courteous service, and well-prepared food.
- **Authentic atmosphere:** Yakitori versus Unicorn
- **Courteous service:** Yakitori versus Unicorn
- **Well-prepared food:** Yakitori versus Unicorn
- Concluding paragraph(s)

On the other hand, Cameron might have used a *block* comparison-and-contrast structure. In this organizational pattern, the outline would be as follows.

- Introductory paragraph(s)
- **Thesis:** Although several friends recommended the Yakitori, we preferred the Unicorn for its more authentic atmosphere, courteous service, and well-prepared food.
- **The Yakitori:** atmosphere, service, and food
- **The Unicorn:** atmosphere, service, and food as compared to the Yakitori's
- Concluding paragraph(s)

● **CHRONOLOGICAL ORDER**   Writers often use chronological order, especially in reviewing a book or a film, to shape parts of their evaluations. Film reviewers rely on chronological order to sketch the main outlines of the plot as they comment on the quality of the acting, directing, or cinematography.

● **CAUSAL ANALYSIS**   Evaluations of works of art, performances, or visuals often measure the *effect* on the audience. Robin Williams and John Tollett, in "Evaluating a Web Site," use several criteria, including using a clear organization and avoiding irritating "chain-yanks." Their evidence illustrates that Web sites should have a positive effect on the user.

- **Criteria:** The organization of a Web site must make information easily accessible for the user.

  EVIDENCE: "Recently I needed to buy a new carafe for my coffee pot. I went to the Web site our local store recommended, and in THREE SECONDS I found exactly the carafe I needed. . . . This site was so well organized that I could scan and find the first topic I needed in about one second. . . . Amazing."
- **Judgment:** The site was very well organized for the user.

- **Criteria:** Web sites should not create false expectations or "chain-yanks" for the user.

  EVIDENCE: "For example, you click next to a graphic that says 'Click here for a larger image.' You click, expecting a larger image and perhaps some additional information, but you get a page with the same image. . . . This makes you feel stupid. Or worse, it makes you think the Web site is stupid."
- **Judgment:** The Web site frustrated the user.

● **TITLE, INTRODUCTION, AND CONCLUSION**   Titles of evaluative writing tend to be short and succinct, stating what product, service, work of art, or performance you are evaluating.

Introductory paragraphs provide background information and description and usually give an overall claim or thesis. In some cases, however, the overall claim comes last, in a concluding "Recommendations" section or in a final summary paragraph. If the overall claim appears in the opening paragraphs, the concluding paragraph may simply review the strengths or weaknesses or may just advise the reader: This *is* or *is not* worth seeing, reading, watching, doing, or buying.

> **66** I have to stop being afraid of being wrong; I can't wait until everything is perfect before the work comes out. I don't have that kind of time. **99**
>
> —SHERLEY ANNE WILLIAMS, NOVELIST AND CRITIC

Research Tips [ ] GO

Before you draft your evaluating essay, stop for a moment and *evaluate your sources* of information and opinion. If you are citing ideas or information from library articles—or especially from the Internet—be skeptical. How reliable is your source? What do you know about your source's reliability or editorial slant? Does the author have a particular bias? Be sure to *qualify* any biased or absolute statements you use from your sources. (See Chapter 11 for additional ideas on evaluating written sources.)

If you cite observations or field sources (interviews, surveys), evaluate the information you collected. Does it reflect only one point of view? How is it biased? Are your responses in surveys limited in number or point of view? Remember: You may use sources that reflect a limited perspective, but *be sure to alert your readers to those limitations.* For example, you might say, "Obviously, these reactions represent only four viewers who saw this film, but . . ." or "Of course, the administrator wanted to defend this student program when he said. . . ."

PEER RESPONSE

The instructions that follow will help you give and receive constructive advice about the rough draft of your evaluating essay. You may use these guidelines for an in-class workshop, a take-home review, or an e-mail computer response.

Writer: Before you exchange drafts, write out the following information about your essay draft.

1. **Purpose, audience, and genre.** Briefly, describe your overall purpose, your genre, and your intended audience. Do you plan to incorporate visuals? If so, where?

2. **Revision plans.** What do you know you still need to work on as you revise your draft?

3. **Questions.** Write one or two questions about your draft that you would like your reader to answer.

Reader: Before you answer the following questions, read the entire draft from start to finish. As you *reread* the draft, do the following.

1. Underline the sentence(s) that state the writer's *overall claim* about the subject.

2. In the margin, put large brackets [ ] around paragraphs that *describe* what the writer is evaluating.

3. On a separate piece of paper or at the end of the writer's essay, make a *three-column log* indicating the writer's criteria, evidence, and judgments. (Does the log include both positive and negative judgments?)

4. Identify with an asterisk (*) any passages in which the writer needs more *evidence* to support the judgments.

5. Write out one *criterion* that is missing or that is not appropriate for the given subject.

6. Assess how well the writer explains the purpose and addresses the intended audience. Do you agree with the writer about his or her revision plans? Finally, answer the writer's questions.

Writer: As you read your peer reviewer's notes and comments, do the following.

1. Consider your peer reviewer's comments and notes. Has your reviewer correctly identified your overall claim? Do you need to add more description of your subject? Does the reviewer's three-column log look like yours? Do you need to revise your criteria or add additional evidence? Do you balance positive and negative judgments?

2. Based on your review, draw up a *revision plan*. Write out the three most important things you need to do as you revise your essay.

> 66 I have rewritten—
> often several times—
> every word I have ever
> published. My pencils
> outlast their
> erasers. 99
> —VLADIMIR NABOKOV,
> NOVELIST

DRAFTING

With your criteria in front of you, your data or evidence at hand, and a general plan or sketch outline in mind, begin writing your draft. As you write, focus on your audience. If your evaluation needs to be short, you may have to use only those criteria that will appeal most effectively to your audience. As you write, check occasionally to be sure that you are including your key criteria. While some parts of the essay may seem forced or awkward as you write, other parts will grow and expand as you get your thoughts on paper. As in other papers, don't stop to check spelling or worry about an occasional awkward sentence. If you stop and can't get going, reread what you have written, look over your notes or sketch outline, and pick up the thread again.

REVISING

Remember that revision is not just changing a word here and there or correcting occasional spelling errors. Make your evaluation more effective for your reader by including more specific evidence, changing the order of your paragraphs to make them clearer, cutting out an unimportant point, or adding a point that one of your readers suggests.

GUIDELINES FOR REVISION

- **Review your purpose, audience, and genre.** Is your purpose clear to your target audience? Should you modify your chosen genre to appeal to your audience?
- **Review possibilities for visuals or graphics.** What additions or changes to images might be appropriate for your purpose, genre, or audience?
- **Criteria are *standards of value*.** They contain categories and judgments, as in "good fuel economy," "good reliability," or "powerful use of light and shade in a painting." Some categories, such as "price," have clearly implied judgments ("low price"), but make sure that your criteria refer implicitly or explicitly to a standard of value.
- **Examine your criteria from your audience's point of view.** Which criteria are most important in evaluating your subject? Will your readers agree that the criteria you select are indeed the most important ones? Will changing the order in which you present your criteria make your evaluation more convincing?
- **Include both positive and negative evaluations of your subject.** If all of your judgments are positive, your evaluation will sound like an advertisement. If all of your judgments are negative, your readers may think you are too critical.
- **Be sure to include supporting evidence for each criterion.** Without any data or support, your evaluation will be just an opinion that will not persuade your reader.
- **Avoid overgeneralizing in your claims.** If you are evaluating only three software programs, you cannot say that Lotus 1-2-3 is the best business program around. You can say only that it is the best among the group or the best in the particular class that you measured.

- **Unless your goal is humor or irony, compare subjects that belong in the same class.** Comparing a Ford Focus to a BMW is absurd because they are not similar cars in terms of cost, design, or purpose.
- **If you need additional evidence to persuade your readers, review the questions at the beginning of the "Collecting" section of this chapter.** Have you addressed all the key questions listed there?
- **If you are citing other people's data or quoting sources, check to make sure your summaries and data are accurate.**
- *Signal* **the major divisions in your evaluation to your reader using clear transitions, key words, and paragraph hooks.** At the beginning of new paragraphs or sections in your essay, let your reader know where you are going.
- **Revise sentences for directness and clarity.**
- **Edit your evaluation for correct spelling, appropriate word choice, punctuation, usage, and grammar.**

POSTSCRIPT ON THE WRITING PROCESS

When you finish writing your essay, answer the following questions.

1. Who is the intended audience for your evaluation? Write out one sentence from your essay in which you appeal to or address this audience.
2. Describe the main problem that you had writing this essay, such as finding a topic, collecting evidence, or writing or revising the draft.
3. What parts or paragraphs of your essay do you like best? Indicate the words, phrases, or sentences that make it effective. What do you like about them?
4. Explain what helped you most with your revision: advice from your peers, conference with the teacher, advice from a writing center tutor, rereading your draft several times, or some other source.
5. Write out one question that you still have about the assignment or about your writing and revising process.

STUDENT WRITING
COURTNEY KLOCKEMAN

Vulgar Propriety

For her evaluative essay, Courtney Klockeman wrote a critical review of the 2001 Oscar Award–winning musical, Moulin Rouge. *The original story is of a young English writer who comes to the Paris of Toulouse-Lautrec in 1899 and falls in love with the nightclub's leading performer and courtesan, Satine. The director's challenge, as Klockeman explains, is to convey the exciting and sensual scene of Montmartre in 1899 for a twenty-first century audience. As you read her essay, see if Klockeman evaluates the film based on clear criteria and evidence that support her thesis that the film "is over the top, but intentionally and meticulously so."*

Baz Luhrmann's rock opera *Moulin Rouge* has been called everything 1 from vulgar and over the top to innovative and spectacular. Love it or hate it, Luhrmann knows how to draw attention. Edward Guthmann calls Luhrmann's vision "two hours of cranked up movie trailers: the volume is punishing, the pacing relentlessly fast and the gestures broad and obvious. Everything is punched up, overstressed" (C1). Indeed, Luhrmann seems to have emulated the things that entertain us: music videos, rock concerts, and "high octane thrill ride" movies. He managed to create a musical romance with the thrills and explosive appeal of all of the above, successfully captivating the A.D.D. MTV generation. The pure opulence of the film, especially the club, might over-stimulate some, but it accurately conveys the exciting lure that the Moulin Rouge has represented since its opening. The film *is* over the top, but intentionally and meticulously so. Each artistic decision reflects careful consideration for historical context and authenticity of costumes and sets while still keeping modern audiences enthralled.

Luhrmann faced a tremendous challenge in trying to shock a desen- 2 sitized generation. He had to convey to a 21st century audience the temptations of the Moulin Rouge to its 19th century audience while still being fairly faithful to the period. In today's world girls walk around in low cut crop tops and high cut shorts on a regular basis, and shows on HBO would have been deemed pornography 30 years ago. The only way to shock us anymore is with excess—vibrant color, ornate detail and flamboyant movement so that we are repulsed yet strangely attracted to the frenzied energy of it all. It is a delicate and complex balance, for which Luhrmann turned to his wife and artistic director Catherine Martin. He had a vision and she made it a reality.

With an ambition for authenticity Martin and her co-costume de- 3 signer Angus Strathie thoroughly researched 19th century France and the Moulin Rouge before beginning production. Their research spanned over several years and included much time in Montmartre and Paris Libraries (Litson 22). The trouble was to reconcile their vision of the film's impact with their research. To remain historically accurate while still connecting to their modern audience, they agreed to follow one main rule: if it existed in the 19th century, even if it wasn't used in every day life, they could use it. For instance, there is a bohemian musician wearing sunglasses

...*continued* Vulgar Propriety, **Courtney Klockeman**

when Christian first arrives in Montmartre. Martin explains that "sunglasses did exist in the 19th century, but they were a specific purpose item. Like if you were climbing Mount Everest and there was a glare from the snow" (Kaye 58). The sunglasses are a tiny stretch, but they make the musician easier for us to relate to, like one we might see on Pearl Street in Boulder.

Through their research, Martin and Strathie also learned that part of the appeal at the actual Moulin Rouge was that the dancers wore knickers that were split down the middle. If some of us were wondering what was so naughty about the cancan . . . mystery solved. Leaving that dirty little detail out was not an option if they were going to stay true to the times and share the shock with us. At the same time an uncensored split knicker cancan would have earned them an R or possibly NC-17 rating, effectively eliminating a large portion of the movie-going public. Martin solved the problem by "conceal[ing] the areas that can be seen [so the girls had] a pink, smooth, Barbie-like area!" (Litson 22). Corsets, of course, were also essential to the costuming. Women used to cinch themselves up so tightly that they would fracture ribs and sometimes damage their internal organs. Naturally, clothing so tight restricts movement and makes dancing extremely difficult. Martin designed smaller corsets to mitigate the issue while keeping the extreme hourglass figures, but Nicole Kidman still cracked a rib during a scene (Litson 22).

Compared to the costumes, the set was fairly straightforward. The original Moulin Rouge was excessive enough that Martin and Strathie needed only to create a replica of it. Even Satine's Hindi elephant was a part of the original (Litson 22). The inside of the dance hall was and still is very much like a circus, as it is portrayed in the film (Mac Devitt). There were some minor changes to the design for the sake of convenience or emphasis. The garden was placed in front instead of to the side of the dance hall to allow for smooth filming in and out of the club. Martin also added the gothic "brothel room." There were such rooms near the notorious dance hall and the dancers were, in fact, prostitutes, but there wasn't one in the hall itself (Litson 22). Martin's addition makes these particulars more assertive by visually and spatially combining the dance hall with its shady brothel aspect.

For some sets Martin sacrificed authenticity for effect. The city of Paris from afar looks more like a picture book than a movie set. Some question the choice to use such post-card like scenery, but the dreamy image with the Eiffel Tower surrounded by quaint little buildings is just a flimsy romanticized façade for the gritty truth. Why not portray it for what it is? Montmartre was, and nightly still is, a seedy district. It is home to pimps and prostitutes, where beatnik artists earn wages on the streets. In the film, Christian seeks the romantic, iconic version and discovers instead the disturbing truth. The styles of the sets represent their distance from or closeness to the truth. During "Your Song" the set becomes surreal with a miniature Eiffel Tower and a singing moon while Satine and Christian dance on the clouds. In that scene, Satine is under the false impression that Christian is the Duke and Christian seems to be naïve of Satine's work as a prostitute. Essentially, they fall in love under false pretenses and the scenery reflects that falseness. Alternately, in the scene where they declare their love with full awareness of each others' identities ("Elephant Love Medley"), realism returns because there is no deception or misunderstanding. The scenes with Christian, Satine, and the Duke once again enter the realm of surreal due to his blissful ignorance of their love affair.

To keep us spellbound, Strathie and Martin replaced a line of girls in matching outfits with a fascinating diversity in color and style to "make [it as] extraordinary for now" as it was in 1899 (Litson 22). They turned an already challenging task into a Herculean feat by designing each individual dancer's costume with a theme in mind. There is a Hindi girl, a baby doll, a Greek goddess, a very heavily tattooed dominatrix, and more than 50 others. They started with sexual fetishes and moved on to nationalities when they ran out (Litson 22). Even in the "Tango de Roxanne," each dancer sports a unique undergarment. By the end of filming, the creative duo had meticulously clothed 15 primary actors, 60 dancers, and more than 600 extras in various scenes. Nicole Kidman alone wears more than 20 costumes throughout (Kaye 58).

The Moulin Rouge seems all the more opulent because of its stark contrast from the outside world. The costumes and sets are more overwhelming in and around the Moulin Rouge than anywhere else. The color scheme is all red, black and gold and everything is heavily ornamented. Away from its influence, Christian's "humble abode" is comparatively minimalistic. It is dominated by whites and light neutrals and has only the bare essentials in furniture. Satine's costumes tend to match the surroundings. In and around the Moulin Rouge she is always corseted and fully accessorized. Like all of the dancers, she is trapped where "the show must go on." At Christian's flat, she is usually wearing only a white sheet or robe, free to be herself—not the temptress of the stage. The view from Christian's flat is the Moulin Rouge, seemingly innocent by day but lit up and dangerously alluring by night. The story's conflict arises in trying to reconcile these apparently incompatible worlds or else leave one behind.

Moulin Rouge may be an "audacious, rapid-fire assault on the senses," but even Guthmann concedes that "it works" (C1). The gaudy display is not without a purpose, exposing us to the lurid temptations of the "tantric cancan" in a way we understand while revealing their destructive consequences. David Ansen and Dan Ephron eloquently conclude that "by reveling in all things artificial, [Moulin Rouge] arrives, giddily, at the genuine" (61). Luhrmann and Martin set out to shock us, thrill us, entertain us, and give us a musical like never before. Even their most "over-stimulated" and conservative critics can't deny that they achieved just that.

Works Consulted

Ansen, David and Dan Ephron. "Yes, 'Rouge' Can Can Can." *Newsweek* 137.22 (2001): 61. *LexisNexis Academic.* Web. 5 Mar. 2009.

Guthmann, Edward. "Red Hot." *San Francisco Chronicle* 1 June 2001 final ed: C1. *LexisNexis Academic.* Web. 5 Mar. 2009.

Kaye, Lori. "Clothes that Cancan." *Advocate* 839 (2001): 58. *Academic Search Premiere.* Web. 5 Mar. 2009.

Litson, Jo. "Rouging It." *Entertainment Design* 35.5 (2001): 22. *LexisNexis Academic.* Web. 5 Mar. 2009.

Mac Devitt, Aedin. "Le Moulin Rouge Cabaret." *About.com.* New York Times, 2008. Web. 5 Mar. 2009.

Moulin Rouge. Dir. Baz Luhrmann. Perf. Nicole Kidman, Ewan McGregor. 2001. 20th Century Fox, 2003. DVD.

? QUESTIONS FOR WRITING AND DISCUSSION

1 In her review, Klockeman explains that the director's main task was to maintain historical accuracy while updating the context, costumes, and sets for a modern audience. If you have seen the film, would you agree that these adjustments do in fact make the film historically real and yet contemporary and exciting for a twenty-first century audience? Explain your response by commenting on scenes that you remember from the film.

2 Reread Klockeman's essay and then write out a three-column log (criteria, evidence, judgments) that she might have used to organize her evaluation. List the pieces of evidence that she uses for each of her criteria. Does she have sufficient evidence from the film to support her judgment of each criterion? Explain.

3 In her title, Klockeman tries to capture the edginess of the film by using the phrase, "vulgar propriety." Is this title effective for the essay? Would other oxymorons or phrases such as "tasteful pornography" also work for her title? Explain your choices.

4 Go online and read other reviews of *Moulin Rouge*. After reading those reviews, do you agree with Klockeman's evaluation? Do these reviews consider other criteria such as acting ability, plot, or character dialogue that you believe are important for evaluating the film? What criteria would you choose for your evaluation of this film?

5 Klockeman wrote her essay primarily for her writing class, but if she wanted to publish her essay, what newspaper, magazine, or online site would be most appropriate? Find two possible publications sites for her essay and explain why Klockeman's style and content would (or would not) be appropriate for that particular audience.

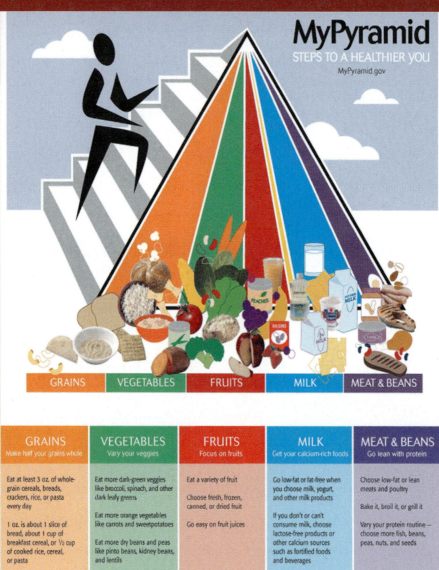

MyPyramid
STEPS TO A HEALTHIER YOU
MyPyramid.gov

GRAINS	VEGETABLES	FRUITS	MILK	MEAT & BEANS
GRAINS Make half your grains whole	**VEGETABLES** Vary your veggies	**FRUITS** Focus on fruits	**MILK** Get your calcium-rich foods	**MEAT & BEANS** Go lean with protein
Eat at least 3 oz. of whole-grain cereals, breads, crackers, rice, or pasta every day 1 oz. is about 1 slice of bread, about 1 cup of breakfast cereal, or ½ cup of cooked rice, cereal, or pasta	Eat more dark-green veggies like broccoli, spinach, and other dark leafy greens Eat more orange vegetables like carrots and sweetpotatoes Eat more dry beans and peas like pinto beans, kidney beans, and lentils	Eat a variety of fruit Choose fresh, frozen, canned, or dried fruit Go easy on fruit juices	Go low-fat or fat-free when you choose milk, yogurt, and other milk products If you don't or can't consume milk, choose lactose-free products or other calcium sources such as fortified foods and beverages	Choose low-fat or lean meats and poultry Bake it, broil it, or grill it Vary your protein routine — choose more fish, beans, peas, nuts, and seeds

For a 2,000-calorie diet, you need the amounts below from each food group. To find the amounts that are right for you, go to MyPyramid.gov.

| Eat 6 oz. every day | Eat 2½ cups every day | Eat 2 cups every day | Get 3 cups every day;
for kids aged 2 to 8, it's 2 | Eat 5½ oz. every day |

The MyPyramid campaign, "Steps to a Healthier You," by the United States Department of Agriculture, is designed to bring healthy diet advice to the American public. After analyzing the graphic and reading the advice in the text, answer Journal Exercise 5 on page 264.

Problem Solving

9

After reading the headlines about the bankruptcies and closings of newspapers across America, you wonder what the future of journalism will be. Citizen journalism has become widespread, so you decide to investigate whether it can solve the problems created by the deterioration of professional print journalism. To replace professional journalists, citizen journalists would need to be able to inform the public and expose corruption and injustice in government and business. You decide to write your research questions and then create a questionnaire to gather information from students at your college about the effectiveness of online citizen journalism. After compiling your survey results and doing research on the current state of citizen journalism, you decide to argue that citizen journalism clearly has the potential to pick up the pieces left by traditional print journalism.

Trying to take notes in your Psych I lecture class—along with 250 other students—you realize that you are completely lost and confused. So you raise your hand to ask a question, but the professor keeps on talking, throwing out more new terms and examples. After class, when you think about how hard you've worked to pay your tuition, you realize that you deserve better classes for your money. The problem, you decide, is in the large lecture format—there are just too many students for the teacher to answer questions and explain difficult concepts. So you decide to write a letter to the head of the psychology department (with a copy to the dean of arts and sciences) outlining your problems with this class and proposing that Psychology I be taught in classes no larger than fifty.

> " This country has more problems than it should tolerate and more solutions than it uses. "
> —RALPH NADER,
> CONSUMER RIGHTS ADVOCATE AND PRESIDENTIAL CANDIDATE

> " Whenever life doesn't seem to give an answer, we create one. "
> —LORRAINE HANSBERRY
> AUTHOR OF *A RAISIN IN THE SUN*

W E DON'T HAVE TO LOOK DILIGENTLY TO LOCATE PROBLEMS IN OUR LIVES. THEY HAVE A HABIT OF SEEKING US OUT. IT SEEMS THAT IF SOMETHING CAN GO WRONG, IT WILL. COUNTRIES ARE FIGHTING EACH OTHER, GREENHOUSE GASES ARE CAUSING climate changes, prejudice is still rampant, television shows are too violent, sports are corrupted by drugs and money, education is too impersonal, and people drive so recklessly that you take your life in your hands every time you go across town. Everywhere we look, someone else creates problems for us—from minor bureaucratic hassles to serious or life-threatening situations. (On rare occasions, of course, we're part of the problem ourselves.)

Once we identify a potential problem, we must critically question and investigate the issue. Just because we think something is a problem does not mean that other people in other social, political, or cultural contexts will agree that it is a problem. For example, let's critically analyze what appears to be a straightforward issue: grade inflation. First, notice the language used to describe the issue. In this case, the word *inflation* suggests a negative bias; we are predisposed to think that any "inflation" is a bad thing. Next, we need to know who is involved in this issue and who has the most to gain or lose by its existence. What different positions are students, teachers, parents, school administrators, admissions officers at colleges, and companies who hire applicants likely to take on this issue? Some of these groups may see grade inflation as a serious problem, while others may not agree that it is a problem or that it even exists. Finally, we must gather the "facts" about grade inflation and the various definitions commonly used to describe it. There are statistics both proving and disproving that grade inflation exists and a variety of definitions for grade inflation.

Once you can identify something that is actually a problem for a specific group of people, the difficult part is to propose a solution and then persuade others that your solution will in fact solve the problem—without creating new problems and without costing too much. Because your proposal may ask readers to take some action, vote in a certain way, or actually work to implement your proposal, you must make sure that your readers vividly perceive the problem and agree that your plan outlines the most logical and feasible solution.

Techniques for Problem Solving

Problem solving requires all your skills as a writer. You need to observe carefully to see if a problem exists. You may need to remember experiences that illustrate the seriousness of the problem. You need to read and investigate which solutions have worked or have not worked. You often have to explain what the problem is and why or how your proposal would remedy the situation. You may need to evaluate both the problem and alternative solutions. To help you identify the problem and convince your readers of the soundness of your proposal, keep the following techniques in mind.

As you start your problem-solving paper, concentrate on ways to *narrow and focus* your topic. When you think about possible topics, follow the advice of environmentalists: "Think Globally, Act Locally." Rather than talk about education or drugs or crime or pollution on a national scale, find out how your community or campus is dealing with a problem. A local focus will help

Techniques for Problem Solving

Technique	Tips on How to Do It
Analyzing the political, social, and cultural *contexts* of the problem	*When, where,* and *why* do some people perceive this issue as a problem? *What* groups of people are affected, and what do they have to gain or lose? *Who* would be most affected by a particular solution?
Identifying and understanding your *audience*	If you want something changed, fixed, improved, subsidized, banned, reorganized, or made legal or illegal, be sure to write to an audience that has the *power to help make this change.*
Demonstrating that a *problem exists*	Some problems are so obvious that your readers will readily acknowledge them: conflicts in the Middle East, air pollution and greenhouse gases in industrialized nations, high childhood obesity rates, high unemployment, and outsized CEO bonuses. Often, however, you must first convince your audience that a problem exists: Are genetically engineered crops a problem or would eliminating them cause even more problems?
Proposing a *solution* that will solve the problem	After convincing your readers that a serious problem exists, you must then propose a *remedy, plan,* or *course of action* that will reduce or eliminate the problem.
Persuading your readers that your proposal *will work*	You need to show that your solution is *feasible* and that it is better than *alternative solutions.* You convince your readers by supporting your proposal with *reasons* and *evidence.*

> **"** You see things; and you say, "Why?" But I dream things that never were; and I say, "Why not?" **"**
> —GEORGE BERNARD SHAW, DRAMATIST

narrow your topic—and provide possibilities for using firsthand observations, personal experience, and interviews.

DEMONSTRATING THAT A PROBLEM EXISTS

A proposal begins with a description of a problem. Demonstrating that the problem exists (and is serious) will make your readers more receptive to your plan for a solution. The following selection from Frank Trippett's *Time* magazine essay "A Red Light for Scofflaws" identifies a problem and provides sufficient examples to demonstrate that scofflawry is pervasive and serious enough to warrant attention. Even if we haven't been personally attacked while driving the Houston or Miami or Los Angeles freeways, Trippett convinces us that *scofflawry*—deliberately disobeying ("scoffing at") laws—is serious. His vivid description makes us aware of the problem.

Demonstrating that a problem exists

Law and order is the longest-running and probably the best-loved political issue in U.S. history. Yet it is painfully apparent that millions of Americans who would never think of themselves as lawbreakers, let alone criminals, are taking increasing liberties with the legal codes that are designed to protect and nourish their society. Indeed, there are moments today—amid outlaw litter, tax cheating, illicit noise, and motorized anarchy—when it seems as though the scofflaw represents the wave of the future. Harvard sociologist David Riesman

Evidence: Authority

suspects that a majority of Americans have blithely taken to committing supposedly minor derelictions as a matter of course. Already, Riesman says, the ethic of U.S. society is in danger of becoming this: "You're a fool if you obey the rules."

Evidence: Examples

The dangers of scofflawry vary wildly. The person who illegally spits on the sidewalk remains disgusting, but clearly poses less risk to others than the company that illegally buries hazardous chemical waste in an unauthorized location. The fare beater on the subway presents less threat to life than the landlord who ignores fire safety statutes. The most immediately and measurably dangerous scofflawry, however, also happens to be the most visible. The culprit is the American driver, whose lawless activities today add up to a colossal public nuisance. The haz-

Evidence: Statistics

ards range from routine double parking that jams city streets to the drunk driving that kills some 25,000 people and injures at least 650,000 others yearly.

The most flagrant scofflaw of them all is the red-light runner. The flouting of stop signals has got so bad in Boston that residents tell an anecdote about a cabby who insists that red lights are "just for decoration." The power of the stoplight to control traffic seems to be waning everywhere. In Los Angeles, red-light running has become perhaps the city's most common traffic violation. In New York City, going through an intersection is like Russian roulette. Admits Police Commissioner Robert J. McGuire: "Today it's a 50–50 toss-up as to whether people will stop for a red light." Meanwhile, his own police largely ignore the lawbreaking.

Evidence: Authority

The prospect of the collapse of public manners is not merely a matter of etiquette. Society's first concern will remain major crime, but a foretaste of the seriousness of incivility is suggested by what has been happening in Houston. Drivers on Houston freeways have been showing an increasing tendency to replace the rules of the road with violent outbreaks. Items from the Houston police department's new statistical category—freeway traffic violence: (1) Driver flashes high-beam lights at car that cut in front of him, whose occupants then hurl a beer can at his windshield, kick out his tail lights, slug him eight stitches worth. (2) Dump-truck driver annoyed by delay batters trunk of stalled car ahead and its driver with steel bolt. (3) Hurrying driver of 18-wheel truck deliberately rear-ends car whose driver was trying to stay within 55 m.p.h. limit.

Evidence: Examples

PROPOSING A SOLUTION AND CONVINCING YOUR READERS

Once you have vividly described the problem, you are ready to propose a solution and persuade your readers. In the following selection from his book *Fist Stick Knife Gun*, Geoffrey Canada proposes ways to create a safer world for our children. Geoffrey Canada is president and CEO of Harlem's Rheedlen Center for Children and Families, an organization that serves at-risk inner-city children. He was recognized in 2009 for his work, with a nomination for *Time* magazine's most influential people. As you read Canada's proposal, notice how he narrows the problem to saving the lives of inner-city children. When he makes a recommendation, he talks about the advantages of his solution, but he talks about *feasibility problems* and real drawbacks. At several points, he gives *reasons* why we must change and supports his reasons with *evidence* from statistics and from his own personal experience.

If I could get the mayors, the governors, and the president to look into the eyes of the 5-year-olds of this nation, dressed in old raggedy clothes, whose jacket zippers are broken but whose dreams are still alive, they would know what I know—that children need people to fight for them. To stand with them on the most dangerous streets, in the dirtiest hallways, in their darkest hours. We as a country have been too willing to take from our weakest when times get hard. People who allow this to happen must be educated, must be challenged, must be turned around.

Personal experience

If we are to save our children we must become people they will look up to. We must stand up and be visible heroes. I want people to understand the crisis and I want people to act: Either we address the murder and mayhem in our country or we simply won't be able to continue to have the kind of democratic society that we as Americans cherish. Violence is not just a problem of the inner cities or of the minorities in this country. This is a national crisis and the nation must *Proposal* mobilize differently if we are to solve it.

Part of what we must do is change the way we think about violence. Trying to catch and punish people after they have committed a violent act won't deter violence in the least. In life on the street, it's better to go to jail than be killed, better to act quickly and decisively even if you risk being caught.

There are, however, things that governments could and should do right away to begin to end the violence on our streets. They include the following:

Specific recommendations *Create a peace officer corps.* Peace officers would not be police; they would not carry guns and would not be charged with making arrests. Instead they would be local men and women hired to work with children in their own neighborhoods. They would try to settle "beefs" and mediate disputes. They would not be the eyes and ears of the regular police force. Their job would be to try to get these young people jobs, to get them back into school, and, most importantly, to be at the emergency rooms and funerals where young people come together to grieve and plot revenge, in order to keep them from killing one another.

Recommendation *Reduce the demand for drugs.* Any real effort at diverting the next generation of kids from selling drugs must include plans to find employment for these children when they become teenagers. While that will require a significant expenditure of public funds, the savings from reduced hospitalization and reduced incarceration will more than offset the costs of employment. . . .

Recommendation *Reduce the amount of violence on television and in the movies.* Violence in the media is ever more graphic, and the justification for acting violently is deeply implanted in young people's minds. The movie industry promotes the message that power is determined not merely by carrying a gun, but by carrying a big gun that is an automatic and has a big clip containing many bullets.

Reason + evidence What about rap music, and especially "gangsta rap"? It is my opinion that people have concentrated too much attention on this one source of media violence. Many rap songs are positive, and some are neither positive nor negative—just kids telling their stories. But there are some rap singers who have decided that their niche in the music industry will be the most violent and vile. I would love to see the record industry show some restraint in limiting these rappers' access to fame and fortune.

Reduce and regulate the possession of handguns. I believe all handgun sales should be banned in this country. Recognizing, however, that other Americans may not be ready to accept a ban on handguns, I believe there are still some things we must do.

Licensing. Every person who wants to buy a handgun should have to pass both a written test and a field test. The cost for these new procedures should be paid by those who make, sell, and buy handguns. . . .

Gun buy-backs. The federal government, which recently passed a $32 billion crime bill, needs to invest billions of dollars over the next ten years buying guns back from citizens. We now have more than 200 million guns in circulation in our country. A properly cared-for gun can last for decades. There is no way we can deal with handgun violence until we reduce the number of guns currently in circulation. We know that young people won't give up their guns readily, but we have to keep in mind that this is a long-term problem. We have to begin to plan now to get the guns currently in the hands of children out of circulation permanently.

The truth of the matter is that reducing the escalating violence will be complicated and costly. If we were fighting an outside enemy that was killing our children at a rate of more than 5,000 a year, we would spare no expense. What happens when the enemy is us? What happens when those Americans' children are mostly black and brown? Do we still have the will to invest the time and resources in saving their lives? The answer must be yes, because the impact and fear of violence has over-run the boundaries of our ghettos and has both its hands firmly around the neck of our whole country. And while you may not yet have been visited by the spectre of death and fear of this new national cancer, just give it time. Sooner or later, unless we act, you will. We all will.

Margin annotations:
- *Recommendation*
- *Recommendation*
- *Recommendation*
- *Statistics*
- *Response to feasibility problems*
- *Evidence*
- *Call to action*

WARMING UP   Journal Exercises

The following exercises will help you practice problem solving. Read all of the following exercises and then write on one or two that interest you most. If another idea occurs to you, write about it.

1. Wishful-thinking department: Assume that you are a member of the student government, and your organization has $10,000 to spend on a campus improvement project. Think of some campus problem that needs solving.

Describe why it is a problem. Then outline your plan for a solution, indicating how you would spend the money to help solve the problem.

2. Reread Frank Trippett's analysis of the scofflaw problem. Write a letter to the city council recommending a solution to one of the problems that Trippett identifies—a solution that the city council has the power to implement.

3. Eldridge Cleaver once said, "You're either part of the solution or part of the problem." Examine one of your activities or pastimes—sports, shopping, cruising, eating, drinking, or even studying. How does what you do possibly create a problem from someone else's point of view? Explain.

4. The following visual, with an accompanying paragraph, appears on the United Nations Children's Fund (UNICEF) Web site at http://www.unicef.org. Analyze the effectiveness of the image and text in demonstrating the problem of child labor. What details in the picture support the argument that child labor is a problem we must solve?

5. Analyze the MyPyramid graphic that appears on the chapter opening page. Then compare those recommendations with a school lunch program in your community or one of the food choices you have on your

> **❝**A good solution solves more than one problem, and it does not make new problems. I am talking about health as opposed to almost any cure, coherence of pattern as opposed to almost any solution produced piecemeal or in isolation. **❞**
>
> —WENDELL BERRY,
> AUTHOR OF *THE GIFT OF THE GOOD LAND*

A small boy sleeps at the table where he was making softballs in the village of Cholomo, Honduras.

Some people say that boycotts—that is, refusing to buy goods made by children—will help put an end to child labour. But boycotts can also hurt working children and their families, as the children lose their jobs, and then their families have even less money to live on. If employers provided parents with jobs at a living wage, fewer children would be forced to go to work. (UNICEF/89-0052/Vauclair) campus. What specific recommendations could you make to one of these menus to help it meet the USDA's MyPyramid guidelines.

6 Changing the rules of some sports might make them more enjoyable, less violent, or fairer: moving the three-point line farther out, introducing the 30-second clock in NCAA basketball, using TV instant replays in professional and college football and basketball, imposing stiffer fines for brawls in hockey games, requiring boxers to wear padded helmets, giving equal pay and media coverage to women's sports. Choose a sport you enjoy as a participant or observer, identify and explain the problem you want to solve, and justify your solution in a letter to the editors of *Sports Illustrated*.

7 The increasing use of sites such as Turnitin.com to check student papers for plagiarism has led to disagreement about how best to respond to possible cases of plagiarism. In the following passage, John Barrie, President of Turnitin.com, says that plagiarism is a "digital problem [that] demands a digital solution." Representing the point of view of many writing teachers, Rebecca Moore Howard claims that the best solution is to prevent plagiarism by teaching students how to access, use, and document sources. Read these two responses and decide which writer proposes the better overall solution.

> **❝** God, give us grace to accept with serenity the things that cannot be changed, courage to change the things which should be changed, and the wisdom to distinguish the one from the other. **❞**
>
> —REINHOLD NIEBUHR, AUTHOR AND THEOLOGIAN

PROFESSIONAL WRITING

Should Educators Use Commercial Services to Combat Plagiarism?

Pro

The following is a summary of John Barrie's argument, which appeared in the CQ Researcher *in 2003. (Mr. Barrie declined to give permission to reproduce his remarks as they appear there.) The entire article can be read on the* CQ Researcher *Web site (http://library.cqpress.com/cqresearcher).*

Mr. Barrie believes that because we all "draw from the past to create the present," our writing and learning in schools and colleges should take advantage of the power of collaboration. Students should, Barrie believes, be able to "share ideas and criticism" as they work to prepare a high school report about a Shakespeare play or a college level paper about Nietzsche's philosophy. "The problem begins," Barrie acknowledges, "when faculty cannot determine whether a student wrote a term paper or plagiarized it from other sources." Barrie cites a recent study by Rutgers University Professor Donald McCabe that concludes that "nearly 40% of college undergraduates admitted to plagiarizing term papers" by lifting information directly from Internet

...*continued* Should Educators Use Commercial Services to Combat Plagiarism?

sources. Solving this growing problem of plagiarism, Barrie argues, requires a solution that goes beyond the "status quo" of campus honor codes, detective work by faculty, and punishments for plagiarism. "Digital plagiarism," Barrie says, "is a digital problem [that] demands a digital solution." According to Barrie, TurnItIn is an important part of that solution. It receives thousands of essays to check each day and finds that "30 percent of those papers are less than original." Barrie concludes by arguing that educators and administrators should not "shirk their responsibility" as educators and should "demand original work" from all students by using plagiarism detection programs such as TurnItIn.

Con

Rebecca Moore Howard

Associate Professor of Writing and Rhetoric, Syracuse University

Teaching, not software, is the key to preventing plagiarism. Today's students can access an array of electronic texts and images unimaginable just 20 years ago, and students' relationship to the practice of information-sharing has changed along with the technology.

But today's students lack extensive training and experience in working carefully from print sources, and they may not understand that they need to learn this skill. They may also find it difficult to differentiate between kinds of sources on the Internet. With information arriving as a cacophony of electronic voices, even well-intentioned students have difficulty keeping track of—much less citing—who said what.

Moreover, the sheer volume of available information frequently leaves student writers feeling that they have nothing new to say about an issue. Hence too many students—one in three, according to a recent survey conducted by Rutgers University Professor Donald McCabe—may fulfill assignments by submitting work they have not written.

Were we in the throes of widespread moral decay, capture-and-punishment might provide an appropriate deterrent. We are, however, in the midst of a revolution in literacy, and teachers' responses must be more complex. They must address the underlying issues: students' ability to conduct research, comprehend extended written arguments, evaluate sources and produce their own persuasive written texts, in explicit dialogue with their sources.

Classrooms must engage students in text and in learning—communicating a value to these activities that extends beyond grades earned and credentials accrued. McCabe, who is a founder of the renowned Center for Academic Integrity at Duke University, recommends pedagogy and policies that speak to the causes of plagiarism, rather than buying software for detection and punishment. In a 2003 position statement, the Council of Writing Program Administrators urges, "Students should understand research assignments as opportunities for genuine and rigorous inquiry and learning." The statement offers extensive classroom suggestions for teachers and cautions that using plagiarism-catching software may "justify the avoidance of responsible teaching methods."

Buying software instead of revitalizing one's teaching means that teachers, like students, have allowed the electronic environment to encourage a reductive, automated vision of the educational experience. As one of my colleagues recently remarked, "The 'world's leading plagiarism-prevention system' is not TurnItIn.com—it's careful pedagogy."

PROFESSIONAL WRITING

The Argument Culture

Deborah Tannen

A professor of linguistics at Georgetown University, Deborah Tannen is also a best-selling author of many books on discourse and gender, including You Just Don't Understand: Women and Men in Conversation *(1990),* Talking from 9 to 5 *(1994),* The Argument Culture: Moving from Debate to Dialogue *(1998), and* I Only Say This Because I Love You *(2001). Throughout her career, Tannen has focused on how men and women have different conversational habits and assumptions, whether they talk on the job or at home. In the following essay, taken from* The Argument Culture, *Tannen tries to convince her readers that adversarial debates—which typically represent only two sides of an issue and thus promote antagonism—create problems in communication. As a culture, Tannen believes, we would be much more successful if we didn't always think of argument as a war or a fight but as a dialogue among a variety of different positions. As you read her essay, does Tannen persuade you that our "argument culture" really is a problem and that her solutions will help solve that problem?*

Balance. Debate. Listening to both sides. Who could question these 1 noble American traditions? Yet today, these principles have been distorted. Without thinking, we have plunged headfirst into what I call the "argument culture."

...*continued* The Argument Culture, **Deborah Tannen**

"What about here? This looks like a good spot for an argument."

The argument culture urges us to approach the world, and the people in it, in an adversarial frame of mind. It rests on the assumption that opposition is the best way to get anything done: The best way to discuss an idea is to set up a debate; the best way to cover news is to find spokespeople who express the most extreme, polarized views and present them as "both sides"; the best way to settle disputes is litigation that pits one party against the other; the best way to begin an essay is to attack someone; and the best way to show you're really thinking is to criticize. [2]

More and more, our public interactions have become like arguing with a spouse. Conflict can't be avoided in our public lives any more than we can avoid conflict with people we love. One of the great strengths of our society is that we can express these conflicts openly. But just as spouses have to learn ways of settling their differences without inflicting real damage, so we, as a society, have to find constructive ways of resolving disputes and differences. [3]

The war on drugs, the war on cancer, the battle of the sexes, politicians' turf battles—in the argument culture, war metaphors pervade our talk and shape our thinking. The cover headlines of both *Time* and *Newsweek* one recent week are a case in point: "The Secret Sex Wars," proclaims *Newsweek*. "Starr at War," declares *Time*. Nearly [4] everything is framed as a battle or game in which winning or losing is the main concern.

The argument culture pervades every aspect of our lives today. Is- 5 sues from global warming to abortion are depicted as two-sided arguments, when in fact most Americans' views lie somewhere in the middle. Partisanship makes gridlock in Washington the norm. Even in our personal relationships, a "let it all hang out" philosophy emphasizes people expressing their anger without giving them constructive ways of settling differences.

Sometimes You Have to Fight

There are times when it is necessary and right to fight—to defend 6 your country or yourself, to argue for your rights or against offensive or dangerous ideas or actions. What's wrong with the argument culture is the ubiquity, the knee-jerk nature of approaching any issue, problem or public person in an adversarial way.

Our determination to pursue truth by setting up a fight between 7 two sides leads us to assume that every issue has two sides—no more, no less. But if you always assume there must be an "other side," you may end up scouring the margins of science or the fringes of lunacy to find it.

This accounts, in part, for the bizarre phenomenon of Holocaust 8 denial. Deniers, as Emory University professor Deborah Lipstadt shows, have been successful in gaining TV air time and campus newspaper coverage by masquerading as "the other side" in a "debate." Continual reference to "the other side" results in a conviction that everything has another side—and people begin to doubt the existence of any facts at all.

The power of words to shape perception has been proved by re- 9 searchers in controlled experiments. Psychologists Elizabeth Loftus and John Palmer, for example, found that the terms in which people are asked to recall something affect what they recall. The researchers showed subjects a film of two cars colliding, then asked how fast the cars were going; one week later they asked whether there had been any broken glass. Some subjects were asked, "How fast were the cars going when they bumped into each other?" Others were asked, "How fast were the cars going when they smashed into each other?"

Those who read the question with "smashed" tended to "remem- 10 ber" that the cars were going faster. They were also more likely to "remember" having seen broken glass. (There wasn't any.) This is how language works. It invisibly molds our way of thinking about people, actions and the world around us.

In the argument culture, "critical" thinking is synonymous with crit- 11 icizing. In many classrooms, students are encouraged to read someone's life work, then rip it to shreds.

...continued The Argument Culture, **Deborah Tannen**

When debates and fighting predominate, those who enjoy verbal 12
sparring are likely to take part—by calling in to talk shows or writing letters to the editor. Those who aren't comfortable with oppositional discourse are likely to opt out.

How High-Tech Communication Pulls Us Apart

One of the most effective ways to defuse antagonism between two 13
groups is to provide a forum for individuals from those groups to get to
know each other personally. What is happening in our lives, however, is
just the opposite. More and more of our communication is not face to
face, and not with people we know. The proliferation and increasing
portability of technology isolates people in a bubble.

Along with the voices of family members and friends, phone lines 14
bring into our homes the annoying voices of solicitors who want to sell
something—generally at dinnertime. (My father-in-law startles phone
solicitors by saying, "We're eating dinner, but I'll call you back. What's
your home phone number?" To the nonplused caller, he explains, "Well,
you're calling me at home; I thought I'd call you at home, too.")

It is common for families to have more than one TV, so the adults can 15
watch what they like in one room and the kids can watch their choice in
another—or maybe each child has a private TV.

E-mail, and now the Internet, are creating networks of human con- 16
nection unthinkable even a few years ago. Though e-mail has enhanced
communication with family and friends, it also ratchets up the
anonymity of both sender and receiver, resulting in stranger-to-stranger
"flaming."

"Road rage" shows how dangerous the argument culture—and espe- 17
cially today's technologically enhanced aggression—can be. Two men
who engage in a shouting match may not come to blows, but if they express their anger while driving down a public highway, the risk to themselves and others soars.

The Argument Culture Shapes Who We Are

The argument culture has a defining impact on our lives and on our 18
culture.

- **It makes us distort facts,** as in the Nancy Kerrigan-Tonya Harding
  story. After the original attack on Kerrigan's knee, news stories
  focused on the rivalry between the two skaters instead of
  portraying Kerrigan as the victim of an attack. Just last month,
  Time magazine called the event a "contretemps" between Kerrigan
  and Harding. And a recent joint TV interview of the two skaters

reinforced that skewed image by putting the two on equal footing, rather than as victim and accused.

- **It makes us waste valuable time,** as in the case of scientist Robert Gallo, who co-discovered the AIDS virus. Gallo was the object of a groundless four-year investigation into allegations he had stolen the virus from another scientist. He was ultimately exonerated, but the toll was enormous. Never mind that, in his words, "These were the most painful and horrible years of my life." Gallo spent four years fighting accusations instead of fighting AIDS.

- **It limits our thinking.** Headlines are intentionally devised to attract attention, but the language of extremes actually shapes, and mis-shapes, the way we think about things. Military metaphors train us to think about, and see, everything in terms of fighting, conflict and war. Adversarial rhetoric is a kind of verbal inflation—a rhetorical boy-who-cried-wolf.

- **It encourages us to lie.** If you fight to win, the temptation is great to deny facts that support your opponent's views and say only what supports your side. It encourages people to misrepresent and, in the extreme, to lie.

End the Argument Culture by Looking at All Sides

How can we overcome our classically American habit of seeing issues 19 in absolutes? We must expand our notion of "debate" to include more dialogue. To do this, we can make special efforts not to think in twos. Mary Catherine Bateson, an anthropologist at Virginia's George Mason University, makes a point of having her class compare three cultures, not two. Then, students are more likely to think about each on its own terms, rather than as opposites.

In the public arena, television and radio producers can try to avoid, 20 whenever possible, structuring public discussions as debates. This means avoiding the format of having two guests discuss an issue. Invite three guests—or one. Perhaps it is time to re-examine the assumption that audiences always prefer a fight.

Instead of asking, "What's the other side?" we might ask, "What are 21 the other sides?" Instead of insisting on hearing "both sides," let's insist on hearing "all sides."

We need to find metaphors other than sports and war. Smashing 22 heads does not open minds. We need to use our imaginations and in-genuity to find different ways to seek truth and gain knowledge through intellectual interchange, and add them to our arsenal—or, should I say, to the ingredients for our stew. It will take creativity for each of us to find ways to change the argument culture to a dialogue culture. It's an effort we have to make, because our public and private lives are at stake.

vo·cab·u·lar·y

In your journal, write the meanings of the italicized words in the following phrases.

- in an *adversarial* frame of mind (**2**)
- the *ubiquity* (**6**)
- *synonymous* with criticizing (**11**)
- with *oppositional* discourse (**12**)
- the *proliferation* (**13**)

- a *contretemps* between Kerrigan and Harding (**18**)
- he was ultimately *exonerated* (**18**)
- imaginations and *ingenuity* (**22**)

QUESTIONS FOR WRITING AND DISCUSSION

1. List three controversial topics currently in the news. Then choose one of those topics and explain the two "sides" of this argument. Now, imagine a third point of view. How is it different from the first two positions? Does coming up with a third position help you think creatively about how to resolve this dispute? Explain.

2. As she writes her essay, Tannen initially outlines the nature of the problem with the "argument culture" before she gives her solution. Which paragraphs most clearly demonstrate the problem? Which paragraphs explain her solution? Does she ignore any aspects of the problem? Would her solution really solve the problem she describes? Why or why not?

3. Critically analyzing the social, political, or cultural context is an important strategy for solving a problem. Where does Tannen explain the context(s) for the problem? Where does she argue that her solution will help resolve social, political, or cultural problems? Are there contexts where her solution might not work? Explain.

4. Read Tannen's advice in the final four paragraphs of her essay. Does she follow her own advice in writing this essay? Which pieces of advice does she follow and which does she ignore? Cite examples from the essay to support your analysis. Would her essay be more effective if she followed her own advice? Explain.

5. As a professor of linguistics, Tannen can write in a formal, academic style, but she can also write in an informal style for general audiences. In this essay, is Tannen writing for academics or for anyone interested in culture and communication? Find examples of Tannen's "academic" style as well as her informal style. Does she successfully integrate the two or is she too informal or too academic? Explain.

6. According to Tannen, the language we choose and the metaphors we use affect our perceptions of the world. Where does Tannen discuss how words

or metaphors shape our perceptions? What examples does she give? In her own argument, does Tannen herself avoid language or metaphors referring to war, violence, or conflict?

7 The *New Yorker* cartoon by BEK, "This looks like a good spot for an argument," did not originally appear with Tannen's essay. Evaluate the appropriateness of this visual image for Tannen's essay. Does the cartoon support Tannen's thesis? Does it contribute to the essay's appeal, or does it distract from Tannen's argument? Citing details from the cartoon and passages from Tannen's essay, explain your response.

8 On the Internet, log on to the Web site of a national news magazine such as *Newsweek* or *Utne* magazine and read their e-mail letters in response to an essay on a controversial topic such as stem cell research, climate change, public transportation, educational testing, and so forth. Read several letters or responses. Can you find at least *three* positions on that issue—rather than just the standard "pro" and "con"? Explain the controversial topic and then write out at least three different positions or points of view which you discover in the responses.

Problem Solving: The Writing Process

ASSIGNMENT FOR PROBLEM SOLVING

Select a problem that you believe needs a solution. Narrow and focus the problem and choose an appropriate audience. Describe the problem and, if necessary, demonstrate for your audience that it needs a solution. State your solution, and justify it with reasons and evidence. Where appropriate, weigh alternative solutions, examine the feasibility of your own solution, and answer objections to your solution.

The problem-solving assignment leads naturally to the genre of a proposal. Some proposals are long, formal documents addressed to knowledgeable readers, while others are short and informal, intended for general audiences. Review your assignment, and then use the following grid to brainstorm possible genres that would meet your purpose for your selected audience.

Continued

Audience	Possible Genres for Problem Solving
Personal Audience	Class notes, journal entry, blog, social networking page
Academic Audience	Academic proposal, analysis, editorial, review, journal entry, forum entry on class site, multigenre document
Public Audience	Column, editorial, article, blog, or critique in a magazine, newspaper, online site, newsletter, or multigenre document

CHOOSING A SUBJECT

If one of your journal entries suggests a possible subject, try the collecting and shaping strategies below. If none of these leads to a workable subject, consider the following suggestions:

- Evaluating leads naturally into problem solving. Reread your journal entries and topic ideas for "evaluating." If your evaluation of your

"I can't think of anything I have no problem with."

subject was negative, consider what would make your evaluation more positive. Based on your evaluation, write a proposal, addressed to the proper audience, explaining the problem and offering your solution.

- Organized groups are already trying to solve a number of national and international problems: homelessness, illegal immigrants, the slaughter of whales, acid rain, abuse of animals in scientific experiments, drug and alcohol abuse, toxic-waste disposal, and so forth. Read several current articles on one of these topics. Then narrow the problem to one aspect that students or residents of your town could help to resolve. Write an essay outlining the problem and proposing some *specific and limited* actions that citizens could take.

- **Community Service Learning.** An important part of any community-service-learning project is collaborating with the agency to assess problems and propose possible solutions. If you have a community-service-learning project in one of your classes, work collaboratively with the agency to assess the community's and/or the agency's needs as well as the knowledge and skills you might bring to the agency to contribute to a possible solution. Working with the agency, decide on a purpose, audience, and genre for your proposal.

- Every day, the news media features images that seem to suggest a problem that needs a solution. Choose one image that you have found in the media and investigate the issue. What problem does the image suggest? What does your research and investigation reveal about the rhetorical situation and cultural context surrounding this image and this issue? Choose a possible audience, genre, and context, and write your own problem-solving essay based on the issue raised by this image.

COLLECTING

With a possible subject and audience in mind, write out answers for each of the following topics. Remember that not all of these approaches will apply to your subject; some topics will suggest very little, while others may prompt you to generate ideas or specific examples appropriate to your problem and solution. A hypothetical problem—large classes that hinder learning—illustrates how these topics may help you focus on your subject and collect relevant ideas and information.

● **IDENTIFY AND FOCUS ON THE SPECIFIC PROBLEM**   Answer the first four "Wh" questions:

WHO: A Psychology I professor; the Psychology Department
WHAT: Psychology I class

When: Spring semester (the structure of this class may be slightly different from previous semesters)

Where: University of Illinois (large lecture classes at one school may be different from those at another)

You may want to generalize about large lecture classes everywhere, but begin by identifying the specific problem at hand.

● **DEMONSTRATE THAT THE PROBLEM NEEDS A SOLUTION**   Map out the *effects* of a problem. (See the diagram.)

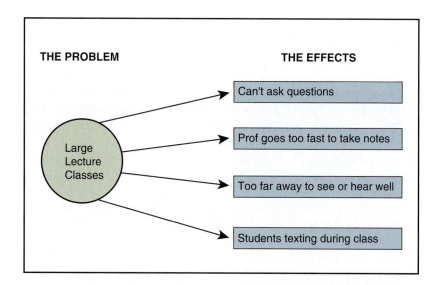

THE PROBLEM / THE EFFECTS

- Can't ask questions
- Prof goes too fast to take notes
- Too far away to see or hear well
- Students texting during class

Large Lecture Classes

You may want to map out both *short-term effects* and *long-term effects*. Over the short term, large lecture classes prevent you from asking questions; over the long term, you may do poorly on examinations, get a lower grade in the class, lose interest in the subject, be unable to cope with your own and others' psychological problems, or end up in a different career or job.

● **DISCOVER POSSIBLE SOLUTIONS**   One strategy is to map out the history or the causes of the problem. If you can discover what caused the problem in the first place, you may have a possible solution. (See the following diagram.)

A second strategy takes the imaginative approach. Brainstorm hypothetical cases by asking, "What if. . . ."

"What if students petitioned the president of the university to abolish all lecture classes with enrollments over 100 students?" Would that work?

"What if students invited the professor to answer questions at a weekly study session?" Would the professor attend? Would students attend?

"What if students taught each other in a psychology class?" How would that work?

"What if all lecture classes were in smart-media classrooms with computer projection, i-clickers, twitter, and in-class videos?"

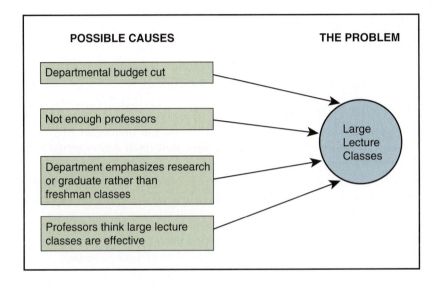

● **EVALUATE POSSIBLE SOLUTIONS**   Apply the "If . . . then . . ." test on each possible solution: Consider whether each proposal would:

    A. actually solve the problem;

    B. meet certain criteria, such as cost-effectiveness, practicality, ethicality, legality;

    C. not create new problems.

"*If* classes were smaller, *then* students would learn more":

If classes were smaller, students might learn more, but a small class size does not necessarily guarantee greater learning.

Although students might learn more, do smaller classes meet other criteria? While they are legal and ethical, are they practical and cost-effective?

Would smaller classes create new problems? Smaller classes might mean fewer upper-level course offerings. Is that a serious new problem?

● **CONVINCE YOUR READERS**   Support your proposed solutions by stating *reasons* and finding supporting *evidence*.

    Reason: Smaller classes are worth the additional expense because students actually engage the material rather than just memorizing for exams.

Evidence: Data from studies comparing large and small classes; personal testimony by students, interviews, or questionnaires; testimony or evidence from authorities on teaching.

● **ANSWER POSSIBLE OBJECTIONS TO YOUR PROPOSAL**   Every solution has a down side or possible drawbacks. You need to respond to the most important objections.

List Drawbacks

Small classes cost more.

Small classes might reduce course offerings.

Small classes might mean less money for research.

List Your Responses

Good education does cost more. The University of Illinois has a reputation as an excellent undergraduate institution, and small classes would help it maintain quality education.

Perhaps some classes with low demand could be cut, but the necessary funds should not be taken out of upper-division classes for psychology majors or research projects.

● **LIST POSSIBLE STEPS FOR IMPLEMENTATION**   If appropriate, indicate the key steps or chronological sequence of your proposal.

1. Poll students and teachers in large lecture classes to confirm that the problem warrants attention.
2. Gather evidence from other colleges or universities to show how they reduced class sizes.
3. Present results of polls and other evidence to the state legislature to request more funds.

● **OBSERVING**   As you gather evidence and examples, use your observation skills. If the problem is large lecture classes, attend classes and *observe* the behavior of students and professors. Are students distracted by noise? Can they ask questions? Does the professor talk too softly to be heard in the back row? Remember that *repeated* observation is essential. If necessary, observe your subject over a period of several days or weeks.

> 66 The best time for planning . . . is when you're doing the dishes. 99
> —AGATHA CHRISTIE, MYSTERY WRITER

● **REMEMBERING**   Use *freewriting, looping,* or *clustering* to help you remember examples from your experience of the problem or of possible solutions. Brainstorm or freewrite about previous class sessions in Psychology I. Do looping or mapping on other small-enrollment classes: What made these classes effective or ineffective? What teaching strategies, projects, or small-group activities were possible in these classes that would not be possible in a class of 250 students?

As you begin researching your problem, don't spend all your time on the Internet or on the library's databases. Remember to interview people who may know about your problem. Use your investigating skills to locate local authorities and interview them in person, via e-mail, or on the telephone. Find out what other people think about this problem. How do they explain or define the problem? What are they already doing to solve the problem? Why are current solutions not working or not working effectively enough? Interview a teacher who knows about the problem, a student who has first-hand experience with the problem, an owner of a local business, or the co-ordinator of a community service or agency. Combining your online and library research with interviews makes your research more interesting, more local and current, and more effective.

● **READING AND INVESTIGATING**   *Use the library* to find books or articles about the particular problem. Other writers have no doubt offered solutions to your problem that you could consider. Articles may even suggest objections to your proposed solution that you need to answer.

Interview participants or authorities on the problem. The professor who is teaching your Psychology I class may have some ideas about a solution. Administration—department chairs, deans, even the president—may agree to answer your questions and react to your possible solutions.

Design a questionnaire that addresses aspects of your problem. Responses to questionnaires provide evidence that a problem is serious, immediate, and in need of a solution. If the results of a questionnaire show that 175 of the 200 people in Psychology I who returned it favor smaller sections, you can include those data in your letter to the head of the department and the dean of the college.

SHAPING

● **GENRES FOR PROBLEM SOLVING**   Initially, you must consider possible genres appropriate for your issue and your particular rhetorical situation. Typical genres used for proposals include articles in magazines, letters to the editor, academic essays, self-help essays, political essays, and business proposals. Depending on the genre and audience you choose, proposals often do the following.

- Identify, analyze, and demonstrate the problem
- Describe and evaluate alternative solutions
- Make proposals
- Give reasons and evidence to support the proposal
- Answer objections; discuss feasibility problems
- Indicate implementation and call for action

Of course, not all problem-solving essays have all six elements. Some do not discuss feasibility in detail or do not describe and evaluate alternative solutions. Adam Richman's essay at the end of this chapter, for example, does not consider alternative solutions to the gradual demise of professional print journalism because his focus is on demonstrating that citizen journalism is a workable solution. Reconsidering your rhetorical situation and genre helps you decide how to shape your proposal.

● **OUTLINES FOR PROBLEM SOLVING**   The following patterns indicate four possible ways to organize a problem-solving essay. One of these patterns may help you organize your proposal.

Problem-Solving Pattern
   I. Introduction
  II. The problem: Identify and demonstrate
III. The solution(s)
IV. Answering possible objections, costs, drawbacks
  V. Conclusion: Implementation plan; call to action

Point-by-Point Pattern
   I. Introduction
  II. The overall problem: Identify and demonstrate
III. One part of the problem, solution, evidence, answers to possible objections, feasibility
IV. Second part of the problem, solution, evidence, answers to possible objections, feasibility
  V. Third part of the problem, solution, evidence, and so on
VI. Conclusion: Implementation; call to action

Alternative Pattern
   I. Introduction
  II. The problem: Identify and demonstrate
III. Alternative Solution 1; why it's not satisfactory
IV. Alternative Solution 2; why it's not satisfactory

V. Alternative Solution 3; why it works best: Evidence, objections, feasibility

VI. Conclusion: Implementation; call to action

Step-by-Step Pattern

I. Introduction

II. The problem: Identify and demonstrate

III. Plan for implementing the solution or how solution has worked in the past:

A. Step 1: Reasons and evidence showing why this step is necessary and feasible

B. Step 2: Reasons and evidence showing why this step is necessary and feasible

C. Step 3: Reasons and evidence showing why this step is necessary and feasible

IV. Conclusion

● **CAUSAL ANALYSIS**   Causal analysis can be used to organize some paragraphs of a proposal. In arguing the benefits or advantages of a proposed solution, you are actually explaining the *effects* of your solution.

- The effects or advantages of smaller class sections in Psychology I would be greater student participation, fewer distractions, more discussion during lectures, and more individual or small-group learning.
- Shortening the work week to thirty-two hours would increase the number of jobs, reduce tensions for working parents, and give employees time to learn new skills.

In each of these cases, each effect or advantage can become a separate point and, sometimes, a separate body paragraph.

● **CRITERIA ANALYSIS**   In some cases, the *criteria* for a good solution are quite clear. For example, cost-effectiveness, feasibility, and worker morale might be important criteria for a business-related proposal. If you work in a fast-food restaurant and are concerned about the increasing number of crimes, for example, you might propose that your manager add a video surveillance system. In order to overcome the manager's resistance to spending the needed funds, you could defend your proposal (and answer possible objections) by discussing relevant criteria.

Proposal: To reduce theft and protect the employees of the restaurant by installing a video surveillance system.

- **Cost-effectiveness.** Citing evidence from other stores that have video cameras, you could prove that the equipment would pay for itself in less than a year. In addition, you could argue that if the life of just one employee—or possibly one manager—were saved, the cost would be worth it.

> 66 Vigorous writing is concise. 99
> —WILLIAM STRUNK, JR., AUTHOR AND TEACHER

- **Feasibility.** Installing a security system would not require any extensive remodeling or any significant training time for employees to learn how to operate the system.
- **Employee morale.** The benefits to employee morale would be significant: Workers would feel more secure, they would feel that the management cares about them, and they would work more productively.

● **CHRONOLOGICAL ORDER**   If your proposal stresses the means of implementing your solution to a problem, you may organize several paragraphs or even an entire essay using a chronological order or step-by-step pattern.

A proposal to improve the reading skills of children might be justified by a series of coordinated steps, beginning by organizing seminars for teachers and PTA meetings to discuss possible solutions; establishing minimal reading requirements in grades K–6 that teachers and parents agree on; offering reading prizes; and organizing media coverage of students who participate in reading programs.

DRAFTING

Using your examples, recorded observations, reading, interviews, results from questionnaires, or your own experience, make a sketch outline and begin writing. As you write, let your own proposal and your intended audience guide you. In your first draft, get as much as possible on paper. Don't worry about spelling or awkward sentences. If you hit a snag, stop and read what you have written so far or reread your collecting and shaping notes.

PEER RESPONSE

Writer: Provide the following information about your essay before you exchange drafts with a peer reader.

1. a. Audience and genre
   b. Statement of problem and context of problem
   c. Possible or alternative solutions
   d. Your recommended solution(s)
2. Write out one or two questions about your draft that you want your reader to answer.

Reader: Read the writer's entire draft. As you *reread* the draft, do the following.

1. Without looking at the writer's responses, describe (a) the essay's intended audience, (b) the main problem that the essay identifies, (c) the possible or alternative solutions, and (d) the writer's recommended solution. What feasibility problems or additional solutions should the writer consider? Why?

2. Indicate one paragraph in which the writer's evidence is strong. Then find one paragraph in which the writer needs more evidence. What additional *kinds* of evidence (personal experience, testimony from authorities, statistics, specific examples, etc.) might the writer use in this paragraph? Explain.

3. Number the paragraphs in the writer's essay and then describe, briefly, the purpose or main idea of each paragraph: paragraph 1 introduces the problem, paragraph 2 gives the writer's personal experience with the problem, and so on. When you finish, explain how the writer might improve the organization of the essay.

4. List the three most important things that the writer should focus on during revision.

5. Respond to the writer's questions in number 2.

Writer: When your essay is returned, read the comments by your peer reader(s) and do the following.

1. Compare your description of the audience, the problem, and the solutions with your reader's description. Where there are differences, try to clarify your essay.

2. Reconsider and revise your recommended solution(s).

3. What additional kinds of evidence will make your recommendations stronger?

4. Make a revision plan. List, in order, the three most important things that you need to do as you revise your essay.

REVISING

When you have a completed draft and are ready to start revising your essay, get another member of your class to read and respond to your essay. Use the peer response guidelines that follow to get—and give—constructive advice on your draft.

Use the following revising guidelines to identify areas for improving your draft. Even at this point, don't hesitate to collect additional information, if necessary, or reorganize your material. If a reader makes suggestions, reread your draft to see if those changes will improve your essay.

GUIDELINES FOR REVISION

- **Review your rhetorical situation.** How can you revise your selected genre to make it more effectively communicate your purpose to your intended audience?

- **Review to make sure you critically analyze the problem.** Don't just assume that everyone will agree with your definition or representation of the problem. Investigate and describe the groups of people who are affected by the problem.

- **Have a classmate or someone who might understand your audience read your draft and play devil's advocate.** Have your reader pretend to be hostile to your solution and ask questions about alternative solutions or weaknesses in your own solution. Revise your proposal so that it answers any important objections.

- **Review your proposal for key elements.** If you are missing one of the following, would adding it make your proposal more effective for your audience? *Remember:* Proposals do not necessarily have to have all of these elements.

  Develop the items that are most applicable to your proposal.

  Show that a problem exists and needs attention.

  Evaluate alternative solutions.

  Propose your solution.

  Show that your solution meets certain criteria: feasibility, cost-effectiveness, legality.

  Answer possible objections.

  Suggest implementation or call for action.

- **Be sure that you *show* what you mean, using specific examples, facts, details, statistics, quotations from interviews or articles.** Don't rely on general assertions.

- **Signal the major parts of your proposal with key words and transitions.**

- **Avoid the following errors in logic and generalization.**

  Don't commit an "either-or" fallacy. For example, don't say that "*either* we reduce class sizes *or* students will drop out of the university." There are more than two possible alternatives.

Don't commit an "ad hominem" fallacy by arguing "to the man" or "to the woman" rather than to the issue. Don't say, for example, that Deborah Tannen is wrong about argument because she is just another pushy woman who should stick to teaching linguistics.

Test your proposal for "If . . . then . . ." statements. Does it really follow that "if we reduce class size, teaching will be more effective"?

Avoid overgeneralizing your solution. If all your research applies to solving problems in large lecture classes in psychology, don't assume that your solution will apply to, say, classes in physics or physical education.

- **If you are citing data or quoting sources, make sure that your material is accurately cited.**

- **Read your proposal aloud for flabby, wordy, or awkward sentences.** Revise your sentences for clarity, precision, and forcefulness.

- **Edit your proposal for spelling, appropriate word choice, punctuation, usage, mechanics, and grammar.** Remember that, in part, your form and audience help determine what are appropriate usage and mechanics.

POSTSCRIPT ON THE WRITING PROCESS

Before you turn in your essay, answer the following questions in your journal.

1. As you worked on your essay, what elements of the rhetorical situation did you revise? How did you change the purpose, audience, or genre elements as you drafted your essay? Cite specific sentences or paragraphs from your essay as examples.

2. List the skills you used in writing this paper: observing people, places, or events; remembering personal experience; using questionnaires and interviews; reading written material; explaining ideas; evaluating solutions. Which of these skills was most useful to you in writing this essay?

3. What was your most difficult problem to solve while writing this paper? Were you able to solve it yourself, or did your readers suggest a solution?

4. In one sentence, describe the most important thing you learned about writing while working on this essay.

5. What were the most successful parts of your essay?

STUDENT WRITING
ADAM RICHMAN

Can Citizen Journalism Pick Up the Pieces?

In a writing class focusing on the future of literacies, Adam Richman decided to write his essay on citizen journalism. He began by assembling research questions that he wanted to answer. Because many traditional newspapers were going bankrupt and ceasing publication, Richman wondered whether citizen journalism might potentially fill the gap left by these disappearing traditional news sources. If citizen journalism could be a solution to the problem, he needed to know whether it was capable of meeting the responsibilities of professional journalism. Citizen journalism must be able to inform the public and serve as a public watchdog for injustice and corruption in government and business. After brainstorming his list of questions, he decided to design a questionnaire that would assess whether citizen journalism—as opposed to professional journalism—kept students informed and whether students thought citizen journalism was as reliable as professional journalism. After tabulating the results of his survey and completing his research, he decided that the evidence showed that citizen journalism definitely had the potential to replace professional journalism. Printed below are some of Richman's research questions, his survey questions, and his essay.

RESEARCH QUESTIONS

Overall Question: Is citizen journalism good for journalism as a whole?

- What percentage of journalism consumers read/watch/listen to a) primarily professional journalism, b) primarily citizen journalism, or c) about an even mix?
- Which of the three groups is best informed on current events?
- Which of the three groups spends the most time consuming news?
- Which of the three groups is the best informed on current events?
- What percentage of journalism consumers says professional journalism has a) more credibility than citizen journalism b) less credibility than citizen journalism, or c) about the same credibility as citizen journalism?
- Which of these three groups is the best informed on current events?
- What percentage of journalism consumers fact-checks the news they consume?

- Which type of journalism gets fact-checked more: professional or citizen?
- What percentage of people considers citizen journalism to be journalism?
- Who is more informed on current events: those who say *yes* above or those who say *no* above?

QUESTIONNAIRE

This questionnaire is part of a research project conducted by Adam Richman. The topics to be covered include encyclopedias, media consumption and current events. Any information you provide will be kept entirely confidential, and your identity will not be requested.

1. **Which of the following do you use more often?**
   A. User-edited encyclopedias (Wikipedia, etc.)
   B. Staff-written encyclopedias (Encyclopedia Britannica, etc.)

2. **Which of the following statements best applies to you?**
   A. To get the news, I primarily use professional journalism (newspapers, TV news programs, news magazines, etc.).
   B. To get the news, I primarily use citizen journalism (weblogs, video logs, etc.).
   C. To get the news, I use an even mix of professional and citizen journalism.

3. **Which of the following has more credibility?**
   A. Professional journalism does.
   B. Citizen journalism does.
   C. They are about the same.

4. **Do you consider citizen journalism (weblogs, video logs, etc.) to be true journalism?**
   A. Yes
   B. No

5. **When reading, watching, or listening to the news, which of the following do you prefer?**
   A. An attempt at objectivity
   B. A transparent bias
   If you answered B, move on to question 6. If you answered A, skip to question 7.

6. **Which of the following statements best applies to you?**
   A. I primarily seek bias I agree with.
   B. I primarily seek bias I disagree with.
   C. I seek an even mix of bias I agree with and bias I disagree with.

...continued Can Citizen Journalism Pick Up the Pieces?, **Adam Richman**

7. **When reading, watching, or listening to the news, how often do you check facts?**

   1 (Never)   2 (Rarely)   3 (Sometimes)   4 (Often)   5 (Always)

8. **Who is the Vice President of the United States?**
9. **Which political party has the majority in both houses of Congress?**
10. **Which radio host has recently been pegged by opposition as the de facto leader of the Republican Party?**
11. **What kind of pet was recently shot and killed by police after the pet mauled its owner's friend?**
    A. Pit bull
    B. Chimpanzee
    C. Bobcat
    D. Horse
12. **Which former First Lady recently underwent open heart surgery?**
13. **Which CNN host recently cancelled his own show?**
14. **Which New York Yankees star has recently come under fire for steroid use?**
15. **Which radio legend recently died?**

ESSAY

Print journalism has recently seen historic cuts. In February, the *Rocky Mountain News* closed just weeks shy of its 150th anniversary. Also that month, Philadelphia Newspapers L.L.C., which owns the city's *Inquirer* and *Daily News,* filed for bankruptcy (Lieberman). Four years shy of its 150th anniversary, the *Seattle Post-Intelligencer* transferred 100 percent of its operations to the Internet (Richman and James). Most recently, Harrisburg's *Patriot-News* announced March 24 that all full-time employees must take 10 days off over the next five months ("Local Newspaper Announces Mandatory Furloughs"). This alarming string of newspaper closings appears to be just the beginning of a fundamental change in journalism. We may well wonder how or if journalism—and our democratic way of life that depends on journalism—can survive these upheavals.

The problem is nothing less than the gradual demise of print journalism. But is there a solution? One possible solution could be the rise of citizen journalists, or "people without professional journalism training using the tools of modern technology and the global distribution of the Internet to create, augment or fact-check media on their own or in collaboration with others" (Glaser). User "djussila" of the citizen journalistic *NowPublic.com* defines journalism as one-third of the democratic equation: Politicians + Public + Publication = Democracy. The publication element is necessary, djussila argues, because direct democracy is obsolete. "People do not really have a say in modern democracy, aside from their vote, unless they are a politician themselves," djussila said. "Journalism serves as a window."

Like a chemical reaction equation, each entity of a functioning 3 democracy needs to remain balanced. But with the gradual reduction of print journalism, the equation becomes unstable. In a piece for the *Washington Post*, Marc Fisher quotes Warren Fiske of the *Virginia Pilot* lamenting the job cuts facing the newspaper industry: "When we had the larger bureaus, you could do the good investigative piece. Most sessions, somebody would find someone doing something wrong," Fiske said. "Now, we can only really cover the flow of legislation."

The number of citizen journalism sites that might replace print jour- 4 nalism has been growing dramatically in recent years. The most popular of these Web sites include the following:

- *NowPublic.com*, one of *Time's* 50 Coolest Web sites of 2007. The magazine said, "Nowhere are the merits of citizen journalism more apparent than at NowPublic.com" ("NowPublic Blog").

- CyberJournalist.net, one of Cnet's Top 100 Blogs. *USA Today* and the *Columbia Journalism Review* have both recommended the site ("About *CyberJournalist.net*").

- *Wanabehuman.blogspot.com*, a UK blog "founded on the principles of participatory or citizen journalism." Their site proudly declares, "We believe every citizen can be a journalist" (*Wanabehuman*: About Wanabehuman).

The growth of these news sources and many others like them 5 raises a key question. Can citizen journalism pick up the pieces being left by professional journalism? To answer this, we first must answer other questions: 1) Can citizen journalism be considered real journalism? and 2) Does citizen journalism have the necessary characteristics to bridge the gap?

According to Mark Pearson's and Jane Johnston's *Breaking into* 6 *Journalism*, news media serves "to inform . . . and to act as a public watchdog over government." If citizen journalism can accomplish these tasks to a degree that meets or exceeds the standards currently set by professional journalism, it can be considered real journalism. A survey I conducted of 100 York College students seems to suggest that citizen journalism may already be meeting the current standards. This survey included an eight-question current events quiz. Those who primarily used professional journalism to get the news answered an average of 3.98 questions correctly. Those who primarily used citizen journalism to get the news answered an average of 4.29 questions correctly. Although it is difficult to generalize this data across the nation, it does suggest that citizen journalism at least has the potential to inform the public to a degree that meets or exceeds the standards set by professional journalism.

In addition to providing the public with civic information, citizen 7 journalism has also demonstrated the potential to act as a public watchdog. In a PBS online article, Mark Glaser showed occasions when blogs have acted as a public watchdog, outlining four events:

- "Trent Lott resigns as majority leader of the U.S. Senate in December 2002 after blogs keep up pressure over a racist remark he made."

- "Conservative bloggers helped discredit documents related to President Bush's National Guard service used in an episode of '60 Minutes II' in 2004. This became known as Rathergate."

- "Various people worked together online to help identify the star of the Lonelygirl15 videos on YouTube as a New Zealand actress."

- "A former Lockheed Martin engineer takes his story about security flaws with Coast Guard ships straight to YouTube after the mainstream media ignored his entreaties. Later, the *Washington Post* wrote about it."

As these cases demonstrate, citizen journalism can indeed serve as a public watchdog.

Because citizen journalism has shown the potential to inform and 8 serve as a watchdog to a degree that meets or exceeds the standards set by professional journalism, it can be considered real journalism. The next question is, "Can citizen journalism solve the problem by bridging the gap left by the fading of professional journalism?"

Professional journalism has three key functions: 1) to offer credible 9 reporting of the news, 2) to report on the deliberations and decisions of state and local government, and 3) to do investigative work on public issues. Currently, there are already weaknesses in all of these areas. The *Columbia Journalism Review's* Web site laments the deterioration of credibility obvious in the media when CNN, Fox News, ABC News, and CNBC all focused heavily on a story revolving around a commercial being shot by Kevin Federline—better known as K-Fed or "Britney's ex," (Colby). Also, a *Washington Post* story explains, "as long as people buy property, look for jobs, send kids to school and pay taxes, they will need credible information about state government." Finally, Fiske says that professional journalism institutions no longer have the resources to commit to investigative reporting (Fisher).

Although there are current weaknesses in professional journalism, 10 both media critics and the public disagree about whether citizen journalism can serve these functions credibly. My survey of York College students suggested a lack of respect for citizen journalism. Seventy-nine percent of respondents said professional journalism is more credible, and fifty-three percent said that citizen journalism isn't even real journalism. Supporting that position, a Virginian politics blogger and maintainer of *RichmondSunlight.com*, Waldo Jaquith, admits an inability to cover local news as objectively as institutional journalists. "What I can't offer on my blogs is the relationships, the institutional memory, the why, the history that reporters who know the capital can bring to their stories," Jaquith said. "Newspapers can describe the candidates for governor in a more balanced, deeper way because you don't have a dog in the race. Webloggers do" (Fisher).

On the other hand, many professionals do support the job that citizen journalists are doing. Dave Berlind, a blogger with *zdnet.com,* denies that blogs lack credibility. "Bloggers and so called 'citizen journalists' have to earn their credibility, and the community at large does a good job of regulating the environment—quality will usually rise to the top." Providers of citizen journalism have earned praise from organizations like *Time, USA Today,* and the *Columbia Journalism Review*. In addition, the citizen journalistic *Chi-Town Daily News* covers Chicago's local happenings in depth, especially compared to the only eight local stories you may find in an average edition of the *Chicago Tribune* ("Investigative Journalism Done Better, Faster and Cheaper Without Newspapers"): "We publish articles written by our team of seasoned beat reporters covering citywide topics like education, the environment, public housing and health," the site's About Us section reads. "Their work is supported by trained volunteer neighborhood reporters." Another Web site, the *Voice of San Diego,* operates similarly. Undeniably, citizen journalism has the ability to cover local news.

One citizen journalism Web site, which was born during the Florida recounts of 2000, has earned praise from *techdirt.com*. "*Talking Points Memo* has been quite successful with its investigative reporting, which does a lot to leverage its community to help out in the process," *techdirt.com*'s 'let's-get-real' department said, "while still employing full time journalists who are doing tremendous investigative reporting—which should only improve as better tools are created to enable more to be done." With this site and others like it—others like those who broke open the four stories bulleted above—it is clear that citizen journalism has the ability to conduct investigative reporting.

Because citizen journalism has shown the ability to adequately accomplish these tasks, the potential exists for new media outlets to fill the vacuum being left by the downturn in professional journalism. Citizen journalism is able to pick up the pieces left by a fragmented and faltering print-based press. The fix will be neither immediate nor perfect, but a solid journalistic foundation supports the very capable field of citizen

...continued Can Citizen Journalism Pick Up the Pieces?, **Adam Richman**

journalism. Potentially life-altering stories may go unnoticed, but for every one of those, another important story will see daylight that professional journalism alone could have never have shown. With every keystroke, with every click of the mouse on a button reading "post," citizen journalism is proving itself to the public. As accessibility to the Internet grows and as professional journalism continues to circle the drain, citizen journalism continues to grow stronger. Thanks to the brand-less brand of journalism that fosters independence, personal responsibility, and healthy skepticism, professional journalism's faltering need not throw the democratic equation off balance—if citizen journalism can meet its potential.

Works Cited

"About *CyberJournalist.net.*" *CyberJournalist.net*. Jonathan Dube, 28 Mar 2009. Web. 28 Mar. 2009.

Berlind, David. "Can Technology Close Journalism's Credibility Gap?" *ZDNet*. CBS Interactive, 19 Jan. 2005. Web. 28 Mar. 2009.

Chi-Town Daily News. Chi-Town Daily News, 28 Mar. 2009. Web. 28 Mar. 2009.

Colby, Edward B. "A Penny 'Saved' Is Media Credibility Burned." *Columbia Journalism Review*. Columbia Journalism Review, 23 June 2006. Web. 28 Mar 2009.

djussila, "The Role of Journalism in a Democracy." *NowPublic*. NowPublic Technologies, 09 Mar. 2009. Web. 28 Mar. 2009.

Fisher, Marc. "Bloggers Can't Fill the Gap Left by a Shrinking Press Corps." *The Washington Post*. Washington Post, 1 Mar. 2009. Web. 28 Mar. 2009.

Glaser, Mark. "MediaShift: Your Guide to Citizen Journalism." *PBS*. PBS, 27 Sep. 2006. Web. 25 Mar. 2009.

"Investigative Journalism Done Better, Faster and Cheaper Without Newspapers." *techdirt*. Floor64, 18 Mar. 2009. Web. 28 Mar. 2009.

Lieberman, David. "Newspaper Closings Raise Fears about Industry." *USA Today*. Gannett, 19 Mar. 2009. Web. 28 Mar. 2009.

"Local Newspaper Announces Mandatory Furloughs." *WGAL News*. WGAL, Lancaster, 24 Mar. 2009. Television.

"NowPublic Blog." *NowPublic.com*. NowPublic News Coverages, 28 Mar. 2009. Web. 28 Mar. 2009.

Pearson, Mark, and Jane Johnston. *Breaking into Journalism*. Crow's Nest, Australia: Allen & Unwin, 1998. Print.

Richman, Dan, and Andrea James. "Seattle P-I to Publish Last Edition Tuesday." *Seattle Post-Intelligencer*. Seattle Post-Intelligencer, 16 Mar. 2009. Web. 28 Mar. 2009.

"Wanabehuman: About Wanabehuman." *Wanabehuman*. Wanabehuman, 28 Mar. 2009. Web. 28 Mar. 2009.

? QUESTIONS FOR WRITING AND DISCUSSION

1. Problem-solving essays need to clearly demonstrate an existing problem. According to Adam Richman, what is the problem facing journalism in America today? In what paragraphs does Adam Richman state this problem? Do you agree with his statement of the problem, or could other forces be creating the problem? Explain.

2. What solution to this problem does Richman propose? In what paragraphs does he state his solution most directly? What evidence does he present to convince you that his solution will work? Which pieces of evidence did you find most persuasive?

3. Richman presents one possible solution to this problem, but there are other alternative solutions to the problem of declining print journalism. Some people say that newspapers can be saved by selling articles online. Others say that newspapers and other print journalism ought to have nonprofit status in order to pay professional journalists to protect our democratic way of life. In addition, critics of citizen journalism say that ordinary citizens are not trained to investigate and deliver news accurately and objectively. Should Richman consider these alternative ideas in order to convince you that citizen journalism has the potential to replace traditional print journalism?

4. Richman is writing for an audience composed of his fellow students at his college. Are the results of this study likely to convince students? Why or why not? If he were writing for an audience of Americans over the age of 50, would this study convince these readers? Why or why not?

Jerome Lawrence and
Robert E. Lee
Inherit the Wind (1960)
Stanley Kramer, Director

STANLEY KRAMER presents SPENCER TRACY | FREDRIC MARCH | GENE KELLY in
"INHERIT THE WIND"
...IT'S ALL ABOUT THE 'MONKEY TRIAL' THAT ROCKED AMERICA...

DICK YORK · DONNA ANDERSON and FLORENCE ELDRIDGE Screenplay by NATHAN E. DOUGLAS and HAROLD JACOB SMITH
Based upon the play by JEROME LAWRENCE and ROBERT E. LEE · Produced and Directed by STANLEY KRAMER · Released thru UNITED ARTISTS

For twelve swelteringly hot days in July 1925, the famous Scopes "Monkey Trial" in Dayton, Tennessee, tested a state law banning the teaching of evolution. The original debate between Clarence Darrow and William Jennings Bryan is recreated in this film version of the play *Inherit the Wind*. Written arguments sometimes recreate the pro–con debate style of a trial, but frequently, they represent multiple points of view, just as parents, teachers, administrators, and students might gather to recommend policy changes at a school or citizens get together to solve problems in the community. This chapter encourages you to imagine multiple situations for written argument as you adapt to different audiences, genres, and social contexts.

Arguing

10

As a recent high school graduate, you decide to write about the increasing number of standardized tests currently required of primary and secondary school students. The question you want to investigate is whether schools are teaching students important skills and making them better members of society or whether schools are just teaching them how to do well on tests. After reading current articles on tests mandated by No Child Left Behind and interviewing your classmates, you decide to write to politicians who are in favor of standardized tests and argue that, while the tests should not be thrown out, they should be changed in order to solve several serious problems they have created for students, teachers, and parents.

After being cited for not wearing a seat belt while operating a motor vehicle, you decide that your rights have been violated. In order to write a convincing argument to your representative that seat belt laws are unfair, you research current articles about the law and interview a law professor on the issue. You decide to claim that seat belt laws should be repealed because they are a fundamental violation of individual liberty. You believe that the opposing argument—that seat belts save lives and reduce insurance rates for everyone—is not relevant to the issue of individual liberty. Because your representative has supported seat belt laws, you present both sides of the issue but stress the arguments supporting your viewpoint.

> " Give me liberty to know, to utter, and to argue freely according to conscience, above all liberties. "
> —JOHN MILTON, POET

> " Freedom of speech is established to achieve its essential purpose only when different opinions are expounded in the same hall to the same audience. . . . The opposition is indispensable. "
> —WALTER LIPPMANN, JOURNALIST

WHEN PEOPLE ARGUE WITH EACH OTHER, THEY OFTEN BECOME HIGHLY EMOTIONAL OR CONFRONTATIONAL. REMEMBER THE LAST HEATED ARGUMENT YOU HAD WITH A FRIEND OR FAMILY MEMBER: AT THE END OFTHE ARGUMENT, ONE PERSON STOMPED out of the room, slammed the door, and didn't speak to the other for days. In the aftermath of such a scene, you felt angry at the other person and angry at yourself. Nothing was accomplished. Neither of you came close to achieving what you wanted when you began the argument. Rather than understanding each other's point of view and working out your differences, you effectively closed the lines of communication.

When writers construct arguments, however, they try to avoid the emotional outbursts that often turn arguments into displays of temper. Strong feelings may energize an argument—few of us make the effort to argue without emotional investment in the subject—but written argument stresses a fair presentation of opposing or alternative arguments. Because written arguments are public, they take on a civilized manner. They implicitly say, "Let's be reasonable about this. Let's look at the evidence on all sides. Before we argue for our position, let's put all the reasons and evidence on the table so everyone involved can see what's at stake."

As writers construct written arguments, they carefully consider the rhetorical situation:

- What is the social or cultural context for this issue?
- Where might this written argument appear or be published?
- Who is the audience, and what do they already know or believe?
- Do readers hold an opposing or alternative viewpoint, or are they more neutral and likely to listen to both sides before deciding what to believe?

> 66 All writing . . . is propaganda for something. 99
> —ELIZABETH DREW, WRITER AND CRITIC

A written argument creates an atmosphere of reason, which encourages readers to examine their own views clearly and dispassionately. When successful, such argument convinces rather than alienates an audience. It changes people's minds or persuades them to adopt a recommended course of action.

Techniques for Writing Arguments

A written argument is similar to a public debate—between attorneys in a court of law or between members of Congress who represent different political parties. It begins with a debatable issue: Is this a good bill? Should we vote for it? In such debates, one person argues for a position or proposal, while the other argues against it. The onlookers (the judge, the members of Congress, the jury, or the public) then decide what to believe or what to do. The chapter opening art, which shows a scene from *Inherit the Wind*, pictures the debate about evolution between Clarence Darrow and William Jennings Bryan during the 1925 Scopes trial. The judge in the picture makes sure the trial follows certain rules, and the audience (not in the picture) decides what or whom to believe.

Written argument, however, is not identical to a debate. *In a written argument, the writer must play all the different roles.* The writer is first of all the person arguing for the claim. But the writer must also represent what the opposition might say. In addition, the writer must think like the judge and make sure the argument follows appropriate rules. Perhaps certain arguments and evidence are inadmissible or inappropriate in this case. Finally, the writer often anticipates the responses of the audience and responds to them as well.

Written argument, then, represents several different points of view, responds to them reasonably and fairly, and gives reasons and evidence that support the writer's claim. An effective written argument uses the following techniques.

Techniques for Arguing

Technique	Tips on How to Do It
Analyzing the *rhetorical situation*	Reviewing your purpose, audience, genre, occasion, and context helps you understand how to write your essay. Pay particular attention to your *audience*. Knowing what your audience already knows and believes helps you convince or persuade them.
Focusing on a *debatable* claim	This claim becomes the *thesis*.
Representing and evaluating the *opposing points of view* on the issue fairly and accurately	The key to a successful arguing paper is *anticipating and responding* to the most important alternate or opposing positions.
Arguing reasonably *against opposing arguments* and *for your claim*	Respond to or refute alternate or opposing arguments. Present the best arguments supporting your claim. Argue reasonably and fairly.
Supporting your claims with sufficient *evidence*	Use firsthand observations; examples from personal experience; results of surveys and interviews; graphs, charts, and visuals; and statistics, facts, and quotations from your reading.

In an article titled "Active and Passive Euthanasia," James Rachels claims that active euthanasia may be defensible for patients with incurable and painful diseases. The following paragraphs from that article illustrate the key features of argument.

Opposing position

The distinction between active and passive euthanasia is thought to be crucial for medical ethics. The idea is that it is permissible, at least in some cases, to withhold treatment and allow a patient to die, but it is never permissible to take any direct action designed to kill the patient. This doctrine seems to be accepted by most doctors. . . .

Claim

However, a strong case can be made against this doctrine. In what follows I will set out some of the relevant arguments, and urge doctors to reconsider their views on this matter.

Audience

Argument for claim

To begin with a familiar type of situation, a patient who is dying of incurable cancer of the throat is in terrible pain, which can no longer be satisfactorily alleviated. He is certain to die within a few days, even if present treatment is continued, but he does not want to go on living for those days, since the pain is unbearable. So he asks the doctor for an end to it, and his family joins in the request.

Example

Example

Suppose the doctor agrees to withhold treatment, as the conventional doctrine says he may. The justification for his doing so is that the patient is in terrible agony, and since he is going to die anyway, it would be wrong to prolong his suffering needlessly. But now notice this. If one simply withholds treatment, it may take the patient longer to die, and so he may suffer more than he would if more direct action were taken and a lethal injection given. This fact provides strong reason for thinking that, once the initial decision not to prolong his agony has been made, active euthanasia is actually preferable to passive euthanasia, rather than the reverse. To say otherwise is to endorse the option that leads to more suffering rather than less, and is contrary to the humanitarian impulse that prompts the decision not to prolong his life in the first place.

Argument against opposition

CLAIMS FOR WRITTEN ARGUMENT

The thesis of your argument is a *debatable claim.* Opinions on both sides of the issue must have some merit. Claims for a written argument usually fall into one of four categories: claims of fact, claims about cause and effect, claims about value, and claims about solutions and policies. A claim may occasionally fall into several categories or may even overlap categories.

● **CLAIMS OF FACT OR DEFINITION**   These claims are about facts that are not easily determined or about definitions that are debatable. If I claim that a Lhasa apso was an ancient Chinese ruler, you can check a dictionary and find out that I am wrong. A Lhasa apso is, in fact, a small Tibetan dog. There is no argument. But people do disagree about some supposed "facts": Are polygraph tests accurate? Do grades measure achievement? People also disagree about definitions: Gender discrimination exists in the marketplace, but is it "serious"? What is discrimination, anyway? And what constitutes "serious" discrimination? Does the fact that women currently earn only seventy-three cents for every dollar that men earn qualify as serious discrimination?

In "*American Gothic*, Pitchfork Perfect," a review of Grant Wood's famous painting, Paul Richard opens with a claim of fact and definition (the complete essay appears in Chapter 8). His claim is that *American Gothic* is an American emblem or icon. Although reviews typically contain claims of value, Richard begins his essay with a claim of fact or definition, arguing that the painting is a visual manifestation of the American dream.

> Is "American Gothic" America's best-known painting? Certainly it's one of them. Grant Wood's dual portrait—with its churchy evocations, its stiffness and its pitchfork—pierced us long ago, and got stuck into our minds. Now, finally, it's here.
>
> "American Gothic," which hasn't been in Washington in 40 years, goes on view today at the Renwick Gallery of the Smithsonian American Art Museum. By all means, take it in—although, of course, you have already.
>
> It should have gone all fuzzy—it's been parodied so often, and parsed so many ways—but the 1930 canvas at the Renwick is as sharp as ever. Its details are finer than its travesties suggest, its image more absorbing. It's also smaller than one might have imagined, at only two feet wide. Wood painted it in his home town of Cedar Rapids, Iowa, showed it only once and then sold it, with relief, to the Art Institute of Chicago—for $300.
>
> The picture with a pitchfork is an American unforgettable. Few paintings, very few, have its recognizability. Maybe Whistler's mother. Maybe Warhol's soup can. Maybe Rockwell's Thanksgiving turkey. They're national emblems, all of them, visual manifestations of the American dream.

CLAIMS ABOUT CAUSE AND EFFECT

- Testing in the schools improves the quality of education.
- Secondhand smoke causes lung cancer.
- Capital punishment does not deter violent crime.

Unlike the claim that grades affect admission to college—which few people would deny—the above claims about cause and effect are debatable. No Child Left Behind requires tests in order to evaluate individual schools. But do these tests ultimately improve students' education, or do they just make students better test-takers? The claim that secondhand smoke causes cancer is behind the rush to make all public and commercial spaces smoke-free. But what scientific evidence demonstrates a cause-and-effect link? Finally, the deterring effect of capital punishment is still an arguable proposition with reasonable arguments on both sides.

In a selection from her book *The Plug-In Drug: Television, Children, and the Family,* Marie Winn argues that television has a negative effect on family life. In her opening paragraphs, she sets forth both sides of the controversy and then argues that the overall effect is negative.

> Television's contribution to family life has been an equivocal one. For while it has, indeed, kept the members of the family from dispersing, it has not served to bring them *together.* By its domination of the time families spend together, it destroys the special quality that depends to a great extent on what a family does, what special rituals, games, recurrent jokes, familiar songs, and shared activities it accumulates.
>
> "Like the sorcerer of old," writes Urie Bronfenbrenner, "the television set casts its magic spell, freezing speech and action, turning the living into silent statues so long as the enchantment lasts. The primary danger of the television screen lies not so much in the behavior it produces—although there is danger there—as in the behavior it prevents: the talks, the games, the family festivities and arguments through which much of the child's learning takes place and through which his character is formed. Turning on the television set can turn off the process that transforms children into people."
>
> Yet parents have accepted a television-dominated family life so completely that they cannot see how the medium is involved in whatever problems they might be having.

● CLAIMS ABOUT VALUE

- Boxing is a dehumanizing sport.
- Internet pornography degrades children's sense of human dignity.
- Toni Morrison is a great American novelist.

Claims about value typically lead to evaluative essays. All the strategies discussed in Chapter 8 apply here, with the additional requirement that you must anticipate and respond to alternate or opposing arguments. The essay that claims that boxing is dehumanizing must respond to the argument that boxing is merely another form of competition that promotes athletic excellence. The claim that pornography degrades children's sense of dignity must respond to the claim that restricting free speech on the Internet would cause greater harm. Arguing that Morrison is a great American novelist requires setting criteria for great American novels and then responding to critics who argue that Morrison's work does not reach those standards.

In "College Is a Waste of Time and Money," teacher and journalist Caroline Bird argues that many students go to college simply because it is the "thing to do." For those students, Bird claims, college is not a good idea.

Nowadays, says one sociologist, you don't have to have a reason for going to college; it's an institution. His definition of an institution is an arrangement everyone accepts without question; the burden of proof is not on why you go, but why anyone thinks there might be a reason for not going. The implication is that an 18-year-old . . . should listen to those who know best and go to college.

I don't agree. I believe that college has to be judged not on what other people think is good for students, but on how good it feels to the students themselves.

I believe that people have an inside view of what's good for them. If a child doesn't want to go to school some morning, better let him stay at home, at least until you find out why. Maybe he knows something you don't. It's the same with college. If high-school graduates don't want to go, or if they don't want to go right away, they may perceive more clearly than their elders that college is not for them. It is no longer obvious that adolescents are best off studying a core curriculum that was constructed when all educated men could agree on what made them educated, or that professors, advisors, or parents can be of any particular help to young people in choosing a major or a career. High-school graduates see college graduates driving cabs and decide it's not worth going. College students find no intellectual stimulation in their studies and drop out.

● CLAIMS ABOUT SOLUTIONS OR POLICIES

- Pornography on the Internet should be censored.
- The penalty for drunk driving should be a mandatory jail sentence and loss of driver's license.
- To reduce exploitation and sensationalism, the news media should not be allowed to interview victims of crime or disaster.

Claims about solutions or policies sometimes occur *along with* claims of fact or definition, cause and effect, or value. Because grades do not measure achievement (argue that this is a fact), they should be abolished (argue for this policy). Boxing is a dehumanizing sport (argue this claim of value); therefore, boxing should be banned (argue for this solution). Claims about solutions or policies involve all the strategies used for problem solving (see Chapter 9), but with special emphasis on countering opposing arguments: "Although advocates of freedom of speech suggest that we cannot suppress pornography on the Internet, in fact, we already have self-monitoring devices in other media that could help reduce pornography on the Internet."

In *When Society Becomes an Addict,* psychotherapist Anne Wilson Schaef argues that our society has become an "Addictive System" that has many characteristics in common with alcoholism and other addictions. Advertising becomes addictive, causing us to behave dishonestly; the social pressure to be "nice" can become addictive, causing us to lie to ourselves. Schaef argues that the solution for our social addictions begins when we face the reality of our dependency.

> We cannot recover from an addiction unless we first admit that we have it. Naming our reality is essential to recovery. Unless we admit that we are indeed functioning in an addictive process in an Addictive System, we shall never have the option of recovery. Once we name something, we own it. . . . Remember, to name the system as addict is not to condemn it: It is to offer it the possibility of recovery.
>
> Paradoxically, the only way to reclaim our personal power is by admitting our powerlessness. The first part of Step One of the AA [Alcoholics Anonymous] Twelve-Step Program reads, "We admitted we were powerless over alcohol." It is important to recognize that admitting to powerlessness over an addiction is not the same as admitting powerlessness as a person. In fact, it can be very powerful to recognize the futility of the illusion of control.

APPEALS FOR WRITTEN ARGUMENT

66 Mere knowledge of the truth will not give you the art of persuasion. 99

—PLATO,
PHAEDRUS

To support claims and respond to opposing arguments, writers use *appeals* to the audience. Argument uses three important types of appeals: to *reason* (logic and evidence support the claim), to *character* (the writer's good character itself supports the claim), and to *emotion* (the writer's expression of feelings about the issue may support the claim). Effective arguments emphasize the appeal to reason but may also appeal to character or emotion.

● **APPEAL TO REASON**   An appeal to reason depends most frequently on *inductive logic,* which is sometimes called the *scientific method.* Inductive logic draws a general conclusion from personal observation or experience, specific facts, reports, statistics, testimony of authorities, and other bits of data.

Experience is the best teacher, we always say, and experience teaches inductively. Suppose, using biologist Thomas Huxley's famous example, you pick a green apple from a tree and take a bite. Halfway through the bite you discover that the apple is sour and quickly spit it out. But, you think, perhaps the next green apple will be ripe and will taste better. You pick a second green apple, take a bite, and realize that it is just as sour as the first. However, you know that some apples—like the Granny Smith—look green even when they're ripe, so you take a bite out of a third apple. It is also sour. You're beginning to draw a conclusion. In fact, if you taste a fourth or fifth apple, other people may begin to question your intelligence. How many green apples from this tree must you taste before you get the idea that all of these green apples are sour?

Experience, however, may lead to wrong conclusions. You've tasted enough of these apples to convince *you* that all these apples are sour, but will others think that these apples are sour? Perhaps you have funny taste buds. You may need to ask several friends to taste the apples. Or perhaps you are dealing with a slightly weird tree—in fact, some apple trees are hybrids, with several different kinds of apples grafted onto one tree. Before you draw a conclusion, you may need to consult an expert in order to be certain that your tree is a standard, single-variety apple tree. If your friends and the expert also agree that all of these green apples are sour, you may use your experience *and* their testimony to reach a conclusion—and to provide evidence to make your argument more convincing to others.

Inductive Logic.   In inductive logic, a reasonable conclusion is based on a *sufficient* quantity of accurate and reliable evidence that is selected in a *random* manner to reduce human bias or to take into account variation in the sample. The definition of *sufficient* varies, but generally the number must be large enough to convince your audience that your sample fairly represents the whole subject.

Let's take an example to illustrate inductive reasoning. Suppose you ask a student, one of fifty in a Psychology I class, a question of value: "Is Professor X a good teacher?" If this student says, "Professor X is the worst teacher I've ever had!" what conclusion can you draw? If you avoid taking the class based on a sample of one, you may miss an excellent class. So you decide to gather a *sufficient sample* by polling twenty of the fifty students in the class. But which twenty do you interview? If you ask the first student for a list of students, you may receive the names of twenty other students who also hate the professor. To reduce human or accidental bias, then, you choose a random method for collecting your evidence: As the students leave the class, you give a questionnaire to two out of every five students. If they all fill out the questionnaires, you probably have a *sufficient* and *random* sample.

Claim	Professor X is an excellent psychology teacher
Reason #1:	Professor X is an excellent teacher because she gives stimulating lectures that students rarely miss. ***Evidence:*** Sixty percent of the students polled said that they rarely missed a lecture. Three students cited Professor X's lecture on "assertiveness" as the best lecture they'd ever heard.
Reason #2:	Professor X is an excellent teacher because she gives tests that encourage learning rather than sheer memorization. ***Evidence:*** Seventy percent of the students polled said that Professor X's essay tests required thinking and learning rather than memorization. One student said that Professor X's tests always made her think about what she'd read. Another student said he always liked to discuss Professor X's test questions with his classmates and friends.

Finally, if the responses to your questionnaire show that fifteen out of twenty students rate Professor X as an excellent teacher, what *valid conclusion* should you draw? You should not say, categorically, "X is an excellent teacher." Your conclusion must be restricted by your evidence and the method of gathering it: "Seventy-five percent of the students polled in Psychology I believe that Professor X is an excellent teacher."

Most arguments use a shorthand version of the inductive method of reasoning. A writer makes a claim and then supports it with *reasons* and representative *examples* or *data*.

● APPEAL TO CHARACTER   An appeal based on your good character as a writer can also be important in argument. (The appeal to character is frequently called the *ethical appeal* because readers make a value judgment about the writer's character.) In a written argument, you show your audience—through your reasonable persona, voice, and tone—that you are a person who abides by moral standards that your audience shares: You have a good reputation, you are honest and trustworthy, and you argue "fairly."

A person's reputation often affects how we react to a claim, but *the argument itself* should also establish the writer's trustworthiness. You don't have to be a Mahatma Gandhi or a Mother Teresa to generate a strong ethical appeal for your claim. Even if your readers have never heard your name before, they will feel confident about your character if you are knowledgeable about your subject, present opposing arguments fairly, and support your own claim with sufficient, reliable evidence.

If your readers have reason to suspect your motives or think that you may have something personal to gain from your argument, you may need to bend over backward to be fair. If you do have something to gain, lay your cards on the table. Declare your vested interest but explain, for example, how your solution would benefit everyone equally. Similarly, don't try to cover up or distort the opponents' arguments; acknowledge the opposition's strong arguments and refute the weak ones.

At the most basic level, your interest in the topic and willingness to work hard can improve your ethical appeal. Readers can sense when a writer cares about his or her subject, when a writer knows something about the topic, about the rhetorical or cultural context, and about the various viewpoints on a topic. Show your readers that you care about the subject, and they will find your arguments more convincing. Show you care by

- using sufficient details and specific, vivid examples.
- including any relevant personal experience you have on the topic.
- including other people's ideas and points of view and by responding to their views with fairness and tact.
- organizing your essay so your main points arc easy to find and transitions between ideas are clear and logical.
- revising and proofreading your essay.

Readers know when writers care about their subjects, and they are more willing to listen to new ideas when the writer has worked hard and is personally invested in the topic.

● **APPEAL TO EMOTION**   Appeals to emotion can be tricky because, as we have seen, when emotions come in through the door, reasonableness may fly out the window. Argument emphasizes reason, not emotion. We know, for example, how advertising plays on emotions, by means of loaded or exaggerated language or through images of famous or sexy people. Emotional appeals designed to *deceive* or *frighten* people or to *misrepresent* the virtues of a person, place, or object have no place in rational argument. But emotional appeals that illustrate a truth or movingly depict a reality are legitimate and effective means of convincing readers.

● **COMBINED APPEALS**   Appeals may be used in combination. Writers may appeal to reason and, at the same time, establish trustworthy characters and use legitimate emotional appeals. The following excerpt from Martin Luther King, Jr.'s "Letter from Birmingham Jail" illustrates all three appeals. He appeals to reason, arguing that, historically, civil rights reforms are rarely made without political pressure. He establishes his integrity and good character by treating the opposition (in this case, the Birmingham clergy) with respect and by showing moderation and restraint. Finally, he uses emotional appeals, describing his six-year-old daughter in tears and recalling his own humiliation at being refused a place to sleep. King uses these emotional appeals legitimately; he is not misrepresenting reality or trying to deceive his readers.

> One of the basic points in [the statement by the Birmingham clergy] is that the action that I and my associates have taken in Birmingham is untimely. Some have asked: "Why didn't you give the new city administration time to act?" The only answer that I can give to this query is that the new Birmingham administration must be prodded about as much as the outgoing one, before it will act. We are sadly mistaken if we feel that the election of Albert Boutwell as mayor will bring the millennium to Birmingham. While Mr. Boutwell is a much more gentle person than Mr. Connor, they are both segregationists, dedicated to the maintenance of the status quo. I have hoped that Mr. Boutwell will be reasonable enough to see the futility of massive resistance to desegregation. But he will not see this without pressure from devotees of civil rights. My friends, I must say to you that we have not made a single gain in civil rights without determined legal and nonviolent pressure. Lamentably, it is an historical fact that privileged groups seldom give up their privileges voluntarily. Individuals may see the moral light and voluntarily give up their unjust posture; but, as Reinhold Niebuhr has reminded us, groups tend to be more immoral than individuals.

Appeals to character and reason

Appeal to reason

Evidence

Appeals to character and reason

We know through painful experience that freedom is never voluntarily given by the oppressor; it must be demanded by the oppressed. Frankly, I have yet to engage in a direct-action campaign that was "well timed" in the view of those who have not suffered unduly from the disease of segregation. For years now I have heard the word "Wait!" It rings in the ear of every Negro with piercing familiarity. This "Wait" has almost always meant "Never." We must come to see, with one of our distinguished jurists, that "justice too long delayed is justice denied."

Appeal to emotion

Appeal to emotion

Appeal to emotion

Appeals to character and reason

We have waited for more than 340 years for our constitutional and God-given rights. . . . Perhaps it is easy for those who have never felt the stinging darts of segregation to say, "Wait." But when you have seen vicious mobs lynch your mothers and fathers at will and drown your sisters and brothers at whim; when you have seen hate-filled policemen curse, kick, and even kill your black brothers and sisters; when you see the vast majority of your twenty million Negro brothers smothering in an airtight cage of poverty in the midst of an affluent society; when you suddenly find your tongue twisted and your speech stammering as you seek to explain to your six-year-old daughter why she can't go to the public amusement park that has just been advertised on television, and see tears welling up in her eyes when she is told that Funtown is closed to colored children . . . when you take a cross-country drive and find it necessary to sleep night after night in the uncomfortable corners of your automobile because no motel will accept you; when you are humiliated day in and day out by nagging signs reading "white" and "colored"; when your first name becomes "nigger," your middle name becomes "boy" (however old you are) and your last name becomes "John" . . . —then you will understand why we find it difficult to wait. There comes a time when the cup of endurance runs over, and men are no longer willing to be plunged into the abyss of despair. I hope, sirs, you can understand our legitimate and unavoidable impatience.

ROGERIAN ARGUMENT

Traditional argument assumes that people are most readily convinced or persuaded by a confrontational "debate" on the issue. In a traditional argument, the writer argues reasonably and fairly, but the argument becomes a kind of struggle or "war" as the writer attempts to "defeat" the arguments of the opposition. The purpose of a traditional argument is thus to convince an undecided audience that the writer has "won a fight" and emerged "victorious" over the opposition.

In fact, however, there are many situations in which a less confrontational and less adversarial approach to argument is more effective. Particularly when the issues are highly charged or when the audience that we are trying to persuade is the opposition, writers may more effectively use negotiation rather than confrontation. *Rogerian argument*—named after psychologist Carl Rogers—is a kind of negotiated argument where understanding and compromise replace the traditional, adversarial approach. Rogerian, or *nonthreatening,* argument opens the lines of communication by reducing conflict. When people's beliefs are attacked, they instinctively become defensive and strike back. As a result, the argument becomes polarized: The writer argues for a claim, the reader digs in to defend his or her position, and no one budges.

Crucial to Rogerian argument is the fact that convictions and beliefs are not abstract but reside in people. If people are to agree, they must be sensitive to each other's beliefs. Rogerian argument, therefore, contains a clear appeal to character. While Rogerian argument uses reason and logic, its primary goal is not to "win" the argument but to open the lines of communication. To do that, the writer must be sympathetic to different points of view and willing to modify his or her claims in response to people who hold different viewpoints. Once the reader sees that the writer is open to change, the reader may become more flexible.

Once both sides are more flexible, a compromise position or solution becomes possible. As Rogers says, "This procedure gradually achieves a mutual communication. Mutual communication tends to be pointed toward solving a problem rather than toward attacking a person or group." Rogerian argument, then, imitates not a courtroom debate but the mutual communication that may take place between two people. Whereas traditional argument intends to change the actions or the beliefs of the opposition, Rogerian argument works toward changes *in both sides* as a means of establishing common ground and reaching a solution.

If you choose Rogerian argument, remember that you must actually be willing to change your beliefs. Often, in fact, when you need to use Rogerian argument most, you may be least inclined to use it—simply because you are inflexible on an issue. If you are unwilling to modify your own position, your reader will probably sense your basic insincerity and realize that you are just playing a trick of rhetoric.

Rogerian argument is appropriate in a variety of sensitive or highly controversial situations. You may want to choose Rogerian argument if you are an employer requesting union members to accept a pay cut in order to help the company avoid bankruptcy. Similarly, if you argue to husbands that they should assume responsibility for half the housework, or if you argue to Anglo-Americans that Spanish language and culture should play a larger role in public education, you may want to use a Rogerian strategy. By showing that you empathize with the opposition's position and are willing to compromise, you create a climate for mutual communication.

Rogerian argument makes a claim, considers the opposition, and presents evidence to support the claim, but in addition, it avoids threatening or adversarial language and promotes mutual communication and learning. A Rogerian argument uses the following strategies.

- **Avoiding** *a confrontational stance.* Confrontation threatens your audience and increases their defensiveness. Threat hinders communication.
- **Presenting your** *character* **as someone who understands and can empathize with the opposition.** Show that you understand by restating the opposing position accurately.
- **Establishing** *common ground* **with the opposition.** Indicate the beliefs and values that you share.
- **Being willing** *to change your views.* Show where your position is not reasonable and could be modified.
- **Directing your argument toward** *a compromise or workable solution.*

Note: An argument does not have to be either entirely adversarial or entirely Rogerian. You may use Rogerian techniques for the most sensitive points in an argument that is otherwise traditional or confrontational.

In his essay "Animal Rights Versus Human Health," biology professor Albert Rosenfeld illustrates several features of Rogerian argument. Rosenfeld argues that animals should be used for medical experiments, but he is aware that the issues are emotional and that his audience is likely to be antagonistic. In these paragraphs, Rosenfeld avoids threatening language, represents the opposition fairly, grants that he is guilty of *speciesism,* and says that he sympathizes with the demand to look for alternatives. He indicates that his position is flexible: Most researchers, he says, are delighted when they can use alternatives. He grants that there is some room for compromise, but he is firm in his position that some animal experimentation is necessary for advancements in medicine.

States opposing position fairly and sympathetically

It is fair to say that millions of animals—probably more rats and mice than any other species—are subjected to experiments that cause them pain, discomfort, and distress, sometimes lots of it over long periods of time. . . . All new forms of medication or surgery are tried out on animals first. Every new substance that is released into the environment, or put on the market, is tested on animals. . . .

States opposing position fairly

In 1975, Australian philosopher Peter Singer wrote his influential book called *Animal Liberation,* in which he accuses us all of "speciesism" —as reprehensible, to him, as racism or sexism. He freely describes the "pain and suffering" inflicted in the "tyranny of human over nonhuman animals" and sharply challenges our biblical license to exercise "dominion over the fish of the sea, and over the fowl of the air, and over every living thing that moveth upon the Earth."

Well, certainly we are guilty of speciesism. We do act as if we had dominion over other living creatures. But domination also entails some custodial responsibility. And the questions continue to be raised: Do we have the right to abuse animals? To eat them? To hunt them for sport? To keep them imprisoned in zoos—or, for that matter, in our households? Especially to do experiments on these creatures who can't fight back?

Acknowledges common ground

Hardly any advance in either human or veterinary medicine—cure, vaccine, operation, drug, therapy—has come about without experiments on animals. . . . I certainly sympathize with the demand that we look for ways to get the information we want without using animals. Most investigators are delighted when they can get their data by means of tissue cultures or computer simulations. But as we look for alternative ways to get information, do we meanwhile just do without?

Sympathetic to opposing position

Suggests compromise position

THE TOULMIN METHOD OF ARGUMENT

In *The Uses of Argument* (1958), British philosopher Stephen Toulmin argued against applying formal logic and the concepts of deduction and induction to written arguments. The six concepts that Toulmin identified are not universal rules but merely guidelines that can be helpful as we analyze the logic of an argument.

- **Data:** The evidence gathered to support a particular claim.
- **Claim:** The overall thesis the writer hopes to prove. This thesis may be a claim of fact or definition, of cause and effect, of value, or of policy.
- **Warrant:** The statement that explains why or how the data support the writer's claim.
- **Backing:** The additional logic or reasoning that, when necessary, supports the warrant.
- **Qualifier:** The short phrases that limit the scope of the claim, such as "typically," "usually," or "on the whole."
- **Exceptions:** Those particular situations in which the writer does not or would not insist on the claim.

● **EXAMPLE OF A TOULMIN ANALYSIS**   We can illustrate each of these six concepts using Cathleen A. Cleaver's argument against Internet pornography in her essay, "The Internet: A Clear and Present Danger?" that appears later in this chapter. The relationship of the data, warrant, and claim are shown here.

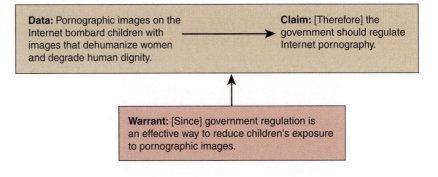

- **Backing:** Government regulation already exists in print, radio, and television media, so it should be extended to the Internet.

- **Qualifier:** *In most cases,* the government should regulate pornography on the Internet. (Cleaver does not actually use a qualifier for her claim.)

- **Exceptions:** Government regulations must protect children, but *where children are not involved, regulation may not be as urgent.* (Cleaver implies this exception, since she focuses her argument only on pornography's effect on children.)

● **USING THE TOULMIN MODEL**   Applying the Toulmin model of argument to written texts can help us as readers and writers if we follow a few guidelines. First, the Toulmin model is especially helpful as we critically read texts for their logical strengths and weaknesses. As we become better critical readers, we are likely to make our own arguments more logical and thus more persuasive. Second, as we critically read texts, not all of us find the same warrant statements, because there can be several ways of explaining a logical connection between the data and the stated claim. Third, applying the Toulmin model and using warrants, backing, qualifiers, and exceptions becomes more important when our readers are likely to disagree with the claim.

Just as Rogerian argument tries to reduce conflict in adversarial situations through mutual communication and a strong appeal to character, the Toulmin model helps communicate in adversarial contexts by being especially reasonable and logical. If our readers already agree that pornography on the Internet is a bad thing, we need to give only a few examples and go straight to our claim. But if readers are members of the ACLU or have a strong belief in free speech on the Internet, we need to qualify our claim and make our warrants—the connections between the data and the claim—as explicit and logical as possible. We may also need to state backing for the warrant and note the exceptions where we don't want to press our case. The more antagonistic our readers are, the more logical we need to be. The Toulmin model is just one approach that can help bolster the logic of our argument.

> ❝ A society which is clamoring for choice [is] filled with many articulate groups, each arguing its own brand of salvation. ❞
> —MARGARET MEAD, ANTHROPOLOGIST

WARMING UP · Journal Exercises

The following exercises will help you practice arguing. Read all of the following exercises and then write on the three that interest you most. If another idea occurs to you, write about it.

1 From the following list of "should" statements, choose one that relates to your experience and freewrite for ten minutes. When you finish your freewriting, state a claim and list arguments on both sides of the issue.

- Bicyclists should be subject to regular traffic laws, including DWI.
- The sale of all handguns should be illegal.
- NCAA football should have playoffs.
- High-quality child care should be available to all working parents at public expense.
- Computer literacy courses should be required at the college level.
- Police should live in the neighborhoods they serve.
- Fraternities and sororities should be forbidden to serve alcoholic beverages.
- Students should work for one year between high school and college.
- Businesses should be required to provide free health insurance for all employees.
- Nonmajor courses should be graded pass/fail.

2 Controversial subjects depend as much on the audience as they do on the issue itself. Make a quick list of things you do every day: the kind of clothes you wear, the food you eat, the books you read, the friends you have, the ideas you discuss. For one of these activities, imagine people who might find what you do immoral, illogical, unjust, or unhealthy. What claim might they make about your activity? What reasons or evidence might they use to argue that your activity should be abolished, outlawed, or changed? Write for five minutes arguing *their* point of view.

3 **Writing Across the Curriculum.** Grades are important, but in some courses, they get in the way of learning. Choose an actual course that you have taken and write an open letter to the school administration, arguing for credit/no-credit grading in that particular course. Assume that you intend to submit your letter to the campus newspaper.

PROFESSIONAL WRITING

The Internet: A Clear and Present Danger?

Cathleen A. Cleaver

Cathleen Cleaver is a former director of legal studies at the Family Research Council, an organization based in Washington, D.C. She has published extensively on issues relating to children and the Internet, in newspapers and magazines such as USA Today, Newsday, *and the* Congressional Quarterly Researcher. *The following essay was originally a speech given at Boston University as part of a College of Communication Great Debate. In this speech, she argues that some industry and government regulation of the Internet is necessary.*

- Someone breaks through your firewall and steals proprietary information from your computer systems. You find out and contact a lawyer who says, "Man, you shouldn't have had your stuff online." The thief becomes a millionaire using your ideas, and you go broke, if laws against copyright violation don't protect material on the Internet. 1

- You visit the Antiques Anonymous Web site and decide to pay their hefty subscription fee for a year's worth of exclusive estate sale previews in their private online monthly magazine. They never deliver and, in fact, never intended to—they don't even have a magazine. You have no recourse, if laws against fraud don't apply to online transactions. 2

- Bob Guccione decides to branch out into the lucrative child porn market and creates a Teen Hustler Web site featuring nude adolescents and preteens. You find out and complain, but nothing can be done, if child pornography distribution laws don't apply to computer transmissions. 3

- A major computer software vendor who dominates the market develops his popular office software so that it works only with his browser. You're a small browser manufacturer who is completely squeezed out of the market, but you have to find a new line of work, if antitrust laws don't apply online. 4

- Finally, a pedophile e-mails your son, misrepresenting himself as a twelve-year-old named Jenny. They develop an online relationship and one day arrange to meet after school, where he intends to rape your son. Thankfully, you learn in advance about the meeting and go there yourself, where you find a forty-year-old man instead of Jenny. You flee to the police, who'll tell you there's 5 nothing they can do, if child-stalking laws don't apply to the Internet.

The awesome advances in interactive telecommunication that 6 we've witnessed in just the last few years have changed the way in which many Americans communicate and interact. No one can doubt that the Internet is a technological revolution of enormous proportion, with outstanding possibilities for human advancement.

As lead speaker for the affirmative, I'm asked to argue that the Internet 7 poses a "clear and present danger," but the Internet, as a whole, isn't dangerous. In fact, it continues to be a positive and highly beneficial tool, which will undoubtedly improve education, information exchange, and commerce in years to come. In other words, the Internet will enrich many aspects of our daily life. Thus, instead of defending this rather apocalyptic view of the Internet, I'll attempt to explain why some industry and government regulation of certain aspects of the Internet is necessary—or, stated another way, why people who use the Internet should not be exempt from many of the laws and regulations that govern their conduct elsewhere. My opening illustrations were meant to give examples of some illegal conduct which should not become legal simply because someone uses the Internet. In looking at whether Internet regulation is a good idea, I believe we should consider whether regulation is in the public interest. In order to do that, we have to ask the question: Who is the public? More specifically, does the "public" whose interests we care about tonight include children?

CHILDREN AND THE INTERNET

Dave Barry describes the Internet as a "worldwide network of univer- 8 sity, government, business, and private computer systems, run by a thirteen-year-old named Jason." This description draws a smile precisely because we acknowledge the highly advanced computer literacy of our children. Most children demonstrate computer proficiency that far surpasses that of their parents, and many parents know only what their children have taught them about the Internet, which gives new relevance to Wordsworth's insight: "The child is father of the man." In fact, one could go so far as to say that the Internet is as accessible to many children as it is inaccessible to many adults. This technological evolution is new in many ways, not the least of which is its accessibility to children, wholly independent of their parents.

When considering what's in the public interest, we must consider 9 the whole public, including children, as individual participants in this new medium.

...continued The Internet: A Clear and Present Danger?, **Cathleen A. Cleaver**

PORNOGRAPHY AND THE INTERNET

This new medium is unique in another way. It provides, through a single   *10*
avenue, the full spectrum of pornographic depictions, from the more
familiar convenience store fare to pornography of such violence and
depravity that it surpasses the worst excesses of the normal human imagination. Sites displaying this material are easily accessible, making
pornography far more freely available via the Internet than from any
other communications medium in the United States. Pornography is the
third largest sector of sales on the Internet, generating $1 billion annu-
ally. There are an estimated seventy-two thousand pornographic sites on
the World Wide Web alone, with approximately thirty-nine new explicit
sex sites every day. Indeed, the *Washington Post* has called the Internet the
largest pornography store in the history of mankind.

There is little restriction of pornography-related activity in cyberspace.   *11*
While there are some porn-related laws, the specter of those laws does not
loom large in cyberspace. There's an implicit license there that exists
nowhere else with regard to pornography—an environment where people
are free to exploit others for profit and be virtually untroubled by legal deterrent. Indeed, if we consider cyberspace to be a little world of its own, it's
the type of world for which groups like the ACLU have long fought but, so
far, fought in vain.

I believe it will not remain this way, but until it changes, we should take   *12*
the opportunity to see what this world looks like, if for no other reason than
to reassure ourselves that our decades-old decisions to control pornography
were good ones.

With a few clicks of the mouse, anyone, any child, can get graphic and   *13*
often violent sexual images—the kind of stuff it used to be difficult to find
without exceptional effort and some significant personal risk. Anyone with
a computer and a modem can set up public sites featuring the perversion of
their choice, whether it's mutilation of female genitals, eroticized urination
and defecation, bestiality, or sites featuring depictions of incest. These pictures can be sold for profit, they can be sent to harass others, or posted to
shock people. Anyone can describe the fantasy rape and murder of a specific person and display it for all to read. Anyone can meet children in chat
rooms or via e-mail and send them pornography and find out where they
live. An adult who signs onto an AOL chat room as a thirteen-year-old girl
is hit on thirty times within the first half hour.

All this can be done from the seclusion of the home, with the feeling of   *14*
near anonymity and with the comfort of knowing that there's little risk of
legal sanction.

The phenomenon of this kind of pornography finding such a wel-   *15*
come home in this new medium presents abundant opportunities for
social commentary. What does Internet pornography tell us about human
sexuality? Photographs, videos, and virtual games that depict rape and the

dehumanization of women in sexual scenes send powerful messages about human dignity and equality. Much of the pornography freely available without restriction on the Internet celebrates unhealthy and antisocial kinds of sexual activity, such as sadomasochism, abuse, and degradation. Of course, by its very nature, pornography encourages voyeurism.

Beyond the troubling social aspects of unrestricted porn, we face 16
the reality that children are accessing it and that predators are access-ing children. We have got to start considering what kind of society we'll have when the next generation learns about human sexuality from what the Internet teaches. What does unrestricted Internet pornog-raphy teach children about relationships, about the equality of women? What does it teach little girls about themselves and their worth?

Opponents of restrictions are fond of saying that it's up to the par- 17
ents to deal with the issue of children's exposure. Well, of course it is, but placing the burden solely on parents is illogical and ineffective. It's far easier for a distributor of pornography to control his material than it is for parents, who must, with the help of software, search for and find the pornographic sites, which change daily, and then attempt to block them. Any pornographer who wants to can easily subvert these efforts, and a re-cent Internet posting from a teenager wanting to know how to disable the filtering software on his computer received several effective answers. Moreover, it goes without saying that the most sophisticated software can only be effective where it's installed, and children will have access to many computers that don't have filtering software, such as those in li-braries, schools, and at neighbors' houses.

INTERNET TRANSACTIONS SHOULD NOT BE EXEMPT

Opponents of legal restrictions often argue simply that the laws just can- 18
not apply in this new medium, but the argument that old laws can't apply to changing technology just doesn't hold. We saw this argument last in the early '80s with the advent of the videotape. Then, certain groups tried to argue that, since you can't view videotapes without a VCR, you can't make the sale of child porn videos illegal, because, after all, they're just plastic boxes with magnetic tape inside. Technological change mandates legal change only insofar as it affects the justification for a law. It just doesn't make sense that the government may take steps to restrict illegal material in *every* medium—video, television, radio, the private telephone, *and* print—but that it may do nothing where people distribute the material by the Internet. While old laws might need redefinition, the old principles generally stand firm.

The question of enforcement usually is raised here, and it often comes 19
in the form of: "How are you going to stop people from doing it?" Well, no law stops people from doing things—a red light at an intersection doesn't force you to stop but tells you that you should stop and that there could be legal consequences if you don't. Not everyone who runs a red light is caught, but that doesn't mean the law is futile. The same concept

holds true for Internet laws. Government efforts to temper harmful conduct online will never be perfect, but that doesn't mean they shouldn't undertake the effort at all.

There's clearly a role for industry to play here. Search engines don't 20 have to run ads for porn sites or prioritize search results to highlight porn. One new search engine even has sex as the default search term. Internet service providers can do something about unsolicited e-mail with hotlinks to porn, and they can and should carefully monitor any chat rooms designed for kids.

Some charge that industry standards or regulations that restrict ex- 21 plicit pornography will hinder the development of Internet technology. But that is to say that its advancement depends upon unrestricted exhibition of this material, and this cannot be true. The Internet does not belong to pornographers, and it's clearly in the public interest to see that they don't usurp this great new technology. We don't live in a perfect society, and the Internet is merely a reflection of the larger social community. Without some mitigating influences, the strong will exploit the weak, whether a Bill Gates or a child predator.

CONCLUSION: TECHNOLOGY MUST SERVE MAN

To argue that the strength of the Internet is chaos or that our liberty depends 22 upon chaos is to misunderstand not only the Internet but also the fundamental nature of our liberty. It's an illusion to claim social or moral neutrality in the application of technology, even if its development may be neutral. It can be a valuable resource only when placed at the service of humanity and when it promotes our integral development for the benefit of all.

Guiding principles simply cannot be inferred from mere technical effi- 23 ciency or from the usefulness accruing to some at the expense of others. Technology by its very nature requires unconditional respect for the fundamental interests of society.

Internet technology must be at the service of humanity and of our in- 24 alienable rights. It must respect the prerogatives of a civil society, among which is the protection of children.

vo·cab·u·lar·y

In your journal, write the meaning of the italicized words in the following phrases.

- steals *proprietary* information (**1**)
- rather *apocalyptic* view (**7**)
- legal *deterrent* (**11**)
- don't have *filtering* software (**17**)

- the law is *futile* (**19**)
- cannot be *inferred* (**23**)
- usefulness *accruing* to some (**23**)
- respect the *prerogatives* (**24**)

QUESTIONS FOR WRITING AND DISCUSSION

1. Before you read or reread Cleaver's essay, write down your own thoughts and experiences about pornography on the Internet. Have you run into sites that you find offensive? Should access to such sites be made more difficult? Do you think children should be protected from accessing such sites—either by accident or on purpose? What do you think are the best method(s) for such regulation: Internet software programs, parental regulation, governmental regulation? Explain.

2. Cleaver begins her essay with several scenarios describing potential abuses and crimes that occur online. Did you find these scenarios effective as a lead-in to her argument? Did they help you focus on her thesis? Should she use fewer scenarios? Why do you think she used all of these examples when only two dealt with child pornography on the Internet?

3. The rhetorical occasion for Cleaver's argument is a debate sponsored by the College of Communication at Boston University. In her essay, can you find evidences (word choice, vocabulary, sentence length, tone, use of evidence, use of appeals) that suggest that her original *genre* was a speech and that her *audience* was college students, college faculty, and members of the community? Cite evidence from the essay showing where Cleaver uses debate elements appropriate for this genre and makes appeals to this audience.

4. Cleaver states her case for government regulation of pornography on the Internet, but who is against regulation, and what are their arguments? What arguments opposing Internet regulation does Cleaver cite? (Are there other opposing arguments that Cleaver does not consider?) How well does Cleaver answer these opposing arguments?

5. Arguing essays make appeals to reason, to character, and to emotion. Find examples of each type of appeal in Cleaver's essay. Which type of appeal does she use most frequently? Which appeals are most or least effective? Does she rely too much on her emotional appeals (see paragraph 13, for example)? For her audience and her context (a debate), should she bolster her rational appeals with more evidence and statistics? Why or why not?

6. Imagine that you are at this debate on the Internet and that your side believes that there should be no or very little regulation of the Internet. What arguments might you make in response to Cleaver? Make a list of the possible pro–con arguments on this topic and explain which ones you will focus on as you respond to Cleaver.

Casebook on Web 2.0

Simson L. Garfinkel, "Wikipedia and the
Meaning of Truth"   [Academic journal article]

Neil L. Waters, "Why You Can't Cite
Wikipedia in My Class"   [Academic journal article]

Mark A. Wilson, "Professors Should
Embrace Wikipedia"   [Online article]

> ❝ The way today's students will do science, politics, journalism, and business next year and a decade from now will be shaped by the skills they acquire in using social media and by the knowledge they gain of the important issues of privacy, identity, community, and the role of citizen media in democracy. ❞
>
> HOWARD RHEINGOLD, AUTHOR OF *SMART MOBS*

The texts in the casebook represent a snapshot of the ongoing conversation and debate about the purpose and value of Web 2.0 learning and communication styles in general, and about Wikipedia specifically. As you read these articles, consider the following questions. Can we define Web 2.0? To what degree are Web 2.0 sites such as Wikipedia replacing traditional print genres? What are the effects of increasing participation in Web 2.0 sites? Do these sites bring increasing democratic participation, a lowering of communication standards, increasing personal communication, decreasing authentic or reliable information, or all of the above?

As you read these texts, maintain a rhetorical perspective: Are these authors making claims of fact or definition, cause-and-effect, value, or policy? Does each document make an argument and consider alternative points of view? What appeals—to reason, to character, or to emotion—do these authors make? Consider also how these writers construct or address their audience: Who do they think their reader is? What do they believe their readers already know or believe? What strategies do they think will convince or persuade their readers?

> ❝ The popularity of Web 2.0 is evidence of a tide of credulity and misinformation that can only be countered by a culture of respect for authenticity and expertise in all scholarly, research, and educational endeavors. ❞
>
> MICHAEL GORMAN, "WEB 2.0: THE SLEEP OF REASON"

PROFESSIONAL WRITING

Wikipedia and the Meaning of Truth

Simson L. Garfinkel

With little notice from the outside world, the community-written encyclopedia Wikipedia has redefined the commonly accepted use of the word "truth." *1*

Why should we care? Because Wikipedia's articles are the first- or second-ranked results for most Internet searches. Type "iron" into Google, and Wikipedia's article on the element is the top-ranked result; its article on the Iron Cross is also first. Google's search algorithms *2* rank a story in part by how many times it has been linked to; people are linking to Wikipedia articles *a lot*.

This means that the content of these articles really 3 matters. Wikipedia's standards of inclusion—what's in and what's not—affect the work of journalists, who routinely read Wikipedia articles and then repeat the wiki-claims as "background" without bothering to cite them. These standards affect students, whose research on many topics starts (and often ends) with Wikipedia. And since I used Wikipedia to research large parts of this article, these standards are affecting you, dear reader, at this very moment.

Many people, especially academic experts, have ar- 4 gued that Wikipedia's articles can't be trusted, because they are written and edited by volunteers who have never been vetted. Nevertheless, studies have found that the articles are remarkably accurate. The reason is that Wikipedia's community of more than seven million registered users has organically evolved a set of policies and procedures for removing untruths. This also explains Wikipedia's explosive growth: if the stuff in Wikipedia didn't seem "true enough" to most readers, they wouldn't keep coming back to the website.

These policies have become the social contract for Wikipedia's 5 army of apparently insomniac volunteers. Thanks to them, incorrect information generally disappears quite quickly.

So how do the Wikipedians decide what's true and what's not? On 6 what is their epistemology based?

Unlike the laws of mathematics or science, wikitruth isn't based 7 on principles such as consistency or observability. It's not even based on common sense or firsthand experience. Wikipedia has evolved a radically different set of epistemological standards—standards that aren't especially surprising given that the site is rooted in a Web-based community, but that should concern those of us who are interested in traditional notions of truth and accuracy. On Wikipedia, objective truth isn't all that important, actually. What makes a fact or statement fit for inclusion is that it appeared in some other publication—ideally, one that is in English and is available free online. "The threshold for inclusion in Wikipedia is verifiability, not truth," states Wikipedia's official policy on the subject.

Verifiability is one of Wikipedia's three core content policies; it was 8 codified back in August 2003. The two others are "no original research" (December 2003) and "neutral point of view," which the Wikipedia project inherited from Nupedia, an earlier volunteer-written Web-based free

---

WIKIPEDIA'S REFERENCE POLICY
en.wikipedia.org/wiki/
Wikipedia:Verifiability

WIKIPEDIA'S "NO ORIGINAL RESEARCH" POLICY
en.wikipedia.org/wiki/Wikipedia:
No_original_research

WIKIPEDIA'S "NEUTRAL POINT OF VIEW" POLICY
en.wikipedia.org/wiki/Wikipedia:
Neutral_point_of_view

WIKIPEDIA'S POLICY ON RELIABILITY OF SOURCES
en.wikipedia.org/wiki/Wikipedia:
Reliable_sources

WIKIPEDIA'S CITATION POLICY
en.wikipedia.org/wiki/Wikipedia:
Citing_sources

encyclopedia that existed from March 2000 to September 2003 (Wikipedia's own NPOV policy was codified in December 2001). These policies have made Wikipedia a kind of academic agora where people on both sides of politically charged subjects can rationally discuss their positions, find common ground, and unemotionally document their differences. Wikipedia is successful because these policies have worked.

Unlike Wikipedia's articles, Nupedia's were written and vetted by experts. But few experts were motivated to contribute. Well, some wanted to write about their own research, but Larry Sanger, Nupedia's editor in chief, immediately put an end to that practice. 9

"I said, 'If it hasn't been vetted by the relevant experts, then basically we are setting ourselves up as a frontline source of new, original information, and we aren't set up to do that,'" Sanger (who is himself, ironically or not, a former philosophy instructor and by training an epistemologist) recalls telling his fellow Nupedians. 10

With experts barred from writing about their own work and having no incentive to write about anything else, Nupedia struggled. Then Sanger and Jimmy Wales, Nupedia's founder, decided to try a different policy on a new site, which they launched on January 15, 2001. They adopted the newly invented "wiki" technology, allowing *anybody* to contribute to any article—or create a new one—on any topic, simply by clicking "Edit this page." 11

Soon the promoters of oddball hypotheses and outlandish ideas were all over Wikipedia, causing the new site's volunteers to spend a good deal of time repairing damage—not all of it the innocent work of the misguided or deluded. (A study recently published in *Communications of the Association for Computing Machinery* found that 11 percent of Wikipedia articles have been vandalized at least once.) But how could Wikipedia's volunteer editors tell if something was true? The solution was to add references and footnotes to the articles, "not in order to help the reader, but in order to establish a point to the satisfaction of the [other] contributors," says Sanger, who left Wikipedia before the verifiability policy was formally adopted. (Sanger and Wales, now the chairman emeritus of the Wikimedia Foundation, fell out about the scale of Sanger's role in the creation of Wikipedia. Today, Sanger is the creator and editor in chief of Citizendium, an alternative to Wikipedia that is intended to address the inadequacy of its "reliability and quality.") 12

Verifiability is really an appeal to authority—not the authority of truth, but the authority of other publications. Any other publication, really. These days, information that's added to Wikipedia without an appropriate reference is likely to be slapped with a "citation needed" 13 badge by one of Wikipedia's self-appointed editors. Remove the badge and somebody else will put it back. Keep it up and you might find yourself face to face with another kind of authority—one of the English-language Wikipedia's 1,500 administrators, who have the ability to place increasingly restrictive protections on contentious pages when the policies are ignored.

To be fair, Wikipedia's verifiability policy states that "articles should *14* rely on reliable, third-party published sources" that themselves adhere to Wikipedia's NPOV policy. Self-published articles should generally be avoided, and non-English sources are discouraged if English articles are available, because many people who read, write, and edit En.Wikipedia (the English-language version) can read only English. . . .

An interesting thing happens when you try to understand *15* Wikipedia: the deeper you go, the more convoluted it becomes. Consider the verifiability policy. Wikipedia considers the "most reliable sources" to be "peer-reviewed journals and books published in university presses," followed by "university-level textbooks," then magazines, journals, "books published by respected publishing houses," and finally "mainstream newspapers" (but not the opinion pages of newspapers). . . .

So what is Truth? According to Wikipedia's entry on the subject, *16* "the term has no single definition about which the majority of professional philosophers and scholars agree." But in practice, Wikipedia's standard for inclusion has become its de facto standard for truth, and since Wikipedia is the most widely read online reference on the planet, it's the standard of truth that most people are implicitly using when they type a search term into Google or Yahoo. On Wikipedia, truth is received truth: the consensus view of a subject.

That standard is simple: something is true if it was published in a *17* newspaper article, a magazine or journal, or a book published by a university press—or if it appeared on *Dr. Who*.

PROFESSIONAL WRITING

Why You Can't Cite Wikipedia in My Class

Neil L. Waters

The case for an online opensource encyclopedia is enormously appeal- *1* ing. What's not to like? It gives the originators of entries a means to publish, albeit anonymously, in fields they care deeply about and provides editors the opportunity to improve, add to, and polish them, a capacity not afforded to in-print articles. Above all, open sourcing marshals legions of unpaid, eager, frequently knowledgeable volunteers, whose enormous aggregate labor and energy makes possible the creation of an entity—Wikipedia, which today boasts more than 1.6 million entries in its English edition alone—that would otherwise be far too costly and labor-intensive to see the light of day. In a sense it would have been technologically impossible just a few years ago; open sourcing is democracy in action, and Wikipedia is its most ubiquitous and accessible creation.

Yet I am a historian, schooled in the concept that scholarship requires accountability and trained in a discipline in which collaborative research is rare. The idea that the vector-sum products of tens or hundreds of anonymous collaborators could have much value is, to say the least, counterintuitive for most of us in my profession. We don't allow our students to cite printed general encyclopedias, much less open-source ones. Further, while Wikipedia compares favorably with other tertiary sources for articles in the sciences, approximately half of all entries are in some sense historical. Here the qualitative record is much spottier, with reliability decreasing in approximate proportion to distance from "hot topics" in American history [1]. For a Japan historian like me to perceive the positive side of Wikipedia requires an effort of will.

I made that effort after an innocuous series of events briefly and improbably propelled me and the history department at Middlebury College into the national, even international, spotlight. While grading a set of final examinations from my "History of Early Japan" class, I noticed that a half-dozen students had provided incorrect information about two topics—the Shimabara Rebellion of 1637–1638 and the Confucian thinker Ogyu Sorai—on which they were to write brief essays. Moreover, they used virtually identical language in doing so. A quick check on Google propelled me via popularity-driven algorithms to the Wikipedia entries on them, and there, quite plainly, was the erroneous information. To head off similar events in the future, I proposed a policy to the history department it promptly adopted: "(1) Students are responsible for the accuracy of information they provide, and they cannot point to Wikipedia or any similar source that may appear in the future to escape the consequences of errors. (2) Wikipedia is not an acceptable citation, even though it may lead one to a citable source."

The rest, as they say, is history. The Middlebury student newspaper ran a story on the new policy. That story was picked up online by *The Burlington Free Press*, a Vermont newspaper, which ran its own story. I was interviewed, first by Vermont radio and TV stations and newspapers, then by *The New York Times*, the *Asahi Shimbun* in Tokyo, and by radio and TV stations in Australia and throughout the U.S., culminating in a story on NBC Nightly News. Hundreds of other newspapers ran stories without interviews, based primarily on the *Times* article. I received dozens of phone calls, ranging from laudatory to actionably defamatory. A representative of the Wikimedia Foundation (www.wikipedia.org), the board that controls Wikipedia, stated that he agreed with the position taken by the Middlebury history department, noting that Wikipedia states in its guidelines that its contents are not suitable for academic citation, because Wikipedia is, like a print encyclopedia, a tertiary source. I repeated this information in all my subsequent interviews, but clearly the publication of the department's policy had hit a nerve, and many news outlets implied, erroneously, that the department was at war with Wikipedia itself, rather than with the uses to which students were putting it.

In the wake of my allotted 15 minutes of Andy Warhol-promised   5
fame I have tried to figure out what all the fuss was about. There is a great deal of uneasiness about Wikipedia in the U.S., as well as in the rest of the computerized world, and a great deal of passion and energy have been spent in its defense. It is clear to me that the good stuff is related to the bad stuff. Wikipedia owes its incredible growth to opensource editing, which is also the root of its greatest weakness. Dedicated and knowledgeable editors can and do effectively reverse the process of entropy by making entries better over time. Other editors, through ignorance, sloppy research, or, on occasion, malice or zeal, can and do introduce or perpetuate errors in fact or interpretation. The reader never knows whether the last editor was one of this latter group; most editors leave no trace save a whimsical cyber-handle.

Popular entries are less subject to enduring errors, innocent or   6
otherwise, than the seldom-visited ones, because, as I understand it, the frequency of visits by a Wikipedia "policeman" is largely determined, once again, by algorithms that trace the number of hits and move the most popular sites to a higher priority. The same principle, I have come to realize, props up the whole of the Wiki-world. Once a critical mass of hits is reached, Google begins to guide those who consulted it to Wikipedia before all else. A new button on my version of Firefox goes directly to Wikipedia. Preferential access leads to yet more hits, generating a still higher priority in an endless loop of mutual reinforcement.

It seems to me that there is a major downside to the self-reinforcing   7
cycle of popularity. Popularity begets ease of use, and ease of use begets the "democratization" of access to information. But all too often, democratization of access to information is equated with the democratization of the information itself, in the sense that it is subject

to a vote. That last mental conflation may have origins that predate Wikipedia and indeed the whole of the Internet.

The quiz show "Family Feud" has been a fixture of daytime televi-   8
sion for decades and is worth a quick look. Contestants are not re-warded for guessing the correct answer but rather for guessing the answer that the largest number of people have chosen as the correct answer. The show must tap into some sort of popular desire to democ-ratize information. Validation is not conformity to verifiable facts or weighing of interpretations and evidence but conformity to popular opinion. Expertise plays practically no role at all.

Here is where all but the most hopelessly postmodernist scholars   9
bridle. "Family Feud" is harmless enough, but most of us believe in a real, external world in which facts exist independently of popular opinion, and some interpretations of events, thoroughly grounded in disciplinary rigor and the weight of evidence, are at least more likely to be right than others that are not. I tell my students that Wikipedia is a fine place to search for a paper topic or begin the research process, but it absolutely cannot serve subsequent stages of research. Wikipedia is not the direct heir to "Family Feud," but both seem to share an ele-ment of faith—that if enough people agree on something, it is most likely so.

What can be done? The answer depends on the goal. If it is to make   10
Wikipedia a truly authoritative source, suitable for citation, it cannot be done for any general tertiary source, including the *Encyclopaedia Britan-nica.* For an anonymous open-source encyclopedia, that goal is theoreti-cally, as well as practically, impossible. If the goal is more modest—to make Wikipedia more reliable than it is—then it seems to me that any changes must come at the expense of its open-source nature. Some sort of accountability for editors, as well as for the originators of entries, would be a first step, and that, I think, means that editors must leave a record of their real names. A more rigorous fact-checking system might help, but are there enough volunteers to cover 1.6 million entries, or would check-ing be in effect reserved for popular entries?

Can one move beyond the world of cut-and-dried facts to check for   11
logical consistency and reasonableness of interpretations in light of what is known about a particular society in a particular historical period? Can it be done without experts? If you rely on experts, do you pay them or depend on their voluntarism?

I suppose I should now go fix the Wikipedia entry for Ogyu Sorai   12
(en.wikipedia.org/wiki/Ogyu_Sorai). I have been waiting since January to see how long it might take for the system to correct it, which has in-deed been altered slightly and is rather good overall. But the statement

that Ogyu opposed the Tokugawa order is still there and still highly misleading [2]. Somehow the statement that equates the samurai with the lower class in Tokugawa Japan has escaped the editors' attention, though anyone with the slightest contact with Japanese history knows it is wrong. One down, 1.6 million to go.

References

1. Rosenzweig, R. Can history be open source? *Journal of American History 93,* 1 (June 2006), 117–146.

2. Tucker, J. (editor and translator). *Ogyu Sorai's Philosophical Masterworks.* Association for Asian Studies and University of Hawaii Press, Honolulu, 2006, 12–13, 48–51; while Ogyu sought to redefine the sources of Tokugawa legitimacy, his purpose was clearly to strengthen the authority of the Tokugawa shogunate.

PROFESSIONAL WRITING

Professors Should Embrace Wikipedia

Mark A. Wilson

When the online, anyone-can-edit Wikipedia appeared in 2001, teachers, especially college professors, were appalled. The Internet was already an apparently limitless source of nonsense for their students to eagerly consume–now there was a Web site with the appearance of legitimacy and a dead-easy interface that would complete the seduction until all sense of fact, fiction, myth and propaganda blended into a popular culture of pseudointelligence masking the basest ignorance. An *Inside Higher Ed* article just last year on Wikipedia use in the academy drew a huge and passionate response, much of it negative. [1]

Now the English version of Wikipedia has over 2 million articles, and it has been translated into over 250 languages. It has become so massive that you can type virtually any noun into a search engine and the first link will be to a Wikipedia page. After seven years and this exponential growth, Wikipedia can still be edited by anyone at any time. A generation of students was warned away from this information siren, but we know as professors that it is the first place they go to start a research project, look up an unfamiliar term from lecture, or find something disturbing to ask about during the next lecture. In fact, we learned too that Wikipedia is indeed the most convenient repository of information ever invented, and we go there often—if a bit [2] covertly—to get a few questions answered. Its accuracy, at least for science articles, is actually as high as the revered *Encyclopedia Britannica,* as shown by a test published in the journal *Nature.*

It is time for the academic world to recognize Wikipedia for what it 3 has become: a global library open to anyone with an Internet connection and a pressing curiosity. The vision of its founders, Jimmy Wales and Larry Sanger, has become reality, and the librarians were right: the world has not been the same since. If the Web is the greatest information delivery device ever, and Wikipedia is the largest coherent store of information and ideas, then we as teachers and scholars should have been on this train years ago for the benefit of our students, our professions, and that mystical pool of human knowledge.

What Wikipedia too often lacks is academic authority, or at least 4 the perception of it. Most of its thousands of editors are anonymous, sometimes known only by an IP address or a cryptic username. Every article has a "talk" page for discussions of content, bias, and organization. "Revert" wars can rage out of control as one faction battles another over a few words in an article. Sometimes administrators have to step in and lock a page down until tempers cool and the main protagonists lose interest. The very anonymity of the editors is often the source of the problem: how do we know who has an authoritative grasp of the topic?

That is what academics do best. We can quickly sort out scholarly 5 authority into complex hierarchies with a quick glance at a vita and a sniff at a publication list. We make many mistakes doing this, of course, but at least our debates are supported with citations and a modicum of civility because we are identifiable and we have our reputations to maintain and friends to keep. Maybe this academic culture can be added to the Wild West of Wikipedia to make it more useful for everyone?

I propose that all academics with research specialties, no matter how 6 arcane (and nothing is too obscure for Wikipedia), enroll as identifiable editors of Wikipedia. We then watch over a few wikipages of our choosing, adding to them when appropriate, stepping in to resolve disputes when we know something useful. We can add new articles on topics which should be covered, and argue that others should be removed or combined. This is not to displace anonymous editors, many of whom possess vast amounts of valuable information and innovative ideas, but to add our authority and hard-won knowledge to this growing universal library.

The advantages should be obvious. First, it is another outlet for 7 our scholarship, one that may be more likely to be read than many of our journals. Second, we are directly serving our students by improving the source they go to first for information. Third, by identifying ourselves, we can connect with other scholars and interested parties who stumble across our edits and new articles. Everyone wins.

I have been an open Wikipedia editor now for several months. I 8 have enjoyed it immensely. In my teaching I use a "living syllabus" for each course, which is a kind of academic blog. (For example, see my History of Life course online syllabus.) I connect students through links to outside sources of information. Quite often I refer students to Wikipedia articles that are well-sourced and well written. Wikipages that are not so good are easily fixed with a judicious edit or two, and many pages become more useful with the addition of an image from my collection (all donated to the public domain). Since I am open in my editorial identity, I often get questions from around the world about the topics I find most fascinating. I've even made important new connections through my edits to new collaborators and reporters who want more background for a story.

For example, this year I met online a biology professor from Centre 9 College who is interested in the ecology of fish on Great Inagua Island in the Bahamas. He saw my additions and images on that Wikipedia page and had several questions about the island. He invited me to speak at Centre next year about evolution–creation controversies, which is unrelated to the original contact but flowed from our academic conversations. I in turn have been learning much about the island's living ecology I did not know. I've also learned much about the kind of prose that is most effective for a general audience, and I've in turn taught some people how to properly reference ideas and information. In short, I've expanded my teaching.

Wikipedia as we know it will undoubtedly change in the coming 10 years as all technologies do. By involving ourselves directly and in large numbers now, we can help direct that change into ever more useful ways for our students and the public. This is, after all, our sacred charge as teacher-scholars: to educate when and where we can to the greatest effect.

QUESTIONS FOR WRITING AND DISCUSSION

1. In "Wikipedia and the Meaning of Truth," Simson Garfinkel explains Wikipedia's standards of "truth." He says that "unlike the laws of mathematics or science, wikitruth isn't based on principles such as

consistency or observability." So, according to Garfinkel, how *is* truth approximated on Wikipedia? Cite specific passages from the article to support your explanation.

2 Neil Waters in "Why You Can't Cite Wikipedia in My Class" and Mark A. Wilson in "Professors Should Embrace Wikipedia" represent nearly opposing points of view. According to each author, what are the proper uses and limitations of Wikipedia? Citing examples from both articles, explain what uses of Wikipedia they agree on and then exactly how their recommendations differ.

3 Reread the sidebar quotations by Howard Rheingold and Michael Gorman at the beginning of this Web 2.0 casebook. Citing examples from texts in the casebook and from your own experience, explain which writer (Rheingold or Gorman) has the more accurate judgment about Web 2.0 technologies. (Is there a third opinion or compromise judgment that would be more accurate?)

Arguing: The Writing Process

ASSIGNMENT FOR ARGUING

For this assignment, choose a controversial and debatable topic that catches your interest or relates to your own personal experience. (Avoid ready-made pro–con subjects such as abortion or drugs unless you have personal experience that can bring a fresh perspective to the subject.) Then examine the topic for possible claims of fact or definition, value, cause and effect, or policy. If the claim is debatable, you may have a focus for your arguing assignment. Next, think about your possible audience. Who needs to be convinced about your argument? Who has the power to change the status quo? Are there multiple perspectives or are there multiple stakeholders involved in this issue? Is there a compromise position you should argue for? (How might your understanding of your audience change your claim?) If possible, narrow your audience to a local group that might be influential. Finally, choose a genre or set of genres that best fits your purpose and audience. Use the following grid of possible audiences and genres to help brainstorm combinations of audience and genre that would be most effective for your purpose and topic.

Audience	Possible Genres for Arguing
Personal Audience	Class notes, journal entry, blog, scrapbook, social networking page
Academic Audience	Academic essay, researched argument, examination essay, debate script, forum entry on class site, journal entry, Web site, or multigenre document
Public Audience	Letter to the editor, column, editorial, blog, article, or critique in a newspaper, online site, magazine, newsletter, graphic novel, Web site, or multigenre document

CHOOSING A SUBJECT

If a journal entry suggested a possible subject, do the collecting and shaping strategies. Otherwise, consider the following ideas.

- Review your journal entries from previous chapters and the papers that you have already written for this class. Test these subjects for an arguable claim that you could make, opposing arguments you could consider, and an appropriate audience for an argumentative piece of writing.

- **Writing Across the Curriculum.** Brainstorm possible ideas for argumentative subjects from the other courses you are currently taking or have taken. What controversial issues in psychology, art, philosophy, journalism, biology, nutrition, engineering, physical education, or literature have you discussed in your classes? Ask current or past instructors for possible controversial topics relating to their courses.

- Newspapers and magazines are full of controversial subjects in sports, medicine, law, business, and family. Browse through current issues or online magazines looking for possible subjects. Check news items, editorials, and cartoons. Look for subjects related to your own interests, your job, your leisure activities, or your experiences.

- Interview your friends, family, or classmates. What controversial issues are affecting their lives most directly? What would they most like to change about their lives? What has irritated or angered them most in the recent past?

- **Community Service Learning.** If you are doing a community-service-learning project, consider one of the following possible

> 66 You can write about anything, and if you write well enough, even the reader with no intrinsic interest in the subject will become involved. 99
>
> —TRACY KIDDER, NOVELIST

topics: (1) Which of the agency's activities best meet the goals of the agency? Write an essay to the agency coordinator recommending a reallocation of resources to the most effective activities. (2) How might agency volunteers more usefully serve the agency in future projects? Write to your project coordinator recommending improvements that would better meet the dual goals of academic learning and agency service.

COLLECTING

● **NARROWING AND FOCUSING YOUR CLAIM**   Narrow your subject to a specific topic, and sharpen your focus by applying the "Wh" questions. If your subject is "grades," your responses might be as follows.

SUBJECT: GRADES

- **Who:** College students
- **What:** Letter grades
- **When:** In freshman and sophomore years
- **Where:** Especially in nonmajor courses
- **Why:** What purpose do grades serve in nonmajor courses?

Determine what claim or claims you want to make. Make sure that your claim is *arguable*. (Remember that claims can overlap; an argument may combine several related claims.)

CLAIM OF FACT OR DEFINITION

- Letter grades exist. (not arguable)
- Employers consider grades when hiring. (slightly more arguable, but not very controversial)
- Grades do not measure learning. (very arguable)

CLAIM ABOUT CAUSE OR EFFECT

- Grades create anxiety for students. (not very arguable)
- Grades actually prevent discovery and learning. (arguable)

CLAIM ABOUT VALUE

- Grades are not fair. (not very arguable: "fairness" can usually be determined)
- Grades are bad because they discourage individual initiative. (arguable)

- Grades are good because they give students an incentive to learn. (arguable)

CLAIM ABOUT A SOLUTION OR POLICY

- Grades should be eliminated altogether. (arguable—but difficult)
- Grades should be eliminated in humanities courses. (arguable)
- Grades should change to pass/fail in nonmajor courses. (arguable—and more practical)

Focusing and narrowing your *claim* helps determine what evidence you need to collect. Use your observing, remembering, reading, and investigative skills to gather the evidence. ***Note:*** An argumentative essay should not be a mathematical equation that uses only abstract and impersonal evidence. *Your experience* can be crucial to a successful argumentative essay. Start by doing the *remembering* exercises. Your audience wants to know not only why you are writing on this particular *topic,* but also why the subject is of interest to *you.*

● **REMEMBERING**   Use *freewriting, looping, branching,* or *clustering* to recall experiences, ideas, events, and people who are relevant to your claim. If you are writing about grades, brainstorm about how *your* teachers used grades, how you reacted to specific grades in one specific class, how your friends or parents reacted, and what you felt or thought. These prewriting exercises will help you understand your claim and give you specific examples that you can use for evidence.

ANALYZING STATISTICS

Whether you are evaluating statistical sources in an essay that you are reading or choosing statistical data to use as evidence for a claim in your own essay, use the following questions to help you determine the relevance, validity, and bias of the statistics.

- Who is the author or the group responsible for gathering or presenting the information? Do they have a bias or point of view?
- What is the date of the study or survey? Are the data still relevant?
- For a survey or poll, what is the sample size (number of respondents) and sample selection (demographic group selected)? Is the sample large enough to give reliable results? Is the group randomly selected? Are certain key groups not included?
- Analyze the wording of the questions asked in the poll or survey. Are the questions relatively neutral? Do the questions lead respondents to a certain conclusion?
- Are the conclusions drawn justified by the data? Are the conclusions exaggerated or overgeneralized?

● **OBSERVING** If possible for your topic, collect data and evidence by observing, firsthand, the facts, values, effects, or possible solutions related to your claim. *Repeated* observation will give you good inductive evidence to support your argument.

● **INVESTIGATING** For most argumentative essays, some research or investigation is essential. Because it is difficult to imagine all the valid counterarguments, interview friends, classmates, family, coworkers, and authorities on your topic. From the library, gather books and articles that contain arguments in support of your claim. *Note:* As you do research in the library, print out articles or make photocopies of key passages from relevant sources to hand in with your essay. If you cite sources from your research, list them on a Works Cited page following your essay. (See Chapter 11 for the proper format.)

SHAPING

As you plan your organization, reconsider your rhetorical situation. Will the *genre* you have selected (letter, researched essay, letter to the editor, blog, Web site, brochure, PowerPoint presentation) help carry out your *purpose* for your intended audience? Is there a relevant *occasion* (meeting, anniversary, or response to news item) that your writing might focus on? What is the *cultural, social,* or *political context* for your writing? Finally, reconsider your *audience.* Try imagining one real person who might be among your readers. Is this person openminded and likely to be convinced by your evidence? Does this person represent the opposing position? If you have several alternative positions, are there individual people who might represent, in your mind, each of these positions? After reconsidering your rhetorical situation, try the shaping strategies that follow.

66 No one can write decently who is distrustful of the reader's intelligence, or whose attitude is patronizing. 99

—E. B. WHITE,
ESSAYIST

● **LIST "PRO" AND "CON" ARGUMENTS** Either on paper or in a computer file, write out your *claim,* and then list the arguments for your position (pro) and the arguments for the opposing positions (con). After you have made the list, match up arguments by drawing lines, as indicated. (On the computer file, move "Con" column arguments so they appear directly opposite the corresponding "Pro" column arguments.)

If some pro and con arguments "match," you will be able to argue against the con and for your claim at the same time. If some arguments do not "match," you will need to consider them separately.

Claim: Grades should be changed to pass/fail in nonmajor courses.

PRO	CON
Grades inhibit learning by putting too much emphasis on competition.	Grades actually promote learning by setting students to study as hard as possible.

Pass/fail grading encourages students to explore nonmajor fields.

Students should be encouraged to compete with majors. They may want to change majors and need to know if they can compete.

Grade competition with majors in the field can be discouraging.

If students don't have traditional grading, they won't take nonmajor courses seriously.

Some students do better without the pressure of grades; they need to find out if they can motivate themselves without grades, but they shouldn't have to risk grades in their major field to discover that.

● **DRAW CIRCLE OF ALTERNATIVE POSITIONS**   If you are considering multiple alternative positions, put your claim in the middle of a circle and indicate the various positions or stakeholders on the outside of the circle. This diagram will help you identify the most important positions in the debate and will help you organize your writing. The example on page 334 is based on the claim that standardized testing in schools should put the students' needs first.

Once you have a diagram for all the major alternative positions or stakeholders, decide the focus of your argument. For your purpose, audience, and context, you may want to focus just on the different goals of teachers, students, and parents. Or you may want to suggest how teachers, students, and parents should organize and force legislators to change the standardized tests or change how schools are funded based on test results.

● **OUTLINES FOR ARGUMENTS**   For more than two thousand years, writers and speakers have been trying to determine the most effective means to persuade audiences. One of the oldest outlines for a successful argument comes from classical rhetoric. The following six-part outline is intended as a guideline rather than a rigid list. Test this outline; see if it will work for *your* argument.

Introduction: Announces subject; *gets audience's interest and attention;* establishes a trustworthy character for the writer

Narration: Gives *background,* context, statement of problem, or definition

Partition: States thesis or *claim,* outlines or *maps* arguments

Argument: Makes *arguments* and gives *evidence* for the claim or thesis

Refutation: Shows why *opposing arguments* are not true or valid

Conclusion: Summarizes arguments, suggests solution, *ties into the introduction or background*

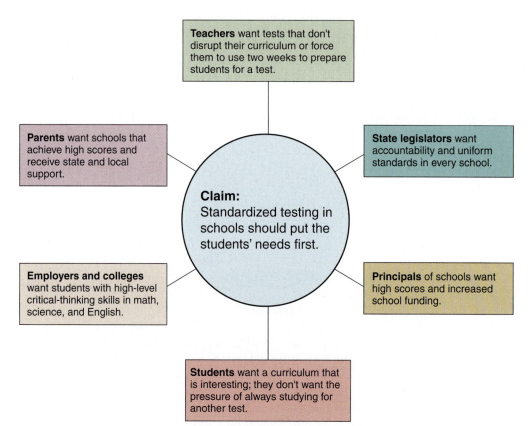

Most arguments have these features, but not necessarily in this order. Some writers prefer to respond to or refute opposing arguments before giving the arguments in support of their claims. When con and pro arguments match, refuting an argument followed by the argument for your claim may work best. As you organize your own arguments, put your strongest argument last and your weakest argument either first or in the middle.

Because most short argumentative essays contain the introduction, narration, and partition all in a few introductory paragraphs, you may use the following abbreviated outlines for argument.

Outline 1   Introduction (attention getter, background, claim or thesis, map)
Your arguments
Refutation of opposing arguments
Conclusion

Outline 2   Introduction
Refutation of opposing arguments
Your arguments
Conclusion

Outline 3   Introduction
              Refutation of first opposing argument that matches your
              first argument
              Refutation of second opposing argument that matches your
              second argument, and so on
              Additional arguments
              Conclusion

For Rogerian arguments, you can follow one of the above outlines, but the emphasis, tone, and attitude are different.

Introduction   Attention getter, background
                        Claim (often downplayed to reduce threat)
                        Map (often omitted)
                        Appeal to character (crucial to Rogerian argument)

Opposing arguments   State opposing arguments fairly
                        Show where, how, or when those arguments may be
                        valid; establish common ground

Your arguments   State your position fairly
                        Show where, how, or when your arguments are valid

Resolution   Present compromise position
                        State your solution to the problem, and show its
                        advantages to both sides

● **DEVELOPING ARGUMENTS**   Think of your argument as a series of *because* statements, each supported by evidence, statistics, testimony, expert opinion, data, specific examples from your experience, or a combination of these.

THESIS OR CLAIM: *Grades should be abolished in nonmajor courses.*

Reason 1   Because they may keep a student from attempting a difficult
            nonmajor course
            Statistics, testimony, data, and examples

Reason 2   Because competition with majors in the field can be discouraging
            Statistics, testimony, data, and examples

Reason 3   Because grades inhibit students' learning in nonmajor fields
            Statistics, testimony, data, and examples

You can develop each reason using a variety of strategies. The following strategies may help you generate additional reasons and examples.

Definition   Define the crucial terms or ideas. (What do you mean
              by *learning?*)

Comparison	Compare the background, situation, and context with another similar context. (What other schools have tried pass/fail grading for nonmajor courses? How has it worked?)
Process	How does or should a change occur? (How do nonmajors become discouraged? How should a school implement pass/fail in grading?)

These strategies may help you develop an argument coherently and effectively. If several strategies are possible, consider which would be most effective for your audience.

Research Tips

When you draft your arguing essay, don't let your citations or direct quotations overpower your own argument. Two tactics will keep you in control of your argument:

1. Always avoid "unidentified flying quotations" by *sandwiching* your quotations. *Introduce* quotations by referring to the author, the source, and/or the author's study. *Follow* quotations with a sentence explaining how the author's evidence supports your argument.
2. Keep your direct quotations *short.* If possible, reduce a long passage to one sentence and incorporate the quoted material in the flow of your own language.

For more on integrating sources into your writing and using quotations, see Chapter 11.

DRAFTING

You will never really know "enough" about your subject or have "enough" evidence. At some point, however, you must stop collecting and start your draft. The most frequent problem in drafting an argumentative essay is delaying the actual writing too long, until the deadline is too close.

For argumentative essays, start with a working order or sequence and sketch an outline on paper or in your head. Additional examples and appeals to reason, character, or emotion may occur to you as you develop your argument or refute opposing arguments. In addition, if you have done some research, have your notes, photocopies of key data, statistics, quotations, and citations of authorities close at hand. As you write, you will discover that some information or arguments simply don't fit into the flow of your essay. Don't force arguments into your draft if they no longer seem to belong.

PEER RESPONSE

Writer: Before you exchange drafts with a peer reader, provide the following information about your essay.

1. a. Intended audience and genre
   b. Primary claim or thesis
   c. Opposing arguments that you refute
   d. Arguments supporting your claim

2. Write out one or two questions about your draft that you want your reader to answer.

Reader: Read the writer's entire draft. As you reread, answer the following questions.

1. **Arguments.** Without looking at the writer's responses above, describe the essay's (a) target audience, (b) primary claim, (c) opposing arguments that are refuted, (d) arguments supporting the claim. Which of these did you have trouble identifying? What additional pro or con arguments should the writer consider?

2. **Organization.** Identify the following parts of the writer's draft: introduction, narration, partition, argument, refutation, and conclusion. Does the writer need all of these for his or her particular subject and audience? Why or why not? Where could the writer clarify transitions between sections? Explain.

3. **Appeals.** Identify places where the writer appeals to reason, to character, and to emotion. Where could these appeals be stronger? Identify sentences where the writer is overly emotional or illogical (see the section "Revising Fallacies in Logic").

4. **Evidence.** Identify at least one paragraph in which the supporting evidence is strong. Then identify at least one paragraph in which the writer makes assertions without sufficient supporting evidence. What kind of evidence might the writer use—first-hand observation, personal examples, testimony from experts, interviews, statistics, or other? Explain.

5. **Revision plan.** List three key changes that the writer should make during the revision.

6. Answer the writer's questions.

Writer: When your essay is returned, read the comments by your peer reader(s) and do the following.

1. Compare your descriptions of the audience, genre, claim, and pro and con arguments with your reader's descriptions. Where there are differences, clarify your essay.
2. Read all of your peer reader's responses. List revisions that you intend to make in each of the following areas: *audience, genre, arguments, organization, appeals, and supporting evidence.*

REVISING

Argumentation is the most public of the purposes for writing. The rhetorical situation (purpose, audience, genre, occasion, and cultural context) plays a crucial role. As you revise, look at this larger context, not just at phrasing, words, or sentences. Test your argument by having friends or classmates read it. Explain your claim, your focus, and your intended audience, genre, and context. Ask them to look for counterarguments that you have omitted or for weaknesses, omissions, or fallacies in logic. But don't automatically change your draft. Take the advice that makes your overall purpose more effective for your audience.

GUIDELINES FOR REVISION

- **When you finish your draft, reconsider the elements of the rhetorical situation** (writer, purpose, audience, genre, occasion, cultural context). Look at the big picture. What needs changing? What needs to be added? What parts are repetitious or not effective?

- **Ask a class member or friend to read your draft to determine the intended audience for your argument.** See which arguments your reader thinks would not be effective for your audience.

- **Use the Toulmin model to evaluate your essay.** Is your claim clearly stated? Does your claim have a qualifier? Do you note exceptions to your claim? Do you have warrant statements explaining how your data support your reasons and claim?

- **Which of your *because* arguments are most effective? Least effective?** Should you change the outline or structure that you initially chose?
- **Revise your draft to avoid fallacies or errors in reasoning.** Errors in logic create two problems: They can destroy your rational appeal and open your argument to a logical rebuttal, and they lessen your credibility—and thus reduce your appeal to your character. (Review the list of fallacies below.)
- **Support your reasons with evidence: *data, facts, statistics, quotations, observations, testimony, statistics, or specific examples from your experience.*** Check your collecting notes once again for additional evidence to add to your weakest argument. Is there a weak or unsupported argument that you should simply omit?
- **Signal the major arguments and counterarguments in your partition or map.** Between paragraphs, use clear transitions and paragraph hooks.
- **Could your essay be improved by visuals or special formatting?** Reconsider your genre and audience. If visuals might make your essay more effective, do a search on the computer. If you need help formatting your essay, check with a peer, a computer lab assistant, or your instructor.
- **If you cite sources in your essay, check the *accuracy* of your statistics, quotations, and source references.** (See Chapter 11 for the proper format of in-text documentation and the Works Cited page.)
- **Revise sentences to improve conciseness and clarity.**
- **Edit sentences for grammar, punctuation, and spelling.**

● **REVISING FALLACIES IN LOGIC**   Listed below are common fallacies in logic. Reread your draft or your peer's draft and revise as appropriate to eliminate these logical errors.

- **Hasty generalization:** Conclusion not logically justified by sufficient or unbiased evidence. If your friend Mary tells you that Professor Paramecium is a hard grader because he gave her a 36 percent on the first biology test, she is making a hasty generalization. It may be *true*—Prof P. may *be* a difficult grader—but Mary's logic is not valid. She cannot logically draw that conclusion from a sample of one; the rest of the class may have received grades of between 80 and 100.
- **Post hoc ergo propter hoc:** Literally, "after this, therefore because of this." Just because Event B *occurred after* Event A does not mean that A *necessarily caused* B. You washed your car in the morning, and it rained in the afternoon. Though we joke about how it always rains after we wash the car, there is, of course, no causal relationship between the two events. "I forgot to leave the porch light on when I

went out last night, and someone robbed my house": Without further evidence, we cannot assume that the lack of light contributed to the robbery. A more obvious cause might be the back door left unlocked.

- **Genetic fallacy:** Arguing that the origins of a person, object, or institution determine its character, nature, or worth. Like the post hoc fallacy, the genetic fallacy is an error in causal relationships.

  > This automobile was made in Detroit. It'll probably fall apart after 10,000 miles.

  > He speaks with a funny German accent. He's really stupid, you know.

  > He started Celestial Seasonings Herb Teas just to make a quick buck; it's just another phony yuppie product.

  The second half of each statement *may* or *may not* be true; the logical error is in assuming that the origin of something will necessarily determine its worth or quality. Stereotyping is frequently caused by a genetic fallacy.

- **Begging the question:** Loading the conclusion in the claim. Arguing that "pornography should be banned because it corrupts our youth" is a logical claim. However, saying that "filthy and corrupting pornography should be banned" is begging the question: The conclusion that the writer should *prove* (that pornography corrupts) is assumed in the claim. Other examples: "Those useless psychology classes should be dropped from the curriculum"; "Senator Swingle's sexist behavior should be censured by Congress"; "Everyone knows that our ineffective drug control program is a miserable failure." The writers must *prove* that the psychology classes are useless, that Senator Swingle is sexist, and that the drug program is a failure.

- **Circular argument:** A sentence or argument that restates rather than proves. Thus, it goes in a circle: "President Reagan was a great communicator because he had that knack of talking effectively to the people." The terms in the beginning of the sentence (*great communicator*) and the end of the sentence (*talking effectively*) are interchangeable. The sentence ends where it started.

- **Either/or:** An oversimplification that reduces alternatives to only two choices, thereby creating a false dilemma. Statements such as "Love it or leave it" attempt to reduce the alternatives to two. If you don't love your school, your town, or your country, you don't have to leave: A third choice is to change it and make it better. Proposed solutions frequently have an either/or fallacy: "Either we ban boxing or hundreds of young men will be senselessly killed." A third alternative is to change boxing's rules or equipment. "If we don't provide farmers with low-interest loans, they will go bankrupt." Increasing prices for farm products might be a better alternative.

- **Faulty comparison or analogy:** Basing an argument on a comparison of two things, ideas, events, or situations that are similar but not identical. Although comparisons or analogies are often effective in argument, they can hide logical problems. "We can solve the meth problem the same way we reduced the DWI problem: Attack it with increased enforcement and mandatory jail sentences." Although the situations are similar, they are not identical. The DWI solution will not necessarily work for drugs. An analogy is an extended comparison that uses something simple or familiar to explain something complex or less familiar. "Solving a mathematics problem is like baking a cake: You have to take it one step at a time. First, you assemble your ingredients or your known data. . . ." Like baking, solving a problem does involve a process; unlike baking, however, mathematics is more exact. Changing the amount of flour in a recipe by 1 percent will not make the cake fall; changing a numeric value by 1 percent, however, may ruin the whole problem. The point, however, is not to avoid comparisons or analogies. Simply make sure that your conclusions are qualified; acknowledge the *differences* between the two things compared as well as the similarities.

- **Ad hominem (literally, "to the man"):** An attack on the character of the individual or the opponent rather than his or her actual opinions, arguments, or qualifications: "Susan Davidson, the prosecuting attorney, drinks heavily. There's no way she can present an effective case." This is an attack on Ms. Davidson's character rather than an analysis of her legal talents. Her record in court may be excellent.

- **Ad populum (literally, "to the people"):** An emotional appeal to positive concepts (God, mother, country, liberty, democracy, apple pie) or negative concepts (fascism, atheism) rather than a direct discussion of the real issue: "Those senators voting to increase the defense budget are really warmongers at heart." "If you are a true American, you should be for tariffs to protect the garment industry."

- **Red herring:** A diversionary tactic designed to avoid confronting the key issue. *Red herring* refers to the practice of dragging a smelly fish across the trail to divert tracking dogs away from the real quarry. A red herring occurs when writers avoid countering an opposing argument directly: "Of course equal pay for women is an important issue, but I wonder whether women really want to take the responsibility that comes with higher paying jobs. Do they really want the additional stress?" This writer diverts attention away from the argument about equal pay to another issue, stress—thus, a red herring.

POSTSCRIPT ON THE WRITING PROCESS

In your journal, answer the following questions.

1. Describe how your beliefs about your subject changed from the time you decided on your claim to when you revised your essay. What caused the change in your views?

2. What opposing argument was most difficult to counter? Explain how you handled it.

3. Which was your strongest argument? Did you use logical appeals and evidence, or did you rely more on appeals to character or emotion? Explain.

4. How did your writing process for the argumentative essay change from the process for your previous essays? What steps or stages took longer? What stages did you have to go back and rework?

STUDENT WRITING

ERIC BOESE

Standardized Tests: Shouldn't We Be Helping Our Students?

As standardized testing has increased in the nation's high schools in recent years, so have the attacks against these tests. Several universities have followed the University of California's lead and deemphasized the SAT test. High school tests, such as the Texas TAAS, California's Stanford 9, Minnesota's MJCA, or Colorado's CSAP, have come under fire because they seem to punish the poorer school districts mainly for having insufficient funds to compete with the wealthy suburban schools. Eric Boese, a student at Colorado State University, decided to write about the problems created by these standardized tests. His purpose, he explains, is to persuade his readers—primarily politicians who set testing policies—that "the use of standardized tests in the education system has to be changed."

Over the past few decades our nation's school systems have progressed   1
with leaps and bounds. We have seen improvements in textbooks, technology, teacher resources, and so much more. The opportunities for children to excel going through primary education are enormous,

greater now than they have ever been. Still we see so many children being held back. Funds are being used inefficiently, and our priorities have become a little mixed up. I'm talking about what it is that we actually teach in primary schools. Are we teaching students skills and giving them knowledge that will make them better members of society or have we decided that it is more important to teach kids how to do well on tests? The answer to this question you may not like, but it is an answer that we can do something about.

To begin working on a solution, we should first locate the source 2 of the problem. As I have said, everything in the world of education is changing, and I have seen that there is one change in particular that can go a long way towards explaining, and solving, our problem. This change is in the use of standardized tests. They have become a more important and more destructive component of our schools. Of course I'm not suggesting that we throw the tests out, for they can be a vital part of education. I hope to show how the current use of these tests is harming the educational process and show how we can use them in a more productive manner in the future.

Over the last ten years in Texas some interesting things have hap- 3 pened. The first was that, in 1990, an exam called the Texas Assessment of Academic Skills (TAAS) was administered for the first time in a number of schools (Weisman). The test was given in grades three through eight and was used as an exit exam early in school. A lot of stress was placed on this test because it was used to determine the longevity of the careers of teachers and administrators. Their jobs depended on the success of their students in taking the exam. In 1994 George W. Bush, the test's biggest supporter, mandated that it be administered statewide. Over six years, the pass rate of the test increased in all student populations (Weisman). The test appeared to be a huge success.

George W. Bush credited the better scores to the test challenging 4 students to do better. I, however, credit it to how the test changed the way the schools function. An alarming article by Jonathan Weisman reviews just this case. He shows how improvements on the TAAS are not correlated to improvements on other standardized tests that were given to the same students. While the TAAS scores went up, the other scores did nothing. The biggest revelation in his article is when he explains why students raised their test scores on that exam and not on others. What he found was that teachers were teaching them how to take the exam. Student learning was compromised because too much stress was put on teachers to make sure their students scored well. Jonathan Weisman knows this to be true:

In a study published by the Harvard Civil Rights Project in January, Professors Linda McNeil of Rice University and Angela Valenzuela of the University of Texas delivered a scathing assessment of the

> TAAS's impact on Texas classrooms, asserting that "behind the rhet-
> oric of the test scores are a growing set of classroom practices in
> which test-prep activities are usurping a substantive curriculum."

Of course it didn't really take experts to figure this out. Anyone involved
in the classrooms of these schools knew that was going on:

> Teachers protested that they were spending eight to ten hours a
> week in test-preparation drills and that their principals were pres-
> suring them to spend even more. Only 27 percent said they believed
> the rising TAAS scores reflected increased learning and higher-
> quality teaching; half said the scores indicated nothing of the sort.
> (Weisman)

This is a situation that is simply unacceptable. Endorsing tests that
have these kinds of side effects is pumping out graduating classes of
test takers. It's causing students to become less capable of meeting
challenges that will face them in college and in the future. Texas isn't
the only place this is taking place, but it is a great example of the way
our nation's schools will turn out if we allow the use of these tests to
continue to spread.

In Texas there are still other factors that cause the test scores to be   5
misleading. There was legislation that allowed schools to exempt spe-
cialed students from taking the test. The number of exemptions increased during the years that the test was administered (Weisman).
From this we see that the students aren't even improving as much on
the tests as the figures show.

The fact that students score better on this kind of exam reveals   6
nothing about their personal improvements. If used differently, however, the exams could be much more effective in meeting students' needs
and less destructive of their education. We could eliminate undue stress
on teachers and create better evaluations of students' abilities.

In other places than Texas, standardized tests are being used in coun-   7
terproductive ways. The biggest problem seems to be that the tests have
too much riding on them. In her article "Test Case: Now the Principal's
Cheating," Carolyn Kleiner gives some examples of how the stakes of
standardized tests have been raised:

> Twenty-eight states now use standard exams to determine gradua-
> tion and 19 to govern student promotion; a growing number also
> dole out performance-based bonuses for schools that show progress
> and threaten intervention, even closure, for those that don't.

Kleiner links the growing importance of the tests to an inevitable side effect, cheating. Of course there are more ways that tests have grown in importance, and yes, more downfalls. The results of standardized tests can have impacts on the jobs of teachers and principals, the money they will make, the reputation of a school or district, and the high school graduation rates. The scores can also affect school funding and various different community issues. People would rather send their children to school somewhere that has a reputation for scoring well on exams and that doesn't have funding problems. In extreme cases, test results can have effects on the property values of residents in a district. George Madaus notes that the test results "don't provide a full picture of a child's—or a school's—accomplishments" and says that "You can't use these tests by themselves to make any decisions" (Kantrowitz et al.). The tests have, however, been used to determine a number of the things above, and as a result, some drawbacks of the tests are that they affect student learning in the classroom, and they cause great stress to students and teachers.

In "Schools for Scandal," Thomas Toch and Betsy Wagner discuss   8 how standardized tests have ultimately led to a problem of educators cheating. The problem of cheating has been one that, until recently, involved students breaking the rules. The new problem we are seeing is that teachers and even principals have started to help their students cheat on some tests. Why would they do this, you ask? It's similar to the situation in Texas—high stakes tests put pressure on them. They are pressured by administrators, principals, and parents alike, all of whom want to see the students get good scores for their own benefit. For parents, good scores are expected, and they see them as being equivalent to their students' doing well in school. In other words, if they see that a school has scored poorly on any given test, they see it as a failure on the part of the school, a further incentive for schools to improve their scores.

It's not something many of us want to hear, but the need for high   9 scores has caused many school officials to encourage cheating as well as raise their school's score by any means possible. "In a national survey of educators in 1990, 1 in 11 teachers reported pressure from administrators to cheat on standardized tests" (Toch and Wagner). On top of the pressures of cheating, there is almost nothing stopping teachers from giving out answers. In most common standardized tests, security monitoring is minimal, answers are available to test givers (who are usually the teachers), and tests are used multiple times. This makes it easy for teachers not only to cheat, but to teach the material that they know will be covered on any given test. Researchers in Colorado found that tests scores dropped dramatically from a first test that teachers had the time to prepare their students for and a very similar test given only a few weeks later. University of Colorado testing expert Lorrie Shepard said, "Teachers are not teaching students skills and concepts. . . . They are teaching specific examples by rote memorization" (Toch and Wagner).

Due to cheating and various other issues, standardized tests reveal *10* less accurate scores each year. In other words, tests are getting worse at what they were designed to do: measure skill levels of students. The reason, Toch and Wagner mention, is that people want high scores. Many tests that challenge students are not being used by schools simply because they yield low scores. The basic skills covered by these tests are inflating scores and forcing teachers to focus on teaching remedial skills and not on the needs of the individual students. In "Education: Is That Your Final Answer?" Jodie Morse gives an example in which the problem is even worse:

> Educators say they have had to dumb down their lessons to teach the often picayune factoids covered by the exams. A study released last month by the University of Virginia found that while some schools had boosted their performance on Virginia's exam, teachers had to curtail field trips, elective courses and even student visits to the bathroom—all in an effort to cram more test prep into the school day. Says the study's author, education professor Daniel Duke: "These schools have become battlefield units."

Causing practices like these to occur in our nation's schools is unjustifiable. The inflation of scores doesn't stop there; tests are being reused to a point where most schools can manage to do very well on them. This creates a false impression of students' skills. The U.S. Department of Education agreed that "with respect to national averages, [school] districts and states are presenting inflated results and misleading the public." How can somebody defend a policy that diminishes the education of students for tests that don't accurately reflect student achievement or, in some cases, even challenge them to think on their own?

So far we have considered some of the many effects of our current *11* testing system. It is equally important to review exactly what materials the tests cover and whether or not they are testing the right things. First of all, 80 percent of standardized tests used in America are produced by corporations (Toch and Wagner). Who says corporations know what should be on these tests in the first place? The relevancy and difficulty of tests are determined by people who have little or no concern for their effects on schools. They are not held accountable for the material covered on their exams and do not feel that security is their concern. Often times, the corporations will make the materials on their tests easier because more schools will buy tests that make themselves look good. In other cases, the corporations simply don't know what to include in their tests for different grade levels. A side effect of corporations writing tests is that they usually recycle their tests and so they rarely "allow schools to return copies of their graded exams to students so they, and their teachers, might learn from their mistakes" (Toch and Wagner). Of the students I surveyed, none claimed that they had ever even learned their own scores on school-mandated standardized tests, and none claimed that they learned anything substantial from the exams that they had taken. On many exams, questions relating to students' advanced-thinking skills are almost nonexistent. Corporations are just not giving tests that are beneficial to students. This is the first change we need to make: either make the corporations answer to a selected group of educational officials or have somebody make tests that have the student in mind.

Along the same lines as above, we need to throw out the tests that are 12 too difficult for students of any particular age group. Only a few people actually oppose this argument. New York State Education Commissioner Richard Mills said that "subjecting 9-year-olds to tests they can't pass is one of the strategies to change things for the better" (Ohanian). I wish somebody would explain this to me. Is this supposed to make students want to work harder because they failed miserably or is it going to discourage them? This may not be an opinion that is held by too many people, but it sure seems to be in some cases. In some states, like Massachusetts for example, students are required to take tests that can last up to 18 hours in order to graduate from high school. We can't expect this much of students who are only 18 years old; not many of them would be able to pass such a test if their classes weren't so focused on preparing them for it, and as we have seen, test preparation often adversely affects student learning.

A level of testing has to be found such that students will be chal- 13 lenged and yet they will not be overwhelmed. Standardized tests should include materials relevant to a student's grade level, some materials that would require the student to explore new ideas, and some questions designed to test a student's advanced-thinking skills. This test would cover materials that would be included in a normal school curriculum and therefore would take up less class time. A teacher could concentrate on students' needs again, and classes could cover more material, explore subjects more deeply and give students the education they deserve. There would be time to do more of what one student claims to love most about school, "getting into great conversations and developing ideas" (Selzer). A test that fits these criteria would give a more accurate evaluation of the student's skills and of the student's potential to succeed in higher-level and college courses. Such a test may not be easy to make, but it would definitely be worth the effort.

It's getting harder and harder to see the positive side of using today's 14 standardized tests. Not only are the tests giving inaccurate evaluations of students' skills, but they are causing corruption in our schools and

...*continued* Standardized Tests: Shouldn't We Be Helping Our Students, **Eric Boese**

diminishing the opportunities for educational excellence of our students. I've discussed ideas for new tests that could be used, but that is not enough to make up for the disturbances involved with the importance of the tests. It is my opinion that we cannot allow these tests to undermine the current system. First of all, funding should not be determined by scores; it should be determined by need. Taxpayers in any given region would also be able to vote to increase funding for the schools that they support. I mentioned that, in Texas, for teachers and administrators the tests held an additional, personal importance. Determining who holds these positions needs a more personal evaluation than looking at test scores. We need to look at how their students are really improving and the effort they put into their students' education.

I'm sure that the public will still have the bias that their students 15 should be getting the best scores, but this is an issue that will have to be faced. They need to be shown that the test scores are a sign for teachers to read to determine the extra attention that some students may require, and this is what the test should be used for. There is no greater purpose for having these tests than for improving education. Many of the problems of the current system will prove to be very difficult to resolve, but any steps towards a new system are ones for the better.

It may all sound difficult now, but the state of our schools is in 16 desperate need of change. Pushing for more tests as so many people are doing is not the answer. I urge you to consider how bright children are being discouraged by an unproductive testing system and to be the person who puts the needs of the children first.

Works Cited

Kantrowitz, Barbara, Daniel McGinn, Ellise Pierce, and Erika Check. "When Teachers Are Cheaters." *Newsweek.* Newsweek, 19 June 2000. Web. 15 Apr. 2001.

Kleiner, Carolyn. "Test Case: Now the Principal's Cheating." *U.S. News &World Report.* U.S. News and World Report, 12 June 2000. Web. 10 Apr. 2001.

Morse, Jodie. "Education: Is That Your Final Answer?" *Time.* Time, 19 June 2000. Web. 15 Apr. 2001.

Ohanian, Susan. "Editorials: Standardized Schools." *Nation.* Nation, 18 Sep. 1999. Web. 10 Apr. 2001.

Selzer, Adam. "High-Stakes Testing: It's Backlash Time." *U.S. News and World Report.* U.S. News and World Report, 3 Apr. 2000. Web. 15 Apr. 2001.

Toch, Thomas, and Betsy Wagner. "Schools for Scandal." *U.S. News and World Report.* U.S. News and World Report, 27 Apr. 1992. Web. 10 Apr. 2001.

Weisman, Jonathan. "Only a Test." *New Republic.* New Republic, 10 Apr. 2000. Web. 15 Apr. 2001.

vo·cab·u·lar·y

In your journal, write the meaning of the italicized words in the following phrases.

- determine the *longevity* of the careers of teachers (**3**)
- test-prep activities are *usurping a substantive* curriculum (**4**)

- a further *incentive* (**8**)
- teach the often *picayune factoids* (**10**)
- preparation often *adversely* affects student learning (**12**)

? QUESTIONS FOR WRITING AND DISCUSSION

1 In your journal, write three short paragraphs explaining your own experience with standardized tests. First, which tests have you taken, and when did you take them? Next, what was the purpose of the tests—to evaluate you or your school? Finally, describe the effect of these tests on your own education. Did they detract from the regular curriculum? Did they give you motivation and incentive to learn? Did they help you get into college?

2 Eric Boese uses a problem-solving format for his arguing essay. Which paragraphs describe the problems with standardized tests? List these problems. Which paragraphs indicate his solutions? What are his solutions? Is his essay clear or would you give him suggestions for improving his organization? Explain.

3 Boese writes that the intended audience for his essay is politicians who are in favor of increased use of standardized tests. Where does Boese address this audience? Where and how could he make his appeal to this audience even stronger? Write out actual sentences Boese could add to his essay.

4 On the Internet, read more recent articles on standardized testing. Has testing in high schools changed since Boese wrote his essay in 2001? Do more or fewer high schools give mandated tests? Has the quality of the tests improved? Do students and teachers like or dislike these tests? Explain.

MAP EVOLUTION EVOLVING

How a controversial entry in Wikipedia has changed over time

The entry for evolution on Wikipedia, the Internet encyclopedia that anyone can edit, was altered 2,081 times by 68 editors between December 2001 and last October. IBM's Watson Research Center produced this image, which tracks the transformation. Each vertical line is a new version; each color is a different editor.

1 DECEMBER 3, 2001
The initial version of evolution, 526 words long, is posted by someone with the user name "Dmerrill." It offers links to pages for creationism and intelligent design but makes no mention of controversy.

2 JULY 13, 2002
An anonymous user redefines evolution as "a controversial theory some scientists present as a scientific explanation." Within two hours, it is changed to read "the commonly accepted scientific theory."

3 OCTOBER 1, 2002
"Graft," shown in yellowish green, makes his debut. He will create 79 edits over three years and spend hours hashing out the content on discussion pages with pro- and antievolution editors. A biology grad student at Harvard University, Graft has edited more than 250 Wikipedia entries.

4 AUGUST 9, 2004
A black line occurs whenever the entire entry is deleted by a vandal. (Entries are also defaced with nonsense or vulgarities.) Editing Wikipedia has become such a popular pastime that, even with more than 1 million entries, about half of all vandalisms are corrected within five minutes.

5 MARCH 29, 2005
The entry reaches its longest point, 5,611 words. That evening, 888 words are excised, causing a

clifflike drop in the graph. The deleted text, a cynical passage about creationists, was cut by proevolution editors who insist on a neutral point of view.

6 SEPTEMBER 19, 2005
A week before the intelligent design trial in Dover, Pennsylvania, begins, an edit war erupts when "Jlefler" writes that "a strong scientific and layman community advocate creationism." The phrase is removed or reapplied eight times in one hour, leaving a narrow yellow zigzag.

Map courtesy of:
Frank Van Ham, Fernanda Viegas, and Martin Wattenberg,
Visual Communication Lab,
IBM Research

In a Web 2.0 environment where users regularly modify site content, researchers need to take extra care in evaluating the source of any information. This graphic shows how the Wikipedia entry on evolution changed over time. See Journal Entry 1 on page 357, which asks you to analyze these changes.

Researching

I n your biology class, you study the Human Genome Project. You discover that this 13-year research project mapped the 20,000–25,000 genes in human DNA. Among the uses of this research are new tests that can predict one's likelihood to contract specific diseases. Though such testing seems like a good thing, you also wonder about its effects—especially since many new commercial ventures offer genetic testing directly to consumers. How will the reliability of these tests be regulated? How would knowing that one is predisposed to an incurable disease affect one's mental well-being? Might these predispositions be used against people by employers or insurers? These questions lead you to investigate the ethical and social implications of genetic testing. You hope that this work will help those interested in having these tests to do so in informed ways—and perhaps encourage further public conversation about the implications of this emerging technology.

After spending two months in France living with a family and trying to understand their dinner conversation, you wonder why you—and other Americans— know so little about foreign languages. After reflecting on your inadequate background in French language and culture, you decide to investigate the current state of foreign-language studies in the United States. During your research, you begin to wonder if Americans know very little about foreign languages and cultures simply because foreign language are rarely required of students either in high school or in college. You decide to study the current state of foreign-language studies and perhaps to demonstrate a need for a consistent foreign-language requirement in public schools. You hope to persuade more students to study foreign languages and encourage some schools to revise their requirements.

> " Research is formalized curiosity. It is poking and prying with a purpose. "
> —ZORA NEALE HURSTON, NOVELIST AND FOLKLORE RESEARCHER

> " You know when you think about writing a book, you think it is overwhelming. But, actually, you break it down into tiny little tasks any moron could do. "
> —ANNIE DILLARD, NATURALIST, AUTHOR, *PILGRIM AT TINKER CREEK*

A LTHOUGH STARTING A RESEARCH PROJECT SOUNDS DIFFICULT AND COMPLICATED, RESEARCH IS REALLY A NATURAL AND ENJOYABLE PART OF OUR EVERYDAY EXPERIENCE, BOTH OUTSIDE AND INSIDE COLLEGE CLASSROOMS. FOR EXAMPLE, WE PRIDE OURSELVES ON BEING GOOD consumers—whether we're window-shopping for a good bargain, finding the best used car, asking co-workers for tips on the best new restaurant in town, or reading up on a new diet. But being a good "consumer" applies to the ways that we interact with information as well. The old saying "Let the buyer beware" applies not only to products we buy, but to information and arguments we "buy" as well. This chapter can help you become better information consumers and users.

The techniques discussed in the previous chapters of this book all involve forms of research. There are specific occasions, however, when you need to do a more thorough job of learning about a topic in order to build a more substantial piece of writing that carefully documents the supporting information. At that point, your initial interest in a topic becomes a set of research questions— questions that you seek to answer by reading a large variety of sources and/or doing sustained and deliberate field research.

Completing a systematic research project requires you to achieve what is often called "information literacy"—the ability to use disciplined methods to find, evaluate, and utilize the wide array of information sources available to you. Four specific skills discussed in this chapter will help you to become information literate.

1. You will need to learn skills for **collecting ideas and information** in the library, on the Internet, and from field research. While many schools have orientations or workshops run by the library, the techniques in this chapter can help you to practice those skills.

2. You will need skills for **critically evaluating** the information you find or generate. The glut of information available on any given topic is a mixed blessing. You need skills that can help you decide which sources are the most reliable, relevant, and useful for your own research. You'll also need to analyze each source for its point of view and potential biases.

3. You will need skills for **smoothly integrating** the information you find into your own writing, introducing the author and source and indicating to your readers how or why that information is relevant to your point. This is important because you are taking information out of its original context; you want your reader to be clear about why *you* are including this information.

4. Finally, you will need skills for **documenting your sources** in the body of your paper and in a Works Cited (MLA) or References (APA) page. Documenting sources not only allows you to give credit where it is due,

but leaves a path for your readers to check the validity of your information or learn more from your sources.

As should be clear by now, a sustained research project takes a good deal of time, planning, reflection, and evaluation and documentation of sources. This chapter outlines the key tasks in this disciplined and reflective process, such as:

- developing a research topic, question, and plan;
- locating, evaluating, and keeping track of your sources of information;
- shaping information to fit your purpose, audience, and genre;
- continually revising your ideas *and* your writing; and
- documenting the sources of your information.

As with other writing assignments presented in this text, the processes for completing a research project are recursive. That is, doing research is not as simple as following a linear set of steps. You will often need to stop and retrace your steps, revise your research question, collect new information, or revise parts of your paper during the writing process. To illustrate the various stages in one writer's process of completing a research project, you will find student writer Kate McNerny's notes, drafts, and documentation interspersed throughout this chapter. At the end of this chapter, you will find the end product of all that work, her paper entitled "Foreign Language Study: An American Necessity," which illustrates important features and forms of a source-based paper in Modern Language Association style.

Techniques for Researching

Since research projects differ from other writing both in process and in the end product—and because much of the writing you do in college will involve research—you need techniques specific to this important form of writing. Here are some of the most important techniques to keep in mind.

> If I find **10,000** ways something won't work, I haven't failed. I am not discouraged, because every wrong attempt discarded is another step forward.
>
> THOMAS EDISON, INVENTOR

Techniques for Researching

Technique	Tips on How to Do It
Use purpose, occasion, audience, genre, and context as your guides for writing.	Remember that research is just a method of collecting and documenting ideas and evidence. The rhetorical situation still directs your writing. *Continued*

Technique	Tips on How to Do It
	Consider not only what *you* are trying to learn, but the final product you want to produce, what you are trying to accomplish, and what readers might already believe, know, or need to know before they read your essay.
Find the most reliable and relevant sources about your subject.	Instead of trying to reinvent the wheel, discover what other people know and then build on it. Ask what you and your readers need to know in order to understand the specific topic, and what sources are most likely to supply that information in the most credible way.
Critically evaluate your sources for accuracy, reliability, and bias.	Consider the author's expertise, the place of publication, possible biases of the author. Be especially careful about Internet sources; though they can be reliable, they often represent people or organizations with a pronounced bias or give inaccurate or misleading information.
Use sources to make *your* point.	As you gather information, you may revise your thesis in light of what you learn, but don't let the tail wag the dog: Don't allow your sources to control you or your paper. Keep your purpose and audience in mind, choosing the pieces of information that are most applicable to your own rhetorical situation.
Document your sources, both in the text and at the end of the paper.	As you are trying to build your own case, citing reliable sources can help you to show the credibility of your information. To document sources effectively, be sure to include in-text citations as you incorporate materials into your draft. Including in-text citations as you write and having electronic or paper copies of each article you use can help you avoid inadvertent plagiarism.

USING PURPOSE, AUDIENCE, AND GENRE AS GUIDES

As you begin your research, you aren't looking for just any information you can find on a given topic; you are looking for information that can help you to illustrate that topic for a specific purpose, for a particular group of readers, and with a particular genre in mind. For this reason, even before you start writing, thinking about your purpose, audience, and genre can help you to find the sources that will support your project.

● **KNOW YOUR PURPOSE** Like any other kind of writing, researched papers have a *purpose.* Reporting, explaining, evaluating, problem solving, and arguing are all purposes for research papers. Keeping an eye on purpose can guide you to the types of information that are most relevant to your area of investigation.

● **ACCOMMODATE YOUR AUDIENCE** Research papers have a defined *audience,* too. If you write a senior research paper in your major, you will write for a professor and for a community of people knowledgeable about your field. If you are a legal assistant or a junior attorney in a law firm, a superior may ask you to research a specific legal precedent and present that research in the most concise form possible. The subject you choose, the kind of research you do, the documentation format, the vocabulary and style you use all should be appropriate for your selected audience.

● **CONSIDER YOUR GENRE** Finally, you must consider what *genre* (particular kind of writing) for presenting your information best fits your purpose and meets the expectations of your audience. If you are researching advances in sports medicine for an audience of experts, you need to use a genre (article, pamphlet, PowerPoint presentation) used by experts in the field. If your paper is an academic article, you may have an abstract at the beginning, a section reviewing and evaluating current research and methodologies, subsections for each of your main points, diagrams and charts for illustration, and an appendix with supplementary materials.

USING THE BEST SOURCES: CURRENCY, RELIABILITY, AND RELEVANCE

It goes without saying that you want the "best" sources that you can find. But what makes something one of the "best" sources? In fact, the "best sources" are those that connect most clearly to your topic but also work for your particular purpose, for your particular audience, and for the particular genre you choose. Within these guidelines of purpose, audience, and genre, you need to judge your sources by three key criteria: currency, reliability, and relevance.

1. By **currency,** we mean that the piece is recent enough to take into account the most up-to-date data and findings of experts.
2. By **reliability,** we mean that the research presented is credible, both because of the qualifications of its author and because of the methods that author has used to collect his or her research.

3. By **relevance,** we mean the degree to which the piece serves your purpose, audience, and genre.

For example, a rich and detailed study of the structure of DNA by a noted biologist might provide current and reliable information on the topic of genetic engineering, and might inform *you* about the topic; but if it does not illuminate the ethical questions you are examining for your paper, you should choose not to include it.

MAINTAINING YOUR VOICE AND PURPOSE: EFFECTIVELY INCORPORATING SOURCES

Completing an effective research project is not only about finding reliable and relevant sources; it is also about how you *use* those sources. The reading you do informs your ideas and positions on a topic. But what sources you *do* choose to cite should be the most relevant, credible, and useful to your discussion—whether they support your position or not.

Including reliable and relevant information shows that you are informed on the subject, offering background information and summarizing what people are (or are not) saying on the subject to capture the various points of view. But sometimes, in the process of including the ideas of others, our own voice can be muted and our own purposes can be de-emphasized. If you start stringing together passages from your sources, you'll be summarizing rather than doing research. You'll be letting the sources tell you what to think, what information is important, or what conclusions to reach. *Write your own paper; don't let your sources write it for you.* It is crucial that you use your sources to make *your* point and that *your* voice still emerges in your writing. You will need to decide how best to incorporate information from your sources in each given case—that is, when it is best to quote, paraphrase, or summarize a source. For more on quotation, paraphrasing, and summary, see Chapter 5 (Reading) as well as the Writing Processes section below.

DOCUMENTING YOUR SOURCES

Documenting your sources is another important part of writing a research paper. The documentation process takes place in three stages:

1. **You must keep careful notes as you collect information.** The note-taking process includes two parts: (1) recording the bibliographic information you will need to document your sources later, and (2) digesting the specific information from each piece that is relevant to your topic, purpose, and audience. This will help you incorporate this information into your own paper as you draft.

2. **As you incorporate source material into your own argument during the writing process, you must include in-text citations to identify that source for your readers.** The in-text citations also signal to your readers that further information can be found at the end of your paper.

3. **At the end of the paper, you should include a list of Works Cited (MLA) or References (APA) that provides your readers with the information they will need to find that source for themselves.** If your readers want more information, or if they doubt a fact or statistic, your documentation enables them to track down the sources. *Note:* Decide on the documentation format (usually MLA or APA style) before you begin your research as you will need to know what relevant bibliographical information to record in your notes.

WARMING UP   Journal Exercises

Do at least one of the following journal exercises to help get yourself into a research frame of mind or to discover a possible research subject.

❶ Look again at the illustration at the beginning of this chapter that graphically "maps" how the debate about evolution developed on the Wikipedia site through revisions to the evolution entry. Assume that you become interested in the ways that Wikipedia, despite its credibility problems, tracks public debates and changing public opinions. First, learn as much as you can about the history and mission of Wikipedia. Then, choose a few topics that interest you. Find the Wikipedia entry for that topic, and click on the "history" tab at the top of the page. Following the instructions there, trace the way that the debate on that topic has developed and see if you can find any trends on particularly controversial topics, in the reliability and tone of the entries, in the ways that biases or political beliefs influence the entries, and so on.

❷ Choose a topic that you are considering for your research project, and find one credible scholarly article that was published very recently—this year if possible. Check the works cited or reference page to see what sources were cited by that author. Starting with the most recent, locate sources that seem closest to your own topic and check their reference pages as well. Record trends in the research on this topic: names of authors who seem to be most often cited, key terms that are important (look especially at titles and abstracts), and any other information you can glean from a quick skimming. Then use this information to help set up your own research plan and search terms. Be prepared to explain in class what other relevant books, articles, or Web sites you found using this research method and how you located them.

3 **Writing Across the Curriculum.** Keep a notebook in your pocket consistently for at least three days. Each time you hear a debate on television, run across a controversial story in the newspaper or on the Internet, hear people debating a topic in a class, around campus, or in social settings, etc., jot down the topic of that debate. Decide which topics seem to you most important, most interesting, and most relevant to your own interests and area of study. If you hear two people discussing the need for alternative energies and you are a marketing major, you might consider studying how such new products might be sold; if you are a biology major, you might consider studying their true environmental impact; if you are a philosophy major, you might study the ethics of using potential food sources for energy purposes. Try to connect whatever topics you find most interesting to areas of study within your own major or discipline—or one that you are considering.

Research Processes

With a computer and the Internet, it is easy to find books, articles, and Web sites that somehow relate to your topic. It is more difficult, however, to determine which sources are credible and appropriate for your audience and purpose. To do so, you need methods for locating the types of information you are seeking and methods for evaluating the sources that you find. Some of those methods apply to all types of sources; others are more specialized depending on the type of source you are seeking or evaluating. You also need to consider the types of sources that exist, and how to choose among them (and combine them) in ways that best serve your own purposes, audience, and genre.

Because a researched essay involves an extended examination of your topic, your audience will expect you to support your thesis and conclusions with substantial and convincing evidence: background information, facts, statistics, descriptions, and other results of interviews and research. And because researched essays are often meant for scholarly purposes and audiences, this type of writing frequently has some strict conventions and expectations that help readers to check the validity of your argument. Supporting sources are cited in the text and included in a Works Cited (MLA) or References (APA) page at the end of the paper. In that sense, a research paper is like a scientific experiment. **The audience of a researched paper will expect to be able to trace your whole experiment—to see what ideas and evidence you worked with, where you found them, and how you used them in your paper.** Therefore, if you are writing for an academic or professional audience, you may want to search specialized databases and indexes such as *Academic Search Premier* and subject indexes such as *Architectural Index, AGRICOLA, Art Abstracts, Biological Abstracts, ERIC, MEDLINE, PsycINFO,* or *Sociological Abstracts.* To find the databases that are most appropriate for specific disciplines or topics, you can consult your reference librarian or faculty members in that discipline.

If, on the other hand, you are taking on a research project that is meant for a popular audience, your research strategy might be somewhat different. For example, if your goal is to determine how direct-to-consumer genetic testing sites market their products to consumers, much of your research might be performed by examining the Web sites of those companies and/or by reading trade journals from the medical profession or marketing firms. In this case, your strategy might be to do a combination of primary research (direct analysis of the sites, interviews with potential users, an experiment in which you show some of the sites to individuals and gauge their reaction) and reading statements about genetic testing by medical practitioners and organizations. You could also read the opinions of experts in medical ethics. If you bring those three sets of sources together, you can develop a strategy that will allow you to summarize previous opinions on this topic *and* add your own analysis of this marketing technique and its ethical implications.

RECORDING BIBLIOGRAPHIC INFORMATION

While you will not complete your Works Cited or References page until you are in the final stages of writing, selecting a documentation style before you begin is crucial as you then will know what bibliographic information you will need to collect (see pages 360–361). If you are writing a paper for the humanities, follow the Modern Language Association (MLA) style set forth in the *MLA Handbook for Writers of Research Papers* (7th ed., 2009). If you are writing a paper in the behavioral sciences, use the American Psychological Association (APA) style as described in the *Publication Manual of the American Psychological Association* (6th ed., 2009). This chapter illustrates both the MLA and APA styles.

USING PRIMARY AND SECONDARY SOURCES

Research sources fall into two general categories: primary and secondary. Some sources—accounts of scientific experiments, transcripts of speeches or lectures, questionnaires, interviews, private documents—are known as *primary sources.* They are original, firsthand information, "straight from the horse's mouth." Secondhand reports, analyses, and descriptions based on primary sources are known as *secondary sources.* Secondary sources may contain the same information, but they are once-removed. For example, a lecture or

Information for a Bibliographic Record

Author(s), if Known	Bergentoft, Rune
Full title and full subtitle of the source *In the case of a book, include the title/subtitle as it appears on the title page; if you are using only one section or chapter, list that title as well.* *In the case of a periodical, list both the title of the specific article and the full title of the journal.*	"Foreign Language Instruction: A Comparative Perspective" *The Annals of the American Academy of Political and Social Science*
Publisher, city/state/country of publication *In the case of a book, list the place and publisher.* *In the case of an electronic publication in a database, list the database name.* *In the case of a Web site, list the sponsoring organization or individual who maintains the site.* *For nonstable online sources, list the URL (you can cut and paste this into your bibliographic file and even make it a hyperlink).*	*Sage Journals Online*
Dates of publication and access *In the case of a journal, list the volume, issue, and date of publication (sometimes the precise date, sometimes the month or season of publication).*	Volume 532 Issue 1
In the case of an electronic source, the date of last revision, usually listed at the bottom of a Web page, and the date you accessed the information.	March 1994
The medium (print, Web, DVD, etc.) in which you accessed the source, and the date for accessing Web sources.	Web, Apr. 24, 2003

Author(s), if Known	Bergentoft, Rune
Beginning and ending page numbers (if available) *With a book, list the page numbers of the portion that you are citing or referencing.* *With a journal article, list the page numbers of the entire article.* *If the article is electronic, record page numbers only if they are stable (as in a PDF) or the page numbers from the print source are identified.*	Pages 8–34

experiment by an expert in food irradiation is a primary source; the newspaper report of that lecture or experiment is a secondary source.

The distinction between primary and secondary sources is important for several reasons. The first reason concerns reliability. Secondary sources may contain errors. The newspaper account, for example, may misquote the expert or misrepresent the experiment. If possible, therefore, find the primary source—a copy of the actual lecture or a published article about the experiment.

One reason for using primary sources is to make your researched document more persuasive through an appeal to character (see Chapter 10, "Arguing"). If you can cite the original source—or even show how some secondary accounts distorted the original experiment—you will gain your readers' trust and faith. Not only does uncovering the primary data make your research more accurate, but your additional effort makes all your data and arguments more credible. So, for example, if you were to cite a newspaper article (a secondary source) that discussed the latest report from the World Health Organization on alcohol consumption, you might also seek out, read, and analyze relevant parts of that report itself, so as to add more depth to the journalistic report—and in some cases, show the shortcomings of the news story. *Unpublished public documents,* such as deeds, wills, surveyors' maps, and environmental impact statements, may contain a wealth of information. *Notes from classes, public lectures,* or *television programs* are also useful sources.

Although the library is an important source of both primary and secondary information, in some types of research projects, it can be useful for you to use another kind of primary source: field research or information that you have generated on your own. This kind of information can be developed through a number of processes:

- *Phone calls* and *letters* to experts, government agencies, or businesses may yield background information, statistics, or quotations.
- *Experiments* can help you to test out your hypothesis or the claims made by others in a controlled environment.

- *Interviews* can be an excellent source of primary information.
- *Focus groups* gather small groups to discuss a few specific questions to see what opinions emerge. It is often worthwhile to use audio or video recording to capture the responses.
- *User tests,* a type of focus group, generate information on how well a product, a set of instructions, or some technology works.
- *Case studies* test a general premise by analyzing a particular situation or set of situations. For example, if you are a business student, you might collect information about the practices of two entrepreneurs in setting up their businesses and compare them.
- *Ethnographies* are similar to case studies, but they take a more holistic approach to your observation of a culture. Both case studies and ethnographies involve the methods discussed in Chapter 3 ("Observing").
- *Surveys* can help you to see general trends and correlate various social practices by posing a series of written questions to a specific group.

While many types of research benefit by primary source information—both that you find and that you generate yourself—nearly *all* research projects require you to do **secondary research.** Even if you are developing your own primary research methodologies or analyzing primary source documents, it is very unlikely that you will be the first one to do so. A careful researcher will investigate how others have done related research, imitate or slightly revise those methods, compare their own results with those of previous studies, and account for those differences. In other cases, secondary research represents the bulk—or even the full spectrum—of your research, either because the topic is not one that lends itself to primary research or because you do not have the resources or the ability to generate new information in a reliable way.

NOTING THE SOURCE'S RELEVANCE, RELIABILITY, AND CURRENCY

Keeping in mind that you want to base your own argument on credible sources, it is important to articulate the reasons a particular source is reliable (and why your audience will consider it so) while you take notes. Jot down the reasons you find this source reliable, based on some of the techniques that follow in this chapter for evaluating sources. You might also note any potential biases in the source. Though there are slightly different criteria for evaluating each kind of source, these are questions that you can ask that apply to all sources of information.*

---

*These criteria are adapted from guidelines designed by Elizabeth E. Kirk, the library instruction coordinator for the Milton S. Eisenhower Library at Johns Hopkins University, and are available at http://www.library.jhu.edu/researchhelp/general/evaluating.

- **Authorship.** Who is the author? Is the author well known? Are the author's credentials or biographical information available on the Internet or elsewhere? Does the author have a reason to be biased? The less you know about the author, the more cautious you need to be about using the source. *If you decide to use a document by a questionable authority, indicate exactly what you know or don't know about the author's credentials.*

- **Publishing organization.** Does the site indicate the organization responsible for the text? Is it published in a "refereed" journal (a journal whose articles are chosen and edited by other experts in the field)? Is there information about the publication, or in the case of an electronic publication, the organization, Webmaster, or designer of the page? Is this organization recognized in its field? *If you know the source is not authoritative or has a commercial basis, indicate the organization's identity if you quote from the site.*

- **Point of view or bias.** Every document or text has a point of view or bias—but some biases may mean that the site's information is not reliable or accurate. Does the author or the organization have a commercial, political, philosophical, religious, environmental, or even scientific agenda? Is the organization selling something? *When you use a source with highly selective or biased information or perspectives, indicate the author's probable bias or agenda when you cite the text.*

- **Reliability and knowledge of the literature.** Reliable sources refer to other texts available or published in that discipline or field. Look for documents that have in-text citations or references to other sources, a fair and reasonable appraisal of alternative points of view, and a bibliography. *Any source that has no references to other key works may simply be one writer's opinion and/or may contain erroneous information. If you have reason to believe the source is not reliable or accurate, find another source.*

CHOOSING AND EVALUATING SOURCES

Although you may begin your search in the reference section, via the library's online catalog, or on the open Web environment, as you narrow and focus your topic or draft sections of your paper, you may come back and recheck the basic references, the online catalog, the periodical indexes, or bibliographies. Along the way, you might also turn to *informal contacts* with friends or acquaintances. Friends, family members, business associates, or teachers may be able to suggest key questions or give you some sources. The bottom line: be nimble by asking lots of questions and pondering who or what might provide the answers you need.

> " Knowledge is of two kinds. We know a subject ourselves, or we know where we can find information upon it. "
> —SAMUEL JOHNSON,
> FROM BOSWELL'S
> *LIFE OF JOHNSON*

What follows outlines the types of sources that are useful for most research projects and gives you some advice on how to use and evaluate each type of source for its relevance, reliability for your topic, and rhetorical situation.

The *librarian* is often the most valuable resource for your research. At some point during your research in the library, probably after you have a focused topic and have collected some sources, talk to a reference librarian. For many writers, asking for help can be really intimidating. To make the process of asking for help as painless—and productive—as possible, try to have some focused questions prepared: "Hi, I'm Kate McNerny. I'm doing a research project for my college writing course. My topic is foreign-language study in the United States. I'm trying to find information about the current state of foreign-language study in the United States and collect some arguments for increasing requirements in secondary schools and colleges. Here's what I've found so far [explain what you've done]. What additional Web sites, indexes, or bibliographies might help me in my research?" The resulting conversation may be the most productive five minutes of your entire library research. After you've talked to the librarian once, it will be easier to return and ask a question when you hit a snag.

● THE 21ST CENTURY LIBRARY: PHYSICAL AND ONLINE SOURCES

After gaining a global understanding of your topic and noting related concepts and search terms, your search for more in-depth information begins. This almost always involves library resources. But what we call a "library" has changed a great deal over the past few decades. While the physical space that contains books, journals, and library staff is still an instrumental research location, what we call a library now also includes the electronic databases that enrich the physical offerings.

● ONLINE DATABASE SOURCES

You will likely find that your library provides access to many different bibliographic databases, which allow you to search efficiently and in many cases retrieve full text of periodical articles and other research materials. EBSCO Academic Search Premier, LexisNexis Academic, and InfoTrac are popular databases that span academic disciplines. Other databases such as ERIC, which focuses on education topics, or PsycINFO for psychology, specialize in materials from a particular discipline. FirstSearch and similar services allow you to search multiple databases at once for the information you need.

When McNerny started her search in her library's online databases, she chose EBSCO Academic Search Premier. After looking at the abstract and the full text of an article by Marion Hines, she decided to email them to herself. Once she had them in electronic form, she reasoned, she could refer to them whenever necessary, search them electronically, and retain an electronic record of the information necessary for completing her bibliographical entry. She could also print them if she liked.

Evaluating a Journal Article

Questions to Ask About Journal Articles	Kate McNerny's Notes
Who is the author? What can you determine about this individual or group?	Hines is the president of a chapter of Delta Kappa Gamma and an assistant professor of Foreign languages. She has also served as a curriculum director in a school system and is a member of many professional organizations.
What is the publication or publisher? What is its purpose?	According to its Web site, the mission of The Delta Kappa Gamma Society International is to "promote professional and personal growth of women educators and excellence in education." The Bulletin "is a professional journal containing articles submitted by members. It keeps members apprised of current educational issues and concerns."
What point of view or biases might that purpose suggest?	While this organization is geared toward women educators, it also is devoted to scholarly publication, and so is less likely to have any specific gender biases. There are none evident in the article itself. However, it is clearly an advocacy organization for educators, so it takes the point of view of teachers.
Does the article draw on serious research, citing literature from the field, or just opinions?	The Reference page includes a number of other authoritative sources including primary sources such as government publications and previous publications by Hines.
How accurate and reliable is the information in the article?	The accuracy can be checked by comparison with other studies and by tracing the sources on the reference page.

The Delta Kappa Gamma Bulletin   15

Foreign Language Curriculum Concerns in Times of Conflict

Marion E. Hines

A Congressional committee on intelligence has declared language as the single greatest limitation in the intelligence community; yet, United States foreign language programs are faced with the paradox of having to justify budgets, prove relevance, and resist marginalization. This article discusses federal intervention to encourage reform in foreign language education in times of conflict, and argues that globalization and national security dictate the inclusion of foreign language study in the core curricula of American schools, colleges and universities.

The United States' chronically weak language resources and lack of linguistic preparedness are invariably exposed when events such as the war in Iraq and the September 11 terror strikes threaten the balance of power, peace or détente in global affairs. In order to regain or maintain a competitive edge, the government offers grants to encourage the restructuring of curriculum, to 'retool' educators, and to infuse new technologies. The efforts have been heroic, but they have not succeeded in correcting the overall problem.

The United States has never adopted a language policy. This has led government and school officials as well as the general public to fall back on reactive instead of proactive decision-making in times of crisis. Paul Simon, former Senator from Illinois and author of the now-classic *The Tongue-Tied American: Confronting the Foreign Language Crisis* states, "In every national crisis from the Cold War through Vietnam, Desert Storm, Bosnia and Kosovo, our nation has lamented its foreign language shortfalls. But then, the crisis 'goes away' and we return to business as usual. One of the messages of September

Marion E. Hines, Ph.D., president of Delta Chapter, Washington, D.C., is an assistant professor in the Department of Modern Languages and Linguistics at Howard University. Dr. Hines is a former curriculum director of foreign language education in the District of Columbia Public Schools. Her professional membership include the American Council on the Teaching of Foreign Languages, the Modern Language Association, the American Association of Teachers of French, and the College Language Association.

Continued

Questions to Ask About Journal Articles	Kate McNerny's Notes
How current is the article?	The article was published in 2003 and references works from 2002, so it is relatively current. However, since educational policies change frequently, it is important to see if there are any new government documents on the topic or responses to Hines' work.
Does the information fit my own purpose and audience? How?	This piece suggests that foreign language study is somehow relegated to a lower priority than math and science. This might provide another point of comparison. Also, since Bergentoft discusses international policies on foreign language education, I can compare U.S. policy with that in other countries.

While library databases usually turn up relatively reliable sources, it is still important for you to evaluate the source using criteria that can help you determine the point of view, currency, and relevance to your project. If you were to find the full text of the Hines article cited on page 364, you could download the piece. The first page provides a great deal of information that you can use to evaluate the source.

Drawing on the citation information, a search of the publication and organizational site, and the biographical information provided, you can do an evaluation of the article's reliability and currency by answering the questions below. You can also start to consider its relevance to your topic and how this piece relates to others you have found.

QUESTIONS FOR EVALUATING JOURNAL SOURCES

- Who is the author? What can you determine about this individual or group?
- What is the publication or publisher? What is its purpose?
- What point of view or biases might that purpose suggest?
- Does the article draw on serious research, citing literature from the field, or just opinions?
- How accurate and reliable is the information in the article?
- How current is the article?
- Does the information fit my own purpose and audience? How?

As this set of questions and the evaluation on page 365 suggest, the evaluation and notetaking process you use as you find library database sources accomplishes several things. It helps familiarize you with each source, it helps you better understand the key organization and publishing sites for information on your topic (especially if you pay attention to the reference pages), and it helps the conversation on the topic that you are trying to enter come into focus as you compare the various sources you find. The process, then, is cumulative and recursive—each new piece of information can help you consider that which you have already found and that which you might look for to further your research.

● **OPEN WEB SOURCES**   It is no longer sufficient to refer to the Internet or worldwide web as a single entity. Those terms really just refer to information that can be accessed through an open Web search engine such as Google. But how and where you find this information—through a Web search engine—is less crucial than the work you must do to choose among the items that those searches turn up.

Using a Search Engine   The first problem we face when doing a search on the open Web is the sheer mass of data that unfocused searches can yield. The second problem is the mixture of source types that an open Web search can produce. A single Google search may turn up scholarly sources, commercial sites, blogs, wikis, personal pages, and Facebook pages. This means that you will need to be especially vigilant as you evaluate the reliability and relevance of the sources you find.

For example, you might do a Google search on "foreign language education" that results in 67 million hits. On the first screen, you will find a number of source types. You are offered the following:

- a link for "scholarly sources" on the topic;
- a statement by the American Council on the Teaching of Foreign Language;
- a paper on the "scandalous" nature of American foreign language policy from the Stanford University Web site, authored by Leon Panetta, currently the CIA director, but previously the assistant to the Director of the Department of Health, Education, and Welfare and Distinguished Scholar for the California Department of Education.
- an opinion piece by U.S. Representative Rush Holt, written for the political liberal online publication, *The Huffington Post*.

On the right side of the page, you'd find a number of commercial sites that offer products and services for foreign language acquisition; if you scrolled down further, you'd find the ubiquitous Wikipedia entry and a number of blogs discussing the topic, with contributors ranging from experts to those with an axe to grind. Evaluating which sources (if any) would be useful can be quite difficult. But if you overlook these sources altogether, you might also miss some potentially useful information. That's why your evaluation process is crucial.

Evaluating Web Sources   Choosing relevant sources from the open Web requires the same care and attention that is required of judging library sources—with an extra dose of patience and diligence. Creating the most focused search terms possible can help a great deal. The active notetaking activities described above can help you to determine whether a source you are considering really fits your own purpose and audience. Discarding those sources that are not directly relevant will pay dividends later as you try to bring together this material within your own writing.

There are also some particular challenges with evaluating Web sources for reliability. For example, we are often unable to judge the context of the information without looking a bit deeper. When we read an article in the *New York Times,* for example, we can expect a certain level of accuracy and reliability that comes from the editorial process; conversely, when we read an article in a supermarket tabloid, we know we should expect very little accuracy. We know not to quote a tabloid article about diet supplements when we are writing an academic paper about health and nutrition. Even on television, we know when we're watching *CNN News* and when we're seeing an infomercial. On the Internet, however, we may have very few context cues to help us judge what we're reading.

All of this is not to suggest, then, that open Web sources are to be wholly avoided. There are excellent resources that can be useful and authoritative. If you adapt the source evaluation techniques discussed in this chapter to Web sites and blogs as well, you can distinguish between those that are appropriate to serious research, and those that are best discarded. Here are some questions to ask about those types of sources.

QUESTIONS FOR EVALUATING OPEN WEB SOURCES

- Who is the author and/or sponsoring organization? What can you determine about this individual or group?
- What is the purpose of the site? What biases might that purpose suggest?
- Is the site presented in an authoritative and thoughtful way? Does it draw upon serious research or just opinions?
- How current is the information?
- Does the information fit my own purpose and audience? How?

Consider, for example, two sites you might find on genetic testing, Medline Plus and DNA Direct. Using the evaluation questions above, you could evaluate these sources as shown on pages 369–370.

Evaluating Web 2.0 Sources The challenges of evaluating open Web sources is increased by the Web 2.0 world in which we live. In Web 2.0, Internet users not only *seek* information, but regularly *post* information to the Web. The most obvious examples of this interactive Web are wikis and blogs, both of which consist of a constant stream of postings by all types of individuals, from top-notch experts to novices, from those who value objective research to those with their own agendas—and those who just like to subvert the process. We have already seen several examples of how wikis work in this chapter.

Another source of information that has driven the Web 2.0 movement is blogs. While blogs began as open, and often personal, journals, they are now sites of public debate. As such, blogs are useful sites for gauging public opinion; at the same time, they require the same critical eye that you would use on any type of Web site, and then some. As part of the Web 2.0 movement, they offer a

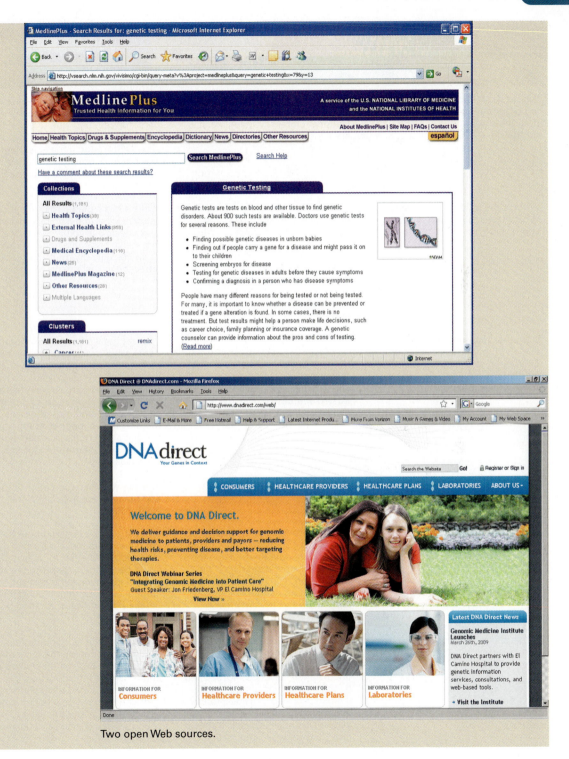

Two open Web sources.

Evaluating Open Web Sources

Questions for Evaluating Open Web Sources	Notes on Medline Plus	Notes on DNA Direct
Who is the author and/or sponsoring organization? What can you determine about this individual or group?	This government site is directed by Dr. Donald A.B. Lindberg, Director, National Library of Medicine. It is sponsored by the National Institutes of Health.	This is a commercial site that states its goal as bringing "the power of personalized medicine to patients, consumers and healthcare professionals" through genetic testing. The board of directors includes more business people than medical professionals.
What is the purpose of the site? What biases might that purpose suggest?	The site "brings together authoritative information from NLM, the National Institutes of Health (NIH), and other government agencies and health-related organizations" and gives "easy access to medical journal articles." The site notes that "there is no advertising on this site, nor does MedlinePlus endorse any company or product."	While it has a Standards page that lists the ways that it helps consumers make decisions about genetic testing, it also has some features that are clearly designed to make its product attractive to customers.
Is the site presented in an authoritative and thoughtful way? Does it draw upon serious research or just opinions?	It provides information "from the world's largest medical library, the National Library of Medicine." And "extensive information from the National Institutes of Health and other trusted sources on over 750 diseases and conditions."	The site makes claims on its Standards page to select only scientifically valid tests supported by the literature. But it also discusses its marketing standards, and much of the site's literature is press releases, news stories, and customer testimonies. It also features many photos that seem more like marketing than serious information for my purposes.
How current is the information?	The site is updated daily.	The site was last updated in 2008, and many of the links are from 2003–2008.
Does the information fit my own purpose and audience? How?	The site provides up-to-date information on genetic testing and links to scholarly data (in readable form) about the latest research on the topic. It can help me to determine the value and dangers of genetic testing directly to consumers.	Since the site is largely about helping consumers make informed decisions about whether to be tested, it could be useful to demonstrate the uses of genetic testing that consumers consider. It is less useful for detailed scientific information on genetic testing.
Is this site reliable and relevant to my project?	This site is useful because of its authoritative sources and the way it attempts to make complex information understandable. It does not seem to be selling anything, though it takes the perspective of medical professionals and scientists with a stake in advancing their field. Overall, it should provide worthwhile information.	It is not reliable as a source of unbiased information on the topic of genetic testing, but I could analyze this and other sites to show how genetic testing is marketed to consumers. That can help to show both the potential benefits and the need for caution when science and business are allied.

voice to any who wish to post, without regard to the expertise of the author (though many blog authors *are* experts) and without the refereeing and editing process of published journals. For that reason, you should consider not only what blogs to select, but how to use them. Using a blog to show the wide range of opinions on a topic can be useful; citing information from them as authoritative (as with wikis) is usually not advisable, unless you then go to the primary sources of information. When evaluating a blog, you should ask these questions.

QUESTIONS FOR EVALUATING BLOGS

- Who is the author and/or sponsoring organization? What kinds of people tend to contribute to this blog?
- What is the purpose of the site? What biases might that purpose suggest?
- Does the owner of the blog manage and vet the postings? Does he/she provide commentary from an expert position?
- How current are the postings? How active is the blog? Is there an archive of past postings?
- Does the information fit my own purpose and audience? How?
- Is this site reliable and relevant to my project?

Some blogs are maintained by experts who provide running commentary on the ideas that are discussed on the site. For example, *Bilingual Talk* is a blog site that is maintained by Liza Sánchez, the founder and Board Chair of *Escuela Bilingüe Internacional* (EBI) in Oakland, California (see page 372). Sanchez is an expert on foreign language education who received her MA in Education at UC Berkeley and who has taught in both public and independent schools. The blog posts news and information on foreign language education (including links to full stories) "for teachers, students, parents and researchers living in a multilingual world" and invites comments from readers.

As a researcher like Kate McNerny, you could use this information in a number of ways. You could read the opinions of Sánchez in light of the other information on the topic you have found, and make note of the reader's comments. You could follow the links she posts, many of which provide an overview of public policy and opinion on multilingual education. But if you want to take full advantage of a blog, and if you start early enough, you could post your own comments and queries to the site as a way of gathering more primary source information—giving you access to ideas and opinions from readers from all over the country (or all over the world, in some cases). You can learn a great deal about public opinion in this way.

When evaluating blogs, you will need to pay special attention to who is contributing to these sources. In many cases, those who would visit and contribute to such a site already have a specific point of view or bias; in this case, it is likely that most of the visitors will already be in favor of multilingual education.

Evaluating a Blog

Questions for Evaluating Blogs	Kate McNerny's Notes on Bilingual Talk Blog
Who is the author and/or sponsoring organization? What kinds of people tend to contribute to this blog?	The author is an expert in multilingual education with an M.A. in education from Berkeley and experience in teaching and educational administration.
What is the purpose of the site? What biases might that purpose suggest?	The site seems to be devoted to promoting multilingual education in the U.S., to monitoring news and policy changes, and to inviting comments and discussion about those changes.
Does the owner of the blog manage and vet the postings? Does he/she provide commentary from an expert position?	Yes, Ms. Sánchez posts news stories and comments upon them, then invites responses.
How current are the postings? How active is the blog? Is there an archive of past postings?	The last posting was two months ago, so it seems a bit spotty. The blog does not seem particularly active, with 0 comments to some postings and only a handful to others. Yes, there is an archive dating back to 2006, but there are often few postings.
Does the information fit my own purpose and audience? How?	The links to the news and policy articles can be useful, though I may need to trace them to the primary source information. Since the comments are so spotty, it will give me less information about public opinion.
Is this site reliable and relevant to my project?	Many of the news articles might be applicable, but since the site is more about English language learners than about native U.S. citizens learning a foreign language, it is not as directly relevant as other sources.

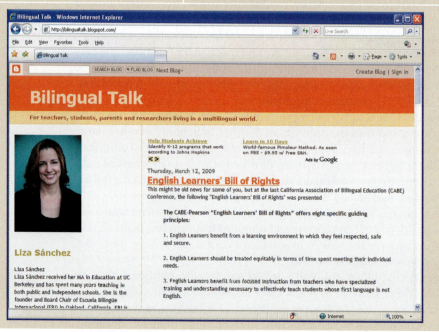

That doesn't necessarily mean that the information is not useful, but it does mean that you'll need to acknowledge the likely biases when you assess the information and again when you incorporate it into your own draft.

In sum, you should treat open Web sources with a healthy skepticism. While it would be shortsighted to ignore the information available via the Web, it is also important that you contextualize that which you find within a variety of other, more authoritative sources. If you combine open Web information with library sources and primary information, you will likely have well-rounded and innovative research. And if you use open Web sources much like you treat reference sources—as a starting point that you will use to drive other research—they can be quite useful.

Writing Processes

While writing a researched project has many similarities to the writing processes discussed throughout this book, the key difference is the need to successfully incorporate the ideas of others toward your own ends. Effective use of sources requires both creativity and scrupulous honesty. On the one hand, you want to use other people's information and ideas when and where they serve *your* purpose and *your* ideas. On the other hand, the sources you cite or quote must be used *fairly* and *honestly.* You must quote accurately, cite your sources in your text, and document those sources accurately. And you must give credit for other writers' ideas and information.

> " Writing a book is not as tough as it is to haul 35 people around the country and sweat like a horse five nights a week. "
>
> —BETTE MIDLER, SINGER, ACTOR, AUTHOR

AVOIDING PLAGIARISM

Considering the amount of time that you have spent reading and studying your topic, it can be hard to distinguish the genesis of an idea—and that can lead to unintentionally forgetting to acknowledge your source. So in the drafting stage and in the revision process, you should be especially vigilant about avoiding plagiarism. Plagiarism occurs when we use the language, ideas, or visual materials from another person or text without acknowledging the source—even unintentionally. Use the following guidelines to avoid plagiarism.

- Do not use language, ideas, or graphics from any essay, text, or visual image that you find *online,* in the *library,* or from *commercial sources* without acknowledging the source.
- Do not use language, ideas, or visuals from *any other student's essay* without acknowledging the source.

Students who plagiarize typically fail the course and face disciplinary action by the college or university.

Sometimes, however, students create problems by rushing or by not knowing how to quote or paraphrase accurately and fairly. You can avoid this *inadvertent* plagiarism by quoting accurately from your sources, by paraphrasing using your own words, and by citing your sources accurately.

Let's assume that you are working with the following passage, taken from the opening paragraph of an article by Marion E. Hines, "Foreign Language Curriculum Concerns in Times of Conflict," which appeared in the *Delta Kappa Gamma Bulletin* in 2003:

Original: The United States' chronically weak language resources and lack of linguistic preparedness are invariably exposed when events such as the war in Iraq and the September 11 terror strikes threaten the balance of power, peace or detente in global affairs. In order to regain or maintain a competitive edge, the government offers grants to encourage the restructuring of curriculum, to "retool" educators, and to infuse new technologies. The efforts have been heroic, but they have not succeeded in correcting the overall problem.

Plagiarism: Every college needs to require a foreign language, in part because we need to communicate better in times of crisis. Events such as the war in Iraq and the terror strikes of September 11 have exposed our lack of linguistic preparedness. Better knowledge of foreign languages would help us communicate with people from different cultures or religions.

Explanation: This writer uses several phrases lifted directly from the source (see highlighted text) without using quotation marks or acknowledging the source.

Proper Citation: Every college needs to require a foreign language in part because we need to communicate better in times of crisis. Marion E. Hines, an assistant professor in modern languages and linguistics at Howard University, argues that "the United States' chronically weak language resources and lack of linguistic preparedness" result in our inability to communicate with people from different cultures or religions (15).

Explanation: In this passage, the writer cites the author before introducing the quotation, uses quotation marks for words and phrases that appear in the article, and uses the proper citation format at the end of the sentence. This article by Marion E. Hines would also be cited in the Works Cited or References page at the end of the essay.

As you take notes and write your drafts, practice using proper citation practices. If at any point you have a question about how to cite your sources accurately, recheck the sections in this chapter or ask your instructor.

DOCUMENTING SOURCES

Both the MLA and APA documentation styles require citation of sources in the text of your paper, followed by a Works Cited (MLA style) or References (APA style) list at the end of your paper. Use footnotes only for content or supplementary notes that explain a point covered in the text or offer additional information. *Note:* MLA in-text documentation and Works Cited documentation are explained here. See pages 381–385 for APA in-text documentation and References format.

● **IN-TEXT DOCUMENTATION: MLA STYLE**   In the MLA style, give the author's name and the page numbers in parentheses following your use of a fact, paraphrase, or direct quotation from a source. These in-text citations then refer your readers to the complete documentation of the source in a Works Cited or Works Consulted list at the end of the paper. As you cite your sources in the text, use the following guidelines.

If you cite the author in the text, indicate only the page number in parentheses.

> According to Vicki Galloway, Project Director for the American Council on the Teaching of Foreign Languages, a student's horizons will not be broadened by "grammar lectures and manipulative classroom exercises" (33).

If the author is unknown, use a short version of the title in the parentheses.

> Most students do not realize that their SAT and ACT scores increase with every year that they study a foreign language (*Knowing Other Languages*).

If the source is unpublished, cite the name or title used in your Works Cited.

> In an informal interview, one university administrator noted that funding of foreign-language study has steadily decreased over the past ten years (Meyers).

If the source is from the Internet or the Web, use the author, or if there is no author, use the title. Include page or paragraph numbers if provided (as, for example, in a PDF document).

> Many Web sites now provide detailed information about how to plan a study-abroad semester or year (*Foreign Language*).

If your bibliography contains more than one work by an author, cite the author, a short title, and page numbers. The following examples show various ways of citing a reference to Paul Simon, *The Tongue-Tied American.*

> In *The Tongue-Tied American*, Simon explains that students can earn a doctorate degree in the United States without ever studying a foreign language (2).

> As Simon notes, "It is even possible to earn a doctorate here without studying any foreign language" (*Tongue-Tied* 2).

> In the United States, one can earn a doctorate degree without studying a single foreign language (Simon, *Tongue-Tied* 2).

Note: Use a comma between author and title, but not between title and page number.

If a source has two or three authors, cite all authors' names in the text or in the parentheses.

> A recent study sampling 536 secondary schools revealed that 91 percent did not require foreign-language credits for graduation (Ranwez and Rodgers 98).

Note: If there are three authors, use commas to separate them, e.g., (Ranwez, Rogers, and Smith 98).

If a source has more than three authors, you may either list all authors' names, separated by commas, or simply give the name of the author listed first followed by the abbreviation *et al.,* meaning "and others."

> Teachers should integrate the study of history, culture, politics, literature, and religion of a particular region with the study of language (Berryman et al. 96).

If you cite several volumes from the same source, precede the page number with the volume number and a colon, as indicated.

> Language and grammar can be taught with real-life contexts or scenarios (Valdman 3:82).

Note: If you cite only one volume of a multivolume work, you need not list the volume number in your in-text citation, but you must list it in your Works Cited.

If you are citing a quotation or information that is itself cited in another source, use the abbreviation *qtd. in* for "quoted in" to indicate that you have used an indirect source for your information or quotation. (If possible, however, check the original source.)

> As Sue Berryman and her colleagues explain, "The course is developed as a world tour during which time the students take a vicarious trip . . . to

become saturated in every aspect of a particular area of the globe" (qtd. in Simon 96).

If you cite two or more authors as sources for a fact, idea, or plan, separate the citations with a semicolon, as follows.

Most recently, two prominent foreign language educators have published plans to coordinate foreign-language studies (Lambert 9–19; Lange 70–96).

● **WORKS CITED LIST: MLA STYLE**   After you have revised your essay and are certain that you will not change any in-text documentation, you are ready to write your list of sources. A Works Cited list alphabetically orders, by author's last name, all published and unpublished sources cited in your research paper. Each citation indicates the medium of publication of the source you consulted, such as print, Web, DVD, television, and so on. If the author is unknown, alphabetize by the first word (excluding *A, An,* or *The*) of the title. Use the following abbreviations for missing information other than an unknown author:

n.p. (no place of publication)
n.p. (no publisher given)
n.d. (no date of publication given)
n. pag. (no pagination in source)

The first line of each citation begins at the left margin, and succeeding lines are indented one-half inch. Double-space the entire Works Cited list.

Following are examples of MLA-style entries in a Works Cited list, organized by kind of source. . . . Use the citations as models for your own Works Cited list. For additional information and examples, see *MLA Handbook for Writers of Research Papers* (7th ed., 2009).

Note: In your essay or manuscript, citations of titles of articles, poems, and short stories should be surrounded by quotation marks ("The Story of an Hour"). Titles of books, plays, novels, magazines, journals, or collections should be italicized (*Caramelo, National Geographic*); note that new MLA guidelines suggest italics instead of underlining.

Print Periodicals: MLA Style

For all articles published in print periodicals, give the author's name, the title of the article, and the name of the publication. For newspapers and magazines, add complete dates and inclusive page numbers. Use the first page number and a plus sign if an article is not printed on consecutive pages. For all professional journals, add volume numbers, issue numbers, years of publication, and inclusive page numbers. Add *Print* as the medium of access for articles in printed periodicals. See pages 379–380 for articles you access on the Web or in online databases.

Article in a Weekly or Biweekly Magazine

Hersh, Seymour M. "Chain of Command." *New Yorker* 17 May 2004: 38–43. Print.

Article in a Monthly or Bimonthly Magazine

Appenzeller, Tim. "The End of Cheap Oil." *National Geographic* June 2004: 80–109. Print.

Morrison, Ann M., Randall P. White, and Ellen Van Velsor. "Executive Women: Substance Plus Style." *Psychology Today* Aug. 1987: 18+. Print.

Article in a Scholarly Journal

According to the newest MLA guidelines, all entries for scholarly publications such as professional journals should now include the volume, issue, year of publication, page numbers (when available), and the medium of access.

Brodkey, Linda. "Writing Ethnographic Narratives." *Written Communication* 9.1 (1987): 25–50. Print.

Swope, Christopher. "Panel OKs Bill to Make English Official Government Language." *Congressional Quarterly Weekly Report* 54.1 (1996): 2128–29. Print.

(For page numbers over 100, use only two digits for the final page citation: 2128–29.)

Article in a Newspaper

Omit the introductory article (*New York Times* instead of *The New York Times*). If the masthead indicates an edition (late ed.), include it in your entry. Newspaper articles do not usually appear on consecutive pages, so indicate the page number on which the article begins and then put a plus sign + to indicate that the article continues on later pages. Indicate section numbers (A, B, C) when appropriate.

Harmon, Amy. "In New Tests for Fetal Defects, Agonizing Choices for Parents." *New York Times* 20 June 2004, natl. ed.: A1+. Print.

Op Ed Piece

Fish, Stanley. "When Principles Get in the Way." *New York Times* 26 Dec 1996, late ed.: A27. Print.

Print Books: MLA Style

Order the information as follows, omitting information that does not apply.

Author's Last Name, First Name. "Title of Article or Part of Book." *Title of Book.* Ed. or Trans. Name. Edition. Number of volumes. Place of Publication: Name of Publisher, date of publication. Publication Medium [Print].

Book by One Author

Cisneros, Sandra. *Caramelo*. New York: Random, 2002. Print.

(The names of well-known publishers are often shortened to the first key word. Thus, "Houghton Mifflin Co." becomes "Houghton," and "Harcourt Brace Jovanovich, Inc." becomes simply "Harcourt.")

Two or More Works by Same Author

Morrison, Toni. *Jazz*. New York: Knopf, 1992. Print.

---. *Song of Solomon*. New York: Knopf, 1977. Print.

Book with Two or Three Authors

Dernado, John, and Emmanuel Rongieras d'Usseau. *Allez, Viens!* Austin: Holt,
    2003. Print.

Padilla, Amando M., Halford H. Fairchild, and Concepcion M. Valadez. *Foreign
    Language Education*. Newbury Park: Sage, 1990. Print.

Book with More Than Three Authors

Abrams, M. H., et al. *Norton Anthology of English Literature*. 7th ed. New York:
    Norton, 2000. Print.

Unknown or Anonymous Author

Encyclopedia of White-Collar Crime. Westport: Greenwood, 2007. Print.

Edited Book

Myers, Linda, ed. *Approaches to Computer Writing Classrooms*. Albany: State U of
    New York P, 1993. Print.

(The words University and Press are commonly shortened to U and P wherever they appear in citations.)

Article or Chapter in an Edited Book

Sophocles. *Electra*. Trans. David Grene. *Greek Tragedies*. Ed. David Grene
    and Richmond Lattimore. Vol. 2. Chicago: U of Chicago P, 1960. 45–109.
    Print.

Work in an Anthology

Chopin, Kate. "The Awakening." *Harper Single-Volume American Literature*. Ed.
    Donald McQuade et al. 3rd ed. New York: Longman, 1999. Print.

Web Sources: MLA Style

As more and more sources are available online, the seventh edition of the *MLA Handbook for Writers of Research Papers* (2009) has made some adjustments, asking you to identify sources you access on the open Web and in online databases using Web as the medium of publication. It has also suggested that URLs are no longer required, though writers are encouraged to include a URL when the citation information is not adequate to allow readers to easily find the source. The current abbreviated basic features of an Internet citation, given below, appear in complete form on the MLA home page at http://www.mla.org; the Purdue Online Writing Lab also provides some useful information on the new MLA guidelines at http://owl.english.purdue.edu/owl/. Use the specific citations following this list as models for your own citations. For additional examples, consult the MLA home page or the most recent edition of the *MLA Handbook for Writers of Research Papers*.

1. Name of author, editor, translator, director, performer, if known
2. Title of article, short story, poem, or short work in quotation marks, or title of a longer work, such as a book, in italics
3. Publication information for any print version of the source if known
4. Title of periodical, database, scholarly project, or Web site (italicized), or for a site with no title, a description such as *home page*
5. Name of the editor of the project or database (if available)
6. The name of any organization sponsoring the Web site
7. Date of electronic publication, update, or posting
8. Medium of access (in these cases, Web) and date when researcher accessed the source or site
9. Electronic address or URL only if the citation does not provide adequate information for readers to access the site.

Web Site

American Medical Association. Home page. Apr. 2007. Web. 12 May 2007.

Document from a Web Site

Trapp, Douglas. "Faces of the Uninsured." *American Medical Association*. AMA, 28 Sept. 2009. Web. 25 Oct. 2009.

Scholarly Project Web Site

Labyrinth: Resources for Medieval Studies. Georgetown U, 2005. Web. 20 June 2009.

Magazine Article

Smith, Dakota. "Black Women Ignore Many of Media's Beauty Ideals." *Women's E-News*. Women's eNews, 17 June 2004. Web. 4 June 2007.

Article from an Online Subscription Database

To cite online material from a database to which a library subscribes, first give the print publication information. Then complete the citation by giving the name of the database (italicized), the medium of access (in this case, Web) and the date of access.

Hines, Marion E. "Foreign Language Curriculum Concerns in Times of Conflict." *Delta Kappa Gamma Bulletin* 70.1 (2003): 15–21. *Academic Search Premier.* Web. 14 Feb. 2009.

Newspaper Article

Safire, William. "The Great Cash Cow."Editorial. *New York Times.* New York Times, 23 June 2004. Web. 25 June 2004.

E-book

Adams, Henry. *The Education of Henry Adams.* Boston: Houghton, 1918. *Bartleby.com.* Bartleby, 1999. Web. 17 June 2009.

Podcast

Brody, Jane. "Health Update." Podcast. *New York Times.* New York Times, 4 June 2007. Web. 14 May 2007.

Blog

Baron, Dennis. "Semantic State of the Union." Blog posting. *Web of Language.* N.p., 24 Jan. 2007. Web. 6 May 2007. <http://webtools.uiuc.edu/blog/view?blogId=25>.

● **IN-TEXT DOCUMENTATION: APA STYLE** In APA style, give the author's name and date when you use a summary or paraphrase. If you quote material directly, give the author's name, the date, and the page number. (Use *p.* for one page and *pp.* for more than one page.) These citations will direct your reader to your References list, where you give complete bibliographical information. As you cite your sources, use the following guidelines.

If you do not name the author in the text, give the author and date in parentheses at the end of the citation. If you are specifically citing a quotation or a part of a source, indicate the page with *p.* (for one page) or *pp.* (for more than one page).

> A recent study of elementary school students studying a foreign language showed that participants from bilingual households "invariably scored higher than participants from English-speaking only households" (Cortes, 2002, p. 320).

If you cite the author in the text, indicate the date in parentheses immediately following the author's name, and cite the page number in parentheses following the quotation.

> According to Vicki Galloway (1984), a student's horizons will not be broadened by "grammar lectures and manipulative classroom exercises" (p. 33).

If you include a long direct quotation (40 or more words), indent the passage one-half inch from the left margin. Omit the enclosing direct quotation marks. Place the period at the end of the passage, not after the parentheses that include the page reference.

> In an article explaining the strategic value of foreign language study, Hines (2003) argues that our response has been inadequate:
>
> The United States' chronically weak language resources and lack of linguistic preparedness are invariably exposed when events such as the war in Iraq and the September 11 terror strikes threaten the balance of power, peace or détente in global affairs. (15)

If you are paraphrasing or summarizing material (no direct quotations), you may omit the page number.

> According to Coxe (1984), many top American businesspeople agree that students who combine some business or economics training with fluency in Japanese have unlimited job possibilities.

If you have previously cited the author and date of a study, you may omit the date.

> In addition, Coxe points out that many top American businesspeople agree that students who combine some business or economics training with fluency in Japanese have unlimited job possibilities.

If the work has two to five authors, cite all authors in your text or in parentheses in the first reference.

> Frith and Mueller (2003) cite another recent example of foreign-language ignorance in marketing. When the California Milk Processor Board wanted an ad agency to translate the "Got Milk?" campaign into Spanish, the unfortunate translation came out as "Are you lactating?" (p. 33).
>
> Two researchers cited another recent example of foreign language ignorance in marketing. When the California Milk Processor Board wanted an ad agency to translate the "Got Milk?" campaign into Spanish, the unfortunate translation came out as "Are you lactating?" (Frith & Mueller, 2003, p. 33).

For subsequent citations, cite both names each time if a work has two authors. If a work has three to five authors, give the last name of the first author followed by *et al.* Include the year for the first citation within a paragraph.

> Shedivy et al. (2004) found similar results.

If a work has six or more authors, use only the last name of the first author and the abbreviation *et al.* followed by the date.

Teachers should integrate the study of history, culture, politics, literature, and religion of a particular region with the study of language (Berryman et al., 1988).

If a work has no author, give the first few words of the title (italicized, if a book or report, or in quotes, if an article or chapter) and the year.

Most students in the United States would be surprised to learn that the Russian government sponsored rock concerts (*A Day in the Life,* 1988).

If the source is an unpublished personal communication (e-mail, letter, memo, interview, phone conversation), provide an in-text citation, but do not include the source in your "References" list.

As Professor Devlin explained, "Foreign-language study encourages students to see their own language and culture from a fresh perspective" (personal interview, September 21, 2003).

If your citation refers to several sources, list the authors and dates in alphabetical order.

Several studies (Frith & Mueller, 2003; Hines, 2002; Simon, 1980) have documented severe deficiencies in Americans' foreign-language preparation.

● **REFERENCES LIST: APA STYLE**   If you are using APA style, you should make a separate list, titled References (no underlining or quotation marks), that appears after your text but before any appendixes. Include only sources actually used in preparing your essay. List the sources cited in your text *alphabetically,* by author's last name. Use only *initials* for authors' first and middle names. If the author is unknown, alphabetize by the first word in the title (but not *A, An,* or *The*). In titles, capitalize only the first word, proper names, and the first word following a colon. As in MLA reference style, begin the first line of each reference flush left and indent subsequent lines one-half inch. Double-space the entire References list. The APA recommends using italics for titles of books, journals, and other documents.

Following are samples of APA-style reference list entries. For additional information and examples, consult the *Publication Manual of the American Psychological Association* (6th ed., 2010).

Periodicals: APA Style

The following examples illustrate how to list articles in magazines and periodicals according to APA style.

> *Note:* Do *not* underline or italicize or put quotation marks around titles of articles. Do italicize titles of magazines or periodicals. Italicize the volume number for magazines, if there is one, and omit the *p.* or *pp.* before any page numbers. If an article is not printed on continuous pages, give all page numbers, separated by commas.

Article in a Weekly or Biweekly Magazine

Hersh, S. M. (2004, May 17). Chain of command. *The New Yorker,* 38–43.

Article in a Monthly or Bimonthly Magazine

Dunbar, D. (1997, February). White noise. *Travel and Leisure, 27,* 106–110, 150–158.

Unsigned Article in a Magazine

E-commerce takes off. (2004, 15–21 May). *The Economist, 371,* 9.

Article in a Newspaper

Use *p.* or *pp.* before newspaper section and page numbers.

Harmon, A. (2004, June 20). In new tests for fetal defects, agonizing choices for
   parents. *New York Times,* p. A1.

Books: APA Style

A Book by One Author

Cisneros, S. (2002). *Caramelo.* New York, NY: Random.

Book by Several Authors

For books with up to six authors, use last names followed by initials and an ampersand (&) before the name of the last author. For books with more than six authors, use last name and initial of the first author followed by "et al."

Corbett, P. J., Myers, N., & Tate, G. (2000). *The writing teacher's sourcebook* (4th
   ed.) New York, NY: McGraw-Hill.

Additional Books by Same Author

List the author's name for all entries. Note that in-text citations are distinguished by copyright year. In the case of two works by the same author with the same copyright date, assign the dates letters *a, b* according to their alphabetical arrangement.

Morrison, T. (1977). *Song of Solomon.* New York, NY: Knopf.

Morrison, T. (1992). *Jazz.* New York, NY: Knopf

Book with an Author and an Editor

Austen, J. (1956). *Pride and prejudice* (M. Schorer, Ed.). Boston, MA: Houghton
   Mifflin.

Note: APA style usually uses the full name of publishing companies.

Work in an Anthology

Chopin, K. (1989). The story of an hour. In E. V. Roberts & H. E. Jacobs (Eds.),
Literature: An introduction to reading and writing (pp. 304–306). Englewood
Cliffs, NJ: Prentice Hall.

Note: Titles of poems, short stories, essays, or articles in a book are not underlined or italicized or put in quotation marks. Only the title of the anthology is underlined or italicized.

Electronic and Internet Sources: APA Style

The World Wide Web and the Internet are still changing, so even the latest APA guidelines, available in the sixth edition of the *Publication Manual of the American Psychological Association* (July 2009), may continue to change. See section 7 of the APA manual for the latest information on citing electronic sources. The basic features of an electronic or Internet citation, given in abbreviated form below, are available for downloading from the APA home page at http://www.apa.org/journals/webref.html. Use the specific citations following this list as models for your own citations.

1. Name of author (if given)
2. Title of article (with APA capitalization rules)
3. Title of periodical or electronic text (italicized)
4. Volume number and/or pages (if any)
5. If information is retrieved from an electronic database (e.g., ABI/FORM, PsycInfo, Electric Library, Academic Universe), give the print information only or the publication's home page URL, if known.
6. When a digital object identifier (DOI) is available, include it instead of the URL.
7. Use the words "Retrieved" (include date here only if the publication is undated) "from" (give the URL). Use the words "Available from" to indicate that the URL leads to information on how to obtain the cited material rather than the complete address of the material itself.
8. Do not use angle brackets around URL.
9. If citation ends with the URL, do not end URL with a period.

Article in a Journal with DOI Assigned

Jackson, B., et al. (2007, May). Does harboring hostility hurt? *Health Psychology,*
26(3), 333–340. doi: 10.1037/0278-6133.26.3.333

Article in a Journal with No DOI Assigned

Brockmeier, J. (2001).Texts and other symbolic spaces. *Mind, Culture, and Activity:*
An International Journal, 8, 215–230. Retrieved from
http://lchc.ucsd.edu/mca/Journal/index.html

Article in an Internet-Only Journal

Twyman, M., Harries, C., & Harvey, N. (2006, January). Learning to use and assess advice about risk. *Forum: Qualitative Social Research, 7*(1), Article 22. Retrieved from http://www.qualitative-research.net

Article in a Newspaper

Greenhouse, L. (2004, June 25). Justices, in 5–4 vote, raise doubts on sentencing rules. *New York Times.* Retrieved June 27, 2004, from http://www.nytimes .com

Work from an Online Subscription Database

Hines, M. E. (2003, Fall). Foreign language curriculum concerns in times of conflict. *Delta Kappa Gamma Bulletin, 70,* 15–22.

Blog

Cambridge, B. (2007, April 24). ACT survey conclusion-more grammar instruction. *NCTE Literacy Education Updates.* Retrieved May 6, 2007, from http:// ncteblog.blogspot.com

STUDENT WRITING

KATE MCNERNY

Foreign Language Study: An American Necessity

Kate McNerny's purpose was to persuade students, administrators, and ordinary citizens that learning the language and culture of a foreign country is important, both to people as individuals and to America as a nation. In this paper, she uses interviews, library research, research on the Internet, and her own experience to alert her readers to the seriousness of the problem and to recommended a solution. She argues the American schools should require students to study at least one foreign language during junior and senior high school. McNerny follows the MLA style for in-text documentation, supplementary notes, and the Works Cited list. The marginal annotations highlight key features of her research paper.

1"

½"

McNerny 1

Kate McNerny

Professor Thomas

English 101

6 May 2003

/double space

/double space

Foreign-Language Study:

An American Necessity

/double space

½"

"Why should I learn a foreign language—everyone speaks English!" "I would never use another language—I never plan to leave the United States." "I had a hard enough time learning English!" These are only a few of the excuses people have given for opposing foreign-language studies, and unfortunately they represent the ideas of more than a few American citizens. In possibly the most multicultural nation in the world, it is ironic that so many people—who themselves have come from foreign cultures and foreign languages—should want to remain isolated from international languages and cultures. A recent indication of the backlash against foreign languages came when the House of Representatives passed legislation recommending that English should be the official language of the U.S. Government.[1] In addition, twenty-three states already have Official English laws on the books (Swope 2128; Torres 51). Because these attitudes are so widespread, we need a national policy supporting foreign-language study in elementary and secondary schools. If we are to continue to develop as a people and a nation, we must be able to communicate with and understand the cultures of people from countries around the globe.

Historically, Americans' attitudes toward foreign languages have swayed from positive to negative, depending on current

1"

1"

1"

For her lead-in, McNerny uses quotations she collected in her informal survey.

McNerny first states her thesis for this problem-solving essay: "We need a national policy supporting foreign-language study." McNerny presents historical background on the problem.

(Proportions shown in this paper are adjusted to fit space limitations of this book. Follow actual dimensions discussed and your instructor's directions.)

McNerny 2

events around the world. Theodore Huebener's study *Why Johnny Should Learn Foreign Languages* shows how attitudes reflect the times. In 1940, in an isolationist period before World War II, a committee of the American Youth Commission issued a report labeling foreign-language studies as "useless and time-consuming" (Huebener 13). An even more appalling statement came from a group of Harvard scholars. They suggested that "foreign language study is useful primarily in strengthening the student's English. . . . For the average student, there is no real need at all to learn a foreign language" (Huebener 14). With such attitudes, it is no wonder that students and administrators ignored foreign language programs during the 1940s and 1950s.[2] Through the years, each international crisis has brought a renewed interest in foreign languages. Just as the advent of Sputnik in the late 1950s was followed by a surge of interest in learning foreign languages, the terrorist attacks of September 11, 2001 have created more interest in languages less commonly taught in the United States (Hines 20).

Despite some occasional surges of interest, however, foreign-language study still holds the weakest position of any major subject in American secondary schools. A recent study of foreign-language programs reports that "only 15 percent of American high school students study a foreign language. Only 8 percent of [American] colleges require credit in a foreign language for admission (down from 34 percent in 1966)" (Unks 24). Because available programs at the junior and senior high school level are generally limited in variety

Ellipsis points indicate material omitted from the source.

The superscript number refers the reader to the "Notes" page for McNerny's comment on the history of the problem.

Square brackets in quoted material indicate a word added by McNerny to clarify the sentence.

McNerny 3

and scope, only a small percentage of those students who
take a foreign language ever become fluent in it. A 1984

"Let me put this in terms you'll understand. First,
you'll have to tell me what language you're speaking."

McNerny included the cartoon at this point to illustrate Americans' stubborn ignorance of foreign language.

study that sampled 536 secondary schools revealed that
most offered a foreign language, but 91 percent did not require
foreign-language credits for graduation (Ranwez and Rodgers 98). In
contrast, most European countries require all students to
learn at least one and often two foreign languages. Norway,
Spain, France, Sweden, Italy, England, Germany, and Finland
all require at least one foreign language. According to Rune
Bergentoft, currently a Mellon Fellow at the National Foreign
Language Center, "Several [European] countries require
knowledge of two foreign languages for entry to the upper

In-text citation for a source with two authors. Note also how McNerny makes use of key statistics, a powerful form of evidence.

Noting Bergentoft's qualifications adds reliability to the quotation that follows.

McNerny 4

secondary school; in the Netherlands, the requirement is three foreign languages" (18).

The United States cannot continue to lag behind other countries in language capability. As two foreign-language researchers noted, "We are members of a world community consisting of hundreds of nations, and our fates are closely intertwined" (Long and Long 366). It is time to change attitudes and to recognize that in order to successfully interact with its "world community," the United States must drastically change its foreign-language practices and policies. American students should be encouraged to start their language studies in elementary school and required to study at least one foreign language during their six years of junior and senior high school.

How do we encourage more students to study a foreign language in our elementary and secondary schools? The solution requires changes on the part of administrators and teachers, changes in the attitudes and experiences of students themselves, and changes in our state and national foreign language policies.

School administrators across the country often oppose the idea of requiring foreign languages because they cannot see the contribution these studies make to the overall goals of the schools' curriculum. In a recent survey, New Jersey secondary school administrators "rated social studies objectives as contributing most to the attainment of high priority goals, and foreign language as contributing least" (Koppel 437). These administrators fail to realize that language studies can add a valuable dimension to a social studies program. Educators can use a combined program to

McNerny restates her thesis, using more specific language: "American students should be . . . required to study at least one foreign language during . . . junior and senior high school."

*McNerny's **essay map:** The solution requires changes by administrators, by students, and by national policymakers.*

*Notice **punctuation** for in-text citation: Source appears in parentheses after the quotation marks but before the period.*

McNerny 5

emphasize a global perspective in language and cultural studies. "The world looks and sounds different when one is 'standing in the shoes' of another, speaking another language, or recognizing another's point of view based on an alternative set of values" (Bragaw 37). This global awareness is crucial in our increasingly interdependent world.

Likewise, teachers need to continue to make changes in their foreign-language courses to attract more students. More and more primary and secondary language courses already focus on cultural issues more than grammar, but now they need to use all the computer, on-line, and Internet resources currently available to attract and motivate their students. Linguist Mark Warschauer, in a preface to papers collected at a conference on Global Networking in Foreign Language Learning, asserts that "foreign language learners can communicate rapidly and inexpensively with other learners or speakers of the target language around the world. With the World Wide Web, learners can access a broad array of authentic foreign language materials . . . or they can develop and publish their own materials to share with others across the classroom or across the globe" (ix). Teachers need to make use of the Internet's communication possibilities to help motivate and interest their students.

Of course, students themselves need motivation in order to enroll in foreign-language classes. Many students simply fail to see why they will ever need to use a foreign language. I used to belong to that group. I remember my mom always telling me, "Take French classes. Learn how to speak French so you can visit your cousins in

This use of a direct quotation supports McNerny's point in a compelling way.

McNerny shows how new technologies can make foreign language learning more valuable in current times.

McNerny's transition helps the reader see why she will now discuss a related topic—student motivation.

Though most of McNerny's essay is based on library research, here she adds personal experience to illustrate the need.

Note how McNerny uses open Web sources as evidence that many useful programs already exist.

McNerny 6

France someday." At the time, during junior high, I did take French classes for a while, but then dropped them when my schedule became "too busy." Then, as my mom had promised, I got the opportunity to visit my cousins in France. For some reason, the fact that I couldn't speak French didn't really hit me—until I stepped off the train at Gare du Nord in Paris and couldn't find the relative who was supposed to meet me. After frantically searching the entire station several times, I had to break down and ask for help. At the information desk, a few completely butchered French phrases escaped my lips—only to be received by an unimpressed, unresponsive station attendant. He muttered something about dumb Americans. Then, with a wave of his hand, he gestured toward some unknown destination. I did survive that painful ordeal, but I vowed I wouldn't embarrass myself—and other Americans—again.

Another way to change students' attitudes is to encourage them to participate in exchange programs or study-abroad programs.[3] Again, the Internet and the World Wide Web offer students and their teachers immediate access to a variety of exchange and study-abroad programs. The World Wide Web has hundreds of sites related to foreign-language study that can help both teachers and students. The International House World Organization, at http://www. international-house.org, is "a worldwide network of language schools sharing a common commitment to the highest standards of teaching and training" (*International*). Students wishing to find out about exchange and study-abroad programs should browse the Web, perhaps

McNerny 7

beginning at a site such as the *Foreign Language Study Abroad Service* at http://www.netpoint.net/~flsas. The Foreign Language Study Abroad Service was started in 1971 and is, according to its home page, "the oldest study abroad service in the U.S." (*Foreign*).

Study-abroad programs and exchange programs help students learn the language, but just as important, they enable students to learn about different cultures. In his resource book, *Teaching Culture,* H. Ned Seelye, Director of Bilingual-Bicultural Education for the State of Illinois, cites just one of many cultural lessons that American students—and tourists—need to learn:

1" At a New Year's Eve celebration in an exclusive Guatemalan hotel, one American was overheard telling another, "You see all these people? They're all my wife's relatives. And every damn one of them has kissed me tonight. If another Guatemalan man hugs and kisses me I'll punch him right in the face!" The irritated American was disturbed by two things: the extended kinship patterns of the group and the *abrazo de ano neuvo* as executed by the men (he did not complain of the female abrazos). Both customs—close family ties that extend to distant relatives and the abrazo given as a greeting or sign of affection devoid of sexual overtures—elicited hostility in the American who was bored by unintelligible language and depressed by nostalgia and alcohol. (85)

In order to prevent such linguistic and cultural misunderstandings, more and more Americans should take advantage of study-abroad

McNerny introduces the author, the title of the book, and the author's credentials to lend authority to the quoted passage.

At the end of the quotation, McNerny cites only the page number, since she has already introduced the author. The page number follows the period in indented block quotations.

McNerny does not end her paragraph with a quotation; instead, she keeps her own voice primary by relating it to her own purpose.

McNerny 8

and exchange programs that will acquaint them with a variety of
cultures and languages.

Finally, in order to coordinate our schools' foreign-language
studies, America needs changes in our state and national
foreign-language policies to ensure that every child will receive some
basic instruction in foreign languages and culture. Changes in our
foreign-language requirements would not only promote cultural
understanding but also would strengthen U.S. international relations
in business and diplomacy. International trade is continually
increasing in the United States and has created a demand for
businesspeople competent in foreign languages. Many top American
businesspeople agree that students who combine some business or
economics training with fluency in Japanese have unlimited job
possibilities (Coxe). Company executives simply cannot expect to
make efficient, sound decisions in their international markets without
understanding and speaking the language of the country they are
dealing with (Huebener 45). Educator Gerald Unks points out two
instances in which a lack of language proficiency caused companies
to initiate fatal marketing programs:

> When Pepsi-Cola went after the Chinese market, "Come
> Alive With Pepsi" was translated into Chinese in Taiwan
> as "Pepsi Brings Your Ancestors Back from the Dead." No
> Sale! General Motors sought to sell its Nova in South
> America oblivious to the fact that "No va" in Spanish
> means "It doesn't go." (24)

Another recent example of foreign-language ignorance in
marketing occurred when the California Milk Association

*Note how McNerny
appeals to another portion
of her audience—
businesspeople.*

*These specific examples
illustrate how important
foreign language proficiency
can be for businesses,
appealing to this audience.*

McNerny 9

wanted an ad agency to translate the "Got Milk?" campaign into Spanish. The unfortunate translation initially came out as "Are you lactating?" (Frith and Mueller 33). These examples illustrate that business people need thorough competence in, not just a rudimentary knowledge of, foreign languages.

Finally, proficiency in foreign languages and cultures is important not only for business and trade overseas, but also for jobs in America. Required foreign-language study would help our future citizens understand and appreciate our multicultural heritage—and help them become employable. Verada Bluford, writing in *Occupational Outlook Quarterly*, argues that as our country "becomes more involved in foreign trade, tourism, and international cooperative ventures, the number of jobs open to fluent speakers of a foreign language increases" (25). Bluford explains that there are "language-centered jobs" such as teaching, translating, and interpreting, but there are also "language-related jobs," such as jobs in marketing and finance, engineering, airlines, banking, and government, where language skills are necessary. These "language-related jobs" will go to students who have language skills in addition to some other skill (Bluford 26). A foreign-language requirement, whether mandated by each state or by Congress, would make all Americans better citizens of the world and their own country.

The need for required language study in the United States is urgent. Some states already require schools to introduce children to some foreign language during their grade school years (Kuo). For example, North Carolina, Arkansas, Louisiana, Arizona, and Oklahoma already have laws, and Oregon has a proposed law that

Before quoting from Bluford, McNerny names the author and the journal from which the article is taken.

McNerny begins her conclusion, citing precedents and calling for state and federal administrators to support a foreign-language requirement.

will require all tenth-graders to know a language other than English (Kuo). Since some individual schools and states realize the benefits of foreign-language requirements, Congress should guide all the states and formulate a national foreign-language policy that would make all our schools more like the European model.

Although the ideas and the plans for a national policy exist, often the funds do not. Some funds can be diverted from within school districts, but the federal government must take some initiative. The current administration spends endless time and money subsidizing business interests and propping up weak foreign economies. Since foreign-language knowledge contributes strongly to success in both these areas, however, it would be practical for the administration also to support expansion of language studies. Instead, it continues to reduce funding for special programs, including language studies centers and international teaching facilities (Unks 25). Realistically, a foreign-language requirement in junior and senior high school cannot be initiated without the support of both local school districts and the federal government. Americans must acknowledge the fact that they are not isolated from the rest of the world. Successful interaction in the "world community" depends on our ability, as a nation, to effectively communicate with and understand people from other countries. Understanding, communication, and world peace cannot be achieved without cultural awareness and foreign-language proficiency.

In this paragraph, McNerny addresses potential reader questions about whether her plan is feasible.

McNerny ends with an appeal to the reader's emotions—a desire for a peaceful world.

1/2"
McNerny 11

1"

Notes

1. Americans not only hesitate to take a foreign language but also seem bent on keeping foreign languages officially "out of sight." The debate over "official English" has spilled over into the workplace, in the form of "English-only" rules in business. Robert Brady, writing in *HR Focus*, reviews the two sides of the English-only debate: "Advocates of English-only rules argue that a single language promotes good organizational communications, ensures workplace safety, improves service to the English-speaking customer base, and avoids discrimination." On the other side, Brady says, opponents believe that requiring employees to speak English goes against the melting-pot heritage of our country—and may violate Title VII of the Civil Rights Act. Many opponents from ethnic and civil rights groups believe these bills and rules are racist (McBee 64). Americans' ignorance of foreign languages (and the fear that ignorance breeds) is an important cause of the popularity of both the "official English" laws and the "English-only" rules.

2. One of the most disturbing facts is that although Huebener's study was done in 1961, very little has changed in over forty years. Except for slight changes in statistics, dates, and names of wars, Americans have remained strikingly insular in their attitudes toward foreign languages and foreigners.

3. Recent figures on study-abroad programs illustrate the huge gap between the number of foreign students who study in the United States and U.S. students who study abroad. In an article on language learning and study abroad, Barbara Freed gives the following figures: "Close to half a million international students

1"

1"   **1"**

Content notes are placed on a separate page and double-spaced. Indent the first line of each numbered note one-half inch.

In her notes, McNerny includes her ideas about "English-only" and "official English," which would have been digressive in the text of her paper.

In this footnote, McNerny puts statistics that didn't seem to fit in the flow of her paragraph but are relevant to study-abroad programs.

1"   McNerny 12

came to the United States to study in 1993–94 [while]

approximately 71,000 American undergraduates participated in

study abroad programs" (3). That means that nearly ten times more

foreign students study English in the United States than American

students study foreign languages abroad.

1"   1"

1"

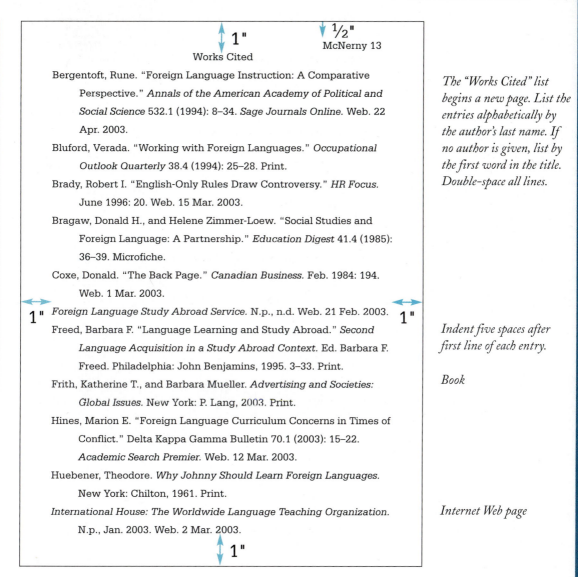

1"

½"

Works Cited

Bergentoft, Rune. "Foreign Language Instruction: A Comparative
Perspective." *Annals of the American Academy of Political and
Social Science* 532.1 (1994): 8–34. *Sage Journals Online.* Web. 22
Apr. 2003.

Bluford, Verada. "Working with Foreign Languages." *Occupational
Outlook Quarterly* 38.4 (1994): 25–28. Print.

Brady, Robert I. "English-Only Rules Draw Controversy." *HR Focus.*
June 1996: 20. Web. 15 Mar. 2003.

Bragaw, Donald H., and Helene Zimmer-Loew. "Social Studies and
Foreign Language: A Partnership." *Education Digest* 41.4 (1985):
36–39. Microfiche.

Coxe, Donald. "The Back Page." *Canadian Business.* Feb. 1984: 194.
Web. 1 Mar. 2003.

1" *Foreign Language Study Abroad Service.* N.p., n.d. Web. 21 Feb. 2003. **1"**

Freed, Barbara F. "Language Learning and Study Abroad." *Second
Language Acquisition in a Study Abroad Context.* Ed. Barbara F.
Freed. Philadelphia: John Benjamins, 1995. 3–33. Print.

Frith, Katherine T., and Barbara Mueller. *Advertising and Societies:
Global Issues.* New York: P. Lang, 2003. Print.

Hines, Marion E. "Foreign Language Curriculum Concerns in Times of
Conflict." Delta Kappa Gamma Bulletin 70.1 (2003): 15–22.
Academic Search Premier. Web. 12 Mar. 2003.

Huebener, Theodore. *Why Johnny Should Learn Foreign Languages.*
New York: Chilton, 1961. Print.

International House: The Worldwide Language Teaching Organization.
N.p., Jan. 2003. Web. 2 Mar. 2003.

1"

*The "Works Cited" list
begins a new page. List the
entries alphabetically by
the author's last name. If
no author is given, list by
the first word in the title.
Double-space all lines.*

*Indent five spaces after
first line of each entry.*

Book

Internet Web page

↕ 1"

↓ ½"

Article from a journal

Koppel, Irene E. "The Perceived Contribution of a Foreign Language to High Priority Education Goals." *Foreign Language Annals* 15.6 (1982): 435–39. *ERIC.* Web. 1 Mar. 2003.

Kuo, Fidelius. "Foreign Language Proposal in Washington State Worthy." *Northwest Asian Weekly.* Northwest Asian Weekly, 9 Dec. 1994: 4. Web. 3 Apr. 2003.

For inclusive page numbers over 100, use only the last two digits in the second number (366–68).

Long, Delbert H., and Roberta A. Long. "Toward the Promotion of Foreign Language Study and Global Understanding." *Education* 105.4 (1985): 366–68. *ERIC.* Web. 22 Mar. 2003.

McBee, Susanna. "A War over Words." *US News.com.* US News & World Report, 6 Oct. 1986. Web. 19 Mar. 2003.

Ranwez, Alain D., and Judy Rogers. "The Status of Foreign Languages and International Studies: An Assessment in Colorado." *Foreign Language Annals* 17.2 (1984): 97–102. *ERIC.* Web. 1 Mar. 2003.

↔ 1"   ↔ 1"

Seelye, H. Ned. *Teaching Culture: Strategies for Foreign Language Educators.* Skokie: National Textbook, 1974. Print.

Swope, Christopher. "Panel OKs Bill to Make English Official Government Language." *Congressional Quarterly Weekly Report* 54.30 (1996): 2128–29. *Academic Search Premier.* Web. 3 Mar. 2003.

Torres, Joseph. "The Language Crusade." *Hispanic.* 9.6 (1996): 50–54. Print.

Unks, Gerald. "The Perils of Our Single-Language Policy." *Education Digest* 41.2 (1985). Microfiche.

Article from a monthly magazine

Warschauer, Mark. Preface. *Telecollaboration in Foreign Language Learning.* Ed. Mark Warschauer. Honolulu: Second Language Teaching and Curriculum Center, 1996. Print.

↕ 1"

Credits

Photo Credits

Index